India and the Romantic Imagination

India and the Romantic Imagination

JOHN DREW

DELHI
OXFORD UNIVERSITY PRESS
OXFORD NEW YORK
1987

Oxford University Press, Walton Street, Oxford OX2 6DP
OXFORD NEW YORK TORONTO
DELHI BOMBAY CALCUTTA MADRAS KARACHI
PETALING JAYA SINGAPORE HONG KONG TOKYO
NAIROBI DAR ES SALAAM CAPE TOWN
MELBOURNE AUCKLAND
and associates in
BEIRUT BERLIN IBADAN MEXICO CITY NICOSIA

Typeset by Taj Services Ltd, Noida, U.P.
Printed by Rekha Printers Private Ltd, New Delhi 110020
and published by R. Dayal, Oxford University Press
YMCA Library Building, Jai Singh Road, New Delhi 110001

Contents

AFTERWORD

Preface

There has been a tendency for Europeans to idealize India. This book attempts to trace the origin and development of this tendency. It is not on the whole concerned with a similar tendency which is prevalent in Asia and elsewhere, nor with other, contrary, tendencies. It is, then, a history of the metaphorical or metaphysical passage to India begun by the Greeks. However successful any form of nineteenth-century materialism may be, I doubt that it will ever invalidate or supersede the universal psychological quest which this passage symbolizes.

In the book an ideal image of India is discovered and used as an organizing principle around which to speculate about the nature of imaginative literature, primarily English. Conversely, imaginative literature has been used as a point of departure from which to speculate about the nature of the passage to India. A dialectic is thus established which perhaps conceals as well as exposes an ambiguity inherent in the subject. There may be places where the reader feels that reference to India has little to do with the Imagination and that, elsewhere in some reference to the Imagination, India is not the crucial factor it is made out to be. Because the two images are used interchangeably and are thus sometimes transposed, there will certainly be occasions (especially in the second half of the book) when it is difficult to say whether a piece of literature represents a passage to India or whether it is being represented *in the context of* that passage. The first half of the book reveals that there are good historical and philosophical reasons for this ambiguity. On account of them, the book itself may be regarded, alternatively, as a work of scholarship or fiction.

Each chapter is a variation on the single theme of the passage to India. There is no chapter on Kipling only because Benita Parry (in *Delusions and Discoveries*, 1972) has already said much of what I should wish to say about his work; no chapter on Blake because his response to India has been considered by, among others, Kathleen Raine (most recently in *Indian Horizons*, 1983). If the pattern of the passage to India established by this book is valid, then it should be generally applicable to the work of these and other writers not only in Britain but in Europe (especially Germany), in the Americas and even in Asia. The chapters I have written are somewhat distended not only because they repeat and elaborate a single idealist argument; they also have a descriptive or expository function. Some of the works crucial to my argument are not widely available and these I have described at some length. While this results in a proliferation of much detail pertinent to cultural contact with India, the intention of the book is to be not comprehensive but coherent, not definitive but speculative. Its essential purpose is to provide the reader with an experience as well as an understanding of the passage to India.

Acknowledgements

Nearly twenty years ago Chris Dade asked me what the significance was of Godbole's song in *A Passage to India*. I could not begin to answer his question. This book is a (sadly) belated attempt to do so—sadly because Chris himself is no longer alive.

The book would never have materialized had it not been for 'that myriad-minded man', John Beer. The original manuscript was drafted under his supervision at Cambridge, 1974–7. Various editors have encouraged me by commissioning articles: John Beer himself (once in conjunction with Gour Das), for books on Forster published by Macmillan; Miron Grindea, for *Adam*; Jon Silkin, for *Stand*; Elinor Shaffer, for *Comparative Criticism*, and Devindra Kohli, for the *Indian Literary Review*. I should also like to thank Sita Narasimhan, who watched much of the book unfold; Peter Dronke, who read over part of it; Bob Grant, for his criticism of its methodology; Partha Mitter, for his comments on one chapter; Kathy Wheeler and Anwar Rizvi for help with translations; and John Ruffle, Keeper of The Oriental Museum, Durham for making available the miniature (reproduced on the jacket) of a holy man being visited by princes. Lastly, I am grateful to a fellow Forsterian at the OUP in New Delhi for saving me from the fate of that character in Ruth Jhabvala's *Heat and Dust* who, having written a monograph on the influence of India on the European consciousness and character, had to publish it 'at his own expense' since 'it was not a subject of much general interest'.

In fact, there *is* enough interest in this subject for the book to fall within an identifiable scholarly tradition—though, for the most part, I have discovered this only since the book was written, perhaps even had to write the book to discover this. It was actually a relief to find that my (apparently eccentric) reading of Shelley's *Prometheus Unbound* in terms of Indian mythology had already been suggested (in an obscure corner of the Bodleian) by S. R. Swaminathan (see chapter 7, n. 156, p. 267). I was also relieved (and delighted) to discover that simultaneously and independently, in different parts of Asia, *A Passage to India* was beginning to be read in terms of neo-Platonism (by Mohammad Shaheen, Vasant Shahane and Edwin Thumboo). It was only recently that I became aware of Garland Cannon's pioneering attempt to establish a link between Jones and the Romantic poets (see chapter 2, n. 160, p. 173)—though that article does leave the way open for a detailed treatment of the subject. More fundamentally, I hope this book will, among other things, not only add an English (and Greek) dimension to Raymond Schwab's seminal study of the effect on Europe of contact with India in the Romantic period (see chapter 7, n. 109, p. 253) but also go some way—a way pointed out, perhaps by Jung and Heinrich Zimmer—to meeting Edward Said's demand for a more 'libertarian' approach to the subject of Orientalism.

I should like to acknowledge the award many years ago of a Commonwealth Scholarship to study under 'Chanchi' Mehta at the Maharaja Sayajirao University of Baroda. I trust this book finally justifies the award. During the writing of it a number of friends have bailed us out with (interest-free) loans: Fred Cogswell, David Jory, Eric Wright; with cash: Sylvane Walters. At various times John Stratton, as well as Eric Wright and Sylvane Walters, provided a roof. John Tackaberry got some of the typing done and Dave Meadows gave me extra precious time by unloading my 5.30 from Ipswich when I was working as a station mails porter. However, the real burden of this book has been borne by my children (now no longer children) and by Rani, to whom it is hereby dedicated.

List of Abbreviations

AHG	*Alexandria: a History and a Guide*, by E. M. Forster (Alexandria, 1922).
AM	*Asiatic Miscellany*, 2 vols, ed. by Francis Gladwin (Calcutta, 1785–6).
AN	*Aspects of the Novel*, by E. M. Forster, Abinger ed. (London, 1974).
AR	*Asiatic Researches*, vols I–XI (London rpt, 1799–1812).
BA	*Brihad Aranyaka* in *The Thirteen Principal Upanishads*, trans. by R. E. Hume, 2nd ed. (London, 1931).
BC	*British Critic*, 1793–1800.
BG	*Bhagavad Gita*, trans. by Juan Mascaro (Harmondsworth, 1962).
BGW	*Bhagvat-Geeta*, trans. by Charles Wilkins (London, 1785).
BL	*Biographia Literaria*, by S. T. Coleridge, ed. by H. N. and Sara Coleridge, 2nd ed., 2 vols (London, 1847).
Colebrooke	*Miscellaneous Essays*, by H. T. Colebrooke, ed. E. B. Cowell, 2nd ed., 2 vols (London, 1873).
CLSTC	*Collected Letters of Samuel Taylor Coleridge*, ed. by E. L. Griggs, 6 vols (Oxford, 1956–71).
CNB	Coleridge, *The Notebooks*, ed. by Kathleen Coburn, 3 vols to date (London, 1957).
CPW	*Complete Poetical Works of S. T. Coleridge*, ed. by E. H. Coleridge, 2 vols (Oxford, 1912).
CR	*Critical Review*, 1780–1800.
Enn.	Enneads, *Plotinus: the Ethical Treatises* etc., trans. and ed. by Stephen MacKenna and B. S. Page, 5 vols (London, 1917–30).
GM	*Gentleman's Magazine*, 1780–1800.

HH	*History of Hindostan*, by Thomas Maurice, 2 vols (London, 1795–8).
IA	*Indian Antiquities*, by Thomas Maurice, 7 vols (London, 1793–1800).
Iamblichus	*Iamblichus' Life of Pythagoras*, trans. by Thomas Taylor (1818; rpt. London, 1926).
Journal	*Mary Shelley's Journal*, ed. by Frederick L. Jones (Norman, 1947).
LPBS	*Letters of Percy Bysshe Shelley*, ed. by Frederick L. Jones, 2 vols (Oxford, 1964).
LWJ	*Letters of Sir William Jones*, ed. by Garland Cannon, 2 vols (Oxford, 1970).
MacKenna	Vol. 1 only of *Plotinus: the Ethical Treatises*, trans. and ed. by Stephen MacKenna and B. S. Page, 5 vols (London, 1917–30).
Menu	*Institutes of Hindu Law, or the Ordinances of Menu*, trans. by William Jones (London and Calcutta, 1796).
MH	*Mahabharata*, trans. attrib. to Pratap Chandra Roy, 11 (unnumbered) vols (Calcutta, 1884–6).
MM	*Monthly Magazine*, 1796–1800.
MR	*Monthly Review*, 1750–1, 1770–1800.
MWJ	*Memoirs of . . . Sir William Jones*, by Lord Teignmouth (London, 1804).
MWTN	*Memoir of . . . the late William Taylor of Norwich*, by J. W. Robberds, 2 vols (London, 1843).
PI	*A Passage to India*, by E. M. Forster (London, 1924).
PL	*Philosophical Lectures*, by S. T. Coleridge, ed. by Kathleen Coburn (London, 1949).
Poems (1772)	*Poems, Consisting Chiefly of Translations from the Asiatick Languages*, by William Jones (Oxford, 1772).
Purchas I–IV	*Purchas his Pilgrimes*, 4 vols (1625).
Purchas V	*Purchas his Pilgrimage*, 4th ed. (London, 1626).
PWPBS	*The Complete Poetical Works of Percy Bysshe Shelley*, ed. by Thomas Hutchinson, rev. by G. M. Matthews, new ed. (London, 1970).
RV	*The Hymns of the Rigveda*, trans. by R. T. H. Griffith, 4 vols (Benares, 1889–92).
SCB	Southey's *Commonplace Book*, ed. by John Wood Warter, 4 Ser. (London, 1849–51).
Staal	J. F. Staal, *Advaita and Neoplatonism* (Madras, 1961).

SWP	*Select Works of Porphyry*, trans. by Thomas Taylor (London, 1823).
TM	*The Missionary*, by Sydney Owenson, Lady Morgan, 3 vols, 2nd ed. (London, 1811).
VP	*Vishnu Purana*, I–V, trans., = vols VI–X of *Works* of H. H. Wilson (see next entry).
Wilson	Horace Hayman Wilson, *Works*, 12 vols (London, 1862–77).
Works (1799)	*Works of Sir William Jones*, ed. by Lady Jones, 6 vols (London, 1799).
WWJ	*Works of Sir William Jones*, ed. by Lord Teignmouth, 13 vols (London, 1807).
Yule	*The Book of Ser Marco Polo*, ed. and trans. by Sir Henry Yule, 3rd ed., 2 vols (London, 1903).

Note on Orthography

For a book on English literature Indian orthography presents a problem. In dealing with Forster's *A Passage to India* it would clearly be nonsense to refer to Krishna as Kŕśtna, say, or Kṛṣṇa. Moreover, a reader interested in Sir William Jones needs to be reminded, perhaps, that Jones used a C (not a K) for Camdeo (Kama-deva), Caul, Cumara-Sambhava, etc. But I *have* altered and standardized the spelling of names used more widely—such as Kashmir and Kalidasa. However, I have *not* altered Mongolian names beginning with K, such as Kublai, to the newly-standardized Q. Moreover, I have amended Jones's much more accurate Zera'tusht to the Zoroaster prevalent in most other—older—writings I have cited. If I have anglicized some names and not others and been inconsistent in my use of the paratal and the retroflex 's'. I hope the purists will forgive me. In retaining many older and outdated (as well as variant) forms, my intention has been to avoid causing obscurity and confusion, especially for anyone wishing to follow up a reference.

Perhaps I should also mention that I have frequently resorted to the capitalization of English words such as Vision, Love and Imagination where, in the absence of a qualifying adjective, they denote the archetypal state of the impersonal or universal and are thereby distinguished from the personal or particular they are (according to the idealist traditions with which this book deals) supposed to supersede or transform.

PART I
THE PASSAGE OUT

'The Road from Colonus' and Death in the Green Tree

in which questions about the passage to India are raised by reference to E.M. Forster's short story.

Therefore let the Reader if he please call it a Romantick Scheam, or imaginary Hypothesis, or what name else best fits his phancy, and he'll not offend me . . . And indeed the Hypothesis as to the main, is derived to us from the Platonists . . .

Joseph Glanvill, *Lux Orientalis, or An Enquiry into the Opinion of the Eastern Sages Concerning the Prae-existence of Souls*

INTRODUCTORY
'The Road from Colonus' and Death in the Green Tree

In 1903, some years before he first went to India, E.M. Forster wrote a short story which, as the similarity of its metaphorical title might suggest, is a prefiguring of *A Passage to India*. In 'The Road from Colonus',[1] as in the Indian novel, a party of English people abroad in an alien landscape are confronted by a psychical experience which their own culture has not prepared them to understand. Of the younger members of the English party little need be said: Arthur Graham is as superficially right about the deviousness of foreigners as Ronny Heaslop will be, and as capable of handling them. Similarly, just as Ronny would have married Adela Quested in the normal course of things, so Arthur Graham will marry Ethel Lucas. Like Adela, Ethel is a sensible girl, dutiful to the older generation, though she, unlike Adela, is more chaperone than chaperoned.

The critical moment of mystical truth in the story belongs to the old man, Mr Lucas, who, in discovering his true identity (apparently) within a hollow tree, experiences enlightenment (only later, on account of having his life saved, to relapse into disillusionment). In Forster's novel, conversely, the old lady, Mrs Moore, during her visit to a cave, will experience disillusionment (only later, following her death, to be 'impelled to that place where completeness is found'). In both story and novel it is not the capable and articulate English but the natives they despise who divine the psychical or metaphysical forces which exist within the physical landscape.

The title of the short story asks us to equate Mr Lucas with Oedipus who, after a life of perversity and disquiet, is permitted in

---

[1] *The Celestial Omnibus and Other Stories* (London, 1911), pp. 143–64.

old age at Colonus to experience a tranquillity which culminates in his total and mystical absorption into a part of the countryside sacred to the mysteries. The earliest Greek drama is rarely far from these mysteries and the association is all the stronger in this story for the central importance of the plane tree and its stream, recalling, as these will, the visitation of the *daemon* of Socrates in the *Phaedrus*. Forster probably intends the reference— whimsically, perhaps, he calls the place Plataniste—and the general mystical effect is in no way diminished by his reference to the inn as a *Khan*, a word evocatively Oriental. Into this setting comes Mr Lucas. The decent social life he has lived in England has been quite meaningless; his visit to Greece, the achievement of a life's dream, equally disappointing. Yet he has made the visit and his discontent, like Mrs Moore's, is determined by a powerful and deliberate force: Providence, it appears, has destined him for enlightenment.

Once he has entered the great green tree Mr Lucas realizes his desire to strip away the forty intervening years since the idealism of his youth: in his great eagerness to possess the spirit of the tree, which has already been entered by man, he is possessed by it and readily gives himself up. There is a moment of pure vision of which, in retrospect, Mr Lucas becomes conscious: 'something unimagined, indefinable, had passed over all things, and made them intelligible and good'. Mr Lucas has discovered 'not only Greece, but England and all the world and life', and it only remains for him, like Oedipus, to be borne 'beyond relapse' and be confirmed 'for ever in the kingdom he had regained'. For the first time he has seen 'his daily life aright' and is aware 'a supreme event' awaits him which will 'transfigure the face of the world'. The silent natives, the murmuring stream and the whispering trees are part of a psychic force urging him to realize his destiny. Of such matters his noisy and articulate companions give themselves neither time nor space to be aware.

Mr Lucas, however, is not so fortunate as Oedipus. It is his fate that his daughter as well as his compatriots will conspire against him and he is forcibly hurried on back to London. Only from Ethel's limited point of view, general as that may be to her culture, does it appear that Mr Lucas would have suffered a worse fate had he remained at Plataniste and been killed by the falling of the tree. The irritating sound of London bathwater is, in Platonist terms, the palest possible reflection of the murmuring of the stream in Greece, and the resumption and prolongation of a meaningless social life in London is an equally impoverished alternative to the cessation of life in a state of enlightenment—which might otherwise have been the destiny of Mr Lucas.

If the whole tone of the story is congenial with the spirit of the Classical Athens of Sophocles and Plato, it is the Classical spirit as it was later understood by Plotinus. It is the constant theme of the *Enneads* of Plotinus that a man who desires mystical vision shall find it and that his soul will secure release if he can withdraw from the noise of the world and discard all that he has hitherto valued. The *Enneads* are particularly pertinent to Ethel's final, ignorant—and, in the context, ironic—reference to Providence. Plotinus draws a critical distinction between the operation of Providence, when the soul acts 'in the light of sound reason', and Fate, when the soul is hindered from self-realization on account of outside interference. It is in the tractates on Providence which immediately follow that Plotinus insists that the cosmos is beautiful if seen (such as Mr Lucas comes to see it) as an image of ultimate reality and, most importantly, concludes his remarks by comparing Providence to a great Tree of Life, a myth which, when he takes it up again later, he invests with precisely the meaning it has in 'The Road from Colonus': namely, that for its essential life and realization the soul is no more dependent on the body of a man than it is on the trunk (branches, or roots) of a tree. Cut either down and the soul will have gone free.[2]

It is a curious coincidence, in view of Forster's later interest in India, that this image of the green tree to be cut down is as central to a whole Indian philosophical tradition as it is to 'The Road from Colonus'. The myth is first elaborated by the Vedic sage Yajnavalkya, whose teaching is reported in the *Brihad Aranyaka* (or Great Forest) Upanishad (*c.* seventh or sixth century BC) and repeated most prominently in the *Bhagavad Gita*.[3] There is nothing to suggest that, at this time of his life, Forster was especially open to Indian influences. It could be that he is indebted for this image, as well as for the intellectual basis of the story, to Plotinus.[4] It could even be that Plotinus, schooled in a city (Alexandria) which was a meeting place of Greek and Indian cultures, was familiar with the teaching of the Upanishad or the *Bhagavad Gita*.

An alternative and not mutually exclusive explanation of the coincidence is that the more visionary an idealistic tradition becomes the more certain it is to discover an archetypal image such as the Tree of this particular myth. When in the *Phaedrus* Socrates

---

[2] *Enn.*, v.ii.2; vi.viii.15.   [3] See chapter 4, p. 131 and n. 43.   [4] See chapter 1, p. 12 and n. 3.

is pressed to name the ancient sages to whose authority he has appealed, he discovers they are not historical but psychological entities: ideas take shape from a source he feels he should be able to and yet cannot identify.[5] Similarly, it is perhaps the imaginative power within Forster which, while discovered by the intellectual tradition that best releases it, itself expands to a mythic importance the image of the tree to be found in both the *Phaedrus* and the *Enneads*. And what Forster discovered individually, as it were, within the context of Hellenism, had already been discovered collectively in the literature of the Hindus.

The question of intellectual influence might hardly seem worth pursuing in this particular instance were it not that the central image used in *A Passage to India* is as evocative of the greatest Greek myth—that of the Cave in Plato's *Republic*—as the image in the short story is of the greatest Indian. Although the Indian landscape is honeycombed with caves formerly inhabited by philosophers, Forster has said that in using the image of the cave in *A Passage to India* he was not conscious of any debt to Indian iconography.[6] If the image was iconic or potentially mythic for Forster it would surely have been on account of the use made of it in Plato's *Republic*. Should we then look to Greek philosophy to discover the basic pattern of *A Passage to India*? Conversely, is it in terms of Indian philosophy that we can best understand 'The Road from Colonus'? Assuming, that is, that literature should be read in terms of any sort of philosophy?

It might appear to be of dubious value to raise these particular questions on the basis of a couple of (common) images. However, the images are here used in the particular context of a concern with the possibility of mystical experience and it so happens that in the West the possibility of mystical experience has been canvassed intellectually by a Platonist tradition which has perennially, if intermittently, associated mysticism with India. What is the nature of this philosophical relationship between Greece and India? What bearing does this relationship have on an understanding of imaginative English literature? It is the purpose of the following pages to explore these questions, and the difficulty of answering them satisfactorily may be determined by the fact that it is not until the final chapter of the book that it will become clear (if then) why these questions have been raised relative to 'The Road from Colonus', and why they are relevant to it.

---

[5] *Phaedrus* 235 B–D. The same thing happens when Socrates is asked to support his belief in metempsychosis (*Phaedo* 70A–73C).   [6] Wilfred Stone, *The Cave and the Mountain* (Stanford, 1966), pp. 301–3.

E.M. Forster: Professor Godbole and a Passage to Alexandria

*in which A Passage to India is read
in the light of the Enneads of Plotinus.*

An Englishman has no conception even of the meaning of a philosophic or religious problem. The notion that the material world could be a mere illusion is one that could never appeal to him as even intelligible (Berkeley, it must be remembered, was an Irishman, and Hume a Scotchman). His religion, when he has one, is a transfigured morality, not a mysticism. He is practical, through and through, in spiritual as well as in material things. Between him and the Indian the gulf is impassable.

G. Lowes Dickinson, *An Essay on the Civilizations of India, China and Japan.*

I want something beyond the field of action and behaviour: the waters of the river that rises from the middle of the earth to join the Ganges and the Jumna where they join. India is full of such wonders, but she can't give them to me.

E.M. Forster (referring to the Sarasvati), 1913.

CHAPTER ONE

E.M. Forster: Professor Godbole and a Passage to Alexandria

FORSTER AND NEO-PLATONISM

Neo-Platonism was an important factor in the intellectual life of E.M. Forster in the mid 1920s. Shortly before Forster finally shaped and published *A Passage to India* he not only wrote about the system of Plotinus with some enthusiasm but spoke of the identities that could be found between it and Indian thought. Shortly after the novel was published he used the same neo-Platonist scheme, as it had been elaborated by Coleridge and Shelley, to point to the imaginative or magical experience he, like them, thought existed at the heart of all great literature.

It is in *Alexandria: A History and a Guide*, published in 1922, that Forster expressly commends the *Enneads* of Plotinus in the translation by Stephen MacKenna.[1] Although Forster is referring to only the first volume of five there are two reasons why, after reading it, he feels confident to speak about the *Enneads* as a whole. The first is that this initial volume, published in 1917, includes (in addition to a translation of the first *Ennead* and Porphyry's *Life*) an invaluable conspectus of the whole Plotinian system composed of important extracts from the later and more mystical *Enneads*.[2] Furthermore, Forster was as well prepared as

---

[1] *AHG*, p. iii.   [2] MacKenna, I, 117–25, 129–58. MacKenna, vol. I, substantially covers the whole ground of the *Enneads*. The basic shape of the neo-Platonist argument is discernible even in (the low-key) *Enn.* I, which is composed of tractates on the Animate and the Man; the Virtues; Dialectic (the Upward Way); True Happiness (including an extensive picture of the ideal sage); Happiness and Time; Beauty (from which Forster quotes in *AHG*); the Primal Good and Secondary Forms of Good; and on the Nature and Source of Evil. Quite apart from this and the Note on Terminology (upon which Forster draws in *AHG*), there is a Conspectus of the Plotinian System which offers extracts from all six *Enneads*, primarily on the Soul and on the Supreme (passages from which particularly

any man to respond to this volume since, previous to MacKenna, the only person who had been able to render the thought of Plotinus into lucid English had been Forster's close friend and companion, Lowes Dickinson.[3] MacKenna's work is particularly relevant to *Alexandria* since Forster believes that in the neo-Platonists the later city found her highest expression and that Alexandria produced nothing greater than the *Enneads*.

It is MacKenna's summary that Forster uses when he himself summarizes the lectures which form the basis of neo-Platonist philosophy. Forster observes that there is an antithetical movement in the *Enneads* as they deal first with the emanation of creation (as it were) out of God and then with its striving to return. He describes the three hypostases (or progressive emanations) of God as, first, the Unity about which nothing can be predicated, including even Its existence, and which is good only as the goal of all striving; second, the Intellectual-Principle, or Mind, containing all thought of all things; and third, the All-Soul, or conceptions of gods, animals, plants and stones graspable by the senses, with matter ('which seems so important to us') being the last and feeblest emanation. At this point creative power comes to a halt. Forster suggests that this scheme may appear abstruse and less attractive than what he calls the more 'emotional' (properly, the devotional)[4] side of the *Enneads* which speaks of the striving of all parts of God, even the stones, to realize their divine potential, something finally achieved only in a concentrated and imageless state apprehended by way of the 'Mystic Vision'.[5]

---

pertinent to my reading I have listed in the notes). Wherever MacKenna's commentaries seem especially pertinent to Forster's novel (and may have influenced it in detail), I refer to this volume under his name.   [3] G. Lowes Dickinson, unpub. Ms., Fellowship Dissertation on Plotinus and Plato, King's College Library, Cambridge. Dickinson is closely appreciative of Plotinus. 'It is patience and sympathy rather than critical and interpretative ingenuity that is needed to unlock his secret' (pp. 3–4).   [4] I think that Forster, upon reflection, might have preferred the word 'devotional'. He knew that Plotinus would not regard it as a compliment to be called 'emotional' since, according to the Platonist scheme, the emotions must be sublimated in Intellect. In *PI* Forster makes a careful distinction between the emotional (Muslims) and the devotional (Hindus). The Muslim Aziz shares in mystical experience only when he grapples 'beneath the shifting tides of emotion which can alone bear the voyager to an anchorage but may also carry him across it on to the rocks' (VII, 65).   [5] *AHG*, pp. 66–7. It is commonly supposed that Plotinus devalued art on the grounds that it constructs an image of an image of Reality and is thus even more illusory than life itself. However, this view derives from a remark Plotinus made in refusing to allow a portrait painter to do (what would probably have been) a simple likeness of him (Porphyry's *Life of Plotinus*, chap. 1, MacKenna, I, 1). Elsewhere, when he wishes

Forster is not the first artist who has been attracted to the *Enneads* for their mystical assertion that matter becomes insubstantial upon recognition of the true spiritual nature of life. Before I argue that this scheme and even the antithetical pattern of the *Enneads* is inherent in *A Passage to India* I should like to demonstrate simply the more general applicability of neo-Platonism to our reading of literature. The theory of the three hypostases (or, as they are seen to be, successive levels of consciousness) suggests that the literary work is more fully realized the closer it gets to the mystical vision. At the least level of achievement there is the work whose images remain disparate, differentiated, fragmented, multiple and as subject to change and chance as anything in the phenomenal world is to ordinary sight. According to this view an imagist approach to literature would not be highly regarded since the purpose of the work should be to locate the unity which underlies diversity, the One which holds together the many and allows the poet quite spontaneously to discover the common identity of unlike images. In the fully realized work the images are indivisible though multiple, the One and the many, the *hen kai pan*.

It might be supposed that by its very nature literature cannot go further than this into some abstract region indefinable in words. In fact, in his critical writings in the mid 1920s, Forster himself suggested that it could and that there are works which not only outstrip others but outstrip even themselves. In the Clark Lectures of 1927 (published as *Aspects of the Novel*) Forster refers to this quality in terms of music;[6] others have preferred to speak in terms of magic. Forster is aware that the neo-Platonists excluded from their writings all references to daily life and that a novelist can (or could then) hardly be expected to do this. None the less in his lectures he regrets the material stuff of the novel[7] as much as he says Plotinus regretted having a body, and the whole thrust of his critical no less

---

to show how Reality is discovered he can find no better image than that of a sculptor at work (*Enn*. I.vi.9; MacKenna, I, 88–9). It is this conception which has been germane to a Romantic theory of art, fostered by, among others, the writers we are here considering. Those writers who value neo-Platonism do so not because it devalues art but, on the contrary, because it provides an explanation of its real worth. Seen imaginatively, neo-Platonism does not suggest that art is an illusion so much as that it remains an illusion, or only relatively real, insofar as it fails to re-arrange the images of life in terms of a coherent all-encompassing Reality. Indian aesthetics draws a nice distinction between *brahmananda* (that is, mystical union) and *rasananda* (the highest aesthetic experience): in *rasananda ahamkara* (that is, egoity, a development or what Plotinus would call 'a throwing outward') subsists (S.K. De, *Sanskrit Poetics as a Study of Aesthetic*, Bombay, 1963, chaps. 4–5).   [6] *AN*, pp. 26, 86, 113–16.   [7] Ibid., esp. chapter II, pp. 17–29.

than his imaginative writing is towards as much of an affirmation of the mystical vision as the negative theology will allow. His perceptive comment that the neo-Platonists were not the disembodied spirits their writing might make them seem but very much human is dependent, I think, on his seeing that their striving for Vision did not constitute a rejection of the ordinary world but an attempt to find the principle which alone could give value to everything within it. For this reason, if we are to read *A Passage to India* in terms of neo-Platonism, the novel may be taken as a comment on its own nature even while it comments on the nature of the universe.

Neo-Platonism is not only the philosophical scheme which has been used most frequently to explicate the nature of imaginative literature: it is also the philosophical scheme which has been used most frequently to explicate the nature of Indian culture. The initial justification for reading *A Passage to India* in terms of neo-Platonism is that when, in *Alexandria*, Forster contrasts the neo-Platonist promise that a man shall *be* God with the Christian one that he shall *see* God, he goes out of his way to liken it to the Indian. Forster was aware that the primary impulse left with Plotinus after his training in Alexandria was to travel East to get in touch with Indian as well as Persian philosophy and points out that, whether or not he actually met Hindus on the quays of Alexandria, his system can be paralleled in the religious writings of India.[8]

That the similarity remained in Forster's mind is evident in his biography of Lowes Dickinson, with whom he travelled on his first visit to India. Forster notes that Dickinson, who in his youth had supposed there was much 'esoteric Buddhism' in the *Phaedrus* and had expressed a wish to vanish into India, had in the event been happy in that country only at Chhattarpur—the scene of J.R. Ackerley's *Hindoo Holiday*.[9] There Dickinson had attuned the prevailing Vaishnavism (or devotional worship of Krishna) to his own

[8] *AHG*, p. 68. Forster had previously referred to the Indian promise that a man shall not see but be God in 'The Gods of India', rev. of *The Gods of India* by Rev. E.O. Martin (1914), rpt in *Albergo Empedocle and Other Writings by E.M. Forster*, ed. George H. Thomson (New York, 1971), p. 222. Forster was almost certainly thinking of the *Bhagavad Gita* (see 'Hymn before Action', 1912, *Abinger Harvest*, London, 1936, pp. 332–4). Forster's statement that Plotinus could have met Hindus on the quays of Alexandria is curiously reminiscent of one made in relation not to Plotinus but to the story of Apollonius of Tyana (see chapter 3, n. 11). Since Apollonius is the central figure in the most important Classical 'passage to India', it is interesting to note that in May 1907 Forster stayed with J.S. Phillimore, whose translation of the biography of Apollonius was published in 1912 (P.N. Furbank, *E.M. Forster: a Life*, 2 vols, London, 1977–8, I, 153).   [9] London, 1932.

Platonism.[10] Since Forster later admitted that he was himself baffled by India in his attempts to write about it,[11] it may be that what he has to say about Dickinson's approach to the worship of Krishna is at least as revealing of his own approach. Bearing this in mind, together with his remarks about Plotinus in *Alexandria*, a reading of *A Passage to India* in terms of the *Enneads* might not only illuminate the novel itself but also determine what, if any, dimension beyond Alexandria India represents.

GODBOLE'S NEO-PLATONISM—AND HIS SONG

The character who in *A Passage to India* accords most closely with the ideal sage of the *Enneads*, the man for whom happiness consists not in action but in wisdom,[12] is Professor Godbole. If we are to argue that neo-Platonism is the key to an understanding of Forster's Hindus and Forster's Hindus are the key to an understanding of his novel, then the argument is going to have to turn very largely on Godbole, and this not in spite of but precisely *because of* the fact that he is largely absent from the novel. Of course Godbole *is* a trifle absurd and Forster will not be taken very seriously when he says that it is in his purple macaroni turban and the patterned clocks on his socks that he reconciles the products of East and West.[13] But then Forster does make the point that according to the Hindu view God, being all-inclusive, participates in practical joking no less than in seriousness,[14] and Forster himself goes on less whimsically to add that the harmony Godbole suggests is 'mental as well as physical'. In fact, it is not in Godbole's wardrobe so much as in his philosophy (which may *appear* equally absurd) that the real harmony between East and West is effected.

Godbole describes his philosophy to Fielding after declining to say whether or not the Marabar expedition has been a catastrophe and whether or not Aziz is innocent. As far as Godbole is concerned legal evidence determines matters of guilt and innocence, but society's laws are no more ultimate than the personal opinion he refuses to give: both are grounded on a faith in individual perceptions. According to his philosophy neither good nor evil are performed in isolation by an individual—they express the whole of the universe. Both are 'aspects of my Lord. He is present in the

---

[10] *Goldsworthy Lowes Dickinson* (London, 1934), pp. 43–4, 137–9.   [11] Note on *PI* in *The Hill of Devi* (London, 1953), p. 155.   [12] *Enn.*, I.v.10 (MacKenna, I, 76–7). See also ibid., I.iv.4 (MacKenna, I, 60–1).   [13] *PI*, VII, 71.   [14] Ibid., XXXIII, 291.

one, absent in the other . . . Yet absence implies presence, absence is not non-existence . . . '.[15] This Hindu position (as baffling to some of Forster's readers as it is to Fielding) is in fact that of Plotinus: 'From none is that Principle (the Good) absent and yet from all; present, it remains absent save to those fit to receive, disciplined into some accordance, able to touch it closely by their likeness and by that kindred power within themselves through which, remaining as it was when it came to them from the Supreme, they are enabled to see insofar as God may at all be seen'.[16] It is as important for Plotinus as it is for Godbole to establish that each several thing in the cosmos is affected by all else by virtue of a common participation in the All, and that life does not look to the individual but to the whole.[17] In that individual souls are one with the Soul of the universe we participate in good; in that we are embodied we all share in the evil abroad in the universe.[18]

Godbole's explanation of this philosophy to Fielding provides a perspective on his song at the tea-party which had proved equally bewildering to the guests there. Again, Plotinus is pertinent. Referring to the All, in a central passage on the One Life, he writes: 'Not that It has to come and so be present to you; it is you who have turned from It'.[19] In the words of Godbole's song Krishna, Indian image of the All, neglects or refuses to come: it is we who have to go to Krishna, or rather, less dualistically, actually take on the form of Sri Krishna, as Godbole aspires to do, and assimilate ourselves to him.

Fielding, exasperated as he is by (what is to his rational perception) Godbole's obtuseness about the Marabars, none the less still wants to have Godbole's opinion about the moral propriety of his resignation from the Club.[20] Godbole's philosophy may be baffling but Godbole attracts just the sort of instinctive trust which Plotinus makes a prerequisite for Vision.[21] On first meeting him we learn that for him tranquillity appears to swallow up everything, whereas the rest of the characters have no reserve of tranquillity to draw upon.[22] Tranquillity is the term used in MacKenna's translation of the *Enneads* to describe the contemplative state the sage must realize if he is to be Vision itself.[23] Neo-Platonism

[15] Ibid., XIX, 177–9.   [16] *Enn.*, VI.ix.4 (MacKenna, I, 157). See also ibid., v.v.8–9; VI.iv.2; VI.ix.7; VI.ix.14. Coleridge, probably with Plotinus in mind, touches on the debilitating experience of 'God present without manifestation of his presence' in *BL*, II, 294.   [17] Ibid., IV.iv.32, 39. The most important philosophical problems arising from this are considered in ibid., VI.ii.21; VI.iii.9.   [18] Ibid., IV.ix.1.   [19] Ibid., VI.v.12.   [20] *PI*, XXI, 193.   [21] Ibid., XIX, 176; *Enn.*, VI.ix.4.   [22] Ibid., VII, 76–7.   [23] *Enn.*, III.viii.6. Cf. Gokal the Brahmin in L.H.

advocates precisely the kind of abstract thought which, we are told, an encounter with Godbole's mind will evoke.[24]

The most strenuous action performed by Godbole in the earlier part of the novel is the singing of the song at the tea-party. To this song may be traced the whole curious course of events thereafter. The song enables us to explain why there would have been no story without it and why the novel we do have, like Godbole himself, slips off just when it seems to be most needed; its words, like those Godbole himself might have uttered at the trial, lacking both basis and conclusion and floating through the air.[25] The song consists of a series of sounds unrelated to known forms of music and it is superseded by an absolute stillness.[26] A study of music may tell us something about the nature of Godbole's song and so may a study of poetry and philosophy. Yet it is none of these. It is the song not of a nightingale (or *bulbul* of Persian poetry) but of an unknown bird and reaches into that silence to which music, poetry and philosophy can all point, being as they are the beauty which is the bloom upon truth. But however elusive the nature of the song itself, its effect within the novel is quite precise. It has been a call to Vision to all those present and they ignore it at their spiritual peril.

Specifically, Godbole's song has been a call to the slumbering spirit, registering only the distinction between pleasure and pain, to break out (like Psyche) from its cocoon of self-enthralment and social endeavour.[27] Speaking to Fielding later, Adela makes the point that the song had left her living at half pressure[28] and suggests that it had exposed the inadequacy of her personal life. As a result of this she develops an irritation against Ronny which is really against herself,[29] breaks off her engagement before animal contact restores it and, still aware that her life is all out of proportion and that there is something to which she has not been attentive enough, goes ill-equipped into the cave.[30]

While Adela resents the apathy which overtakes her after the song has exposed her spiritual inadequacy,[31] Mrs Moore accepts hers. Even before she has heard the song India has impressed upon her that, though we must insist that God is Love, God is not to be so easily located or so readily summoned as Christianity would have us believe.[32] She has become aware of the silence

---

Myers, *The Root and the Flower* (London, 1935), who quotes Plotinus to summarize *his* philosophy (pp. 186, 217).   [24] *PI*, VII, 74.   [25] Ibid., XIX, 176.   [26] Ibid., VII, 77–8.   [27] Ibid., XIV, 133. Cf. *Enn.*, VI.ix.9. See also chapter 4, p. 133.   [28] Ibid., XXVI, 240.   [29] Ibid., VIII, 79.   [30] Ibid., VIII, 81–2, 86, 92; XV, 152–4.   [31] Ibid., VIII, 79; XIV, 133.   [32] Ibid., V, 50–1.

which exists beyond the remotest echo and is therefore somewhat more attuned to the ostensibly negative song Godbole sings. After hearing it she is no longer so committed to the social conviction that has brought her to India, namely, that marriage is efficacious,[33] and on the day of the Marabar expedition she even senses that marriage might actually be a bar to man's happiness, an idea which strikes her in the image of a person trying to take hold of her hand.[34] That idea is personified in the novel as Godbole and, metaphorically speaking, if any character may be said to offer his hand (or mind) to Mrs Moore, it is Godbole.

An explanation of why the two English ladies have been wrong-footed by India may be offered by reading one incident on the journey to the Marabars in terms of the *Enneads*. The sunrise fails. The sun, we are told, has power but no beauty, it is not 'the unattainable friend', 'the eternal promise', 'the never-withdrawn suggestion that haunts our consciousness'.[35] But if virtue has appeared to fail in the celestial fount[36] and Adela gets sunstroke it is because she has sought in the sunrise, as in India generally, something of scenic, or material, interest. Plotinus, taking the sun as an image for godhead, says that it is always difficult to tell (as it is difficult to tell approaching the Marabars) whether or not the sun has risen but that this is all the more reason to await it with tranquillity, confident that it is capable of filling the contemplating Intellect—above which alone it can dawn—with a power which is also beautiful.[37] The women have been looking at India in the wrong way. Like Forster when he began his novel, they have expected India to provide answers through its external forms (they have turned their souls outwards, as Plotinus would say) and become ensnared by the magic (or *maya*) of appearances. According to Plotinus only the Self-intent, those absorbed in inward contemplation, go free of this magic.[38] He specifically names caring for children and planning marriage (activities designed to establish personal relationships and ensure the regeneration of matter as it participates in human form) as examples of the bait which causes people to fall under a spell which deludes them, and it is precisely these which have brought Mrs Moore and Adela to India.[39]

Fielding also feels the effect of Godbole's song. But in spite of Godbole's prompting ('it was as if someone had told him there was such a moment') he misses his chance of Vision (the Marabars

---

[33] Ibid., VIII, 93.   [34] Ibid., XIV, 135.   [35] Ibid., X, 113.   [36] Ibid., XIV, 138. The women, disappointed, suppose that there has been 'a false dawn'.   [37] *Enn.*, v.v.8. This passage from Plotinus Coleridge uses centrally in *BL*, I (pt. II), 248–9.   [38] Ibid., IV.iv.40, 43–4 (MacKenna, I, 151). See also IV.viii.8.   [39] *PI*, III, 25; VIII, 93; XIV, 135.

transformed) just after he has asserted the innocence of Aziz.[40]
The best he can do is to see the Marabars as romantic, a perception associated with the ultimately abortive pantheism of 'dearest
Grasmere', as spiritually unproductive for Fielding as it has been
for Ronny.[41] The *Theos* is not to be sought in the *pan*. The reflection about the true nature of the echo remains forever at the verge
of Fielding's mind.[42] Similarly, the significance of Godbole's song
eludes him to the end, though not the recollection of it, which still
preoccupies him during his final meeting with Aziz.[43]

BEYOND HUMANISM

A Passage to India is not essentially a humanistic novel. It reveals that
the very best sort of humanism ('good will plus culture and
intelligence')[44] is incapable of sustaining a single friendship, let
alone the whole world. Forster makes the point that Fielding, like
Adela, remains a dwarf without the apparatus for judging whether
or not the hundred Indias are one.[45] Once more it is Plotinus who
can suggest why this is. Fielding is an atheist and, according to the
Enneads, the whole question of visionary experience cannot even
be discussed with those who have 'drifted far from God'.[46] If the
Englishwomen are in India to foster personal relationships, Fielding is concerned with 'teaching people to be individuals, and to
understand other individuals'.[47] It is basic to the *Enneads* that the
individual in any form, 'while more readily accessible to our cogni-
zance', does not in fact exist.[48] Earlier on Fielding could at least
say of himself that, minus the critical holiness, he resembled a holy
man in that he was not 'planning marriage'[49] and so was free—in
another phrase which echoes the *Enneads*—of 'the desire for
possessions'.[50] By the end of the novel, when, unlike Mrs Moore,
he has been able to return to a European world which takes him
farther than ever from India, he cannot even say that: he is married, about to have a child and Aziz has become for him merely 'a
memento'.[51] He remains closed to the spirit of Hinduism, ignorant
of the fact that Aziz, far from being able to enlighten him as 'an
Oriental',[52] will be unable to do so precisely because he accepts
that limiting definition of himself.[53]

[40] Ibid., xx, 191–2.   [41] Ibid., VIII, 82; XIV, 138; XXVIII, 259; XXXII, 284.
[42] Ibid., XXXI, 277.   [43] Ibid., XXXI, 278; XXXVII, 322.   [44] Ibid., VII, 60.   [45] Ibid.,
XXIX, 264–6.   [46] *Enn.*, VI.ix.5.   [47] *PI*, XI, 119.   [48] *Enn.*, VI.iii.9. Plotinus
takes up this subject in ibid., II.i.1–2.   [49] *PI*, XI, 119.   [50] Ibid., XXVI, 242.
Plotinus refers to the divine state where nothing can induce 'the desire of
possession' (*Enn.*, I.ii.1).   [51] Ibid., XXXVII, 320–1.   [52] Ibid., XXXVII,
322.   [53] Ibid., II, 21; XXVII, 255; XXXVI, 313.

The mosque, we are told, also misses the universe which Fielding has missed or rejected.[54] Aziz traces his culture back to the Mughal emperors, the first of whom, Babur, found India alien.[55] The Muslims value the Plotinian secondaries of Form and Beauty: the arts of architecture and poetry and the gracefulness of speech and gesture which are 'the social equivalent of Yoga'.[56] The God to which they point becomes a social formulation, even a pun,[57] and consequently religious devotion is too easily reduced to its social form of personal emotion. Plotinus speaks of the way that the soul's seeing is baulked 'by the passions and by the darkening that matter brings to it'.[58] Emotion determines the way the Muslims use words, not literally like the British but as an expression of mood, and it causes Aziz—again concerned, as Plotinus suggests it is fatal to be, with marriage (Fielding's)—to build his life on a mistake.[59] Aziz is already involved in the Islamic social obligation of 'caring for children',[60] which Plotinus regards as part of the delusory magic. The concern for 'the society of the future' which this represents combines with his personal experience to drive him to care for something else Plotinus asserts that a wise man will ignore: 'colonizations and the founding of states . . . or the ruin of his fatherland'.[61]

It may be evident by now that I am arguing for a reading of *A Passage to India* in terms of neo-Platonism not simply on the grounds of an identity between Godbole's philosophy and that of Plotinus but also because Forster makes all the characters in his novel subject to the philosophy which Godbole embodies. It is in the light of the same neo-Platonist scheme that the final ride of Aziz and Fielding may be read. In answer to the question of whether the two men can be friends, the earth in its hundred voices says: 'No, not yet' and—to show that the timing of their reconciliation is not, as Aziz suggests, dependent on the coming of

[54] Ibid., XXXI, 277.   [55] Ibid., XXXVI, 308. Cf. the essay on Babur written in 1921 and published in *Abinger Harvest* (pp. 292–6) where the Mughal love of detail is set over against the ways of a race 'which has never found either moral or aesthetic excellence by focussing upon details'. Eventually Babur, like Aziz, is drawn into the orbit of Hindu mysticism.   [56] Ibid., II, 16–18; IX, 103–4; XXVII, 252–3. Note that the Muslims appreciate a poetry of nostalgia ('Gone, gone'), as opposed to that of appeal ('Come, come'), ibid., XXX, 270.   [57] Ibid., XXXI, 277.   [58] *Enn.*, I.viii.4 (MacKenna, I, 96).   [59] *PI*, XXXI, 272; XXXV, 304–5. Fielding had earlier taken notice of this emotional use of language (ibid., VII, 70). The Marabar expedition itself would not have taken place had not Aziz found his words being taken literally instead of as an expression of mood (ibid., VII, 67–8, 72).   [60] Ibid., XI, 117, 119.   [61] Ibid., XXX, 269; XXXVII, 323–4; *Enn.*, I.iv.7 (MacKenna, I, 64–5). Godbole concurs with Plotinus on the subject of patriotism (*PI*, XXXIV, 295–6). See also *Enn.*, III.ii.15 (MacKenna, I, 154–5).

political independence to India[62]—the sky says: 'No, not there'.[63] On the face of it Forster is being even more relentless than Kipling, who at least excepted 'strong men' from his conclusion that East and West should not meet before earth and sky stood together on Judgment Day.[64] In *Aspects of the Novel*, however, Forster insists that the chronological ending of a novel is far from being its real conclusion.[65] He may well have had his own last novel in mind.

The place which is holding Aziz and Fielding apart is diversified India, the India of a hundred voices.[66] To this India the two men are subject because, in direct proportion to the share of action they have in the novel, they remain ignorant of the One India. Like the hundred Krishnas of Godbole's song[67] the hundred Indias have to be apprehended as an abstract or imageless One. The One India, no less than the hundred, being inclusive of them, denies that reconciliation is to be contained in a particular time or place. Unlike the negation of the many Indias, however, that of the One (in common with the One of the *Enneads*) implies infinite possibility and does not regard time or place as ultimate.[68] It is for this reason that Forster comes to recognize that India is not, as he had earlier supposed, a promise (that man definitely will realize his divine identity with all things) but an appeal (to man to aspire towards its possibility in the abstract).[69] Forster's novel, like Godbole's song, may cease upon 'the sub-dominant' but it does not conclude there.

Before considering further the hypothesis that *A Passage to India* is not so much about several Indias mutually at variance as about One India in various stages of Self-realization, I should stress that literature, being composed of words which are images and of images which symbolize ideas, is not on the face of it mystical abstraction. If mystical experience is imageless and self-contained then it would seem that the materials of a literary work could at best only point to the possibility of its existence. Yet it is equally true that the possibility of the existence of something abstract and self-contained can be predicated only by some form more tangible than itself. Furthermore, the mystic vision which is all-encompassing cannot by definition exclude the ideal and imaginary world of literature. If a novel cannot contain mystical ex-

[62] Ibid., XXXVII, 324.   [63] Ibid., XXXVII, 325.   [64] 'The Ballad of East and West', first and last stanzas, *Rudyard Kipling's Verse: Inclusive Edition*, 3 vols (London, 1919), I, 308, 313–14.   [65] *AN*, pp. 26–8, 60, 66–7.   [66] *PI*, XXIX, 264; XXXVII, 325.   [67] Ibid., VII, 78.   [68] e.g. *BA*, 2.3.6; 3.9.26; 4.2.4.   [69] *PI*, XIV, 137.

perience, it could, perhaps, by a process of assimilation, be totally transformed by it. Were this to happen to a novel its condition, as Forster hoped, might approximate to that of poetry or music.[70]

Godbole provides a perfect analogue for the novelist because his religious rites stand in much the same relationship to mysticism as literature may do. In a way which is not incongruous to the syncretistic Indian mind,[71] he is simultaneously an *Advaitin* (espousing the philosophy that there is no duality of either matter and spirit or man and God) and a *bhakta* (or religious devotee who asserts that an apprehension of total union is actually dependent on a sense of the distinct separateness of lover and beloved).[72] Godbole's song reconciles this apparent contradiction. He takes on the persona of 'a milkmaiden' (that is, a *gopi*, here presumably Radha) who calls on Krishna to come to her only and so be united in love. Short of being granted such an exclusively personal relationship she implores Krishna to multiply himself a hundredfold and appear to others as well as to herself. But, as Godbole explains to Mrs Moore, Krishna does not come in this, or in any other, song. According to Godbole's philosophy if a second distinct image appeared it would circumscribe the infinite potential of an abstract, or mystical, One. His song remains one of pure aspiration.

Because *bhakti* cuts the Gordian knot of metaphysics and uses images of separateness, and especially that of separated lovers, it may be particularly appealing to a novelist, whose novel must necessarily live among the manifold and diverse images of the world and whose theme, according to Forster, is invariably that of love.[73] It should be noticed, however, that *bhakti* is no less abstruse than the Advaita in that, in this context at least, it uses the image of separateness to indicate not actual separateness but, on the contrary, potential Union. For its part, although it forswears duality, Advaita can depict Absolute Reality only in terms of a realm of relative reality. Plotinus, likewise, has to resort to imagery drawn from the sensible world in order to indicate the nature of the Intellectual. Moreover, as Forster notes, Plotinus, by virtue of his profession as philosopher, has to indicate the comprehen-

---

[70] The reference here is to the argument made in *AN*   [71] Staal, p. 224.   [72] If Godbole may be read as a neo-Platonist sage, it is not because he is any the less an Indian Brahmin whose portrait is so meticulously drawn that from a few lines we can deduce his caste (Chitpavan), his philosophy (Advaita) and his religion (a Vaishnavite *bhaktin* follower of Tukaram). Cf. *PI*, VII, 65, 70–1; XIX, 177–9; XXXIII, 285–93; XXXIV, 295 to J.H. Hutton, *Caste in India*, 2nd ed. (Bombay, 1951), pp. 20, 278 and to Staal's remarks. See also G.K. Das, 'The Genesis of Professor Godbole', *Review of English Studies*, XXVIII, No. 109 (Feb. 1977), 56–60.   [73] *AN*, p. 38.

siveness of mystical experience by means of an elaboration of the gradations of matter. Forster is particularly sensitive to this since, by virtue of *his* profession, he too uses language as the material medium through which to discover the comprehensive nature of Reality. As both Plotinus and Forster were aware, the capacity of any sort of material, including language, to do this can be gauged only by the extent to which it has been transformed into something relatively immaterial, or insubstantial. The ironical paradox is that, in art at least, aspiration towards an infinite dimension may itself be the infinite dimension.

If for the *bhakta* God's presence not only is but *can* only be implied through absence, so for the novelist the immaterial or aethereal not only is but *can* only be implied through the material. Forster, like the *bhakta*, uses images of separateness to imply not separateness but potential unity. He is as abstruse as he says Plotinus is. It is not simply that in *A Passage to India* nightmare implies vision and disillusionment implies enlightenment; it is that in each case the former is a necessary concomitant of the latter. The way an opened Marabar cave points on to the abstract conception of an absolute void represented by an unopened cave forces us to conceive of Absolute Reality in terms of something more abstract than the images in Godbole's Vision (or those in Forster's novel). The caves may be regarded not as a negation of Vision but as a necessary postulate of it, indicating not the primacy of matter but the non-exclusive (and therefore potentially all-inclusive) nature of spirit.

Even by those who are prepared to concede to Godbole a paramount place in the novel the caves are frequently seen as offering a challenge too great to be contained by him. He is 'silenced' by mention of them and does not confront them physically.[74] Matter, so the argument runs, has proved too intransigent for even Godbole's refined consciousness. At the heart of things there is only a meaningless void. In *Alexandria* Forster noted that it never seemed to have occurred to the philosophers there that God might not exist.[75] It might seem that in the Indian novel Forster is confronting Godbole and, through him, neo-Platonism with a brute materialism for which their idealism cannot account. In fact, if a Marabar cave is subjected to the same sort of neo-Platonist reading we gave to the sun rising over the Marabars we will see that the Marabars have only as much power as is permitted them by the perceptions of the onlookers. The *Enneads* of Plotinus only exist at all to confront philosophically the problem posed by material-

[74] *PI*, VII, 74.   [75] *AHG*, p. 60.

ism. Plotinus uses the imagery of a sterile and unproductive land to describe spiritual desolation and, following Plato's great myth, he repeatedly uses imagery evocative of the Cave to illustrate the deceptive appearance of matter. Far from the Marabar Caves providing a dimension which was ignored by Plotinus it seems that, if anything, Forster's description of them contains many echoes of the *Enneads*.[76]

For Plotinus matter is 'Essential Evil', 'Authentic Non-Existence'.[77] It is bodiless and formless and it is only when (like an opened Marabar cave) it is penetrated by form that it pretends to a participation in Being it does not really have: 'Its existence is but a pale reflection and less complete than that of the things implanted in it'.[78] Since matter is an absolute lack of all Being its initial imaging will be so faint as to be a mockery:

Its every utterance, therefore, is a lie . . . it is like a mirror showing things as in itself when they are really elsewhere, filled in appearance but actually empty, containing nothing, pretending everything. Into it and out of it move mimicries of Authentic Existents, images playing upon an image devoid of Form, visible against it by its very formlessness . . . they might be compared to shapes projected so as to make some appearance upon what we can only know as the Void.[79]

Of matter participating in form Plotinus says: 'The entrant Idea will enter as an image, the untrue entering the untruth'. This is

a pseudo-entry into a pseudo-entity—something merely brought near, as faces enter the mirror, there to remain just as long as the people look into it . . . All that impinges upon this Non-Being is flung back as from a repelling substance; we may think of an Echo returned from a repercussive plane surface; it is precisely because of the lack of retention that the phenomenon is supposed to belong to that particular place and even to arise there.[80]

Although the whole universe is aspirant it is limited by its own corporeal nature: 'this is no more than such power as body may have, the mode of pursuit possible where the object pursued is debarred from entrance; it is the motion of coiling about, with ceaseless return upon the same path—in other words, it is circuit'.[81] Of all forms of life stone is the least susceptible to an upward tendency, and in a corporeal substance which participates as little in Being

---

[76] A central reference point in English literature regarding the significance for Platonists of caves is to be found in the essay 'On the Cave of the Nymphs', §§ 2–4, *SWP*, pp. 174–7.   [77] *Enn.*, II.iv.10–16; II.v.2–5.   [78] Ibid., VI.iii.7.
[79] Ibid., III.vi.7. (MacKenna, I, 148).   [80] Ibid., III.vi.13–14.   [81] Ibid., IV.iv.16.

and is so little aspirant as a Marabar cave it follows that the coiling will be 'too small to complete a circle'.[82]

This whole conception of matter as being really a void which at the moment it is first penetrated by form takes on the appearance of a mirror which mimics, lies, repels, coils and throws back an echo in such a way as to suggest it has qualities of its own is, I would have thought, extraordinarily evocative of Forster's description of the inside of a Marabar cave. Be that as it may, there still remains the question of whether Forster's Marabars can be dismissed as totally as Plotinus dismisses matter: 'Though Matter is far-extended—so vastly as to appear co-extensive with all this sense-known Universe—yet if the Heavens and their content came to an end, all magnitude would simultaneously pass from Matter with, beyond a doubt, all its other properties'.[83]

In the opening chapter of the 'Caves' section of his novel Forster envisages the world before the advent of the gods as a primal ocean, pure matter 'older than all spirit'.[84] But this conception is not foreign to Plotinus; he too conceives of the universe before it was ensouled: 'It was stark body—clay and water—or, rather, the blankness of Matter, the absence of Being, and, as an author says, "the execration of the Gods" '.[85] If an unopened Marabar cave appears to be the centre of a wholly material universe, it may be remembered that the extreme idealist position, which denies any reality to the effect, is so perfectly the converse of materialism, which denies any reality to the cause, that *their terminology is identical*: the Essential Existence of Plotinus is defined in terms of negatives.[86] It is with good reason Plotinus writes that eventually 'you must turn appearances about or you will be left void of God'.[87]

This need to turn appearances about seems to be quite as important to a reading of *A Passage to India*: the peculiar train of events in the novel *does not make coherent sense* until one does so. Godbole is not, as it appears, being perverse when he refuses to admit

[82] *PI*, XIV, 148.   [83] *Enn.*, III.vi.16.   [84] *PI*, XII, 123–4.   [85] *Enn.*, v.i.2. (MacKenna, I, 131–2). Cf. also the remarks of Plotinus on 'the lower realm' where 'the underlying ground is sterile' and fails 'to attain to the status of Being'—'the world of Appearance' (*Enn.*, VI.iii.8) with the countryside approaching the Marabars (*PI*, VIII, 86–8, 92, 97; XIV, 136, 140; XXVIII, 259). The British do not understand this countryside (ibid., XX, 181).   [86] Plotinus notices the materialist converse in ibid., III.viii.10. Among the Indian materialists are the Svabhavavadins who hold 'that all things arise from inherent properties—both good and evil . . . and since all this world thus arises spontaneously, therefore also all effort of ours is vain . . .' (Asvaghosa, cited in N.N. Bhattacharyya, *History of Indian Cosmogonical Ideas*, New Delhi, 1971, p. 102).   [87] *Enn.*, v.v.11.

that the visit to the Marabars has been unsuccessful.[88] In fact the caves have actually provided the non-Hindus who visit them with a critical opportunity to confront their spiritual limitations. The cycle Aziz is to feel himself caught in is that of 'mosque, caves, mosque, caves',[89] but as the novel moves on from 'Mosque' and 'Caves' to 'Temple' we increasingly have to consider just how totally Forster is not only following the antithetical movement evident in the *Enneads* but has accepted Plotinus at his most abstruse and followed him out of antithetical thinking altogether: 'Without evil the All would be incomplete. For most or even all forms of evil serve the Universe'.[90]

After her visit to the caves Mrs Moore concludes (exactly contrary to Plotinus) that matter alone has existence and that it is from the huge scenic background of the heavens that all magnitude has passed.[91] Yet she understands that nothing evil (in the Christian sense) has been in the cave.[92] She has experienced the emptiness of the universe and concluded that God is non-existent in it. She is totally disillusioned with marriage, love and all personal relationships.[93] Yet her tirade on this subject (picked up as 'sounds' by a Hindu *mali* outside)[94] is the basis for Adela's moment of Vision at the trial and for the deification of Mrs Moore herself. The cynicism it expresses about any form of personal relationship provides an impersonal perspective on anything Adela supposes might have happened to her, whether in a cave with Aziz or in a church with Ronny.[95] For the first time Adela doubts if any other person was involved in the experience which had resulted from her going into the cave bored with sight-seeing, doubting the propriety of her own marriage and asking Aziz an unconsciously offensive question about his.[96]

For her part Mrs Moore has completely cut adrift from the personal values she had hitherto brought to her social and religious

[88] *PI*, XIX, 176.   [89] Ibid., XXXVI, 313.   [90] *Enn.*, II.iii.18. The same point is made in ibid., III.ii.5 (MacKenna, I, 150).   [91] *PI* XXIII, 208. Even before their experience in the cave, Mrs Moore and Adela have both begun to doubt the efficacy of their activities, Mrs Moore in a general, and therefore impersonal, way (ibid., XIV, 135) and Adela in personal terms (ibid., VIII, 81–3; XV, 152–3).   [92] Ibid., XIV, 148. Initially Mrs Moore, like Adela later, suffers from the delusion that she has been attacked by a *person*.   [93] Ibid., XIV, 150.   [94] Ibid., XXII, 203. Ronny is quite right in thinking there is something subversive about the *mali* picking up 'sounds' but is unaware that this activity is as cosmic in its implications as that of his peon, Krishna, who, in his mundane way, imitates the god, his namesake, by neglecting to come at call (see this chapter, p. 38).   [95] Ibid., XXII, 202. See also ibid., XXII, 206. Adela has also begun to experience this sense of the inadequacy of personal relationships (ibid., XXII, 198). Adela eventually speaks of her *debt* to India (ibid., XXXVI, 310).   [96] Ibid., XV, 152–4; XXIV, 228; XXIX, 264.

life, has broken out of the cocoon which had enveloped her. Her former life has become a dream[97] and she has laid herself open to the Impersonalism which not only promises nothing but which, in its earlier stages, is more likely to be productive of nightmare than vision.[98] While she did not hear Godbole explain to Fielding that God's absence implies his presence, she heard him express the same thing in a different way in the song at the tea-party; she will experience the truth of the same remark at the Marabar trial, where her own absence proves to be a more powerful psychical presence than her physical presence could ever have been; and, become at that time part of a god, she will be further impelled to that place where completeness is found when she impinges on Godbole's consciousness during the visionary frenzy at Mau.

THE SPIRIT BEHIND THE FRIEZE?

There is one concept which is of vital importance to a neo-Platonist reading of the novel. According to the *Enneads* the universe is ensouled,[99] an idea so abstract that for purposes of discussion we have to image out the soul in terms of sight (Vision) or, as Plotinus often prefers, sound.[100] The universal soul, or cosmic sound, is all-pervasive. Once again we are asked to turn appearances about. God is not in space, as art depicts: space is in God.[101] Strictly speaking, God knows no partition and it is as much an illusion of the corporeal realm to say that a soul is part of a god as to say that it is individual.[102] Partibility, however, can be attributed to soul which still participates in form and, after the Marabar trial, Mrs Moore is still only part of a god in the sense that she is worshipped in particular forms at particular places.[103] Forster, therefore, is consistent with Plotinus when he suggests that Mrs Moore, having acquired 'an invisible power' by appealing to the imagination of the country, has been deified not as 'a whole god, perhaps, but part of one', taking a place in that hierarchy of gods which contributes to 'the philosophic Brahm'—identical as Brahm is with 'That Other' sought by the lesser gods of Plotinus.[104]

---

[97] Ibid., XXII, 206.   [98] Ibid., XIV, 135.   [99] *Enn.*, IV.iii.20 (MacKenna, I, 153–4).   [100] Ibid., VI.iv.12. The Hindu Sphota is described by Colebrooke as the object of mental perception which ensues upon the hearing of an articulate sound (Colebrooke, I, 331–2. See also ibid., I, 372, 397). It points on to the absolute Nada-Brahman.   [101] Ibid., VI.viii.11.   [102] Ibid., VI.iv.14 (MacKenna, 1, 152). The argument is developed in ibid., VI.v.4–5.   [103] *PI*, XXVIII, 257–8.   [104] *Enn.*, VI.v.12.

This elevation of the soul is not inevitable. According to the *Enneads* there are two phases of the soul; the lower, tied to sense impressions, and the higher, freed of them. When the soul is set on self (that is, on individuality and personality) it produces 'its lower, an image of itself—a non-Being—and so is wandering, as it were, into the void, stripping itself of its own determined form'.[105] It may liberate itself from this descent and become illuminated by assimilating itself to the soul above it:

When the two souls chime each with each, the two imaging faculties no longer stand apart; the union is dominated by the more powerful of the faculties of the soul, and thus the image perceived is as one; the less powerful is like a shadow attending upon the dominant, like a minor light merging into a greater: when they are in conflict, in discord, the minor is distinctly apart.[106]

This conception might account for the disparity between Adela's initial perception of what happened to her in the cave (when her vagrant shadow self stands apart and something tangible or physical appears to have taken place) and the integrated vision which comes to her in court following the cessation of the chanting of Mrs Moore's name and of her own insidious echo (evil reflection, as that is, of her own self-centred thoughts). Adela's higher or impersonal soul has been assimilated to the impersonalism of Mrs Moore above it; her lower or personal soul which takes the cosmic personally is not now dominant but subordinate—and so Aziz does not appear in the cave.

The difficulty for the novelist, of course, is to find some way of depicting these subtle spiritual forces at work in the universe. No wonder Forster regretted that the novel had to tell a story. In fact he follows Plotinus in using the imagery of a cosmic sound audible to those receptive enough to let the hearings of sense go by and keep the soul's perception open to sounds from above.[107] These sounds Forster refers to as 'messages from another world'.[108] Previous to the trial Adela 'hears' Mrs Moore state her belief in ghosts[109] and in the innocence of Aziz, although nothing has been said,[110] and at the trial itself, among the 'sounds, which gradually grew more distinct', none has such 'a natural leading power over the soul'[111] as the name of Mrs Moore[112] which, when chanted by the Hindus, not only helps Adela to be rid of her echo and attain

[105] Ibid., III.ix.2.   [106] Ibid., IV.iii.31. The two-fold nature of the soul discussed in *Enn.*, IV is considered by MacKenna, I, 145.   [107] Ibid., v.i.12.   [108] *PI*, XXIX, 266.   [109] Ibid., VIII, 95–6.   [110] Ibid., XXII, 204–5.   [111] *Enn.*, IV.iv.40 (MacKenna, I, 151). See also ibid., IV.ix.3.   [112] *PI*, XXIV, 219, 224–6. See also ibid., XXIV, 221; XXIX, 264.

Vision[113] but helps Mrs Moore herself further along the road of spiritual enlightenment—to which, as Plotinus says, death is no barrier.[114]

Even the atheistical Fielding begins to believe that Mrs Moore has an existence after death.[115] Aziz is certain of this[116] and on account of it is able to continue to partake in the spiritual growth her name represents. The belief in ghosts which he denies verbally but which runs in his blood was evoked by Mrs Moore's first appearance in the mosque[117] and sustains his faith in her long after she has abandoned him to the fateful cave and their personal friendship is over.[118] He fancies she is present at the trial,[119] it is on account of her that he renounces his claim against Adela for compensation,[120] and when after that he opts, like Akbar, to accommodate himself to Hindu India[121] he remains open to those intimations from the Unseen which cause him to love not emotionally but in an impersonal way. Hearing the chant of the Hindu crowd at Mau, which now links the two names, Radha and Krishna, that remained separate in Godbole's original song, Aziz identifies it with the chant of the Hindus during his trial and this revival of the name of Mrs Moore causes him to change his attitude to her son Ralph.[122] Finally, unlike Fielding, he is responsive to the even more subtle prompting—in his case 'not a sight, but a sound'—which flits past him and causes him to promise Adela he will associate her thereafter with the irreproachable Mrs Moore.[123]

Plotinus suggests that even forms of life which are receptive to a significant, or sacred, sound do not necessarily apprehend the significance of it.[124] Aziz can revere the name of Mrs Moore without knowing why and the sound of it has a partial but not total effect

---

[113] Even Adela's surname may be interpreted in terms of a line in the *Enneads*: those who seek the Authentic, we are told, do not necessarily find it: 'it chooses where it will and enters as the participant's power may allow . . . it remains the *quested* and so in another sense never passes over' (ibid., VI.iv.3). See also ibid., VI.iv.8. Mrs Turton particularly remarks on Adela's surname (*PI*, III, 26). In the Paris Review interview (*Writers at Work*, intro. Malcolm Cowley, London, 1958, ser. 1, p. 30), Forster notes that Quested is a country name. He had used it previously in chap. IX of *Howards End*, Abinger ed. (London, 1973), p. 75. It may be interesting to note that in chap. XVI of this novel, Forster has Leonard Bast conceive of the Schlegel sisters as 'a composite Indian god whose waving arms and contradictory speeches were the product of a single mind' (p. 137).   [114] *Enn.*, IV.vii.15(20). The true soul is loosed from the body either by death or by a life of philosophic contemplation (MacKenna, I, 154).   [115] *PI*, XXVII, 254.   [116] Ibid., XXVII, 256.   [117] Ibid., II, 18.   [118] Ibid., XIV, 151; XXII, 206.   [119] Ibid., XXVII, 254–5.   [120] Ibid., XXIX, 262.   [121] Ibid., XXXV, 298.   [122] Ibid., XXXV, 305; XXXVI, 313–14, 316.   [123] Ibid., XXXVII, 322.   [124] *Enn.*, VI.iv.15.

upon him. He perceives that she has penetrated to the Orient. In fact Mrs Moore has penetrated further than the Orient (presupposing, as that does, dualistically, a separate Occident) and it is only the Hindus who are capable of understanding that she has penetrated to the silence and nothingness which underlie the universe.

Contemplative and disinclined to action, the Hindus are not such stuff as novels are made of. For the most part in *A Passage to India* they stand as still and silent as figures in a frieze,[125] but, paradoxically, for that very reason they personify collectively, as Godbole does individually, the spirit behind the frieze. Forster takes a cosmic view of the Hindu social system: 'The fissures in the Indian soil are infinite: Hinduism, so solid from a distance, is riven into sects and clans, which radiate and join, and change their names according to the aspects from which they are approached'.[126] Plotinus, writing of the way Unity takes on the aspect of diversity in the universe, writes: 'We see the Unity fissuring, as it reaches out into Universality, and yet embracing all in one system so that with all its differentiation it is one multiple living thing'.[127]

In their festival the Hindus seek through a mystical inner state not only to embrace all that is in India but to make that passage to more than India which Whitman refers to as the secret of the earth and sky.[128] The final injunction of the *Enneads* that the mystic must leave 'the temple images behind' receives outward ceremonial expression in the novel in the procession to the lake at Mau. There 'earth and sky leant toward one another, about to clash in ecstasy'.[129] Eventually, 'a wild tempest started, confined at first to the upper regions of the air. Gusts of wind mixed darkness and light . . . .'.[130] The tempest engulfs heaven and earth and immerses people of all religions alike. The emotional centre of all this, Forster tells us, could be located no more than could the heart of a cloud. But what he may really be pointing to is suggested by a passage in Plotinus where the radiance within the enlightened soul is compared to the light of a lantern 'when fierce gusts beat about it in a turmoil of wind and tempest'.[131] The Hindu servitor at the

---

[125] *PI*, III, 25; v, 45.   [126] Ibid., XXXIV, 294.   [127] *Enn.*, III.iii.1. At VI.vii.13 it is said that the Intellectual-Principle, on account of being both Collective Difference and Collective Identity, by its very nature modifies into a universe. The matter is discussed in MacKenna, I, 133.   [128] 'Passage to India', Section 9, 11.233–4.   [129] *PI*, XXXVI, 308.   [130] Ibid., XXXVI, 316–17.   [131] *Enn.*, I.iv.8 (MacKenna, I, 65). Cf. *RV*, VII.97.1.

lake,[132] together with the water-chestnut gatherer[133] and the punkahwallah,[134] composes a single archetypal god, emerging, re-emerging and being submerged with the chain of sacred sounds which, first heard in Godbole's song and then again at the trial, reverberates with enough effect at Mau to allow us to suppose that this is the cosmic thread upon which the elements of the novel are strung.

GODBOLE'S VISION—AND FORSTER'S

The description of the festival at Mau is a literary attempt to reflect what Plotinus tried to reflect in philosophy: the mystical vision. It appears to be the climax of the novel and yet, if the novel is to sustain our philosophical reading, this is not so: India does not admit of a climax.[135] Why not? Because neither reader nor writer can say when and where the mystical vision has been achieved: it does not 'fall under' the rules of place any more than of time[136] and, in the event of its achievement, it would cover not just the part but the whole, entire. I have already suggested why the novel should, perhaps, be read as a visionary work. None the less, it is the festival which especially lends itself to being read in terms of a single paragraph from Plotinus. There he explains how the soul obtains its vision of the Good, being stirred towards Intellectual Beings for the radiance about them 'just as earthly love is not for the material form but for the Beauty manifested upon it . . . The soul taking the outflow from the divine is stirred; seized with a Bacchic passion, goaded by these goads, it becomes Love'.[137] Forster describes the festival as an orgy not of the body but of the spirit,[138] and that this particular reference to Bacchus may have been in his mind is the more likely since no European legend has been more frequently associated with India.[139]

Forster's familiarity with the passage in the *Enneads* seems even more evident from his description of the Hindu villagers as they glimpse the image of Krishna: 'A most beautiful and radiant expression came into their faces, a beauty in which there was nothing personal, for it caused them all to resemble one another during the moment of its indwelling, and only when it was withdrawn did they

---

[132] *PI*, XXXVI, 317.   [133] Ibid., VII, 77.   [134] Ibid., XXIV, 218.   [135] Ibid., XXXVI, 318.   [136] Ibid., XXXIII, 290. See the opening sentence of the Temple section (ibid., XXXIII, 285). For terminology, cf. *Enn.*, VI.iii.3.   [137] *Enn.*, VI.vii.22.   [138] *PI*, XXXIII, 290.   [139] See chapter 5, pp. 172–3.

revert to individual clods'.[140] Plotinus says that if the soul remains in the Intellectual-Principle the Vision is not complete: 'The face it sees is beautiful no doubt but not of power to hold its gaze because lacking in the radiant grace which is the bloom upon beauty'.[141] Earlier Plotinus has spoken of Vision (of which the beauty and radiance are a manifestation) as pertaining to 'the self-indwelling Soul'.[142] In the light of Plotinus Forster's passage may be read to suggest that, in so far as any onlooker can ever know, the villagers have become Love and do enjoy the mystical Vision. That is, until they fall under 'the rules of time' and revert to 'individual clods': 'Individuals have their separate entities, but are at one in the (total) unity'.[143]

However close Forster may be in his description of the Hindu festival to the terminology as well as to the sentiment of the *Enneads*, we still have to decide whether he is himself quite so unreserved about neo-Platonism. His initial qualification that the onlooker can never know when the mystical vision has been achieved is, in fact, taken to a further abstract level when he interjects to say that even the adept himself cannot say: 'How can it be expressed in anything but itself'?[144] This remark is pertinent to what happens to Godbole at the festival. The argument that ultimately the Hindus exclude nobody and nothing else in the novel ('foreigners, birds, caves, railways and the stars')[145] and that Forster's viewpoint may be identified with Godbole's might be thought to depend on our certainty that Godbole has enjoyed a complete vision. Yet Godbole's experience appears to be abortive. His soul is 'a tiny reverberation', part of 'the chain of sacred sounds' which evoke Vision. At Mau certain definite images impinge on his memory and he remembers, in a progressive descent through creation, Mrs Moore, a wasp and a stone, images which the novel has already linked in a chain of association.[146] At this point Godbole is returned to his immediate environment and we

[140] *PI*, XXXIII, 286.   [141] *Enn.*, VI.vii.22. Plotinus also associates the terms beauty and radiance with Vision in ibid., v.viii.10; VI.vi.18; VI.vii.21, 36. Plotinus, at his least 'Greek', has to conclude that, while beauty and form emanate from Unity and depend on it, the One is beyond both (see ibid., v.v.10–13; VI.vii.32–3).   [142] Ibid., III.viii.6. MacKenna's translation of Porphyry's Life of Plotinus (chap. 10) records that Plotinus 'had for indwelling spirit a Being of the more divine degree' (I, 11).   [143] Ibid., VI.ii.21.   [144] *PI*, XXXIII, 290.   [145] Ibid., XXXIII, 289–90. This reflects on the contrary exclusiveness of Christianity (ibid., IV, 36). A similar eclectic list of beings which depend on the One is to be found in *Enn.*, VI.ix.i (see also MacKenna, I, 141).   [146] Ibid., III, 33; IV, 36; XXXIII, 288, 293. Burra, in his Introduction to the Everyman edition (pp. xviii–xix), noticed one recurrence of the wasp and other critics have elaborated on this.

are told that 'he had been wrong to attempt the stone, logic and conscious effort had seduced'.[147] What has gone wrong? Has Godbole's philosophy failed him and thereby invalidated our reading of the novel in terms of it? If Plotinus is to continue to be our guide it will be seen that it is not the philosophy which has proved inadequate. In a central passage on the nature of the One Life Plotinus speaks of that intellectual or imaginative state where the one soul holds within it all souls or intelligences, with every item standing forth distinctly, multiple yet indivisible.[148] But, he adds (and the *but* is very important), this association of 'item after item' is not identity[149] and the soul must speed to 'something greater to its memory' which acts not by seeing and knowing but by loving.[150] For that the lover must elaborate within himself an immaterial image,[151] the soul must be kept formless.[152] Godbole allowed himself to be distracted by his religious duties, by externals: the need for a new hymn and the re-adjustment of his pince-nez.[153] Plotinus specifically warns against 'throwing outward' during the looking.[154] It is precisely the tiny fragments of Godbole's consciousness that attend to 'outside things' which permit 'tiny splinters of detail', distinct images, to emerge from the imageless vision, or 'universal warmth'.[155] Thereafter item can follow item, however affirmative the under-standing, and ultimately one image will prove exclusive of the rest.

To the humanist Fielding it does not seem possible 'for one human being to be sorry for all the sadness that meets him on the face of the earth, for the pain that is endured not only by men, but by animals and plants, and perhaps by the stones'.[156] The image which proves resistant to Godbole is stone and it is consistent with Plotinus to say that this is because stone, the mineral by which the void of a Marabar cave is contained, is of all creation the least aspirant. Forster seems to follow Plotinus very closely in his re-marks on the life of stones (a subject rarely considered by others)[157] and it is evident that he too regards stone as the visible form least receptive to Vision. It does not follow from this, however,

---

[147] Ibid., XXXIII, 286-8.   [148] *Enn.*, VI.iv.14; VI.ix.5. See also MacKenna, I, 133.   [149] Ibid., v.iii.17.   [150] Ibid., VI.vii.22, 35; VI.ix.4 (MacKenna, I, 157).   [151] Ibid., VI.vii.33.   [152] Ibid., VI.ix.7.   [153] *PI*, XXXIII, 287.   [154] *Enn.*, VI.ix.7. The need to hold the Vision within is also stressed in ibid., v.iii.9 (MacKenna, I, 155); v.vii.10-11; VI.v.10.   [155] The need for the soul to take 'warmth' is mentioned in *Enn.*, VI.ix.4 (see MacKenna, I, 157).   [156] *PI*, XXVI, 248.   [157] Cf. Plotinus on 'the indwelling earth-principle' in 'the growing and shaping of stones, the internal moulding of mountains as they rise' (*Enn.*, VI.vii.11) with Forster on the Marabars (*PI*, XII, 123). Cf. also Plotinus on boulders and stones (*Enn.*, IV.iv.27) with Forster (*PI*, XV, 151).

that any inherent power should be attributed to stone or that we
should see the Marabars as weighing anything at all in the balance
against Godbole's philosophy. Quite the reverse. Plotinus goes out
of his way to explain that you cannot use a stone by way of contrast
to the One: the One 'is not like a stone, some vast block lying
where it lies, covering the space of its own extension, held within
its own limits, having a fixed quantity of mass and of assigned
stone-power'.[158] The One, says Plotinus, is wholly free of attributes and qualities.[159] It is fallacious ever to conceive of the
metaphysical in terms of the physical. If we do, once again we shall
have failed to turn external appearances about. Spirit operates by
way of all conceivable principles but lies outside them all and encompasses them all. For this reason Plotinus says: 'Seeking Him,
seek nothing of Him outside: within is to be sought what follows
upon Him; Himself do not attempt'.[160] Godbole should not have
'attempted' stone not only because stone is physically ultimately
most resistant to absorption into the metaphysical but because the
metaphysical Ultimate, which alone could absorb it, should not be
attempted. The ultimate vision (which isn't really Vision but Union) will not be achieved by conscious effort any more than by
logic. It will come, beyond image and idea, in a mystical state in
which there can be no perception but only the existence of infinite love. It is for this reason that Godbole was initially 'silenced'
by mention of the Marabar Caves and avoided either talking about
them or visiting them.

The title of Forster's novel is apposite. As he says, the passage
to *more than* India (to the universal mystical experience which India has made central to its culture) is 'not easy, not now, not here,
not to be apprehended except when it is unattainable'.[161] Plotinus
also says that to grasp the nature of Unity is 'not easy' but that we
have a way through the Ideas. He suggests further that the difficulty for the soul is that the nature of what it is trying to grasp (the
Formless) and its means to grasping it (assimilation by means of
identity) preclude knowledge of attainment.[162] If the passage is

[158] *Enn.*, VI.v.11.   [159] Ibid., VI.v.12 (MacKenna, I, 146). See also ibid., v.v.13.
Plotinus suggests we should speak of Being 'without any attribute' (ibid., III.vii.6).
The point is again made in ibid., VI.iv.1; VI.viii.11; VI.ix.3. See MacKenna, I, 141
and compare terminology with *PI*, XXXVI, 316.   [160] Ibid., VI.viii.18. The peculiar
use of the word 'attempt' here in relation to Vision, like the conception of God
'without attributes' and that of mystical experience 'falling under' the rules of
Time, together with that of the soul trying to 'attain' and 'apprehend', suggests that
in conceiving of the Hindu festival Forster was indebted to MacKenna even for his
terminology.   [161] *PI*, XXXVI, 317. Cf. terminology with *Enn.*, VI.ix.3–5,
11.   [162] *Enn.*, VI.ix.3–4. (MacKenna, I, 156–7).

not to be apprehended except when it is unattainable, neither is it to be attained except when it is inapprehensible. What Forster appreciates, consistently with Plotinus, is that in an approach to mysticism the novel can operate only at the level of Ideas, of the Imagination, of 'India'. The closest it could come to indicating the abstract mystical state which is said to contain the secret of the earth and sky would be to show an enlightened mind at the level equivalent to its own capacity—that where the images are indivisible but multiple—and to depict all the disparate images in the novel in terms of that mind, i.e. Godbole's. According to my reading *A Passage to India* does just this and on that account we may argue that Forster is not being sceptical of the neo-Platonist position but entirely consistent with it when, like Plotinus,[163] he says that it is impossible to tell whether the mystical vision has succeeded.[164] Language forces him no less than Plotinus to resort to the negation of infinite possibility[165] and all he can properly do as a novelist is portray an India aspirant to something more than India.

This reading of the novel suggests that it is not essentially the study of personal or even inter-racial relationships it is often taken to be but of an Impersonalism which reaches out into the common ground not merely of humanity but of existence. The best English Romantic poems may be more fruitfully read not as exercises in egotistical sublimity but as visions of those objective truths which lie in the Imagination, or (in modernized Platonist parlance)[166] the Collective Unconscious. That Forster's India stands as an image for the Imagination is an idea which receives support from the literary criticism he wrote in the mid 1920s. I have already referred to the Clark lectures where, again using that antithetical shape which begins with the material and moves towards the immaterial, he argues that only by touching a mystical region can a novel release the tremendous current which, after the reading of it is over, allows every item to lead a larger existence than was possible at the actual time of reading.[167] Less diffuse than the Clark lectures and

---

[163] Ibid., IV.iv.6. Of adepts, Plotinus writes: 'It is that they see God still and always, and that as long as they see, they cannot tell themselves they have had the vision; such reminiscence is for souls that have lost it'.   [164] *PI*, XXXIII, 290.   [165] *Enn.*, VI.viii.8. (MacKenna, I, 143).   [166] C.G. Jung, *The Archetypes and the Collective Unconscious*, trans. R.F.C. Hull (London, 1959), pp. 4, 33, 75–6. This work also owes much to the mandalas of Mahayana Buddhism and places Jung within that synthesizing tradition which has approached the East by way of Platonism.   [167] *AN* supports a neo-Platonist approach to the novel in a number of ways. Forster's initial and essential point is that the novel, if it is to penetrate to life's mysteries (pp. 60–1, 70–1), must go free of the time sequence to

closer in time to the writing of *A Passage to India* is 'Anonymity: an Inquiry' (1925), an essay in which Forster quite overtly takes his lead from the Romantic poets, Coleridge and Shelley, who, like him, were responsive to neo-Platonism.[168]

What he really values in writing, Forster says in 'Anonymity', is the power words have not simply to quicken our blood but also to do something else that, could it be defined, would explain the secret of the universe: namely, create a world which seems more real and solid than daily existence. This world

> created by words exists neither in space nor time though it has semblances of both, it is eternal and indestructible . . . *We can define it best by negations*. It is not this world, its laws are not the laws of science or logic, its conclusions not those of common sense. And it causes us to suspend our ordinary judgments.[169]

which it is inevitably tied (chaps. I, II). The successful novel is not to be read as 'a chronological chart' but, like life, valued for 'a few notable pinnacles' (p. 19). It is space, and not time, which is 'the lord' of *War and Peace* (p. 27). To comprehend this, the reader must keep an ear open to hear the novelist's 'voice' (pp. 27, 29). For Plotinus, Space is the Soul, within which Time (the life of the soul in movement) is reabsorbed into Eternity'(*Enn.*, III.vii.11–12). As we have seen, he, too, insists that the initiate must be receptive to 'sounds from above', and Forster here conceives of the novelist as God-like (p. 39). If love (so important to Plotinus also) predominates in fiction, it is because this is indicative of the state of mind in which the novelist creates (p. 38). He makes visible the invisible life of his characters and makes the unexplained appear explicable (p. 44). He goes beyond the evidence (p. 44); his world is not that of the law courts (p. 59 – vide, the strange course of events in Chandrapore). The song of Godbole and the singing of the Hindus may seem more important in the light of Forster's respect for fiction which has a prophetic quality, 'a song' (pp. 93, 94) which, unlike fantasy, not only implies but expresses the supernatural (p. 78): 'The extension, the melting, the unity through love and pity occur in a region which can only be implied, and to which fiction is perhaps the wrong approach' (p. 92). Given this expansion, every item in the novel can lead a larger existence than was possible at the time of reading (pp. 91, 116). From the outset, when he evokes the mystics (pp. 19–20, 28), Forster, though not himself to be identified with Tolstoy (p. 27) or Dostoyevsky (pp. 91–94) any more than with Gide (p. 71) or Lawrence (p. 99), is constantly concerned with the difficulty fiction has in approaching a mystical dimension.   [168] *Two Cheers for Democracy*, Abinger ed. (London, 1972), pp. 77–86. Forster starts with Coleridge and refers to him throughout (pp. 77, 79, 81, 82, 83, 84). For his conclusion about the power of Imagination he simply quotes Shelley (p. 86). The importance of Shelley for Forster can be seen from a reference relating to *PI*. In 'Notes on the English Character' (1920), Forster narrates the original of the incident where Aziz chides Fielding for regarding emotions as a commercial commodity (*PI*, XXVII, 255). The one Englishman Forster can think of who, like his Indian friend, regards the spirit and the emotions as endless and not to be measured and weighed like potatoes, is Shelley (*Abinger Harvest*, pp. 5–6).   [169] Ibid., p. 81 (my italics). The reference here is unmistakably to Coleridge's 'suspension of disbelief'. Cf. MacKenna, I. 141.

The surface personality of the author who creates such a work is wholly eliminated, as is that of the responsive reader who is transformed towards the condition of the author. This common ground where they meet is called God by the mystics.[170] Such a vision of literature is not possible, I would have thought, to a man who is *sceptical* about the passage Godbole makes.

If I advocate an identification of Forster with Godbole in particular it is not because the other characters in *A Passage to India* have no significance. It is that they take on what significance they do have only in terms of the philosophical outlook which Godbole embodies. In their own right they are nothing compared to what Godbole has us see they—and we—potentially are. Forster's Godbole is thus what Forster says Dostoyevsky's Mitya is: at once the novelist's creation and his prophetic vision.[171]

FORSTER: SCEPTICAL OR SPECULATIVE?

In the light of previous readings of *A Passage to India* this reading may appear to be at one—theosophical—extreme. Was Forster not influenced by Indian thought? Doesn't *A Passage to India* display considerably more scepticism than this idealistic reading suggests? If I turn to these questions now it is for three related reasons. First, I want to show that this reading has not been done in ignorance of these objections and that to take them into account does not necessarily lead to *alternative* readings of the novel. Second, they are the sort of objections which are bound to recur throughout this book and to confront them now may remove an obstacle to further reading. Third, the answer given to these questions will determine what, if any, special dimension attaches to the image of India.

At the best of times idealism is productive of scepticism—but it requires hardly any scepticism at all on the part of the reader to question whether Forster's point of view in *A Passage to India* is to be so wholly identified with that of Godbole, who is after all only *one* of his characters. It might be argued instead that Forster keeps his detachment and that this is particularly evident in his use of irony, wry or comic as that may be. While it may not matter much, Godbole's socks *are* absurd and, while his philosophy may be profound, it certainly *sounds* nonsense to the sympathetic and, after all, reasonable Fielding.[172] The caves may be muted but their echo

---

[170] Ibid., pp. 83, 86.   [171] *AN*, p. 92. For a distinction between Dostoyevsky's and Forster's 'prophetic' voices, see this chapter, n. 182.   [172] *PI*, VII, 71. Forster's whimsicality has allowed Nirad Chaudhuri to characterize Godbole as a clown

continues to be heard, Aziz and Fielding have salvaged something but not everything and the author, sceptical though not cynical, is prepared to settle for a world which is as much a muddle as a mystery. A reading such as this which regards Forster's novel as even marginally sceptical rather than wholly idealistic is conditioned, I would suggest, by an assumption that idealism is *positively* enlightening. We have seen that the idealism of Plotinus is much more abstruse than this and that, precisely because his idealism must embrace all matter as well as all spirit, he has (and is aware he has) to use exactly the same language as the materialist to indicate the nature of ultimate reality.

The way the novel mirrors this idealist dichotomy may be seen from the simple example of Krishna the peon, who in his mundane way imitates his namesake the god by neglecting to come at call.[173] Is the cosmic concept of the absent Krishna here parodied and reduced to the level of the comic? Or is the comedy of Krishna the peon raised to a cosmic level, which absorbs the mundane? What Forster discovered in Hinduism and what he specifically says in the novel he found lacking in Christianity was precisely this capacity of the cosmic to embrace the comic.[174] The irony in the novel is not just the comic irony of the sceptic; it is the cosmic irony of the idealist who has discovered that the formulations of language do not permit idealism to be differentiated from materialism—or mysticism from scepticism.

In conjecturing whether Forster was ever so idealistic as to be identifiable with Godbole I am discounting biography as absolutely as Forster does in his essay 'Anonymity', where he argues that all first-rate literature has a mystical dimension. The Forster who writes about politics in the 1930s and 1940s frequently does have the quiet sceptical voice of the thoughtful intellectual and even the Forster who whimsically imagines himself being compared to Blake and Beethoven[175] does so with the wry scepticism of a writer who is aware that his short stories about the Unseen frequently fail to rise above the merely fanciful.[176] None the less, there is some reason for regarding *A Passage to India* as work of a different order, as one of those imaginative achievements in the Romantic tradition in which Forster, like the Socrates of the *Phaedrus*, surpassed himself in approaching that region about which no earthly

('Passage to and from India', *Encounter*, II, No. 6, June 1954, 21). The context of the remark is a consideration of the treatment of Indians as 'individuals'. The article, contrary to this chapter, argues that the novel's tacit assumption is that 'Indo-British relations presented a problem of personal behaviour and could be tackled on the personal plane'. (p. 23).   [173] Ibid., VIII, 95.   [174] Ibid., XXXIII, 291.   [175] 'My Own Centenary' (1927), *Abinger Harvest*, pp. 59–61.   [176] For a definition of fantasy, see *AN*, VI, 76.

poet has yet sung (but which, note, Fielding thinks the Hindus have perhaps found).[177] In 'Anonymity', where Forster speaks about the difficulty of apprehending the central thing about a work, he manifestly follows Coleridge in referring to the need for a suspension of disbelief. This suspension can be achieved only if scepticism is superseded or subverted. Furthermore, Forster is not being purely iconoclastic or negative when, in the same essay, he argues that while information about a writer's life is wholly irrelevant to the central mystery of any first-class work he has done, a study of the work itself is not going to take the student much closer to its essential spirit. This critical position has quite practical literary implications. These are evident in an essay Forster wrote that same year (1925) in tribute to John Keats.[178]

In the essay on Keats the name of Keats is not actually mentioned until the final paragraph and both the life and work are wholly ignored except in so far as a few biographical details and a bit of doggerel are pertinent to the bourgeois sense of propriety of his guardian, Mr Abbey. The central mystery about poetry which the name of Keats symbolizes is defined exclusively in terms of what poetry is not. The essay makes a successful statement about poetry precisely because it deals not with Keats but with Mr Abbey, not with poetry but with (what according to Shelley is) its antithesis: Mammon. Forster concentrates his attention on Mr Abbey not because he is sceptical of the achievement of Keats but because he is sceptical of the capacity of language to indicate the mystical nature of that achievement other than through an exposition of its very concrete opposite. The aesthetic questions Forster confronts in 1925 are, I suggest, a direct outgrowth of his own imaginative experience as a novelist in the period preceding the publication of *A Passage to India* in 1924. The definition of Keats in terms of Mr Abbey is not done to give Mr Abbey the sort of standing enjoyed by Mr Wilcox in *Howards End*. Mr Abbey is there simply as a way of beginning to define Keats, just as information about a tram stop in 'Anonymity' is used as a way of beginning to define the central mystery of poetry. This may lend some plausibility to the suggestion that, just as Plotinus uses matter (which, for him, really has no existence other than as unrefined consciousness) to define spirit, Forster uses the Marabar Caves to indicate the indefinable experience to which Godbole aspires.

The argument that the Forster who wrote *A Passage to India* was so imaginative as to become mystical is not made in ignorance

---

[177] Cf. *PI*, xxxi, 278; *Phaedrus* 247C.   [178] 'Mr and Mrs Abbey's Difficulties' (1925), *Abinger Harvest*, pp. 225–33.

of the fact that the voice of the more prosaic Forster was sometimes that of the rational sceptic. It does not preclude the fact that
the sceptical note can be heard in *A Passage to India* itself. The
point about true scepticism, however, is that its note is unequivocally dominant. On the other hand the existence of mysticism, as
Forster intervenes in his novel to say, is never unequivocal. At
best, the possibility of its existence can be postulated but, unlike
scepticism, never proved. It might seem from this that the only indication there is that the wondering of the sceptic has become the
wonder of the mystic is that the possibility of the latter alternative
actually exists at all. None the less, there is reason to believe that
in *A Passage to India* such a transition has occurred, most notably
because it is not the rational, sceptical ethos of the British—for
whom information is great and shall prevail[179]—to which the rest
of the characters and the action of the novel are subject.

Moreover, this novel, unlike Forster's earlier novels, seems to
have pushed the author beyond any conscious intentions he may
have had. The awkward shape of *A Passage to India*, especially the
mystical 'lump'[180] of its 'Temple' section, suggests that in his experience of 'India' Forster, like his own Adela Quested,[181] found
he was no longer 'examining life but being examined by it'. The
fact that Coleridge was in a trance when he wrote 'Kubla Khan'
has encouraged critics to consider quite impersonally the mystical
figure in that poem. While writing *A Passage to India*, Forster referred to it as 'a meditation',[182] and being written in a meditative
frame of mind is perhaps the closest a novel can come to being
written in a trance. If, furthermore, the novel is a meditation on
the power of meditation—and the contemplative power of Forster's Hindus is actually more *effective* on the course of action than
any conceivable action could have been—it would not be surprising if the mysteries were hid from even the (adept) writer.

I am not arguing that *A Passage to India* must be read in this
way. On the contrary I have used the neo-Platonist intellectual
scheme to raise the possibility that the multiplicity of disparate images which go to make up the muddle of Forster's India, being representative not just of India but of 'the whole world's trouble',[183]

---

[179] *PI*, xx, 191.　　[180] Paris Review interview, p. 27.　　[181] *PI*, xxvi,
245.　　[182] Furbank, ii, 107. Forster is less emotional than he says Dostoyevsky is
and more 'reflective' about 'a poetic and emotional philosophy' as he says Hardy
and Conrad are. Unlike Dostoyevsky, he is not a committed Christian 'reaching
back into love and pity'; he has something of the contrasting 'detachment' of 'an
ancient Greek or a modern Hindu'. In this he is, as he says, 'an eclectic' (*AN*, pp.
86–101 *passim*).　　[183] *PI*, xiv, 137.

can be given coherence in terms of the philosophical mystery to which Godbole·holds the key. This is, however, an abstract conception, and just as neo-Platonist philosophy asserts that art may reflect but is not in itself mystical experience, so does Indian philosophy emphasize that mystical experience is not an Indian but a universal prerogative. The concern of both is with man's universal potential. My reading of the novel has been concerned with its mystical potential and, paradoxically, the more valid this reading is, the greater should be the number of possible readings of the novel in terms of its actual images and ideas.

A PASSAGE BEYOND ALEXANDRIA?

There have been many fine studies which have shown how *A Passage to India* may be read in terms of Forster's actual experience of India.[184] It has been the point of this chapter to complement and not to confound these studies by showing that the Indian images in the novel might *equally well* be read in terms of neo-Platonism. That is not to exclude the possibility that the novel can also be read in terms of Indian philosophy. The extensive parallels that exist between neo-Platonism and the Indian Vedanta (in particular) have been noticed and examined by others besides Forster. An academic study of these parallels undertaken not long ago by J.F. Staal in *Advaita and Neoplatonism* concludes that the schools which crystallize around Sankara and Plotinus both

assert the existence of an Impersonal Absolute, The Good omnipresent and beyond ordinary morality, the possibility of whose existence can be realized within the individual by means of contemplation;

warn against the danger of that type of pantheism where an attempt is made to apprehend the *Theos* by way of the *pan* and not vice versa;

speak of the magical or deceptive nature of the phenomenal or natural world and consider action to be a weakened form of that contemplation which is the proper act of the soul;

regard knowledge as self-luminous and thus conceive of evil as simply nescience;

and accept the exoteric belief in metempsychosis, along with consonant conceptions such as that Time is cyclical and the power of prayer impersonal.

Staal suggests that the only difference between Advaita and neo-

---

[184] The best of these are listed by Frederick P.W. McDowell, 'Forster Scholarship and Criticism for the Desert Islander', *E.M. Forster: A Human Exploration*, ed. G.K. Das and John Beer (London, 1979), esp. pp. 276–9.

Platonism is one of emphasis, with the *Enneads* of Plotinus laying
stress on the hierarchy of Being up to the One while Advaita so
stresses the perfection of the One that any consideration of the
partial in isolation is a relatively unreal exercise. Each system gives
secondary importance to the primary concern of the other and the
paradox of this distinction is that it serves only to stress how similar must be the type of mysticism to which the two metaphysical
systems point.[185] The Advaita is not the only school of the Vedanta,
just as the Vedanta is not the only philosophical system in India,
but it is true to say that it typifies a dominant thrust in Indian philosophy, being developed not only out of the older Upanishads but
by way of the metaphysics of Mahayana Buddhism, especially the
Madhyamika school. It may therefore be considered representative of Indian thought.

Since such close parallels undoubtedly exist, is there any reason
to suggest that the passage to India is essentially anything more
than a passage to Alexandria? Forster's experience suggests the
possibility of making one very fine distinction which may or may
not be generally true. In *Alexandria* Forster identified the Indian
with the neo-Platonist promise that a man shall be God; in the
novel, however, he makes the distinction that India is not anything
so positive as a promise but only something as elusive as an
appeal.[186] In the interim had Forster discovered that Indian idealism is more speculative than he had supposed, its language indistinguishable from that of scepticism? Or had his meditation on
'India' given him a more refined understanding of neo-Platonism?
Had he made a return passage to Alexandria and realized that its
idealism was more subtle than he had originally thought? Either
way, India survives potentially as an image for an even more
refined mysticism than Alexandria represents. As epigraph to
Alexandria Forster cites Plotinus to the effect that to any vision
must be brought an eye adapted to what is to be seen. In a sense
this makes nonsense of questions of influence. Perhaps we cannot
see more of India than was seen in Alexandria. But then in Alexandria might there not also be asked the speculative question: is
there more to India than meets even the Alexandrian eye?

[185] Staal, p. 231.   [186] *PI*, xiv, 137.

CHAPTER TWO

Sir William Jones: *Asiatic Researches* and the Platonizing of India

in which Jones's literary work in India
is re-evaluated in terms of the metaphysics
of the Vedanta to which he was attracted.

He came; and, lisping our celestial tongue,
Though not from Brahma sprung,
Draws orient knowledge from its fountains pure,
Through caves obstructed long, and paths too long obscure.

Jones (on himself), 'Hymn to Surya'.

CHAPTER TWO

Sir William Jones: Asiatic Researches and the Platonizing of India

in which Jones's literary work in India
is re-evaluated in terms of the metaphysics
of the Vedanta to which he was attracted

He came, and, lisping our celestial tongue,
Though not from Brahma sprung,
Draws orient knowledge from its fountains pure,
Through caves obstructed long, and paths too long obscure

Jones (on himself), 'Hymn to Surya'

CHAPTER TWO
Sir William Jones: *Asiatic Researches* and the Platonizing of India

In 1783 Colonel James Capper published his *Observations on the Passage to India*.[1] The passage had become an important one for the British and was made that same year by the man who, more than any other Briton, made it possible for the phrase to assume a literary and metaphysical dimension: Sir William Jones. Jones had achieved a considerable reputation as a poet and Oriental scholar long before he left England for India and there was an air of expectation about what he might achieve not only in his chosen field of jurisprudence but as a man of letters.[2] More than a decade previously Jones had written that 'the descendants of Tamerlane carried into India the language, and poetry of the Persians; and the Indian poets to this day compose their verses in imitation of them'.[3] This remark, made in an essay, 'On the Poetry of the Eastern Nations',[4] in which Jones suggested that poetry in Asia was livelier and more inventive because in Asia the passions remained uncorrupted amid natural surroundings,[5] was not to be Jones's final word on Indian poetry. None the less, even after he had done more than any man to make the treasures of classical Indian literature accessible to Europe and had specifically warned against following 'the muddy rivulets of Muselman writers on India, instead of drinking from the pure fountain of Hindu learning',[6] his earlier response to Asiatic poetry did not so much change as find its real focus farther East.

In retrospect, Jones would have considered himself wholly

---

[1] London, 1783. [2] *MR*, LXXI (Nov. 1784), 357; ibid., LXXVI (May 1787), 416. See also *MWJ*, pp. 232, 242. [3] 'On the Poetry of the Eastern Nations', *Poems* (1772), p. 198. [4] Ibid., pp. 173–99. [5] Ibid., pp. 174, 177–8, 181. [6] 'On the Musical Modes of the Hindus', *AR*, III, 65.

ignorant of India before he took passage to Bengal in 1783. At the
time he was not considered so. Edmund Burke consulted Jones on
Indian affairs before he left London,[7] while Burke's great adver-
sary Hastings gave Jones every encouragement the moment he
reached Calcutta to extend and institutionalize his personal pre-
dilections by the formation of the Asiatic Society of Bengal.[8] The
deference shown by both men to Jones suggests how much they
shared, not only with him but with each other, in their almost mystical respect for Indian culture as it was embodied in the traditional
institutions of the country.[9] In his perspective on India Jones
sometimes appears to have been as hedged in as any man by his
sense of the superiority of European culture,[10] by his acknowledgement of the prior claims of Christian revelation[11] and, one
might add, by his cultivated eighteenth-century mind no less than
by his dedication to the legal profession.[12] None the less he seized
so successfully on the relatively few Sanskrit works which came his
way that, in spite of subsequent disparagement and the discovery
of so many more texts central to the tradition, it is possible to
argue that few Europeans since have penetrated further to the essence of Hindu culture or seen more clearly its significance for their
own civilization. The work done by Jones removed any excuse Englishmen had ever had for suffering from that optical illusion *vis-à-
vis* India which Burke said made a briar at their noses appear of
greater magnitude than an oak five hundred yards away.[13]

[7] Thomas W. Copeland, ed., *The Correspondence of Edmund Burke*, 9 vols
(Cambridge, 1958–70), IV, 352; *LWJ*, Letter 277, II, 478–9; Letters 306, 307, II,
520–4. See also Letters 381, II, 630–2 and 387, II, 642–5.   [8] Introduction, *AR*, I,
vii–viii and *LWJ*, Letter 379, II, 628–9. That Hastings had a genuine interest in
Indian literature is further evident from Jones's letters to him, *LWJ*, Letter 395, II,
658–60, Letter 446, II, 717–19, and Letter 566, II, 899–900. See also *MWJ*, pp.
237–9.   [9] Cannon speculates about the lost possibilities of their co-operation
(*LWJ*, Letter 395, II, 659, n.4).   [10] 'The Second Anniversary Discourse', *AR*, I,
406. The curious way in which Jones is absorbed in Asian civilization even while he
asserts the superiority of the European is equally evident in his earliest and latest
work (*Poems*, 1772, pp. vi–viii; and 'On the Philosophy of the Asiatics', *AR*, IV,
176–8).   [11] In the essay 'On the Gods of Greece, Italy and India' (*AR*, I, 225,
238, 246, 272–3, 275) and in the eighth, ninth and tenth discourses (ibid., III, 15–16,
486–7 and IV, xiv).   [12] In closing his (unpaginated) preface to *The History of
Nader Shah* (London, 1773), Jones says a farewell to literature and an occasional
poem written in 1781, *The Muse Recalled* (Strawberry Hill), is conceived as a
momentary return to poetry. See also the preface to his translation, *Sacontala, or
the Fatal Ring* (London, 1790), p. xi; *LWJ*, Letter 527, II, 848–9 and William
Hayley, *An Essay on Epic Poetry* (London, 1782), Epistle IV, 11, 373–82, pp.
88–9.   [13] *The Works of Edmund Burke* (Bohn Classics ed.), 8 vols (London,
1854–89), III, 125.

JONES'S PROSE

The first seminal essay written by Jones after his arrival in India and published in the first volume of *Asiatic Researches* was 'On the Gods of Greece, Italy and India'.[14] This is the most detailed of a number of comparative studies of classical civilizations already begun in England by Sir William Temple a century previously,[15] in which the possibility is mooted that India, far from being peripheral to European civilization, might shed light on its origins. Such researches, like those into Chinese civilization, were frequently used to undermine the exclusive claims of Christianity[16] and Jones's biographer, Lord Teignmouth, a stalwart of the Clapham Sect, is at some pains to present him as a Christian. While there is justification for his view there is also reason for his pains. In a private letter of 1787 Jones wrote: 'I am no Hindu; but I hold the doctrine of the Hindus concerning a future state to be incomparably more rational, more pious, and more likely to deter men from vice, than the horrid opinions inculcated by Christians on punishments without end'.[17] A decade later William Taylor, referring to Herder as the Plato of the Christian world, suggested that had Jones been the founder of a new sect (a thought in itself indicative) he would have instituted a paganized Christianity like Herder's in which the feared gods of the vulgar were transformed into the beloved divinities of the cultivated.[18]

Although Jones publicly acknowledged his faith in the revelation of Jesus Christ as the fulfilment of the prophecies of Isaiah,[19] this did not preclude his penning a prayer on 1 January 1782, partisan to no religion, which Teignmouth was candid enough to publish.[20] It begins: 'Eternal and incomprehensible mind, who, by thy boundless power, before time began, created'st innumerable worlds . . .' and continues, 'we, thy creatures, vanish into nothingness before thy supreme majesty . . . we see thee only through thy stupendous and all-perfect works; we know thee only by that ray of sacred light, which it has pleased thee to reveal. Nevertheless . . . let us humbly supplicate thee to remove from us that evil, which thou hast permitted for a time to exist, that the ulti-

---

[14] *AR*, I, 221–75.   [15] Sir William Temple, 'An Essay upon the Ancient and Modern Learning', *Miscellanea, the Second Part*, 3rd ed. (London, 1692), pp. 1–72. For the importance given to the Brahmins, see pp. 13–19, 22–3, 68–9.   [16] In the unpaginated preface to volume IV of his *IA*, Thomas Maurice specifies particularly Voltaire, Bailly and Volney.   [17] *LWJ*, Letter 467, II, 766.   [18] *MR*, N.S., Appendix to XXVII (1798), 566. Herder was indebted to Jones's *Sacontala* for confirming the idyllic image he had of India.   [19] *AR*, I, 225, 275. See also *LWJ*, Letter 464, II, 758 and n. 2.   [20] *MWJ*, pp. 357–8.

mate good may be complete . . .', before concluding, 'so, in all future states, to which we reverently hope thy goodness will raise us,
grant that we may continue praising, admiring, venerating, worshipping thee more and more, through worlds without number,
and ages without end!' Such a mind, speculative rather than
dogmatic, stands behind Jones's Hindu 'Hymn to Narayena',[21]
which opens:

> Spirit of Spirits, who, through ev'ry part
> Of space expanded and of endless time,
> Beyond the stretch of lab'ring thought sublime,
> Badst uproar into beauteous order start,
> Before Heaven was, Thou art . . .

In the prefatory argument to that poem Jones suggests that the intellectual tradition which governs his response to 'the Vayds and
Purans of the Hindus', as well as 'the remains of Egyptian and Persian theology' is that of 'the Ionick and Italick Schools'.

   This speculative attitude based on Platonism is evident near the
beginning of the essay 'On the Gods of Greece, Italy and India',
when Jones promises to remember 'that nothing is less favourable
to inquiries after truth than a systemical spirit' and says he will 'call
to mind the saying of a Hindu writer, "that whoever obstinately
adheres to any set of opinions, may bring himself to believe that
the freshest sandal-wood is a flame of fire" '.[22] The essay, which
contains many striking instances of myths shared by the Hindus
with the Greeks and Romans, as well as the Egyptians, makes
pointed reference to a subject with which, as its author says, it is
not properly concerned: namely, the identity of the Vedanta and
Platonic philosophies. Arguing that one of the four sources of
mythology is the 'metaphors and allegories of moralists and metaphysicians', Jones, after referring to *Maya* as 'the Mother of universal Nature'—the word explained by some Hindu scholars as
' "the first Inclination of the Godhead to diversify himself . . . by
creating Worlds" '—goes on to say that it has

a more subtile and recondite sense in the Vedanta philosophy, where it
signifies the system of perceptions, whether of secondary or of primary
qualities, which the Deity was believed by Epicharmus, Plato, and many
truly pious men, to raise by his omnipresent spirit in the minds of his creatures; but which had not, in their opinion, any existence independent of
mind.[23]

[21] *AM*, I, 22–8.   [22] *AR*, I, 223–4.   [23] Ibid., I, 223.

That Jones has an accurate idea of the Advaita Vedanta is evident when he says later in the same essay:

It must always be remembered, that the learned Indians, as they are instructed by their own books, in truth acknowledge only One Supreme Being, whom they call Brahme, or the Great One, in the neuter gender: they believe his Essence to be removed from the comprehension of any mind but his own; and they suppose him to manifest his power by the operation of his divine spirit, whom they name Vishnu, the Pervader, and Narayan, or Moving on the Waters, both in the masculine gender, whence he is often denominated the First Male; and by this power they believe, that the whole order of nature is preserved and supported: but the Vedantis, unable to form a distinct idea of brute matter independent of mind, or to conceive that the work of Supreme Goodness was left a moment to itself, imagine that the Deity is ever present to his work, and constantly supports a series of perceptions, which, in one sense, they call illusory, though they cannot but admit the reality of all created forms, as far as the happiness of creatures can be affected by them.[24]

Later still, he adds in passing: 'To destroy, according to the Vedantis of India, the Sufis of Persia, and many philosophers of our European schools, is only to generate and reproduce in another form . . .'[25] Finally, in comparison with the sensual paradises of Indra and Muhammed, he writes that

The Mucti, or Elysian happiness of the Vedanta School is far more sublime; for they represent it as total absorption, though not such as to destroy consciousness, in the Divine Essence; but, for the reason before suggested, I say no more of this idea of beatitude, and forbear touching on the doctrine of transmigration, and the similarity of the Vedanta to the Sicilian, Italick, and old Academick Schools.[26]

This identification of the foremost school of Indian philosophy with the philosophy of Pythagoras and Plato informs Jones's whole approach to classical Indian culture and this, together with the sympathetic nature of his response, is perhaps Jones's most important contribution to English letters.

From the outset of his career Jones had hoped that a study of Oriental cultures might help reinvigorate European culture.[27] It was the hope of one who, even at the heart of his great preoccupa-

---

[24] Ibid., I, 242–3.   [25] Ibid., I, 250.   [26] Ibid., I, 266. Jones makes the same point in his influential correspondence with Lord Monboddo (*LWJ*, Letter 499, II, 818). In an earlier letter (*LWJ*, Letter 388, II, 646) Jones suggested Plato might have been familiar with Hinduism through Egypt. He was reading the *Yogavasistha*, a Vedantin appendix to the *Ramayana* in which he discovered 'much of the Platonick metaphysics and morality'.   [27] *Poems* (1772), pp. vii–viii, 198–9.

tion with the law, was essentially a literary man, an active member of Dr Johnson's Club. The quite exceptional eclecticism which permits the deist in Jones to co-exist with the Christian, the mystic with the utilitarian, the Orientalist with the Classicist and the republican with the monarchist[28] is evident also in his literary work where an eighteenth-century sensibility is leavened with an aesthetic decidedly Romantic. One perennial ambition which possessed Jones was the composition of a specifically national epic such as Spenser and Milton had proposed. After Jones had had some experience of India the plan of this poem, 'Britain Discovered', first conceived of in 1770,[29] acquired the machinery of Hindu gods who, because (like the gods in Kipling's story, 'The Bridge-Builders')[30] they foresaw the potential threat to their existence posed by British paramountcy in India, sought to oppose the original establishment of Britain's genius in Albion.[31] If this conception seems somewhat odd in retrospect it should be remembered that, soon after this, William Taylor was to suggest to Southey an epic in which Vishnu would undertake a new incarnation to fight beside Captain Campbell at Seringapatam and 'the ancient divinities of Hindostan, in alliance with the Christian sainthood' would assist the English army to achieve a victory for trinitarianism over Islam.[32]

At this time identifications were also being sought between the Druids, as Caesar had described them,[33] and the Brahmins, whose myths and forms of worship were used to supply the key to the ancient religious life of Britain. An association of the Druids with, among other Oriental philosophers, the Brahmins had been made in Classical times by both Clement of Alexandria[34] and Diogenes Laertius[35] and was later revived (in conjunction with a reference to Apollonius of Tyana) in *The Anatomy of Melancholy*.[36] It was now not only again mentioned by men with an experience of India like J.Z. Holwell[37] and Alexander Dow[38] but, following the specula-

[28] This disparity gave rise to the singular inclusion of Jones in 'Neglected Biography', *The Annual Biography and Obituary for 1817* (London, 1817), pp. 444–76. See p. 444n.   [29] *MWJ*, Appendix A, pp. 475–89. The plan to make use of the Hindu gods was actually conceived before Jones arrived in India (ibid., p. 228n).   [30] *The Day's Work* (London, 1898), pp. 1–44.   [31] Abstract of Book II, *MWJ*, p. 484. The goddess Ganga, especially, has a similar role.   [32] *MWTN*, Taylor to Southey Letter 19, I, 357. See also ibid., Southey to Taylor Letter 7, I, 262–3.   [33] *De Bello Gallico*, VI, 13–14.   [34] *Stromata*, I.xv.   [35] *Lives of Eminent Philosophers*, I, 1.   [36] Robert Burton, *The Anatomy of Melancholy* (Oxford, 1621), Democritus to the Reader, p. 17.   [37] *Interesting Historical Events, relative to the Provinces of Bengal and the Empire of Indostan*, 2nd ed., 3 pts (London, 1766–71), III, 26.   [38] *The History of Hindostan*, 3 vols (London, 1768–72), I, xxi and I.

tions of Reuben Burrow in *Asiatic Researches*,[39] investigated by Thomas Maurice with a view to demonstrating an ancient Indian influence on Britain.[40] Col. Vallancey, in correspondence with Jones while preparing his dictionary of Old Irish, drafted 'an epitome of the ancient history of Ireland, corroborated by . . . discoveries in the *Puranas* of the Brahmins . . .',[41] and as late as 1829 there could still appear in London *The Celtic Druids*, a book subtitled 'An attempt to show that the Druids were the priests of Oriental Colonies, who emigrated from India'.[42] The idea was not incongruous to a man such as Jones who, just as Burke spoke of the Indians as a people for ages 'cultivated by all the arts of polished life, whilst we were yet in the woods',[43] could suggest that *Sakuntala* was written when 'the Britons were as unlettered and unpolished as the army of Hanumat' (i.e. monkeys).[44] Nor did this approach appear incongruous to the Germans who, uninhibited by imperial attitudes, responded so enthusiastically to Indian intimations of their 'Aryan' roots that their research into Indian culture in the nineteenth century actually, if undeservedly, obscured the earlier work of the British Orientalists.[45]

In a letter of 1770, writing about a play he has begun, Jones says that 'the story is full of the most affecting incidents, and has more sublimity even than the tragedies of Aeschylus, as it abounds in Oriental images'.[46] Fifteen years later, in the second Anniversary Discourse to the Asiatic Society of Bengal, he was still maintaining (if backhandedly) the superiority of the Asiatic imagination: 'we may decide, on the whole, that reason and taste are the grand prerogatives of European minds while the Asiaticks have soared to loftier heights in the sphere of imagination'.[47] The fact that Jones remained a Hellenist did not prevent him from suggesting that contemporary European letters stood to benefit from a familiarity with Asiatic imagery.[48] His earlier advocacy of the importance to poetry of the passions is again evident when he avows that 'the Hindu system of musick has, I believe, been formed on truer principles than our own', being directed to 'the natural ex-

[39] 'A Proof that the Hindoos had the Binomial Theorem', *AR*, II, 488–9.   [40] *IA*, VI, pt. I, Preface and 18–247.   [41] Charles Vallancey, *Prospectus of a Dictionary of the Language of the Aire Coti, or Ancient Irish* (Dublin, 1802). See *LWJ*, Letter 467, II, 768–9.   [42] Godfrey Higgins, *The Celtic Druids* (London, 1829).   [43] *The Works of Edmund Burke*, II, 182.   [44] *Sacontala*, Preface, p. vii.   [45] R.M. Hewitt, 'Harmonious Jones', *Essays and Studies by Members of the English Association*, XXVIII (1942), 42–5, 59.   [46] *MWJ*, pp. 72–3. Teignmouth's translation is here preferred to that in *LWJ*, Letter 25, I, 45, as being closer to the sort of English Jones might have used.   [47] *AR*, I, 407. See *Poems* (1772), p. 181.   [48] *Poems* (1772), pp. vi–iii, 198–9.

pression of strong passions'. Even the ruins of Indian architecture
might 'furnish our own architects with new ideas of beauty and
sublimity'.[49] Among those who read Jones in Germany, Herder
and Friedrich Schlegel responded to the idea that Sanskrit literature had an immediate relevance for European writers,[50] while in
England Thomas Maurice (who followed Jones's researches very
closely) could conceive of his *Indian Antiquities* as exploring 'a
new path in literature'.[51]

On the face of it, however, the effects of Jones's researches into
Indian culture are less visible on literature than on the related
fields of philology and mythology. While the work of Jones in the
development of comparative studies is generally acknowledged, it
is usually qualified as that of a pioneer whose findings have necessarily been superseded. Such a view, reasonable as it is, misses
what may be the real significance not only of Jones's work but of
comparative studies themselves. Jones, as he was aware, was only
one of many 'learned investigators of antiquity' who were 'fully
persuaded that a very old and almost primaeval language' had
once existed among the 'Scythians' and that from this were derived
the principal languages of Asia and Europe.[52] It was only Jones,
however, who had both the authority and the audience to establish
Sanskrit as the key to philology, just as it was his knowledge of the
Hindu pantheon which acted as catalyst for a study of comparative
mythology.[53] For Jones himself, it should be stressed, comparative
studies, like the acquisition of languages, were only a means and
not an end. It is hardly surprising that a man who refused to learn
Armenian because he had not heard of any original compositions
in it,[54] and Zend and Pahlavi because he doubted if genuine books
in either still existed,[55] should say that he valued philology little
when 'considered apart from the knowledge to which it leads'.[56]
He also, for all his talents as a linguist, refers to languages as 'mere
instruments of knowledge'.[57]

Moreover, it is clear from the passages he chose to translate
from the Sanskrit that Jones would not attach much value even to
literature were it not, according to his old dictum, 'a delight of the

---

[49] *AR*, I, 410–11. For the effect of Indian architecture, see Mildred Archer,
Indian Architecture and the British, 1780–1830 (Feltham, 1968).   [50] Ronald Taylor,
'The East and German Romanticism', *The Glass Curtain between Europe and Asia*,
ed. Raghavan Iyer (London, 1965), pp. 188–96.   [51] *IA*, I, dedicatory
page.   [52] *LWJ*, Letter 165, I, 285.   [53] *AR*, I, 421–4; 'On the Persians', ibid., II,
49–58; ibid., I, 221–75. See also N.B. Halhed, *A Grammar of the Bengal Language*
(Hooghly, 1778), p. iii.   [54] *AR*, III, 12.   [55] Ibid., II, 51.   [56] *LWJ*, Letter 251, I,
442.   [57] *AR*, II, 51. See also the Preliminary Discourse, ibid., I, xiv.

soul'.[58] In closing a commentary appended to an essay on Hindu literature which, typically, he had commissioned from a native *pandit*, the Kashmiri Goverdhan Caul,[59] he writes that, since 'wherever we direct our attention to Hindu Literature, the notion of infinity presents itself' (a remark Thomas Maurice felt might be applied with even greater justice to Hindu theology),[60] it is necessary 'to select the best from each Sastra, and gather the fruits of science, without loading ourselves with the leaves and branches'.[61] The image is significant. Jones had begun his commentary with a reference from the *Bhagavad Gita* to the Fig Tree of which the Vedas, otherwise 'considered by the Hindus as the fountain of all knowledge, human and divine', are but leaves, the holy tree itself being 'the Incorruptible One . . . with its roots above and its branches below'. Furthermore, Jones did not fail to quote the sentence which too much learning sometimes tends to invert: 'He who knows this tree knows the Vedas'.

Much as Jones insists on the utility to British rule of a study of Asian civilization[62] and much as he insists on the uniqueness of the prophecies in the Mosaic books, the whole thrust of his researches leads on to what may be regarded as the esoteric truth which, according to the tenets of the Advaitins and neo-Platonists, must be the end and completion of all comparative studies undertaken in an impartial spirit, namely, the apprehension of a common identity. In his third Anniversary Discourse—on the Hindus—Jones was prepared to conclude that it was not possible 'to read the Vedanta, or the many fine compositions in illustration of it, without believing that Pythagoras and Plato derived their sublime theories from the same fountain with the sages of India'.[63] Already he had compared Pythagoras to Kapila, the founder of the Samkhya system, Plato to 'Vyasa', to whom the compilation of the Veda and the foundation of the Vedanta was then ascribed, and Zeno to Patanjali, the author of the *Yoga Sutras*.[64] Previously, the eleventh-century Muslim historian al-Biruni had noticed how like the traditions of both Pythagoras and Plato and Sufism was the attitude to the soul expressed in Patanjali's *sutras* and in the *Bhagavad Gita*.[65] Abu-l-Fazl, Akbar's prime minister, had also associated these three strains of what those immersed in them might regard as a

---

[58] *Poems* (1772), p. 210.   [59] 'On the Literature of the Hindus', *AR*, I, 340–55.   [60] *IA*, IV, 417–18.   [61] *AR*, I, 354.   [62] Ibid., I, 407–8; *Menu*, Preface, p. xvi. Jones does define utility in a larger sense in *AR*, IV, xi–xiii.   [63] *AR*, I, 425.   [64] Ibid., I, 352–3.   [65] Edward C. Sachau, ed., and trans., *Alberuni's India*, 2 vols (London, 1888), I, 68–88 *passim*.

common tradition,[66] and by Akbar's time Sufism was quite practically discovering on Indian soil its identity with the Vedanta. This it continued to do during the rich period of speculative syncretism for Islam in India which came to an end with the execution by Aurangzeb of his rival to the throne, the mystical Dara Shikoh, whose translation of the Upanishads (which he had taken to be the secret scriptures referred to by the *Koran*)[67] Jones had also read.[68] This Islamic ambience was the more important for Jones since the conclusions he drew about the origins of civilization in Asia were underpinned by the *Dabistan*, a work of comparative religion written during that same syncretistic period by a *sufi* who, like other Muslims of his persuasion, was particularly attracted to Kashmir as a home of religious mysticism.[69]

It is Jones's reliance on the *Dabistan* for the earlier history of Persia which permitted later scholars, who were by then better informed and could discredit it, to discount Jones thereby.[70] Yet the conclusion towards which Jones was drawn by his reading of this book has never been disputed: namely, that there had been an early Indo-Iranian culture which would prove relevant to an understanding of European civilization.[71] In his sixth Anniversary Discourse—on the Persians—in which Jones, again typically, acknowledges his debt to Mir Muhammed Hussain (by whom he had been introduced to the *Dabistan*) and to Bahman, a Parsee whom he had taken into his house as a Persian reader, he speaks of 'a nation of Hindus' ruling and practising Brahminism in Iran anterior to Zoroaster.[72] The term 'Hindu' used by Jones in this context was consciously chosen as a preferable alternative to 'Cu-

---

[66] Francis Galdwin, trans., *Ayeen Akbery*, by Abu-l-Fazl, 3 vols (Calcutta, 1783–86), III, 96. The same association was made in another important source of the eighteenth-century attitudes to India, François Bernier, 'The Gentils of Indostan', IV, 176–8 [177]. *A Continuation of the Memoires of M. Bernier*, trans. H.O., 2 vols, III–IV (London, 1672), Jones refers to both Al-Biruni and Bernier in his essay, 'A Description of Asia' (*WWJ*, XII, 364, 390). [67] Aziz Ahmad, *Studies in Islamic Culture in the Indian Environment* (Oxford, 1964), pp. 192–3. The period here referred to is covered by pp. 167–200. [68] *AR*, I, 346; 'On the Primitive Religion of the Hindus', *Works* (1799), VI, 415. Possibly it is Dara's translation which is referred to in *AR*, I, 429. He is also mentioned in the preface to *Menu*, p. x. Halhed and Anquetil-Duperron both knew the Upanishads through his translation. [69] *AR*, I, 349; II, 48. The *Dabistan* is still sometimes attributed not to Mohsen Fani but to Mubid Shah as it was in T.W. Beale's *Oriental Biographical Dictionary*, new ed., rev. Henry George Keene (London, 1894), s.v. Mubid Shah. [70] *The Dabistan*, trans. D. Shea and A. Troyer, 3 vols (Paris, 1843), I, lxxiv–lxxvi. Notice the reservations expressed in *CR*, LXX (Sept., 1790), 280. [71] Maurice consolidated this conception of an early Indo-Iranian culture, *IA*, I, 123–5. Later it was to be discovered that large parts of the *Rig Veda* and the *Zend Avesta* were identical. [72] *AR*, II, 43–66.

sian, Casdean, or Scythian' and, far from being ridiculous, antici-
pates the direction taken by his successors who would use the Indian to indicate the true character of the old Persian religion. He
also makes one distinction crucial to a study of the influence of
Oriental thought on the West when he suggests that although
Zoroaster 'travelled into India that he might receive information
from the Brahmans in theology and ethics', he differed from them
in his doctrines (which the Parsee Bahman, himself possibly under
Vedantin influence, denied were his) of two coeval principles, the
supremely good and supremely bad.[73] The older worship in Persia,
he thought, was to be deduced by reference to the Vedas and to
the manners and customs of the contemporary Brahmins, such as,
for example, their interest in astrology with its correspondent veneration of the sun and stars.

It is in their religious philosophy that the Persians most resemble
the Indians:

They are said also to have known the most wonderful powers of nature,
and thence to have acquired the fame of magicians and enchanters: but I
will only detain you with a few remarks on that metaphysical theology
which has been professed immemorially by a numerous sect of Persians
and Hindus, was carried in part into Greece, and prevails even now
among the learned Muselmans, who sometimes avow it without reserve.
The modern philosophers of this persuasion are called Sufis . . . their fundamental tenets are, that nothing exists absolutely but God; that the human soul is an emanation from his essence, and though divided for a time
from its heavenly source, will be finally reunited with it; that the highest
possible happiness will arise from its reunion; and that the chief good of
mankind in this transitory world, consists in as perfect an union with the
Eternal Spirit as the incumbrances of a mortal frame will allow . . .

Jones then elaborates on the nature of this state in terms of the images used by the *sufi* poets who assert that 'for want of apt words
to express the divine perfections and the ardour of devotion, we
must borrow such expressions as approach the nearest to our
ideas, and speak of Beauty and Love in a transcendent and mystical sense . . . '. Such, says Jones,

is the wild and enthusiastic religion of the modern Persian poets, especially of the sweet Hafiz and the great Maulavi: such is the system of the
Vedanti philosophers and best lyric poets of India; and, as it was a system
of the highest antiquity in both nations, it may be added to the many other
proofs of an immemorial affinity between them.

If Jones is to be faulted at all for his scholarship it is primarily on

[73] Ibid., II, 60–1. See also ibid., I, 349. See chapter 3, p. 106.

account of a slight displacement: he has used, among other things, philosophical affinities to draw conclusions about history. In the event he may not be far wrong, but the philosophical traditions with which he is dealing themselves assert that the Imagination is not necessarily subject to, though it may be inclusive of, the movement of influences. In the opening sentence of his essay 'On the Mystical Poetry of the Persians and Hindus', Jones writes:

A figurative mode of expressing the fervour of devotion, or the ardent love of created spirits toward their Beneficent Creator, has prevailed from time immemorial in Asia; particularly among the Persian theists, both ancient Hushangis and modern Sufis, who seem to have borrowed it from the Indian philosophers of the Vedanta school; and their doctrines are also believed to be the source of that sublime, but poetical, theology, which glows and sparkles in the writings of the old Academicks.[74]

In his suggestion, albeit tentative, that it is as an historical source that India is key to a mystical state evident also among the Persians and Greeks, Jones has exposed himself to newer historical evidence and been discredited.

It is in his observations thereafter on poetry (where history is not a prime consideration) that Jones, a man of an essentially poetic sensibility, finds his true forte. First, he warns against misinterpreting the eroticism of mystical poetry, arguing, consistently with the aesthetic he had himself propounded twenty years earlier, that the devotion natural to the undepraved nature of man is bound to express itself in metaphors and allegories which extend beyond 'the bounds of cool reason, and often to the brink of absurdity'. Jones quotes extensively from Barrow' 'the deepest theologian of his age', on Love and comments that the passage

differs only from the mystical theology of the Sufis and Yogis, as the flowers and fruit of Europe differ in scent and flavour from those of Asia, or as European differs from Asiatick eloquence; the same strain, in poetical measure, would rise up to the odes of Spenser on Divine Love and Beauty, and in a higher key with richer embellishments, to the songs of Hafiz and Jayadeva, the raptures of the *Masnavi*, and the mysteries of the *Bhagavat*.

Following the insertion of a passage from another European writer, this time Necker, Jones says of them both together:

If these two passages were translated into Sanscrit and Persian, I am confident, that the Vedantis and Sufis would consider them as an epitome of their common system; for they concur in believing that the souls of men

[74] Ibid., III, 165.

differ infinitely in degree, but not at all in kind, from the divine spirit, of which they are particles, and in which they will ultimately be absorbed; that the spirit of God pervades the universe, always immediately present to his work, and consequently always in substance; that he alone is perfect benevolence, perfect truth, perfect beauty; that the love of him alone is real and genuine love, while that of all other objects is absurd and illusory; that the beauties of nature are faint resemblances, like images in a mirror, of the divine charms; that, from eternity without beginning, to eternity without end, the supreme benevolence is occupied in bestowing happiness, or the means of attaining it; that men can only attain it by performing their part of the primal covenant between them and the Creator; that nothing has a pure absolute existence but mind or spirit; that material substances, as the ignorant call them, are no more than gay pictures, presented continually to our minds by the sempiternal artist; that we must beware of attachment to such phantoms, and attach ourselves exclusively to God, who truly exists in us, as we exist solely in him; that we retain, even in this forlorn state of separation from our beloved, the idea of heavenly beauty, and the remembrance of our primeval vows; that sweet musick, gentle breezes, fragrant flowers, perpetually renew the primary idea, refresh our fading memory, and melt us with tender affections; that we must cherish those affections, and, by abstracting our souls from vanity, that is, from all but God, approximate to his essence, in our final union with which will consist our supreme beatitude.

This passage is virtually identical in shape with that already cited from the sixth Anniversary Discourse, but here the philosophical or mystical ambience is considered exclusively in its relationship to poetry: 'From these principles flow a thousand metaphors and other poetical figures, which abound in the sacred poems of the Persians and Hindus, who seem to mean the same thing in substance, and differ only in expression, as their languages differ in idiom'.

I have quoted at length from Jones's writings because long neglect of them requires it be made manifestly clear that Jones responded to India not just scholastically in terms of the Platonist tradition but as a man whose literary sensibilities had been touched by the spirit of Indian literature. His essay on the mystical poetry of Persia and India illustrates better than any the true nature of the contribution he made to English letters. In treating of classical Persian and Hindu poetry as a by-product of mystical experience, it provides an important perspective on the nature of civilization in the Indo-Iranian East. At the same time, it offers a Romantic view of the nature of poetry and suggests the milieu in which Jones himself was enough immersed to write, among his other hymns to the Hindu deities, a poem as impressive as the 'Hymn to Narayena'. Moreover, the essay is itself an introduction to a fine (albeit bowdlerized) translation of the *Gita Govinda*,[75] the Sanskrit classic on the loves of Krishna which is perhaps un-rivalled in its evocation of the spiritual in terms of sensual love. And finally, more generally if no less significantly, the essay re-commends the Hindus to European perception as a people among whom may still be found 'the same emblematical theology, which Pythagoras admired and adopted'.

JONES'S POETRY

The conviction that poetry depends on a mystical experience which lies deeper than idiom or expression is stated in verse in Jones's 'Hymn to Surya' which, like the *Gayatri*,[76] is an invocation to the sun as the visible symbol of the 'Eternal Mind'. Jones, having prayed the sun to represent him as one who had drawn 'orient knowledge from its fountains pure', goes on to say:

> Yes; though the Sanscrit song
> Be strown with fancy's wreathes,
> And emblems rich, beyond low thoughts refin'd,
> Yet heav'nly truth it breathes
> With attestation strong,
> That, loftier than thy sphere, th'Eternal Mind,
> Unmov'd, unrival'd, undefil'd,
> Reigns with providence benign.[77]

It is the concern, clearly expressed here, not just with the imagery of Indian poetry (much as Jones recommended Oriental imagery to the European poets) but with the mystical philosophy which pervades the imagery which encouraged Jones to write his hymns to the Indian deities.

This is evident also in the best of the hymns, that to Narayana, where Jones invokes the 'Spirit of Spirits':

> Oh! guide my fancy right;
> Oh! raise from cumbrous ground
> My soul in rapture drown'd,
> That fearless it may soar on wings of fire;
> For Thou, who only knowst, Thou only canst inspire.[78]

It is no accident that this particular hymn is the most successful since it is evocative of an abstract power existing beyond the world

---

[75] Ibid., III, 185–207. See also, 'On the Chronology of the Hindus', ibid., II, 119–21.   [76] *Menu*, Preface, p. xvi; *Works* (1799), VI, 417.   [77] *AM*, II, 170–1.   [78] Ibid., I, 24.

of name and form and the poetry is able to escape the catalogue of unfamiliar Hindu names which Jones, rather mistakenly, had supposed would prove a refreshing alternative to the exhausted Classical pantheon.[79] Few British poets of this time use the Pindaric Ode[80] to suggest the spontaneous beauty of creation as effectively as does Jones in the stanza which opens:

> Omniscient Spirit, whose all-ruling pow'r
> Bids from each sense bright emanations beam;
> Glows in the rainbow, sparkles in the stream,
> Smiles in the bud, and glistens in the flow'r
> That crowns each vernal bow'r . . .

The diction may be eighteenth century but not many eighteenth-century poets have a comparable sense of the mystical source which alone gives life to the ephemeral, if exhilarating, world of Nature. Other than in Milton (and the Buddhist scriptures), the world has rarely been transfigured into a noetic cosmos so convincingly as in the final stanza of the 'Ode to Narayena' when Jones invokes, above the sea, the sky:

> Blue crystal vault, and elemental fires,
> That in th'ethereal fluid blaze and breathe

and, above the meadows,

> Mountains, whose radiant spires,
> Presumptuous rear their summits to the skies,
> And blend their em'rald hue with sapphire light

before the phenomenal is rejected in what is also a poet's repudiation of the image:

> Hence! vanish from my sight:
> Delusive Pictures! unsubstantial shows!
> My soul absorb'd One only Being knows,
> Of all perceptions One abundant source,
> Whence ev'ry object ev'ry moment flows:
>   Suns hence derive their force,
>   Hence planets learn their course;
> But suns and fading worlds I view no more:
> God only I perceive; God only I adore.

For Jones the power of the Omniscient Spirit which 'glows in the rainbow, sparkles in the stream' also 'glows and sparkles in the

---

[79] *Poems* (1772), pp. vii–viii, 198–9. See *MR*, LXXVI (May 1787), 418; LXXVI (June 1787), 481; Appendix to LXXXI (1789), 653.   [80] Prefatory argument to the two 'Hymns to Pracriti', *Works* (1799), VI, 321–2; *MWJ*, pp. 266–7.

writings of the Old Academicks'.[81] It is also the nectar which 'glows and sparkles on each fragrant lip'[82] in 'The Hymn to Indra', conceived as that is as a unique vision of the mountain paradise of the gods vouchsafed to the Indian poet Vyasa. What is distinctive in all three instances is that it is Indian philosophy and mythology which, for Jones, best illuminates or is illuminated by that power.

The paradoxes of mysticism are usually less obtrusive in poetry than in philosophy since a poem, unlike a philosophical argument, is frequently stronger rather than weaker for its apparent contradictions.[83] It is therefore a nice irony, if not a further paradox, that while art as a part of the world of name and form which has no ultimate reality *in itself* is (from one point of view) devalued in the metaphysical systems of the Vedanta, and (to a lesser extent) neo-Platonism, it is through the medium of art that something of the mystical experience advocated by those metaphysical systems has been most generally apprehended.[84] If Jones's translation of the *Gita Govinda* made available to Europe a most important lyrical poem, his translation of *Sakuntala* made available a most celebrated Sanskrit play. The language of his translation indicates that Jones viewed the play in a mystical light and his view may be sustained by reference to classical Indian poetic theory.[85]

According to Bharata's *Natya Sastra*, recognized as an Upaveda or lesser Veda,[86] drama in India exists for the education of those who are not permitted access to the sacred scriptures. Theoretically it is designed, therefore, to educate the uninitiated in the recondite truths of metaphysics.[87] This Jones knew through his acquaintance with Goverdhan Caul[88] and it is not surprising, then, that he should view *Sakuntala* as a drama designed to raise 'the mind by devotion to the felicity of the Divine Nature'.[89] The story of Sakuntala, as it was extrapolated by Kalidasa from the *Mahabharata*,[90] is that of the daughter of a sage and a heavenly

---

[81] *AR*, III, 165.   [82] *AM*, II, 156.   [83] A. Barth, *The Religions of India*, trans. J. Wood, 3rd ed. (London, 1891), pp. 192–3.   [84] Staal, pp. 208–19. See chapter 1, n. 5. The point that neo-Platonism's main influence in England has been in the field of literature is stressed by R.T. Wallis in his standard work, *Neoplatonism* (London, 1972, p. 174).   [85] Dushyanta, the king, stresses that what happens to him is part of some magic to which those who are attached to life are subject. The idealized life of the sages in the drama is the touchstone for his view.   [86] *AR*, I, 340.   [87] Adya Rangacharya, *Introduction to Bharata's Natya-Sastra* (Bombay, 1966), pp. 3–6.   [88] *AR*, I, 353–4.   [89] Ibid., I, 340–1.   [90] *MH*, Sections LXXI–LXXIV in the Sambhava of the Adi Parva, pp. 211–28. Fatma Moussa-Mahmoud notes that this episode was translated and published by Sir Charles Wilkins (*Sir William Jones and the Romantics*, Cairo, 1962, p. 49 and n. 83).

nymph who, discovered in a forest hermitage by a king out hunting, is given a ring in plight of his troth before he returns to his
palace. Sakuntala, her mind so taken up by thought of the king,
overlooks the arrival of a visiting sage who, thus neglected, lays
the curse on her that whoever has so firmly taken hold of her mind
will forget her, a curse modified by the proviso that it will be lifted
when the bestower again sees his ring. Sakuntala sets out for the
king's palace but mislays the ring while crossing a river. The king,
laid under the curse, fails to recognize her and a tragic ending
seems inevitable. However, a fisherman finds the ring inside a fish
and brings it before the king, and the sight of the ring restores the
king's memory. By this time the disowned Sakuntala has not only
borne the king a son but been transported into the heavens. Eventually, she and the king are reconciled.

Jones had no sooner translated this play from Sanskrit into Latin
and from Latin into English than it went through repeated editions
in Germany and has since had many other English translations,
even though it is sometimes felt to be alien to European taste.
Herder, writing a preface to the second edition of Georg Forster's
translation, suggested that the play was not European in spirit in
that, being the production of a culture which believed the divine
penetrated the core of human existence, it demanded to be read in
tranquillity and deep meditation.[91] This attitude was partly shared
by the reviewer in the *Annual Register* who, though he (like his
counterpart in the *Monthly Review*)[92] located the Indianness of the
play in its impassioned quality, also referred to the spell it cast so
that judgement was suspended until reason had returned.[93] These
responses deserve to be considered against the canons of classical
Indian aesthetics. In terms of Bharata's *rasa* theory expounded in
the *Natya Sastra*, the purpose of *Sakuntala* is to induce in the audience an agonizing awareness of one predominant sentiment:
pathos at the separation of the girl and her lover.[94] All other sentiments are subordinate to that. *Sakuntala* is as close as Sanskrit drama may be expected to come to what Europeans know as tragedy.
Since the characters are but working out the will of the gods, here,
as in Indian drama generally, the final scene exists so that the characters may be reconciled to each other and the audience to itself.
Whatever sentiment has been stirred in the audience must be
stilled: the play is over. From what is, incidentally, about the time
of Sankara or shortly before, Indian aesthetic theory has widely

---

[91] Cited by Ronald Taylor, pp. 190–1.   [92] *MR*, N.S., IV (Feb. 1791),
124.   [93] *Annual Register* (1791), Account of Books, p. 194.   [94] Rangacharya,
pp. 67–75.

recognized that underlying the predominant *rasa* of the play should be the even more fundamental *santarasa*, or perfect quietude.[95]

It has been a common European reaction to express disgust at a metaphysic which describes Creation in terms of a drama which plays itself out. The *Dabistan* notes that, according to the Vedanta, the created world is called '*Maya*, that is "the Magic of God", because the universe is his playful deceit, and he is the bestower of imitative existence, Himself the unity of reality. With this pure substance, like an imitative actor, he passes every moment into another form'.[96] This description should clarify how even the shape of an Indian play may reflect a metaphysical truth: namely, that the pain and misunderstanding of separation is ultimately illusory, arising from a forgetfulness that there is only harmony. Tragedy arising from an irreconcilable conflict does not easily exist in a culture where the predominant philosophical tradition discountenances the ultimacy of pairs of opposites: spirit and matter, good and evil. In view of this, it may seem inapt that Jones should refer to Kalidasa as 'the Shakespeare of India'.[97] In fact, Jones is not giving way here to an effusive and shallow comparison. In his essay 'On the Musical Modes of the Hindus', where he speaks of the allegorical concept whereby the six primary *ragas*, or modes, are said to be wedded to five further modes, the *raginis*, and to father others, Jones comments: 'The fancy of Shakespear, and the pencil of Albano, might have been finely employed in giving speech and form to this assemblage of new aerial beings, who people the fairyland of Indian imagination . . . .'.[98] Jones later specifies that he is thinking of *A Midsummer Night's Dream*[99] but the reference to 'aerial beings' may additionally call to mind *The Tempest*, a play which, while at Harrow, Jones had once transcribed from memory

---

[95] The reference, in the context of Advaita, to Abhinavagupta is made in Staal, p. 182. Rangacharya indicates that this was a later concept, pp. 74–5. The way in which the *rasa* theory was elaborated by the *dhvani* school to lift the artistic to a philosophical level, stressing the importance for artist and audience of an inner intuitional experience akin to the mystical, is discussed in De, pp. 48–79. Since it was the Kashmiri Goverdhan Caul who first acquainted Jones with Sanskrit aesthetics, it is quite likely Jones was familiar with Abhinavagupta and conceived of the Abhijnana-Sakontala (The Re-cognition of Sakuntala) in terms of his theory of art as Vision, designed to induce peace and reconciliation following a cycle of ignorance and divisiveness. See also the chapter on Sanskrit Drama and Indian Thought in Henry W. Wells, *The Classical Drama of India* (London, 1963), pp. 42–51.   [96] *Dabistan*, II, 91.   [97] *Sacontala*, Preface, p. viii. See also *LWJ*, Letter 467, II, 766. In Letter 489 (ibid., II, 806) Jones says that he would have thought Shakespeare had studied Kalidasa.   [98] *AR*, III, 73–4.   [99] Ibid., III, 83. See also *LWJ*, Letter 467, II, 766. Wells notes that *A Midsummer Night's Dream* has been the most popular of Shakespeare's plays in India (p. 13).

to provide the script for a production in which he acted the part of Prospero.[100]

The reference to Shakespeare gives rise to one further point which is of some importance to any assessment of Oriental influences in the eighteenth century. Augustus Wilhelm Schlegel actually commented that, had not the fidelity of the translation of *Sakuntala* been attested to by Orientalists, it must have appeared that Jones's love of Shakespeare had been too much for him.[101] From the outset its authenticity had been doubted.[102] This reaction indicates, among other things, just how much of the earlier European Orientalism is genuinely Oriental in spirit. An Oriental poem by Jones, 'The Palace of Fortune', written in 1769—long before India absorbed his attention—may serve as a case in point. A girl, appropriately named Maia, who, somewhat like Sakuntala, lives a simple life in a cell near a fountain, wishes she lived in a palace. Celestial beings attendant on the goddess Fortune spirit her away in an aerial car drawn by peacocks to a heavenly paradise garden. Here there is a lake

> And on a rock of ice by magick rais'd
> High in the midst a gorgeous palace blaz'd;
> The sunbeams on the gilded portals glanc'd,
> Play'd on the spires, and on the turrets danc'd . . .
> High in the centre of the palace shone,
> Suspended in mid-air, an opal throne . . .[103]

Maia is told she may live there so long as she does not again fill her mind with vain desires. Pleasure is the first of several personifications who, for her edification, pass before her sight:

---

[100] *MWJ*, p. 17. In reference to Indian cosmogony, Thomas Maurice (*IA*, v, 935) thought of the famous passage in *The Tempest* when Prospero's magic is complete and the actors, 'all spirits'

> Are melted into air, into thin air:
> And, like the baseless fabric of this vision,
> The cloud-capp'd towers, the gorgeous palaces,
> The solemn temples, the great globe itself,
> Yea, all which it inherit, shall dissolve,
> And, like this insubstantial pageant faded,
> Leave not a rack behind . . .
>
> (IV.i.149–156)

It is congenial to classical Indian aesthetics to believe that we are such stuff as dreams are made on and that drama is an imitation of life serving to remind us that life itself is as much an 'insubstantial pageant' as a play.   [101] A.W. Schlegel, *A Course of Lectures on Dramatic Art and Literature*, trans. John Black, 2 vols (London, 1815), I, 25.   [102] *LWJ*, Letter 564, II, 894.   [103] *Poems* (1772), pp. 15–16.

> The floating ringlets of his musky hair
> Wav'd in the bosom of the wanton air.

The 'nectareous dew' of sensual pleasure he requests as a favour from Fortune soon turns to poison on his lips and Glory and Riches fare no better when they, likewise, obtain the fulfilment of their desires. Maia herself loses her paradise when she covets a ring which initially proves as baneful to her as the king's ring did to Sakuntala:[104]

> Sudden the palace vanish'd from her sight
> And the gay fabric melted into night . . .

By the time the genius of the ring appears, Maia has learnt that the realization of vain imaginings leads only to misfortune. It is not true to say that this is simply an eighteenth-century moral tale with nothing particularly Indian about it.[105] It is, after all, not only worked up out of, but accords very closely with, one of Dow's translations from the Persian of Inatulla of Delhi,[106] whose stories, like so many Persian stories long previous to his, were 'taken from the writings of the Brahmins'.[107]

Even of a poem which Jones wrote when he was in India, 'The Enchanted Fruit', it has been said that 'divested of its exotic trappings, the poem is a regular eighteenth-century moral tale in heroic couplets'.[108] This is undoubtedly true—but, returned to the exotic trappings it actually does have, the poem is a regular Hindu moral tale taken from the *Mahabharata*.[109] 'The Palace of Fortune' may be reminiscent of Pope,[110] but there again Draupadi, the lady protagonist in 'The Enchanted Fruit', is also the protagonist in a Sanskrit play known to Jones as *The Seizure of the Lock*.[111] To see an influence stemming from Pope—or Chaucer—is not necessarily to preclude an Oriental influence but rather to suggest the possibility that the earlier English writers also lay within the sphere of such an influence. In the preface to 'The Palace of Fortune' itself, Jones had pointed out that many of the Italians, including Petrarch, wrote very much in the spirit of the Asiatic poets, the

---

[104] Jones gives to *Sacontala* the subtitle 'The Fatal Ring', a phrase he had used in 'The Palace of Fortune' (*Poems*, 1772, p. 35).   [105] Moussa-Mahmoud, p. 16.   [106] Alexander Dow, trans., *Tales translated from the Persian of Inatulla of Delhi*, 2 vols in 1 (London, 1768), II, 56–102. Notwithstanding his assertion to the contrary, Jones did not even change the moral.   [107] Ibid., I, Preface, vii.   [108] Moussa-Mahmoud, p. 46.   [109] *AM*, I, 191, n.q.   [110] E. Koeppel, 'Shelley's "Queen Mab" und Sir William Jones's "Palace of Fortune"', *Englische Studien*, XXVIII (1900), 50–3.   [111] *Sacontala*, Preface, p. ix. The reference is to *Venisanhara*, no. 46, Catalogue of Oriental Manuscripts (*Works*, 1799, VI, 451), See Wilson, XII, 335–44.

form as well as the spirit of whose work he believed was brought into Europe by the Arabs.[112] In the 1790s it was the collection of Inatulla's tales which put Richard Hole on to the idea that there might be classical Indian analogues not only for the *Arabian Nights*[113] but also for some English works, including several of Chaucer's *Canterbury Tales*, an observation which later research has confirmed.[114] If Hole, reading Inatulla's story of the fifth Veda, conceived of a debt owed by Chaucer,[115] a contemporary reviewer thought of that owed by Pope.[116] When Jones suggests that a correct idea of Indian religion and literature could not be formed prior to the publication of Wilkins' translation of the *Bhagavad Gita* in 1785,[117] that is not to say that the Hindu tradition could not have left some mark on English literature, especially by way of Persia and Arabia, long before members of the Asiatic Society of Bengal took their torches into what one contributor to the *Quarterly Review* sombrely referred to as 'the dark caverns of Sanscrit literature'.[118]

---

[112] *Poems* (1772), Preface, pp. iv–v.   [113] Richard Hole, *Remarks on the Arabian Nights' Entertainments* (London, 1797), pp. 221–2, 229, 248–9. William Franklin had already remarked that *The Loves of Camarupa and Camalata*, which he translated from the Persian in 1793, was originally an Indian tale from which one of the Sindbad stories was derived (*BC*, I, July, 1793, 307). A correspondent in *Oriental Collections*, I, No. III (July, Aug., Sept., 1797), p. 298, noted that as early as 1711, M. Pétis de la Croix had suggested his Persian tales were based on Indian dramas. The identification of scenes in Sindbad stories with particular localities was later attempted in R.H. Major, ed., *India in the Fifteenth Century* (London, 1857), Introduction, pp. xxx–xlv.   [114] Hole, pp. 239–48. Hole was thinking of the Merchant's Tale and the Squire's Tale. Classical Indian analogues have since been established for the tales of the Franklin, the Pardoner and the Shipman (F.N. Robinson, ed., *The Works of Geoffrey Chaucer*, Boston, 1957, pp. 722, 729, 732). Reuben Burrow (*AR*, II, 489) had already suggested an Indian influence on the *Treatise on the Astrolabe*, a thesis wild in detail but not so wholly incredible in view of, for example, Kirtland Wright's demonstration of Indian influences on al-Khwarizmi and other Arab astronomers whose works were known in Europe in Chaucer's day, *The Geographical Lore of the Time of the Crusades* (New York, 1925), p. 82. Burrow's remarks might bear on a reading of the Squire's Tale, though it has yet to be determined whether there is a specifically Indian origin for this and other tales of a generally Oriental provenance or for the structure, metaphysical in its import, whereby, as William Taylor observed (*MWTN*, Taylor to Southey Letter 45, II, 107), stories like Pilpay's fables, shown by Wilkins to be those of Vishnusarman (*The Heetopades*, Bath, 1787, Translator's Preface, *passim*), are told 'in nests of boxes, one within another'.   [115] Hole, p. 239; *Tales of Inatulla*, I, 213–75.   [116] *MR*, N.S., XXXII (July 1800), 235. The review is of Scott's, not Dow's, translation.   [117] *AR*, I, 355.   [118] *Quarterly Review*, I (Feb. 1809), 54. The same article refers to Indian cosmology in words similar to those Macaulay was to use in his 1835 'Minute on Education'.

THE IMPORTANCE OF JONES'S INDIAN WRITING

At the outset of his eleventh Anniversary Discourse to the Asiatic Society Jones apologized that, in spite of his belief that 'all nations in the world had poets before they had mere philosophers', he would deal first not with the imaginative power of the mind manifest in the fine arts of Asia but with the reasoning power evident in the abstract sciences, or philosophy, of the continent.[119] Before he could deliver what surely would have been his finest, as it was intended to be his final,[120] discourse—on the poetry of Asia—he was dead. Adjectives like 'great' and 'good' came to the mind of Coleridge when he later thought of Jones and Wilkins.[121] With Coleridge Jones shared a thoughtful commitment to the Mosaic books as inspired prophecy and to the incarnation of Jesus as a divine revelation unique in history. None the less, as it so often seems with Coleridge also, the finest flights of Jones's writing come when his mind is attuned to something more mystical and less exclusive than Christian theology. Additionally, Jones had too great a knowledge and love of the literature of Asia to disparage or misrepresent its religious beliefs. This is evident in his discourse 'On the Philosophy of the Asiatics' when, citing proverbs in Chinese, Sanskrit, Arabic and Persian (as well as in Greek), he warns Protestant missionaries against underrating the ethical content of Asian literature. The peroration of his discourse is devoted to the proposition that the diverse civilizations of Asia are pervaded by a common religious idealism, of which the Vedanta provides the most imaginative as well as the most influential expression.

Earlier in the same discourse Jones had gone so far as to say that until an accurate translation of Sankara's commentary on the Vedanta appeared in a European language, 'the general history of philosophy must remain incomplete'. Thereupon he offered an epitome of what he called 'the most celebrated Indian school':

The fundamental tenet of the Vedanti school, to which in a more modern age the incomparable Sancara was a firm and illustrious adherent, consisted not in denying the existence of matter, that is, of solidity, impenetrability, and extended figure (to deny which would be lunacy) but, in correcting the popular notion of it, and in contending that it has no essence independent of mental perception; that existence and perceptibility are convertible terms; that external appearances and sensations are illusory,

---

[119] *AR*, IV, 165–6.   [120] Ibid.; IV, 166. 184–5.   [121] John H. Muirhead, *Coleridge as Philosopher* (London, 1930), p. 283. The same adjectives are applied to Jones by a correspondent in *GM*, LXV, pt II (Sept. 1795), 715.

and would vanish into nothing, if the divine energy, which alone sustains them, were suspended but for a moment . . .

This sort of idealism, Jones adds, has had adherents in the West in both Classical and modern times. It is

an opinion, which Epicharmus and Plato seem to have adopted, and which has been maintained in the present century with great elegance, but with little public applause; partly because it has been misunderstood, and partly because it has been misapplied by the false reasoning of some unpopular writers, who are said to have disbelieved in the moral attributes of God, whose omnipresence, wisdom and goodness, are the basis of the Indian philosophy.

While he demurs from subscribing to the Vedanta doctrine himself, Jones is defensive of it:

I have not sufficient evidence on the subject to profess a belief in the doctrine of the Vedanta, which human reason alone could, perhaps, neither fully demonstrate, nor fully disprove; but it is manifest, that nothing can be farther removed from impiety than a system wholly built on the purest devotion; and the inexpressible difficulty which any man, who shall make the attempt, will assuredly find in giving a satisfactory definition of material substance, must induce us to deliberate with coolness, before we censure the learned and pious restorer of the ancient Veda . . .

Jones, who reminds us at this point that he was living in a part of India where not the Vedanta but the Nyaya was the prevailing philosophical system, reserved his real warmth for mysticism not as it was intimated in 'mere' philosophy but as it was felt through the imagery of Asiatic poetry. As it is, it is a passage from the *Taittiriya Upanishad*—Varuna speaking to his son—which (apart from his hopeful promise of the further discourse he was destined never to deliver) constitutes Jones's parting words to the Asiatic Society of Bengal: ' "That Spirit, from which these created beings proceed; through which, having proceeded from it, they live; toward which they tend, and in which they are ultimately absorbed, that spirit study to know; that spirit is the Great One" '.

If it is the essential contribution of Jones to literature to assert that it is in the mystical spirit of Persian and Indian poetry and music that Asian civilization receives its highest expression and that the best European response to this may be discovered through the Platonist tradition, this is a comment not merely on the nature of imagery but on the Imagination itself. Jones could make his claims for the Asiatic imagination (always strongest when he is writing, writing about or translating poetry) without being any less of a Hellenist, or even a Christian. His work makes it clear that an extended response to Asia was possible in terms of ideas concerning the mystical state already existent within the European tradition. It was Jones's hope that Asia could offer European poetry fresh images for these ideas in place of the well-worn Classical imagery.[122] Left at this, the suggestion could be that of an eighteenth-century sensibility, however much refined by a unique acquaintance with the literature of Asia. There are, however, moments when Jones's writing fulfils the canons of his own aesthetic criticism, when passion, not imitation, informs his work and permits it to glow and sparkle with the power he had recognized in the writings of 'the old Academicks'.

It is in such moments that Jones brought the intellectual tradition of Europe to the very edge of a realization about India and its relationship to the Imagination, the expression of which falls short, as it necessarily must, in his ordinary prose even while its effect is felt in his more poetic utterance. While his discourses on the peoples of Asia evolved towards the proposition that Iran could stand as image for the original home of mankind,[123] his increasing preoccupation with India and its ancient literature ensured that it was the Hindus who came to stand as image for the state of mankind before its dispersal.[124] Later research would concede the importance to civilization of an Indo-Iranian people but not of the conception of them as a single source of world civilization. Considering, however, that Jones's original attraction to the East was through poetry[125] and that his heart lay with the Oriental fable even while he tried to extricate history from it,[126] it is possible to read his conclusions about the original state of mankind as the miscarriage of a poetic apprehension, the full import of which becomes deflected when stated in terms of history and geography: namely, that India is an appropriate image for the oneness of mankind in that Hindu culture accords mystical monism more importance and its practice is, and has long been, carried on more intensively there than anywhere else.[127]

The deflection of this observation—possibly on account of a recurring Christian concern with historicity, though probably more

---

[122] The Hindu hymns are clearly a practical expression of this theory.   [123] *AR*, II, 64–6; III, 479–80, 490–1.   [124] Ibid., I, 349; II, 55, 58–63.   [125] Most notably, *Poems* (1772), at once a collection of poems and a poetic manifesto, and *Poeseos Asiaticae Commentariorum* (London, 1774).   [126] Self-evident in his essay 'On the Gods', in his appreciation of the allegorical representation of the Hindu musical modes and in his attraction to the *Gita Govinda* and *Sakuntala*.   [127] What I am basically arguing here is that, in terms of De Quincey's famous distinction, Jones' essays can be read as a part not only of the literature of knowledge but of the literature of power.

on account of a failing of the imaginative powers—led to such a rapid decline in Jones's reputation that it is difficult even now to see how high it once stood. It is as pertinent to this subsequent obscurity as it is indicative of how apposite an image India is for a tradition which regards the image as ephemeral that, contemporaneously with Jones, Thomas Taylor could labour to make the neo-Platonists known to the English in their own language with as little reference to India as Jones made to Plotinus and Porphyry in his exposition of the Vedanta. Yet when the theosophical societies which established themselves in England at this time were reconstituted in the nineteenth century, they based themselves on the identities inherent in these two traditions, deriving the term 'theosophy' from Porphyry[128] but finding in Indian thought a more extensive as well as a more exotic frame of reference. Madame Blavatsky, with a reading of the earlier volumes of the *Asiatic Researches* behind her, was led to reformulate Jones's old thesis about a race of Ur-Hindus as the source of civilization.[129]

In this, if in nothing else, Madame Blavatsky shares with some historians a concern to represent Indian mystical practice in temporal terms. The nineteenth-century French historians, Simon and Vacherot,[130] following H.H. Wilson,[131] both attempted to establish in more precise historical terms an Indian influence on the neo-Platonists. But precision eluded them, as it has eluded other historians since who have sought to explain similarities in ideas, images and practices between the Indians and the neo-Platonists in terms of Oriental influences coming in either through Hellenistic Alexandria or pre-Socratic Athens. Plotinus himself, in consonance with the more mystical dialogues of both Plato and the Upanishads, provides the reason why this should be so when he suggests that to any vision must be brought an eye adapted to what is to be seen.[132] In a larger sense this philosophical proposition makes nonsense of the question of historical influence. In a lesser sense, however, some sort of information regarding India would have had to have reached the Mediterranean for India to exist at all as an image in the Western Imagination, even though at best it could never be more than an image for the mystical state, the

---

[128] Eusebius, *Praeparatio Evangelica*, IV, 6.   [129] H.P. Blavatsky, *The Secret Doctrine*, 2 vols (London, 1888).   [130] Jules Simon, *Histoire de l'École d'Alexandrie*, 2 vols (Paris, 1845), I, 102–7; Étienne Vacherot, *Histoire Critique de l'École d'Alexandrie*, 3 vols (Paris, 1846–51), I, 307. Both historians consider Apollonius of Tyana as key to the meeting of Greek and Oriental traditions. Vacherot sees him as the man who transformed Platonism.   [131] Wilson, VI, xiii–xv. See also ibid., VI, cx–cxi, 11 n.2, 13 n.1.   [132] See chapter 1, p. 42.

source of which is not in India but, as the one (very central) Upanishad Jones himself translated makes clear,[133] in the Self. To
search in India with the expectation that India *per se* will offer enlightenment is to confuse exterior image with interior mystical
state and for many of Jones's fellow countrymen this has inevitably
led only to disillusionment.[134]

THE DIFFUSION OF JONES'S WORK

Jones's own work and that which he inspired among members of
the Asiatic Society was diffused most widely in the early 1790s
through the *Asiatic Researches*,[135] a journal almost wholly an
outgrowth of his mind. The earlier volumes of the journal, given
over particularly though not exclusively to Indian antiquities—and
as likely to contain an article Jones had commissioned from a
Kashmiri *pandit*,[136] an interview he had had with an Abyssinian[137]
or a letter he had received from a Chinese friend[138]—include authoritative articles by Jones himself on orthography, mythology,
literature, chronology, chess, linguistics, the zodiac, botany,
music, poetry, the lunar year and natural history.[139] Few, if any,
Englishmen since have desired to acquire, as did Jones, 'a complete
knowledge of India',[140] let alone shown such a comprehensive
grasp of Indian civilization taken on its own or any other terms.
There is some ground for saying that Jones's authority has never
been superseded, a claim based not only on the extensiveness of
his knowledge displayed in the *Asiatic Researches* but on the insight evident in his poems published in a shorter-lived journal
often confused with *Asiatic Researches*, the *Asiatic Miscellany*.[141]

---

[133] *WWJ*, XIII, 374. The translation of the *Isavasyam* is followed by one from
Yajnavalkya's teaching in the 'White' *Yajur-Veda* (ibid., XIII, 378), a tradition of
which it is part (see chapter 4, p. 129).   [134] A most notable recent example of this
is Arthur Koestler's *The Lotus and the Robot* (London, 1960).   [135] The edition
used here is a London reprint of the Calcutta ed: vols I–II (1801); III–V (1799); VI
(1801); VII (1803); VIII (1808); IX (1809); X (1811); XI (1812). Note that vols III–V are
an earlier reprint and that in the early reprints there are not only discrepancies in
punctuation but, especially in vols III and IV, in pagination.   [136] *AR*, I,
340–4.   [137] Ibid., I, 383–6.   [138] Ibid., II, 204.   [139] Respectively, ibid., I, 1–56;
I, 221–75; I, 344–55; II, 111–47 and 389–403; II, 159–65; II, 207–23; II, 289–306; II,
345–52, 405–417; IV, 108–120, 234–323; III, 55–87; III, 165–207; III, 257–93; IV,
137–42. Besides the discourses, other contributions by Jones appeared in ibid., I,
142–4, 383–8; II, 77–107, 195–203; III, 39–53, 463–8.   [140] *LWJ*, Letter 526, II,
848.   [141] See ibid., Letter 468, II, 770 and n. 3; *MWJ*, p. 265. In *A Discourse on
the Institution of a Society* (London, 1784), Jones had spoken of his plan to publish
an 'Asiatick miscellany', a piece of intelligence prominently advertised in *MR*, LXXI
(Nov. 1784), 335. Hence the confusion.

Neither journal was readily available in England and the shortage of copies gave rise in the 1790s to a series of reprints, mainly of Jones's work and mainly from *Asiatic Researches*, entitled *Dissertations and Miscellaneous Pieces relating to . . . Asia.*[142] At least partly on account of their scarcity, if more particularly because of their intrinsic merit, periodicals like the *Monthly Review* and the *British Critic* especially, and to a lesser extent the *Critical Review*, reprinted considerable extracts from Jones's articles.[143] The *Monthly Review* had praised Jones's earliest work at Oxford[144] and not only waited in anticipation of the work expected of him in India and reviewed all by him or inspired by him that came to hand but, in 1787, published one of the most effusive panegyrics to be delivered on a living author.[145] In its very first number the *British Critic* remarked that wherever literature was held in honour Jones was never mentioned without reverence.[146] The *Critical Review* spoke of having the highest veneration for his learning and talents.[147] After his death both the *Gentleman's Magazine* and the *Monthly Review* incorporated William Ouseley's tribute to Jones in their respective reviews of the *Persian Miscellanies*,[148] while the *Annual Register* reproduced John Shore's extensive eulogy in what was ostensibly a review of the third and fourth volumes of *Dissertations and Miscellaneous*

[142] Four vols (London, 1792–1796). The scarcity of copies of *AR* is noticed in the preface to vol. I of this miscellany and, among other places, in *GM*, LXIII, pt I (Jan. 1793), 56 and *BC*, I (June 1793), 117.   [143] *MR* reviewed all works of any importance on India and devoted more space to them than any other magazine. More than 100 pages were given over to the first 3 vols of *AR*; sixteen pages, mainly of excerpts, were reserved for *Sacontala* (N.S., IV, Feb. 1791, 121–37). *CR* offered less space to works on India but invariably entertained the idea that India and not Egypt was the original home of philosophy and science (LXIX, May 1790, 528–9, 532, LXIX, June 1790, 620; LXX, Sept. 1790, 278; N.A., I, Jan. 1791, 18; I, April 1791, 450; III, Dec. 1791, 463–4; VII, April 1793, 428–9; XV, Nov. 1795, 308. Like *MR* (N.S., V, July, 1791, 241–50; VIII, July 1792, 250–2), *CR* reviewed the second as well as the first edition of Craufurd's *Sketches of the Hindoos* (N.A., I, April 1791, 449–54; II, May 1791, 52–6; VII, April 1793, 427–36). *BC*, which commenced publication only in 1793, paid considerable attention to India. Nearly fifty pages were devoted to *AR*, III, alone. The magazine was appreciative of Thomas Maurice, to whose work it set aside 100 pages in its first four years of publication.   [144] Reviews of work by Jones had appeared in XI.II (Appendix to 1770), 508–9; XI.IV (June 1771), 425–32; XI.V (Dec. 1771), 498; XLVI (Jan. 1772), 36–43; XI.VI (Feb, 1772), 81–92; XI.VI (May 1772), 508–17; XI.IX (Oct. 1773), 280–6; LI (July 1774), 21–4; LVII (Oct. 1777), 326; LX (June 1779), 452–9; LXIII (Aug. 1780), 142–3; LXVI (April 1782), 298–300; LXVI (June 1782), 442–3; LXVII (Aug. 1782), 148–9; LXIX (Oct. 1783), 296–7.   [145] *MR*, LXXVI (April 1787), 414–16.   [146] *BC*, I (May 1793), 2, 13.   [147] *CR*, N.A., IX (Sept. 1793), 97.   [148] *GM*, LXVI, pt I (April 1796), 318–19; *MR*, N.S., XX (June 1796), 121–7.

Pieces.[149] The *Gentleman's Magazine* had also published a notice
by Shore on Jones's funeral in which he was described as 'the most
eminent Oriental scholar in this or perhaps any other age', one
whose name was known wherever literature was cultivated.[150] It is
significant that a correspondent who wrote to take issue with this
notice by the man who was to be Jones's first biographer did so on
the grounds that it failed to recognize that Jones's compositions,
whether in verse or prose, were essentially those of a poet.[151]

It is the poetic spirit in Jones which has survived the outdating of
his scholarship as well as the conventionality of some of his verse,
and it is no accident that the real tributes to Jones assumed a poetic form. Thomas Maurice published one elegy[152] and, shortly
afterwards, William Hayley published another, refusing to apolo-
gize for the repetition on the grounds that the literary excellence of
Jones required some kind of homage from every man of letters.[153]
Both poems were widely reviewed and extracts reprinted in all the
leading periodicals.[154] When the *Monthly Magazine* began publication shortly after, it too included a further commemorative
poem, this time a sonnet, very possibly written by William
Taylor.[155] As one reads the praise accorded Maurice's poem it is
not always easy to tell if it is essentially a response to Maurice, to
Jones or to some poetic quality common to both and embodied in
Maurice's imaginative figure of the 'Genius of Antient Asia' on the
banks of the Ganges delivering her own eulogium on Jones. It was
Jones's poetic sensibility which, combined with his extraordinary
gift for languages,[156] had enabled him 'to woo the Asiatic
Muses'[157] long before he arrived at the mouths of the Ganges. In a
single decade following that landfall he evoked an image of India
which then shone as brightly, as it was later to be as eclipsed, as his
own literary reputation.

---

[149] *Annual Register*, 1797, Account of Books, pp. 498–504.   [150] *GM*, LXV, pt I
(April 1795), 347.   [151] Ibid., LXV, pt II (Sept. 1795), 715.   [152] Thomas Maurice,
An Elegiac Poem, sacred to the Memory and Virtues of Hon. Sir William Jones
(London, 1795).   [153] *An Elegy on the Death of the Hon. Sir William Jones*
(London, 1795), Advertisement, n.p.   [154] e.g., *BC*, V (May 1795), 510–14; VI
(Dec. 1795), 604–7; *MR*, N.S., XVII (June 1795), 194–6; XVIII (Nov. 1795), 292–4;
CR, N.A., XIV (June 1795), 175–7; XVII (July 1796), 289–91; *GM*, LXVI, pt I (March
1796), 228. Stanzas from Maurice's poem also appeared in the *Annual Register*,
1795, Poetry, pp. 147–8.   [155] *MM*, I (June 1796), 404. The sonnet is not included
among the many contributions listed as being made by Taylor to the magazine
(*MWTN*, I, 155ff). However, it associates Jones with Selden and Milton, something
which Taylor does in a letter to Southey of 28 Jan. 1799 (*MWTN*, Taylor to Southey
Letter 5, I, 251). Jones, who admired both men, also once coupled their names in a
letter (*LWJ*, Letter 86, I, 147–8).   [156] *MWJ*, p. 376n. Jones had some knowledge of
twenty-eight languages; thirteen he knew well.   [157] *MR*, LXXVI (April 1787), 415.

Six of the nine hymns Jones wrote in honour of the Hindu
deities appeared in the two volumes of the *Asiatic Miscellany*, designed to interest 'lovers of poetry' as well as 'the learned and the
curious',[158] and one further hymn in its equally short-lived successor, the *New Asiatic Miscellany*.[159] These hymns are not, as may at
first appear, simply Neoclassical English poems making polite use
of Indian mythology. In his earliest essay on Eastern poetry Jones
had said he hoped a greater familiarity with Asiatic literature
would not only furnish English poets with new imagery but afford
a more extensive insight into the history of the human mind.[160] In
the other essay on poetry published in conjunction with this in
1772, Jones elaborated on his meaning when he wrote that original
poetry, being a natural expression of passion, was governed not by
imitation but by 'a very different principle; which must be sought
for in the deepest recesses of the human mind'.[161] Jones's later acquaintance with Hindu mythology did not merely supply him with
the rich and novel alternative to Classical imagery he had guessed
it might but made him doubly aware of the common spirit which
had inspired in diverse cultures a not dissimilar pantheon. Concealed beneath the alien nomenclature of the Hindu deities there
is a rebarbative effect to Jones's hymns, primarily because Jones
picked on those figures of Indian mythology which embody creative or inventive powers. The poems, therefore, implicitly deal

---

[158] *AM*, II, vi.   [159] Ibid.; I included the Hymns to Camdeo (18–21), Narayena
(22–8), Sereswaty (179–87) and Ganga (257–66). *AM*, II included the Hymns to
Indra (152–61) and Surya (162–71). *The New Asiatic Miscellany*, I (1789), opened
with the Hymn to Lacshmi (1–12) but no further hymns were published in the
second and final volume, which appeared in the same year. From his introduction
to the two Hymns to Pracriti (those to Bhavani and Durga) it is clear that Jones
intended them for publication together with his translation of the first Nemean Ode
of Pindar (*Works*, 1799, VI, 321–22).   [160] *Poems* (1772), pp. 198–9. Prevailing
scholarly opinion concerning the influence of Jones on literature is fairly summed
up by S.N. Mukherjee in *Sir William Jones: a Study in Eighteenth Century British
Attitudes to India* (Cambridge, 1968, p. 141): 'He made very little impact on
European thought . . . His impact on the Romantic poets was negligible'. Even
Moussa-Mahmood, who writes a whole book devoted to the subject of Jones and
the Romantics, has to admit that, apart from a few images in Southey and Moore
derived from Jones, there was a 'poor harvest of literary works inspired by Indian
literature' (p. 102). My own, quite contrary, hypothesis is based on two factors
they neglect: (1) The space devoted to Jones and the Indian researches he
inspired in the English literary periodicals of the 1780s and 1790s, and (2) The
possible effect on poetry of (what Mukherjee calls) 'the attitude of mind' Jones left
behind him: 'a profound reverence for men irrespective of their race and their
different cultural backgrounds'. For a pioneer statement of this hypothesis, see
Garland Cannon, 'The Literary Place of Sir William Jones', *JAS*, II, I (1960),
47–61.   [161] Ibid., p. 202.

with their own nature even while they deal explicitly with the nature of existence.

In one way or another all the hymns are concerned with the mysterious relationship between the beautiful yet transient manifestations of the Supreme Being in Nature and the awesome One, 'wrapt in eternal solitary shade'.[162] While this is stated most clearly and poetically in the 'Hymn to Narayena', it is implicit also in the hymns to Camdeo or Kamadeva (the god of love, especially important since Nature and Art are both conceived of as God's mystic Love); to Sarasvati (the goddess of Invention and Imagination); to Ganga (the sacred river sent from heaven to revivify the dead); to Indra (perceived, as in a poet's vision, upon his mountain paradise, dispensing nectar and music); to Surya (the sun, to whom, Jones says, is ascribed the power originally and properly attributed to the one eternal Mind); to Lakshmi (the Indian Aphrodite, who is the active power of Vishnu, the Preserver); to Durga (the goddess who traces the daemonic Siva to his retreat on the mountaintop); and to Bhavani (where Matter, as goddess, is evoked as the aethereal energy of God).[163] The hymns are remarkable for a sense of delight in the natural world: love and music abound in sky and ocean, in mountain and on plain, and mineral, vegetable and animal as well as spiritual life assume an importance usually denied them in the anthropocentric universe of the humanist. In the hymns the principal forms of Nature are generally represented, consonant with the *puranas*, as goddesses, female embodiments of the active power of the primary, passive God. Every aspect of the natural world—and therefore of the poetry which, according to Jones, is itself a natural expression of the power, Love, which gave rise to the natural world—thus speaks of the mystical power which sustains it from within.

The first hymn to be published, that to Camdeo, was introduced by the editor as being 'translated from the Hindu [*sic*] into Persian, and from the Persian into English'.[164] This led some to believe (erroneously) that the poem was a direct translation of a Sanskrit hymn. That misconception corrected,[165] others have stressed how much the hymns lie within the English poetic tradition.[166] Jones himself, in the extensive arguments or prefaces to the hymns, freely

[162] *AM*, I, 24.   [163] *Works* (1799), VI, 317–35.   [164] *Discourse* (1784), title page.   [165] Once it had been represented as such in its original publication, the error was reproduced in the *Annual Register* (1784–5, *Poetry*, pp. 137–8) and was still current a decade later when, in 1796, Eliza Hamilton published *Letters of a Hindoo Rajah* (see preface to 2nd ed., 2 vols, London, 1801, I, xxviii–xxix). It was corrected by a reviewer of the book (*MR*, N.S. XXI, Oct. 1796, 181). Jones did translate *a* Hymn to Cama (*AR*, III, 278).   [166] V. de Sola Pinto, 'Sir William Jones and English Literature', Bulletin of *SOAS*, XI (1943–6), 692.

acknowledges his debt to both Indian and European sources, the former more often for subject matter, the latter for stanza forms.[167] What is clear is that in dealing with Hindu mythology Jones allows himself the freedom of invention of an English poet. At the same time, the Hindu *puranas* permit considerable imaginative licence and Jones, whose subject is, as he suggested in his argument to the 'Hymn to Narayena', common to both traditions, is rarely unfaithful to the Indian spirit. His 'Hymn to Ganga', which deviates considerably from the Indian conceit, is perhaps the least eclectic in this respect.

The 'Hymn to Durga', on the other hand, is a wholly authentic though condensed rendition of Kalidasa's *Cumara Sambhava*.[168] In it the great ascetic Siva is invoked:

> Dread Iswara; who loved o'er awful mountains,
> Rapt in prescience deep, to roam,
> But chiefly those, whence holy rivers gush,
> Bright from their secret fountains,
> And o'er the realms of Brahma rush.

The seasons cannot affect the mountains or their personified Lord, Himalaya:

> Nor e'en the fiercest summer heat
> Could thrill the palace, where their monarch reign'd
> On his frost-impearled seat,
> (Such height had unremitted virtue gain'd!).

The daughter of Himalaya, Parvati, or the mountain-born, is fated (for reasons on which the good of the world depends) to become devoted to Isvara, or Siva,

> the God, who fix'd in thought
> Sat in a crystal cave new worlds designing.[169]

However, Siva, having reduced to ashes the God of Love who disturbs him in his meditation, flees to Mount Kailasa. Parvati is distraught at this and is about to destroy herself in a mountain torrent when she is confronted by a Brahmin wizard who urges her to turn to a less boorish god. When by way of answer Parvati throws herself from a crag, breezes bear up 'her floating locks and waving robes' and she is transported to 'a mystick wood'. The wizard had

---

[167] A considerable number of Hindu texts (besides Oriental thought and mythology in general) are cited as sources for subject matter; there are acknowledgements for form to Gray and Pindar, though Jones does not disguise his own stylistic innovations.   [168] This poem has since been translated by R.T.H. Griffith, *The Birth of the War-God*, 2nd ed. (London, 1879). Jones had heard the original recited orally (*Works*, 1799, VI, 317–18).   [169] *Works* (1799), VI, 323–4.

been Siva himself. As we have seen, every god, even (or especially) an ascetic one with contained daemonic powers, is destined to have a *sakti* or active form in the shape of a goddess, and Parvati is married to Siva, Love is restored and the goddess celebrated by her alternative name of Durga, meaning 'of difficult access'.

The paradigm of emanation, which in its philosophical application informs Jones's hymns, might well be used more mundanely to describe the way the hymns reached the public. The 'Hymn to Camdeo', for example, was first published in a pamphlet together with Jones's 'Discourse on the Institution of the Asiatic Society' and his 'First Charge to the Grand Jury in Calcutta' (1784).[170] It was reprinted in the *Asiatic Miscellany* of 1785[171] and from that again reprinted in *Dissertations and Miscellaneous Pieces* (1792).[172] In the mean time, not only had stanzas from the poem appeared as part of appreciative reviews in the *Monthly Review*[173] and the *Critical Review*[174] but it had been republished in full in the *Annual Register*[175] and in full but for fifteen lines in Craufurd's *Sketches of the Hindoos* (1790),[176] itself enlarged, republished and re-reviewed two years later. Likewise, the 'Hymn to Narayena' was first published in the *Asiatic Miscellany*[177] and was reprinted from there in both the *Gentleman's Magazine*[178] and *Dissertations and Miscellaneous Pieces*.[179] Long stanzas from the hymn had once again appeared as part of laudatory reviews in the *Critical Review*[180] and the *Monthly Review*[181] and the whole poem was judiciously edited by Craufurd for inclusion in *Sketches of the Hindoos*.[182] Maurice also reproduced one stanza.[183] Although these poems were favourably received and two stanzas of a third hymn, that to Sarasvati, were reproduced from the *Asiatic Miscellany*[184] in the *Monthly Review*[185] and an edited version of the whole hymn appeared in Craufurd,[186] none of the other hymns sems to have reached print outside the *Asiatic Miscellany* before 1799.[187]

Quite apart from that, it is difficult to estimate what effect the Hindu hymns may have had since their strength comes from a quality associated with the mythology which develops out of the

[170] *Discourse* (1784), pp. 25–33.   [171] *AM*, I, 18–21.   [172] *Dissertations*, II, 347–50.   [173] *MR*, LXXI (Nov. 1784), 354–7.   [174] *CR*, LIX (Jan. 1785), 19–21.   [175] *Annual Register*, 1784–5, Poetry, pp. 137–8.   [176] *Sketches* (1790), pp. 165–7. See chapter 6, pp. 213, 217 and nn. 104, 126.   [177] *AM*, I, 22–8.   [178] *GM*, LVII (Feb. 1787), 108–10.   [179] *Dissertations*, II, 351–6.   [180] *CR*, LXIII (April 1787), 266–9.   [181] *MR*, LXXVI (May 1787), 418–19.   [182] *Sketches* (1790), pp. 140–1.   [183] *IA*, IV, 456n.   [184] *AM*, I, 179–87.   [185] *MR*, LXXVI (June 1787), 481–2.   [186] *Sketches* (1790), pp. 150–5.   [187] *Works* (1799), VI, 313–92.

Orphic no less than the Hindu tradition.[188] It is almost certainly this quality and not, as it seems, their imagery which excited William Taylor and led him to urge Southey to build his 'edifice of immortal name on Hindoo ground'.[189] A concern with merely the imagery of the hymns could lead only to a vapid, if pleasant, imitation like the poem published by the Exeter Society, 'To the Gods of India',[190] written on the departure for India in 1793 of Sir John Shore, Jones's future biographer, and Hubert Cornish. The real strength of the hymns lies in the spirit sometimes denominated Oriental, although (as was to be strikingly demonstrated in poetry by a soldier about whom George Cornish, Hubert's brother, passing through Reading shortly afterwards with Lady Shore, was so solicitous)[191] the spirit is not confined to the so-called Orient— even though it may be discovered by an acquaintance with the Orient and find its expression through Oriental imagery.

OTHER 'PASSAGES' OF THE TIME

Following the death of Jones, Henry Thomas Colebrooke, his real heir as a Sanskritist, wrote: 'It must be long before he is replaced in the same career of literature, if he is ever so. None of those who are now engaged in Oriental researches are so fully informed in the classical languages of the East; and I fear that, in the progress of their enquiries, none will be found to have such comprehensive views'.[192] The fear was well-founded. In an essay in which he makes the argument that Colebrooke was an incomparably greater Sanskrit scholar than Jones, Max Müller suggests that Jones was essentially a literary man of great originality and highly cultivated taste.[193] The very basis of that comparison, fair as it is, indicates how, from the time of Colebrooke on, Sanskrit studies and their fruits were to be the property not of literary men but of professional scholars and philologists.

In any study of the place occupied by India in English literature, Jones is a seminal figure not only because Orientalism was for him

---

[188] While working on his hymns, Jones did have the Orphic in mind (*LWJ*, Letter 412, II, 678). [189] *MWTN*, Taylor to Southey Letter 22, I, 375. Taylor recognized the Platonic dimension to Jones's Indian work (*MR*, Appendix to XXVII, 1798, 565–7). [190] This poem, by A.Y., was printed in full in a review of *Essays by a Society of Gentlemen at Exeter* (1796) in *MR*, N.S., XXII (Jan. 1797), 4–5. [191] *CLSTC*, Letters 40–1, I, 72–3. See also Letter 20, I, 38–41. [192] Sir T.E. Colebrooke, *The Life of H.T. Colebrooke* (London, 1873), pp. 71–2. [193] Max Müller, 'Colebrooke', *Biographical Essays* (London, 1884), pp. 268–71. In a letter written to Wilson in 1827 (*The Life*, p. 356), Colebrooke speaks of them both as having followed in the footsteps of Jones.

a literary activity and was taken as such by his contemporaries but because the Orientalism of his day was ultimately centred on the translation of classical Sanskrit texts. Jones himself cites the publication of Wilkins' translation of the *Bhagavad Gita* in 1785 (later the subject of a drawing by Blake)[194] as the event which made it possible for the first time to have a reliable impression of Indian religion and literature. But Jones also supposed that there had been a genuine Greek contact with India. Colebrooke, when he praised Wilkins, spoke of him as having acquired more knowledge of the Hindus than any man since the days of Pythagoras[195] and Jones, in one of his hymns about India, refers to 'orient knowledge' having been drawn from 'its fountains pure' there in Classical times.[196] In the intervening years, however, Jones felt that these fountains had too often been muddied by an ignorance of Hindu religion and philosophy stemming from an ignorance of Sanskrit.

What Jones says about 1785 being a turning point is so obviously true that it is surprising to discover that in one way it is not true at all. It is true that one may contrast the convincing *Letters of a Hindoo Rajah* (1796) written by Eliza Hamilton,[197] the sister of a founding member of the Asiatic Society, with Chesterfield's *The Oeconomy of Human Life* (1750),[198] which, though ostensibly a Brahmin book, has nothing particularly Indian about it. The year 1785 will seem to have been a turning point, too, if one compares Jones's own Hindu hymns with the *Indian Odes* of W.B. Stevens (1775)[199] or Jones's direct translation from the Sanskrit of Manu's Code of Hindu Law with that done earlier by his literary friend Halhed,[200] who worked from a Persian translation. On the other hand, if we judge by Jones's own work, the new familiarity with Indian culture did not create a new impression of it so much as confirm an old one. It is significant that Jones should refer to one

---

[194] No. x, 'A Descriptive Catalogue, 1809', *The Complete Writings of William Blake*, ed. Geoffrey Keynes (London, 1966), p. 583. Flaxman did a monumental drawing of Jones collecting information from the *pandits* for his Digest of Hindu and Mohammedan Law (Hayley's *Elegy*, p. 35, note xviii).   [195] *The Life of H.T. Colebrooke*, p. 28.   [196] *AM*, II, 170.   [197] First published London, 1796. Charles Hamilton, author of a book on the Rohilla Afghans and a translation of the *Hedaya*, was the brother. The influence of Jones is acknowledged and greatly evident.   [198] Eleventh ed., London 1767. As soon as the book was first published (1750), Chesterfield was identified as the author (*MR*, IV, Nov. 1750, 64–70).   [199] Georgina Galbraith, ed., *Collected Poems of William Bagshaw Stevens* (London and Chichester, 1971). The odes, for a copy of which Southey asked William Taylor (*MWTN*, Southey to Taylor Letter 52, II, 134–5) were printed at Oxford. Most notable is the first stanza of an Ode to the Sun, supposedly sung by a Chorus of Brahmins (pp. 61–2).   [200] N.B. Halhed, *A Code of Gentoo Laws* (London, 1776); *LWJ*, Letter 26, I, 47 n. 1.

of his Indian informants as an 'old gymnosophist'.[201] A Platonist
approach to India had already been developed by the Greeks and
survived into the Middle Ages. Not only did the original Classical
accounts figure largely in the minds of Jones and his contemporaries (whose literary sensibilities were, of course, grounded in the
Classics) but they had frequently been reinforced by the findings
of Europeans following renewed contact with India in the late sixteenth century. An authoritative comparison of Pythagorean to
Brahminical thought by the Jesuit de Nobili appeared in
Purchas[202] and a similar comparison by another Jesuit, Bouchet,
specifically said to have been written in response to enquiries from
Europe, was published in Picart's widely-read *Religious Ceremonies and Customs*.[203]

By a peculiar irony J.Z. Holwell, Governor of Bengal, whose
account of the 'Black Hole' of Calcutta first shaped an image of
India as Hell which the 1857 'Mutiny' was to consolidate,[204] took
claims for a Brahminical influence on Pythagoras so seriously that he
advocated his countrymen join him in adopting a Brahminical way of
life.[205] Holwell was read and used by Voltaire[206]—just as the Jesuit
relations were cited by the French deists—in support of the view that
the Brahmins had enjoyed the benefits of natural religion prior
to the birth of Christ. This very issue spurred the search for authentic Sanskrit texts[207] but the discovery of those texts in the last
decade and a half of the eighteenth century did not
create an approach to India much different from that already
evident a century earlier in a literary source as influential as *The
Letters Writ by a Turkish Spy*. The *Turkish Spy* is not only the first
work in which the Orient serves as the basis for a satire on Euro-

---

[201] *AR*, II, 290–1. This was the mathematician Ramachandra. Jones is said to
have viewed the Hindus as a living picture of antiquity' (*MWJ*, p.
233).   [202] Purchas, v.v.558–9.   [203] Bernard Picart, ed., *The Religious Ceremonies and Customs of the Several Nations of the Known World*, 6 vols (London,
1731–7), IV, 159–87. Jones (*AM*, I, 191 n.o.), Maurice (*IA*, V, 1010–13), Craufurd
(1792 ed., I, 65n, 219n) and Southey (*SCB*, Ser. 4, p. 42; Kenneth Curry, ed., *New
Letters of Robert Southey*, 2 vols, New York, 1965, I, 204) all acknowledge a debt to
Bouchet.   [204] *A Genuine Narrative of the Deplorable Deaths of the English
Gentlemen, and others, who were suffocated in the Black Hole* (London,
1758).   [205] The third part of *Interesting Historical Events* was entitled *A
Dissertation on the Metempsychosis, commonly though erroneously called the
Pythagorean doctrine*, q.v. III, 147–227. One reviewer suggested it might be classed
with the reveries of Jacob Boehme and his followers (*MR*, XLV, Dec. 1771,
428).   [206] First letter of Voltaire, J.S. Bailly, *Lettres sur l'Origine des Sciences, et
sur celle des Peuples de l'Asie* (London and Paris, 1777), pp. 3–4; fourth letter of
Voltaire, J.S. Bailly, *Lettres sur l'Atlantide de Platon et sur l'Ancienne Histoire de
l'Asie* (London and Paris, 1779), pp. 2, 6, 14. Voltaire read Holwell in English. A
French translation of Holwell's work appeared in 1768.   [207] *AR*, I, 413.

pean manners and morals but also one which reserves a special place for the Brahmins, whose way of life is seen to be Pythagorean and whose books, written in 'the Primeval Speech of Mankind', are thought to hold the secrets of man's temporal and eternal origins.[208] Doubly ironical as the Turkish Spy's Indian letters may be, the account of Indian cosmology and philosophy is accurate and who can say that the passage to India, hallmarked by its usual ambiguity, has not, in fact, been made?

The publication of Wilkins' translation of the *Bhagavad Gita* occasioned excitement because it meant Europeans would have direct access to those primeval books of the Brahmins said by the Turkish Spy to contain the secrets of mankind's existence. Yet the very many translations which have followed have still not resolved the issue of whether or not they do contain those secrets. The works of Thomas Maurice,[209] perhaps the most influential on literature of Jones's followers, show how access to the books themselves would change neither the attitude Christianity necessarily had to take towards them nor the old recurrent Hellenist approach to Hinduism. While Maurice, as a Christian minister, was bound to read the *avatars* of Vishnu in terms of the coming of Christ, he used the neo-Platonists Porphyry and Celsus to explicate Indian 'mysteries' such as cave-worship and Saivite penances.[210] By using neo-Platonism to interpret Indian culture and Indian culture to interpret the civilizations of the ancient world, Maurice did much to establish theosophy (a word used by Coleridge in relation to the

[208] G.P. Marana, W. Bradshaw *et al.*, *The Eight Volumes of Letters Writ by a Turkish Spy*, 8 vols (London, 1694), I, Preface, n.p. Indian wisdom is extolled and knowledge shown of Indian philosophy in letters III.II.xxi; III.III.xiii; V.II.iii; V.III.xviii; VI.III.v; VI.III.xvii; VI.III.xviii; VII.I.xxi; VII.III.vi; VII.III.xi; VIII.IV.xi; VIII.IV.xii. India is also referred to in ibid., IV.II.xiv; IV.III.i; IV.IV.xiv; VIII.IV.iv. Among the Spy's sources on India are Porphyry (II.I.xxvii), Apollonius of Tyana (I.III.ii; IV.IV.ix; VII.IV.v) and Bernier (II.II.xxvii; VI.III.vi). There may be a further debt to Jesuit relations.   [209] Previous notes have already referred to *IA*, the dates for the seven vols of which are variously given as 1791–7 (Allibone), 1792–7 (Robert Watt) and 1793–1800 (*DNB*). Reference to the *Memoirs of the Author of Indian Antiquities* (3 pts, London, 1819–21, III, 85ff) does not fully resolve this matter nor, as a letter to me of 16 August 1977 from Mr J.H. Fuggles of the British Library suggests, is it easy to establish which volumes of the two sets owned by the Library enjoy a priority. I have preferred to avoid confusion by referring to the earliest dated volume generally available: namely I, 1794 (pp. 12–314); II, 1794 (pp. [1]–400); III, 1793 (pp. [i]–vii, 343–540; IV, 1794 (pp. 403–772); V, 1794 (pp. 773–1091); VI, 1796 (pp. [i]–xv, [18]–440); VII, 1800 (pp. [443]–895). Maurice's other chief work is *A History of Hindostan*.   [210] *IA*, I, 119; II, 174–7. Maurice supposed that through Pythagoras the whole tradition of Platonism originated in India (ibid., II, 378; IV, 706–7; V, 816–20; 1001). Vaishnavism and cave worship are considered in vol. II, penances in vol. V.

Brahmins)[211] on an older, forgotten basis.[212] Maurice may seem to us, as he did to Southey, to be a synonym for obscurity.[213] However, his response is typical of the enthusiasm towards the new Orientalism centred on India, and the space given to him by the periodicals in the 1790s is as much as that given to the *Asiatic Researches*.[214]

The new note of enthusiasm for things Indian had been sounded first by Warren Hastings when, as Governor-General of India, he introduced the translated *Bhagavad Gita* by saying that long after the British dominion in India had ceased to exist the Hindu scriptures would continue to be read.[215] This remark found an echo in England a decade later when the *Monthly Review*, reviewing the achievements of the Asiatic Society in that brief period, suggested that after the Empire was forgotten the *Asiatic Researches* would be remembered as the work of

a learned society placed in the midst of a people preserving, at the close of the eighteenth century, the pristine dogmata of the primeval ages: from whom Pythagoras derived the tenets which he transmitted to the philosophers of the Italic school; and by whom the same tenets are still taught, that were taught to Pythagoras.[216]

The British Empire forgotten. The Hindu scriptures remembered. Such a complete antithesis would have been unthinkable to an offi-

---

[211] See chapter 6, p. 224. The spiritual abstraction of the Brahmins is likened to that of 'the ancient ascetics and modern Behmenists' in *GM*, LV, pt II (Dec. 1785), 955. The divine raptures of the Brahmins are likened to those of the Swedenborgians in *IA*, V (1794), 1001, as also in *BC* III, (Feb. 1794), 156.   [212] In *The Wonder that was India* (3rd ed., London, 1967), p. 485, A.L. Basham refers to the Theosophical Society as propagating 'a modernized Hinduism'. This is true of Madame Blavatsky's work in so far as she, like Maurice (whom she had read), undertakes a comparative study of ancient civilizations in the light of Indian culture. She frequently cites Bailly, Voltaire, Jones, Wilford and other late-eighteenth-century authorities who first used the new knowledge of the Brahmins, their literature and language to argue in favour of an Oriental origin for civilization. In literature this tradition surfaces most notably in Yeats (Harbans Rai Bachchan, *W.B. Yeats and Occultism*, 2nd ed., Delhi, 1974, pp. 217–57) and A.E. Russell (Henry Summerfield, *That Myriad-Minded Man*, Gerrards Cross, 1975, pp. 28–58).   [213] *MWTN*, Southey to Taylor Letter 46, II, 95.   [214] *BC*, which between 1793 and 1797 gave over more than 100 pages to reviews of Maurice's work, referred to him as Jones's successor (*BC*, IX, March 1797, 232). More justly, *CR* remarked that he shared with Jones a knowledge of the ancient literature of other civilizations with which the Indian could be compared (*CR*, N.A., XV, Nov. 1795), 308.   [215] Letter of Hastings to Nathaniel Smith, *BGW*, p. 13. Both Wilkins in India (*BGW*, pp. 19–20) and Maurice in England (*IA*, I, 106–7) testify to Hastings' knowledge of Indian culture and it is appropriate that a temple raised in his honour on English soil in 1800 was built in the style of Hindu architecture (Mildred Archer, p. 17).   [216] *MR*, N.S., XXIII (Aug. 1797), 408.

cial of the nineteenth-century British *raj*. Yet the work of Jones and his fellow Orientalists is invariably seen in the context of later nineteenth-century developments. A rather different picture emerges when we take a longer view and see Jones's Indian researches, as Jones and his contemporaries frequently did, in terms of the traditional Greek approach to India.

CHAPTER THREE

Apollonius of Tyana: A Neo-Pythagorean and the Indianizing of Plato

in which the description of India in
the romantic biography of Apollonius
is assessed in terms of Indian culture
contemporaneous with it.

And ideas behave like rumours,
. . . every Plotinus we read
is what some Alexander looted
between the malarial rivers.

A.K. Ramanujan, 'Small Scale Reflections on a Great House'.

Good men by a sort of natural affinity will accept the truth.

Apollonius, Epistle XLVIII.

CHAPTER THREE

Apollonius of Tyana: A Neo-Pythagorean and the Indianizing of Plato

The original 'passage to India' which quite unequivocally lauds or idealizes India and its philosophy is to be found in the romantic biography of Apollonius of Tyana written by Philostratus in the third century AD. The *Life of Apollonius of Tyana*[1] takes its whole impetus from the initial journey undertaken by Apollonius to India and Apollonius emphasizes the central significance of that journey during the two other most crucial episodes in the book—at the time of his visit to the Ethiopians and on the occasion of his trial before the emperor Domitian. Whatever reservations various critics have had about the romantic nature of the biography or its subject, the fact remains that in its presentation of India, Indian manners and Indian philosophy, the book, according to all that is now known about India at that time, offers a remarkably authentic view of that culture.

Traditionally, the biography of Apollonius has been read for the significance it has had for Christianity. The attitude of the Church towards the book was determined by Eusebius, who delivered a well-conducted attack on the claims made for Apollonius as a thaumaturge[2] and as late as 1680 Blount, the earliest English translator, following the publication of the first two books, claimed to have suppressed the rest for fear of giving further

---

[1] So called in the translation of Edward Berwick (London, 1809). This has been used in collation with the more modern editions and translations of F.C. Conybeare, *The Life of Apollonius of Tyana*, 2 vols (London, 1912; vol. II, rev. 1950) and J.S. Phillimore, *In Honour of Apollonius of Tyana*, 2 vols (Oxford, 1912). Conybeare's edition includes the Epistles of Apollonius and the Treatise of Eusebius.   [2] Conybeare, II, 484–605.

offence to Christians.[3] In actual fact had not Hierocles written his polemic[4] to establish Apollonius as a miracle-worker and thereby canonize the *Life* as a pagan alternative to the Gospels, it is difficult to believe that the book would have aroused controversy. Even in Blount's time there were readers who were left wondering less about a parallel between Apollonius and Christ than between Apollonius and Pythagoras.[5] A modern reader has all the more reason to remove the biography from the context of subsequent controversy and consider its original significance in the history of Platonism, especially in the relationship of Platonism to India.

The *Life* has enjoyed some literary currency among those interested in Platonism. In the seventeenth century the Cambridge Platonists More and Cudworth both paid the figure of Apollonius considerable attention, and More, perhaps on account of his close association with the first English chronicler of Indian antiquities, John Marshall,[6] was quick to stress the importance to the *Life* of the Indian episodes.[7] As late as the mid nineteenth century, when John Henry Newman drafted a sketch of Apollonius,[8] historians thought of him as the philosopher who had played a decisive part in introducing Oriental influences into Platonism.[9] Keats writes of him in an altogether different context in *Lamia* but he was a figure of interest also to Coleridge, who commended his morality, and to Southey, who took notes on two editions of the biography.[10]

The place of Apollonius in English literature, however, is no easier to pin down than that of India. Metaphysicians tend to be as elusive as metaphysics and it has been doubted whether Apollonius ever actually went to India.[11] Even as a figure out of romance he has surfaced in the literary tradition in some appropriately mysterious ways. Coleridge and Southey, for example, may well have felt the further impress of Apollonius while read-

---

[3] *The First Two Books of Philostratus, Concerning the Life of Apollonius Tyaneus*, trans. Charles Blount (London, 1680), Preface.   [4] *Philalethes*. It was this which elicited the reply from Eusebius.   [5] Berwick, pp. iv–vi.   [6] *John Marshall in India*, ed. Shafaat Ahmad Khan (London, 1927). Marshall's work, which was expressly intended for Henry More (see pp. 2, 27, 245), represents Indian philosophy in terms of the Vedanta (pp. 177–202, *passim*).   [7] Ralph Cudworth, *The True Intellectual System of the Universe*, 4th ed., 2 vols (London, 1743), I, 265–70; a most important comparison between Apollonius and Christ is made by Henry More in *An Explanation of the Grand Mystery of Godliness* (London, 1660), Bk. IV, pp. 96–136 *passim*. For the consideration of the importance of India for Apollonius, see ibid., III, 58–9.   [8] *Historical Sketches*, 2nd ed. (London, 1873), pp. 305–31.   [9] See chapter 2, n. 130.   [10] *PL*, II, 103; VII, 240; *SCB*, 3rd ser., 497–9.   [11] Osmond de Beauvoir Priaulx, *The Indian Travels of Apollonius of Tyana* (London, 1873), p. 62.

ing about the sage Calasiris in *The Aethiopian Story* of Heliodorus.[12] Shelley, likewise, may have felt it in reading about Peregrinus Proteus in a translation of Wieland's book of that name.[13] Both Calasiris and Peregrinus are often supposed to have been romanticizations of Apollonius. The fascination of a figure such as Apollonius lies precisely in this capacity for inspiring and generating further such fabulous figures. The romantic story of Apollonius travelling to India is of essential interest in this book because of the powerful impetus it gave to the myth of 'a passage to India'. Without the story of Apollonius would there ever have been the story of Plotinus trying to go there? More important, would the story of Pythagoras going there ever have received the currency it did?

THE PASSAGE TO INDIA

Apollonius is a neo-Pythagorean.[14] He accepts the rule of Pythagoras, renouncing possessions and gifts, vowing abstinence and continence, rejecting the use of animals for food and clothing, becoming hirsute and observing a five-year vow of silence. He acquires the knowledge invariably associated with this mode of life: that is, knowledge of his previous incarnations, of the languages of men and animals, of the innermost thoughts of men and of how to pacify the angry and disturbed.[15] Given this sort of love of wisdom, he is soon drawn by his daemon to visit the wise men of India.[16] His journey is made by way of the well-tried, widely-recorded overland route taken by Alexander the Great. He passes the cave of Prometheus, crosses the Caucasus, sees the

---

[12] In the Introduction to his translation of Heliodorus (London, 1961, p. x), Sir Walter Lamb suggests that Calasiris may have been closely modelled on Apollonius. It is likely that both Coleridge and Southey knew *The Aethiopian Story* (J.B. Beer, *Coleridge the Visionary*, Cambridge, 1959, p. 255).   [13] *Peregrinus Proteus*, which Shelley read to Mary in 1814, which she found 'an exceedingly profound irony against Christ' and which she re-read in 1818 (*Journal*, 25 Nov. 1814; 4 July 1818), is the story of a man whom William Taylor of Norwich suggests Wieland—and it may be Lucian—conceived as being in the mould of Apollonius. This is possible since Wieland was to make Apollonius the subject of an even more important novel, *Agathodaemon* (William Taylor, *Historic Survey of German Poetry*, 3 vols, London, 1828–30, II, 269, 482–6, 490).   [14] St Jerome says Apollonius was called a philosopher by such as followed Pythagoras, Letter LIII, § 1.   [15] Berwick, Bk. I, chap. ii, p. 4; I.vii.12–13; I.xii.22; I.xiv.23–4; I.xv.25–7; I.xx.34–5. Apollonius overtly declares himself a Pythagorean in I.xxxii.53–4; VI.xi.317–19. See also Epistle LIII (Conybeare II, 448–9). Iamblichus refers to a book on Pythagoras by Apollonius (Iamblichus, XXV, 130–1).   [16] Ibid., I.xviii.30–1.

temple of Bacchus on Nysa, records diverse theories about the origin of Bacchus, discourses on the elephant, compares the Indus and the Nile and speaks of Porus, the Indian king defeated by Alexander.[17] There is virtually nothing up to this point which is not a standard part of the Classical accounts of Alexander's march into India.

One passage in the text, however, merits special mention here. Crossing the Indian Caucasus (or Hindu Kush) Apollonius does not, like the other Greeks, talk about the physical conditions—the icy cold and the barrenness. Instead, after being told that the barbarians esteem the mountains as the dwelling-place of the gods, he launches into a metaphysical disquisition. It is not by climbing mountains, he says, that one understands the nature of the Supreme Being and of goodness and virtue. When the pure soul makes these things the object of its contemplation it will rise far higher than the mountains.[18] The Buddhist sage Nagasena had told King Milinda (or Menander) much the same thing in very nearly the same place not long previously.[19] The need to surmount or ignore the mountain tops of even the highest paradises is a point often made in Buddhist scriptures.[20] It is an argument made in favour of concentrating the mind on something more intensely abstract than imagery. In the sun-temple at Taxila and later in Ethiopia Apollonius himself will argue against temple images on the grounds that 'the mind forms to itself a something which it delineates better than what any art can do'.[21]

At Taxila, and thereafter in going on to the Ganges, Apollonius covers ground beyond that known to the historians of Alexander. A new and detailed picture of India emerges. At Taxila Apollonius is entertained by the king, Phraotes, whose life accords closely with that stipulated for kings by Indian law.[22] Though the temple in the city is lavish, the palace of the king is simple and an account is given of the king reclining on leaves, taking a meal, followed by an entertainment provided by acrobats. The king's name discovers him to be one of the Parthians who could have ruled in north-west India close to the commencement of the Christian era.[23] He is a convincing figure whose regard for

[17] Ibid., II.iii.69–70; II.viii–ix.76–8; II.xi–xvi.79–90; II.xviii–xix.91–2; II.xx–xxi.94–6.   [18] Ibid., v.73.   [19] IV.8.88, *The Questions of King Milinda*, trans. T.W. Rhys Davids, 2 vols (Oxford, 1890–4), I, 203–4.   [20] Sir Monier Monier-Williams, *Buddhism* (London, 1889), pp. 206–13; L.A. Waddell, *The Buddhism of Tibet* (London, 1895), pp. 77–8, 83–5; chapter 5, p. 169. For Plotinus on No-Form, see *Enn.*, VI.ix.3.   [21] Berwick, II.xxii.96–9; VI.xix.333–6.   [22] Ibid., II.xxv–xxvi.100–1. Cf. *Manu Smriti*, VII.   [23] Strabo, *Geographia*, XV.i.36; Arrian, *Anabasis*, V.29.4.

philosophy and attitude towards those who become adept in its practice is traditionally Indian: he defers to the sages as his superiors.[24] Furthermore if, on account of the rediscoveries of modern scholarship, it is possible to know that his conduct is in accordance with the *varnasramadharma*, so too is it possible to know that his knowledge of the Greek language and Greek literature is compatible with the existence of the Indo-Greek Gandhara civilization. It is now known, too, that the sun-temple in Taxila visited by Apollonius actually did exist conformable with the description given of it.[25]

By this point in the *Life* we have already learnt that the Indians wear cotton clothes and shoes of bark rather than animal skins and that, except at sacrifices, the king takes neither meat nor wine. A further similarity to Pythagorean customs is to be observed in the way music is played before the king retires in order that his dreams may be favourable and he will arise with the best interests of his subjects at heart.[26] When Phraotes tells Apollonius that this 'mirth' is permitted in accordance with the law of the land, he could be citing the *Yajnavalkya Smriti*.[27] Another similarity between the Pythagorean and Indian ways of life is evident when the king informs Apollonius—in a variation on information already made available to the Greek world by Megasthenes[28]— that a youth who wishes to join a community of philosophers presents himself for admission at the age of eighteen, upon which extensive inquiries are made into his family, his conduct towards his parents, his powers of memory and his susceptibility to pleasure and passion. Also, a minute investigation is made of his looks, in which a skilled philosopher might read his disposition.[29]

Apollonius is now directed to the king's spiritual preceptor, Iarchas, who lives on a Hill of Sages some days journey to the East. Apollonius, who has hitherto been absolutely confident of his own spiritual self-sufficiency, at once expresses his conviction that he is about to confront philosophers whose knowledge, compared with that of the Greeks, is of 'a higher and more divine character'. He is therefore quite content to acquiesce when, after being welcomed by an Indian with (what is perhaps) the distinguishing *tilak* mark on his forehead, he is given orders in the

---

[24] Cf. Berwick, II.xxvii.102; II.xli.121–2 and *Manu Smriti*, VII.37–43; *Yajnawal-kya Smriti*, Bk. I, trans. Srisa Chandra Vidyanava (Allahabad, 1913), XIII, vv. 312–16.   [25] Ibid., II.xx.94; II.xxiv.99–100; George Woodcock, *The Greeks in India* (London, 1966), p. 130.   [26] Ibid., II.xxxiv.112; Iamblichus, XV, 32.   [27] *Yajnawalkya Smriti*, XIII, 331.   [28] Strabo, xv.i.59.   [29] Berwick, II.xxx.105–7. Cf. Iamblichus, XVII, 37–8. For the importance given to memory by the Pythagoreans, see ibid., XXIX, 88 and Diodorus Siculus x.5.1.

authoritarian manner to which a Pythagorean was accustomed: *autos epha*. The Indian sages do not keep their knowledge exclusive from him, Iarchas asserting that 'the communication of knowledge is much more becoming the character of philosophy, than the invidious concealment of what ought to be known'. Apollonius is invited to make himself privy to the knowledge and powers of the sages by questioning them. His first question is the old Greek one: do the sages know themselves? The answer is typically Hindu: 'We know all things because we know ourselves'. This answer only makes sense if the word 'self' in this context is construed to mean not the individual personality but the impersonal Upanishadic *atman*, the divine within. That this reading is probably correct is confirmed by the next answer given by Iarchas: namely, that the sages think of themselves as gods.[30]

This idea of a universal divine immanence is germane also to the doctrine of the transmigration of souls which Iarchas asserts was taken from India into Egypt by the Ethiopians, a claim for Indian influence which gained some credit in the Hellenistic world and became current again in the late eighteenth century. The *adrastian* law as it is interpreted by both Apollonius and Plotinus is identical with the Indian law of *karma*: that is, that the nature of a man is determined by the deeds accruing to him as a result of his experience in previous lives.[31] The *Yajnavalkya Smriti* elaborates on this in such a way as to correct a common European misapprehension of fatalism: 'The fulfilment of an action rests between destiny and human effort. Of these two, the destiny is the manifestation of the human effort of the past incarnation'.[32] That the sages worship the sun by day and its rays by night is also conformable with the idea behind the Indian practice of meditation on the setting sun whereby the initiate seeks to absorb the power of the sun before it retires for the night to Mount Meru.[33] Some knowledge of Indian cosmology is also apparent when it is reported that the Indians regard the Hill of Sages as the navel of the world in the middle region of India—presumably a reference

[30] Ibid., III.xi–xx.135–47. [31] Ibid., VIII.vii.440; *Enn.*, III.ii.13. There is a similar Sanskrit word describing the concept of unseen merit and demerit: *adrishta* (S. Radhakrishnan, *Indian Philosophy*, 2nd ed., 2 vols, London, 1929–31, II, 291). [32] *Yajnawalkya Smriti*, XIII, 349. Cf. 'It is said, fate is nothing but the deeds committed in a former state of existence; wherefore, it behoveth a man vigilantly to exert the powers he is possessed of'. *The Heetopades* (Wilkins), p. 6. [33] Berwick, III.xv.140–1; III.xxxiii.163. According to the *Manu Smriti*, a Brahmin in the first stage of life should adore God at sunrise and sunset and in the third stage should go down to the waters to bathe at sunrise, noon and sunset (II.222; VI.22).

to the mythological concept of Mount Meru in Jambudvipa.[34]

Indian physics, as related (reliably) by Iarchas and again previously made known to the Greeks by Megasthenes, is also agreeable to the Pythagorean: the world is composed not of four but of five elements, the fifth being the quintessence, the seminal aether, or *akasa* of the Hindus. The world is an androgynous animal, coalescing to produce all living things. It is directed by an all-pervasive God and its several parts are governed, as the poets put it, by minor deities. Water is the primal element.[35] These cosmogonical ideas are as old as the Vedas; they are also evident in the reputedly Pythagorean *Timaeus*.[36] Only one (perhaps surprising) difference between the Indians and the Pythagoreans is emphasized: Apollonius notes that the Indians are not concerned with number, Iarchus suggesting that virtue is more worthy of preservation than number. Apollonius reiterates this position when he tells the Ethiopians that 'the pleasure which springs from Philosophy harmonized, as Pythagoras prescribed, and enriched with that divine temperature which his Indian friends gave it, is not of short duration, for it extends *ad infinitum*, and is unbounded by number'.[37] Since it is generally conceded that the nine numerals with zero and place value were invented in India[38] and allowing that the development of a conception of abstract number is grounded in metaphysics, the difference is the more surprising. However, the Indians, like the Pythagoreans, recognized a division between esoteric and exoteric doctrines.[39] In this case we might suppose that Iarchas has so far abstracted from number as to be aware only of *sunya* (literally, nothingness), the Sanskrit word from which, by way of the literal Arabic translation *sifr* and its Italian corruption *zephirum*, is derived the English zero.[40]

Eusebius remarks that on his return from the East Apollonius displays miraculous powers as if he has been turned into a divine being.[41] Eusebius does not deny the existence of miracles: it is the

[34] *VP*, II, II, II, 109–26.   [35] Berwick, III.xxxiv–xxxvii.165–9.   [36] *BA*, 3.6; 5.5.1; *Timaeus* 30B, 92C. See also Alexander Polyhistor's account of the Pythagorean system preserved in Diogenes Laertius VIII.25–35.   [37] Berwick, III.xxx.159–60; VI.xi.321   [38] Walter Eugene Clark, 'Hindu-Arabic Numerals', *Indian Studies in Honour of Charles Rockwell Lanman* (Cambridge, Mass., 1929), pp. 217–36.   [39] Iamblichus, XVIII, 41–8. W.K.C. Guthrie suggests there is a distinction between those concerned with number-doctrine and those concerned with mysticism (*Orpheus and Greek Religion*, London, 1935, p. 219).   [40] David E. Smith and L.C. Karpinski, *The Hindu-Arabic Numerals* (Boston and London, 1911), pp. 57–62. Sir John Woodroffe suggests that the algebraic zero may be equated with pure consciousness (*The Serpent Power*, 8th ed., Madras, 1972, p. 339).   [41] 'The Treatise of Eusebius', XXIII, Conybeare, II. 540–1.

object of his work to stress that miracles are dependent on divinity. What the Christian finds unacceptable is the position, common to the Pythagoreans and the Hindus, which attributes potential divinity to all beings. The practice of phenomenal austerities has perennially been directed to the individual's acquisition of mastery over his body, his senses and desires: the superman in spirit is freed from his bondage to matter. The power of the Indian sages encountered by Apollonius is demonstrated in several forms. They practice levitation—according to the gloss of Damis—'not for the purpose of exciting admiration, of which they are not guilty, but from an idea that what they do in such an approximation to the sun, is done in the way most acceptable to that luminary'.[42] They have knowledge of their own past lives, of other people's lives and experience prescience:[43] according to this tradition a man who strives to realize himself, the divine within himself, will find the barriers of time, space and individuality increasingly surmountable (or, rather, dissoluble) and will acquire what are popularly known as psychical powers. Speaking of divination, Iarchas makes clear that it can be reliable only in a man who keeps himself 'pure, and free from all mental strain and turpitude whatever'. His power will be used only for the instruction of the ignorant and for the good of mankind.[44]

This last qualification calls to mind one of the oldest and best-known Indian stories: that of the Vedic sage Vasistha who, living alone in the forest with nothing beside but his cow Nandini, daughter of Kamadhenu (literally, Granter of Desires), was able to provide a feast when the hermitage was visited by the king, Visvamitra, and his hunting party. Visvamitra, amazed by this miraculous appearance of food and other gifts from the cow, tried to procure Nandini for himself first by persuasion and then by force.[45] The salutary lesson he learned was that such a cow could belong only to a sage who, free of desire himself, would desire things solely on behalf of others. Apollonius witnesses a similar, if less moral or allegorical, incident when a king, rather ignorant and somewhat of a contrast to Phraotes, comes to pay his respects to the sages and is entertained to a meal which appears from nowhere.[46]

It is possible to remain as sceptical about the miraculous powers of adepts as about the journey of Apollonius to India and still be faced with the inescapable conclusion that in the Mediterranean

---

[42] Berwick, III.xv.140.   [43] Ibid., III.xii.136; III.xxi–xxiii.149–51.   [44] Ibid., III.xlii.173–4.   [45] *MH*, Section CLXXVII in the Chaitra-ratha of the Adi Parva, pp. 501–4. A variant of this story is told in the *Raghuvamsa* of Kalidasa. It is sometimes said to originate in *RV*, VII.18.4.   [46] Berwick, III.xxvi–xxvii.155–7.

early in the third century AD there was considerable knowledge of Indian culture—its legends, its law codes and its *sutras*. Iarchas, for example, is apparently an exponent of the system of yoga usually attributed to Patanjali. Yogi-Yajnavalkya is another *yogi* of this period who taught a method of realization of the identity of the individual and universal soul such as later commentators sometimes claim was taught by the Vedic sage Yajnavalkya, and it is just conceivable that it is from his name that the Greeks, who had difficulty with Indian names, derived the diminutive Iarchas.[47] Yoga follows the teaching of the Vedic sage in advocating mental withdrawal and contemplation whereby the ordinary consciousness is refined to a spiritually more intense state. The new development of the yoga of Patanjali is its enumeration of the physical exercises which permit the adept to abstract from the phenomenal world. Hence the *yogi* is said to be no longer subject to gravitation or, as Bhaskaracharya calls it, the attractive power of the earth:

He can walk and ascend in the sky, as if he were suspended under a balloon. He can, by this intuitive process, inform himself of the mysteries of astronomy and anatomy . . . He may call to recollection the events of a previous life. He may understand the language of brute creation. He may obtain an insight into the past and future. He may discern the thoughts of others, himself vanish at pleasure, and, if he choose to do so, enter into his neighbour's body, and thus take possession of his living skin.[48]

These are *siddhi*, or supernatural powers, implicit in any tradition of idealism where the spirit is thought to achieve mastery over the body: the theurgic practices of Iamblichus and Proclus presuppose the philosophical position of Plotinus. Yet Patanjali also stresses, as do the older *Vedanta Sutras* (and Mahayana Buddhism), that such supernatural powers are but by-products of the higher life and only by disregard of them can liberation be won.[49]

The Indian part of the biography of Apollonius raises many questions. At times it may appear that this book, like many of its eighteenth-century successors, is referring to an Oriental country less for its own sake than as a pretext for commenting unfavourably on life in the West. For example, Phraotes chides Apollonius

---

[47] *Yoga-Yajnavalkya*, ed. Prahlad C. Divanji (Bombay, 1954). This treatise is an elaboration of the teaching of the Vedic sage from whom the *yogi* takes him name. The Vedic sage Yajnavalkya is also the figure W.B. Yeats singles out as the originator of the cultural milieu which gave rise to Patanjali (see chapter 4, pp. 128–9 and n. 32). This accords with a view taken in *MH*, Sections CCCXI–CCCXIX of the Çanti Parva, pp. 624–54.   [48] Patanjali's Sutra III, in K.M. Banerjea, *Dialogues on the Hindu Philosophy* (Calcutta, 1861), p. 69; Radhakrishnan, II, 366–8.   [49] Colebrooke, I, 263, 386–93; Monier-Williams, p. 246; Radhakrishnan, II, 367

with the fact that the Greeks will punish counterfeiters but not sophists.[50] Iarchas tells Apollonius: 'Troy was destroyed by the Greeks who sailed to its shores, and you are destroyed by the stories told of it. For from an idea that the men who fought at Troy were the only men to be esteemed, you overlook many of a more divine character born in your country, in Egypt and India'.[51] The morality of Greek poetry is also arraigned when Iarchas points out that whereas the Greek poets have maligned Tantalus for his gift of immortality, the Indians have justly blessed him for it.[52] Not one of these remarks would appear to be authentic to India—and yet it is not beyond the bounds of possibility that each of them is. Long before Phraotes, an Indian king—Bindusara, the father of Asoka—had showed enough interest in the place of sophists in the Greek world to ask Antiochus I, the Greek king of Syria, to send him one.[53] So too, while the attitude towards Greek epic poetry expressed by Iarchas is, as we know from Diogenes Laertius, that of the Pythagoreans,[54] Homer's work was quite possibly known in India at this time and, if it was, would almost certainly have provoked a similar reaction.[55] Nor is there any reason why the Indian Tantalus—especially in view of the context in which he is later evoked by Apollonius—could not be Dhanvantari, the physician of the gods who brought up the cup of nectar at the Churning of the Ocean.[56]

Whether the *Life* is to be regarded as biography or as romance, there is an admixture of anecdote and legend customary to both these literary genres. Quite unequivocal is the reason given (by Apollonius in his eloquent discourse to the Ethiopian gymnosophists) why the passage to India, be it literal or metaphorical, was made. The discourse opens with a persuasive account of the attractions of the Pythagorean precepts and their preferability to those of other philosophical sects. Apollonius then says that he was curious to know the origin of an art clearly 'the invention of men who

---

[50] Berwick, II.xxx.105.   [51] Ibid., III.xix.146.   [52] Ibid., III.xxv.153–5.
[53] Woodcock, p. 51. In *Believe as You List*, Massinger has Antiochus III disappear among the gymnosophists of India. In his curious story of Iambulus, Diodorus Siculus refers to the friendliness displayed towards the Greeks by the Indian king of 'Palibothra' (II.60.2–3).   [54] Diogenes Laertius, VIII.21.   [55] Dio Chrysostom (*Oration* LIII.6–7) and Plutarch (*Moralia*, 328D) both suggest Homer was read in India. While this may indicate a Greek confusion between the Indian epics and their own, it is possible that Indians who spoke Greek (as Nicolaus Damascenus reports) or an Indian king who was a Philhellene (as Diodorus mentions) might not only exist but also read Homer. The establishment of flourishing Greek colonies in the north-west of the sub-continent lends credence to this possibility (R.A. Jairazbhoy, *Foreign Influence in Ancient India*, London, 1963, pp. 97–101).   [56] *MH*, Section XVIII in the Astika of the Adi Parva, pp. 80–1.

excelled in divine knowledge, and searched deeply into the nature of the soul, whose immortal, and immutable essence, is the true source from whence it flows'. Though such knowledge is evident in Plato, Apollonius believes it is clear from a contrary tendency at work that Athens is not the home of 'knowledge of the soul'. 'Hence it became necessary for me to inquire, whether any nation, or people existed, amongst whom not one or two men were of this, or that opinion concerning the nature of the soul; but to find out where its immortality had in all times been the universal opinion'. He discovers such a place in India: 'I have seen men living upon the earth and not upon it: defended without walls, having nothing, and yet possessing all things'. Of the powers of the Indian *yogis*, especially levitation above the earth, he says: 'This exaltation is what is wished for by all, but it can only be effected by the Indians'.[57] The basic assumption of this discourse, that the Indians enjoy a priority in philosophy, is essential to any argument in favour of the proposition that India has a special place within the Imagination.

Apollonius is quite adamant that he is the first Greek to visit the real Indian sages, those adjacent to the Ganges, beyond the limits of Alexander's conquest. Whatever credit is given to that claim, Apollonius is equally sure that Pythagoras did *not* acquire his philosophy in India. According to Apollonius, Pythagoras had been instructed in Indian philosophy by the Ethiopians before such time as they sought to conceal their Indian origin by adopting Egyptian rituals. If Apollonius is right, we should have to read accounts of the journey of Pythagoras to India metaphorically. Of course, in some sense we also have to read the journey of Apollonius metaphorically—but the metaphor here is not exclusive of a possible literal dimension.

There is good historical reason for suggesting that, even if Pythagoras never went to India, the account of Apollonius has to be treated as something more than mere romance. The argument that the early books of the *Life* constitute a projection of Pythagorean ideals on to a distant and unknown country such as India is by no means convincing. Why should a Pythagorean seek to make such a projection on to India? It is no answer to say that he might have hoped thereby to dignify his philosophy through associating it with an ancient source of wisdom. It was primarily those sympathetic to the Pythagorean tradition to begin with, who first elaborated the image of India as a source of wisdom. Furthermore,

---

[57] Berwick, VI.xi.319–22. Cf. Apollonius on levitation in the sunlight to Colebrooke, I, 262.

however much the *Life* may strain even credulity, nothing could be more far-fetched than the idea that it is simply fortuitous that the beliefs and manners of the sages of the country chosen for such a projection do in fact coincide in almost every detail with the Pythagorean. A modern scholar, a Brahmin conversant with both cultures, has written: 'A student of Orphic and Pythagorean thought cannot fail to see that the similarities between it and the Indian religion are so close as to warrant our regarding them as expressions of the same view of life. We can use the one system to interpret the other'.[58]

The Pythagoreans, like the Indians, subscribe to a coherent system, a world-view in which mysticism, metaphysics and magic are intimately and organically related. Although it is magical practices which dominate the Indian episodes of the *Life*, these (especially in the context of fiction, or story-telling) should not be seen apart from the metaphysical view of which they are a visible manifestation or expression. Whether or not the letters attributed to Apollonius are apocryphal, they were attributed to him for the reason that they express views consistent with his final utterance on the immortality of the soul made, according to the last chapter of the *Life*, in a posthumous appearance in a vision.[59] If one of the letters, written to a man whose son has died, seems impersonal it is because the philosophy purveyed in it is concerned with the universal Self:

There is no death of anyone save in appearance only, even as there is no birth of anyone or becoming, except only in appearance. For when a thing passes from essence into nature we consider that there is a birth or becoming, and in the same way that there is death when it passes from nature into essence; though in truth a thing neither comes into being at any time nor is destroyed. But it is only apparent at one time and later on invisible, the former owing to the density of its material, and the latter by the reason of the lightness or tenuity of the essence, which however remains always the same, and is only subject to differences of movement and state. For this is necessarily the characteristic of change caused not by anything outside, but by a conversion of the whole into the parts, and by a return of the parts into the whole, due to the oneness of the universe.

That the position ascribed to Apollonius is close to that of Plotinus becomes even more evident when he explains why there can be an alternation between visibility and invisibility:

[58] S. Radhakrishnan, *Eastern Religions and Western Thought*, 2nd ed. (London, 1940), p. 143. This remark is a curious, if more applicable, re-rendering of one made in relation not to Indian but to Persian religion by F.M. Cornford (*From Religion to Philosophy*, London, 1912, p. 176).   [59] Berwick, VIII.xxxi.489–91.

It is characteristic of each of the several genera of things here, when it is full, to be apparent to us because of the resistance of its density to our senses, but to be unseen in case it is emptied of its matter by reason of its tenuity, the latter being perforce shed abroad, and flowing away from the eternal measure which confined it; albeit the measure itself is never created nor destroyed.

Apollonius then considers why it is that 'error' has passed un-refuted on such a scale:

The reason is that some imagine that they have themselves actively brought about what they have merely suffered and experienced; because they do not understand that a child brought into the world by parents, is not begotten by its parents, any more than what grows by means of the earth grows out of the earth; nor are phenomenal modifications or affec-tions of matter properties of the individual thing, but it is rather the case that each individual thing's affections are properties of a single phe-nomenon. And this single phenomenon cannot be rightly spoken of or characterized, except we name it the first essence. For this alone is agent and patient, making itself all things unto all and through all, God eternal, which in so far as it takes on the names and person of individuals, forfeits its peculiar character to its prejudice. Now this is of lesser importance; what is of greater is this, that some are apt to weep so soon as ever God arises out of mankind, by mere change of place and not of nature. But in very truth of things, you should not lament another's death, but prize and reverence it . . .[60]

This philosophical position is close not only to that of Plotinus but also to the non-dualist idealism of contemporary Indian Vedan-tins. It is perhaps significant that when al-Biruni, the eleventh century Muslim historian of India, came to explain the doctrine of the unity of all creation, both material and immaterial, as declared in the *Bhagavad Gita*, it was to Apollonius of Tyana that he turned for a comparison.[61]

Wherever Apollonius goes after his return to the Mediterra-nean, India is never far from his mind and frequently he refers to his debt to the Indian sages.[62] The emperor Domitian speaks

---

[60] Epistle LVIII, Conybeare, II, 454–7.   [61] Sachau, I, 40.   [62] Even before Apollonius visits Ethiopia to reveal the Indian origin of the gymnosophists there, we hear of his using Indian prayers (IV.xvi.202) and Indian practices (V.xxx.281). Not only does he write widely-known treatises on astrology and sacrifices based on what he has learned in India (III.xli.172–3) but he warmly recommends the Indian refusal to sacrifice animals (V.xxv.273), delights Emperor Vespasian with his account of India (V.xxxvii.293) and praises a youth for speaking as if he had been instructed by Indians (VI.iii.304).

not only for himself but for many of his subjects when he bursts out in irritation: 'I beg you may not turn the conversation to Indians. . .'[63] This remark is made at the trial of Apollonius in Rome which dominates the last part of the *Life*. The mystical philosophy of the Indians remains the touchstone for the attitude of Apollonius towards politics, just as it does for both Kipling and Forster in their classic novels about India. Apollonius asserts that not he alone but philosophy is on trial, and moreover a particular philosophy which holds that a wise man, because he knows himself in the sense Iarchas suggested, can do nothing against his better judgement. He tells his friends that he would not have the gall to face his Indian preceptors if he did not go to Rome to face trial and he goes bearing in mind the advice given him by Phraotes that tyrants, like lions, should be treated neither with too much severity nor too much gentleness.[64] The non-dualism of the mystic, evident earlier in the treatment by Apollonius of both parties in the civil dispute at Aspendus,[65] seeks to reconcile the oppressor to his better self and thereby to the oppressed. In our own time politicians have found Gandhi obtuse for taking this same approach to politics which, according to Aristotle, the Pythagoreans took when they asserted that if a man's conduct in private life was virtuous he would be virtuous in public life.[66] In the *Republic* Plato wrote of the difficulty a man educated in abstract virtue would have in the court-rooms of the Law[67] and Apollonius strikes an equally Platonist note in prison awaiting trial—when he seeks to console his fellow prisoners with the information that their condition is a cosmic archetype.[68]

Not only the manner of the defence but its matter also is illuminated by the Indian experience of Apollonius. The most important charge against him is that he is called a god. Unlike Christ, Apollonius makes no unique claim to divinity but upholds the doctrine, which Philostratus points out he had learnt among the Indians, that all good men are entitled to that appellation.[69] In the defence prepared by Apollonius but never in fact used, he defends this doctrine by reference to the concept of a Demiurge:

This doctrine is that of the Indians and Egyptians. The latter blame the Indians in some things, and call in question certain of their precepts

---

[63] Berwick, VII.xxxii.413.   [64] Ibid., VII.xiv.385–8; VII.xxx.409. Apollonius again points out he could have sought asylum in India, VII.xix.395.   [65] Ibid., I.xv.25–7.   [66] It was typical of Gandhi to let political policy be determined by a pure life and inner vision; Louis Fischer, *The Life of Mahatma Gandhi* (New York, 1950), *passim*.   [67] *Republic* 517D.   [68] Berwick, VII.xxvi.403–6.   [69] Ibid., VIII.v.429.

touching morality; but the doctrine which the philosophers of the East hold of the Demiurgus, or maker of all things, is so approved of by the Egyptians, that they instruct others in its tenets, notwithstanding it is of Indian origin. This doctrine acknowledges God to be the author of nature and of all existence; and makes his goodness the efficient cause of all things. If, then, goodness is so intimately connected with the Divinity, I cannot avoid considering myself founded in the opinion of good men partaking of the Divine nature. By the world, which depends on God as its great Demiurgus, we understand all things in heaven, and in earth, and in the sea, of which all men equally partake, though their several conditions as to fortune may be very different. But there is a world in every good man's power, the regulation of which does not exceed the limits of human wisdom, which you will allow, O Emperor! requires a man like unto a God to govern.[70]

The prepared defence suggests a further reason why Apollonius is enamoured of India. In Rome, as they would never have been in India, the Pythagorean precepts are regarded as peculiar, so much so that they have to be defended in court. In the part of his oration in which he argues that men are forgetful of their debt to the earth in slaughtering animals for food, clothing and sacrifice, Apollonius says that Pythagoras derived his disapproval of such conduct from the Brahmins by way of the gymnosophists of Egypt. It is owing to this dietary restriction, he argues, that he is able to gain the advantage of knowing the previous incarnations of his soul.[71]

APROPOS APOLLONIUS AND INDIA: PORPHYRY AND VEGETARIANISM

To call Apollonius a neo-Pythagorean is not to distance him in any way from the neo-Platonists, who (Porphyry makes clear) were consciously seeking out the more Pythagorean elements in Plato's thought.[72] This is seen in their concern with every aspect of the practical philosophical life, and central to Porphyry's treatise *On Abstinence* is his remark: 'The Pythagorean is more pleasing than the Socratic banquet'.[73] In this treatise Porphyry shows that he, like Apollonius on trial in Rome, is aware that an adherence to a vegetarian diet as part of a philosophy involving non-violence and a belief in the transmigration of souls has long been associated with India. Porphyry's main concern in the treatise, however, is not with India but with Pythagoras, whom he conceives of as having tried to re-establish a golden age when animals were neither

---

[70] Ibid., VIII.vii.445–6. For Plotinus on the Demiurge, *Enn.*, v.i.10.   [71] Ibid., VIII.vii.439–42.   [72] 'On the Life of Plotinus', chaps 18, 20, MacKenna, I, 15–16, 20.   [73] 'On Abstinence from Animal Food', Bk. III, § 26, *SWP*.

killed nor eaten. Unlike Apollonius, he never does consider whether Pythagoras came under an Indian influence. The matter is of interest here because the figure of Pythagoras is as obscure as the question of Indian influence on him and it is pertinent to ask whether neo-Platonism reached a concurrence with Indian thought by refining Pythagoras through reference to his Greek successors—or whether Pythagoras was at this time being reinterpreted or recreated in terms of the already refined Indian tradition with which the neo-Platonists had become familiar.

The argument made by Apollonius at his trial that there is an intimate connection between a vegetarian diet and enlightenment or, as he puts it, the discovery of divinity, is argued in full by Porphyry in *On Abstinence*. Probably Porphyry is thinking especially of India when he writes of the need to be 'a gymnosophist of the spirit', divesting the spirit no less than the body of its 'manifold garments'.[74] When he goes on to suggest that all sentient beings have a 'language', he indicates the diversity of languages by making reference both to the differences between those of the Greeks and of the Indians[75] and to the way Apollonius could understand the language of animals.[76] The *Life* clearly left its mark on Porphyry. He refers to Apollonius both in his biography of Pythagoras and in his treatise on the Styx, in the latter as part of a commentary on the description of an androgynous *ardhanarisvara* (Siva-sakti) statue in an Indian cave preserved from Bardaisan.[77]

It is in Book IV of *On Abstinence* that Porphyry deals with the simplicity, peace and healthiness of the Golden Age and refers to those peoples who had attempted to realize it. A most detailed treatment is given to the Indians. Drawing on contemporary as well as widely-available traditional sources, Porphyry speaks of

---

[74] Ibid., I.31. Taylor quotes the Pythagorean Demophilus to similar effect, ibid., p. 83 n.x. See also *Enn.*, I.vi.7 and the words of an Indian *yogi* reported by Marco Polo (Yule, II.III.xx.366).   [75] Ibid., III.4. The original reference to the Indian jackal is in Ktesias and, as Lassen observes, probably helps establish the antiquity of Indian animal fables (*Ancient India as described by Ktesias the Knidian*, trans. J.W. McCrindle, London, 1882, p. 75).   [76] Ibid., III.3. Eusebius associates Apollonius and Porphyry as the authorities for the opinion that no sacrifices should be offered to the One God (*Praeparatio Evangelica*, IV.12–13). Porphyry expresses this view in ibid., II.34.   [77] 'De Vita Pythagorae', §.2, p. 5, Iamblichus, *De Vita Pythagorica* (Amsterdam, 1707); Stobaeus, *Physica*, Bk. I, c.iii, s.56, *Ioannis Stobaei Eclogarum Physicarum et Ethicarum*, ed. Augustus Meineke, 2 vols (Leipzig, 1860), I.40; H.J.W. Drijvers, *Bardaisan of Edessa* (Assen, 1966), p. 173. The embassy to the court of Emperor Elagabalus at the time when Philostratus was writing his biography of Apollonius at the commission of the former empress inspired Richard Garnett's story, 'The Wisdom of the Indians', *The Twilight of the Gods* (London, 1927), pp. 114–23.

the *rishis* up in the Indian mountains who live on ripe fruits, milk and herbs and of others by the Ganges who survive on fruit and rice. He mentions that they are not only vegetarian but pursue a solitary life of silence. He speaks also of those who abandon home and family to take up an abstemious monastic life outside the cities. The Brahmins and the *Samanaeans* (probably either Buddhists or Jains) provide Porphyry with as concrete an example as he can find of the life of the Golden Age and, again in reference to the vulgar who ask what would happen if all men lived like the Indians, cites the saying of Pythagoras that if all men were kings life would be difficult, yet the regal life is not on that account to be avoided.[78]

That Porphyry had more than a passing interest in India is suggested by St Augustine, himself perhaps the most important channel through which neo-Platonism passed into the Christian tradition. Augustine, referring to Porphyry's first treatise (now lost), *On the Return of the Soul*, quotes him as saying that 'no one system of thought has yet embraced a doctrine that embodies a universal path to the liberation of the soul, no, neither the truest of philosophies, or the moral ideas and practices of the Indians, nor the initiation of the Chaldeans, nor any other way of life. . .'.[79] In whatever way Augustine, arguing in favour of Christianity as 'the universal path', cares to construe this passage and whatever Porphyry initially did or did not know about India, clearly the Indians, as practical philosophers, command considerable respect.

APROPOS APOLLONIUS: PLOTINUS AND THE METAPHYSICAL PASSAGE

If any passage to India which may or may not have been made, literally or metaphorically, has been subject to more controversy than that of Apollonius of Tyana, it is that of Plotinus. According to Porphyry, Plotinus set off from Alexandria eager to investigate Persian philosophical methods and the system adopted among the Indians. This is said to have been a direct result of making great progress in philosophy under the guidance of his teacher, Ammonius Saccas, a philosopher called the 'God-taught' who discouraged the propagation of his doctrine and is thought to have been concerned 'more with establishing a way of life than in pursuing intellectual knowledge for its own sake'.[80] If, as some scho-

---

[78] 'On Abstinence', I. 17–18. [79] *De Civitate Dei*, X.xxxii. [80] 'On the Life of Plotinus', chap. 3, MacKenna, I, 3; *Plotinus: the Six Enneads*, trans. Stephen

lars have claimed,[81] Plotinus is to be read exclusively in terms of the Greek tradition, it does seem peculiar that not only could he not find a satisfactory teacher in Alexandria before meeting Ammonius but also that the primary impulse left with him after being the student of Ammonius was to gain first-hand knowledge of the philosophical practices of Persia and India.

If Plotinus is exclusively indebted to the Greeks, his metaphysics must derive essentially from the Eleatics, from Pythagoras and Plato, although also from Aristotle: after the *Enneads* it was possible for Aristotle to become largely neo-Platonized in the Muslim intellectual tradition while in Europe there have been times when the term Platonism has become synonymous with neo-Platonism. Neither mystical thought nor practice, however, came to dominate European culture, being the dimension of neo-Platonism which usually remained beyond the pale both of the Christianity it permeated and the Renaissance it stimulated. In Europe, therefore, the scholastic tradition has been the readier to demonstrate that Plato and Aristotle are *not* the mystics which neo-Platonism made of them. Paradoxically, this anti-mystical tradition is as responsible as the more peripheral mystical one for promoting the idea that Plotinus was indebted to the Orient—although in this case the implication is pejorative. Either way, mysticism, for precisely the reasons given by Apollonius, is associated more with India than with Greece. The association is understandable: in India the Vedanta, unlike neo-Platonism in Europe, has proved to be a mystical strain strong enough to contain (in every sense) the more popular theistic and dualistic movements which are the closest Indian equivalent to Christianity.

Whether or not the philosophy of Plotinus is to be explicated wholly in terms of the Greek tradition, it was certainly possible for a philosopher in Alexandria to be familiar with Indian ideas.[82] That there was contemporary knowledge in the Mediterranean world not only of the Brahminical way of life but also of the mystical philosophy of the Brahmins is evident from a passage by Bishop Hippolytus:

Throughout life they go about naked, saying that the body has been given by the Deity as a covering for the soul. They hold that God is light, but not such light as we see with the eye, nor such as the sun or fire, but God is with them the Word,—by which term they do not mean articulate speech,

---

MacKenna and B.S. Page (Chicago, 1952), biographical note on Plotinus, p. v.   [81] Most notably, A.H. Armstrong, see Staal, pp. 236–9.   [82] See the penultimate paragraph of this chapter, p. 112, and the first paragraph of chapter 5, pp. 145–6.

but the discourse of reason, whereby the hidden mysteries of knowledge are discerned by the wise. This light, however, which they call the Word, and think to be God, is, they say, known only by the Brachhmans themselves, because they alone have discarded vanity, which is the outermost covering of the soul. The members of this sect regard death with contemptuous indifference . . . With regard to the Word, which they call God, they hold that it is corporeal, and that it wears the body as its external covering, just as one wears the woollen surcoat, and that when it divests itself of the body with which it is enwrapped it becomes manifest to the eye . . . The Brachhmans, therefore, when they have shuffled off the body, see the pure sunlight as fish see it when they spring up out of the water into the air.[83]

This passage reveals a clear contemporary knowledge of the Indian Vedanta such as is not again evident in European records until Bernier's rather similar exposition of it in the seventeenth century.[84]

Striking parallels have been established between the metaphysical systems of Plotinus and Sankara.[85] However, it is not to Sankara, whose commentaries were written some centuries later, but to the *Vedanta Sutras* (or *Brahma Sutras*) of Badarayana (and his precursors) that we should turn if we are to talk of *Vedantins* who could have 'influenced' Plotinus. Badarayana himself appears to accept a monistic view of the universe whereby the world is thought to have evolved out of and to be reabsorbed into the single Reality. This Reality is both the material and the instrumental cause of the world and is to be realized through intuitional knowledge, itself made possible by means of devotion and meditation. Badarayana does not resolve the question of whether or not the soul is identical with the Absolute. He does refer, however, to earlier Vedantins who offer varying solutions to philosophical problems which are themselves elaborations, as Badarayana admits, of positions established some centuries earlier by the sages of the Upanishads.[86]

[83] *The Refutation of All Heresies*, trans. J.H. MacMahon (Edinburgh, 1868), Bk. I, xxi, 59–60. See also Staal, pp. 243–5.   [84] 'The Gentils of Indostan', IV, 176–71 (in error for 180), Bernier (1672). A letter from Charles Blount, the first English translator of the story of Apollonius, to the Earl of Rochester remarks that Bernier's account of the Hindu opinion concerning the immortality of the soul agrees very well with that of Apollonius (Thomas Burnet, *Archaeologiae Philosophicae*, new ed., trans. Foxton, 2 pts., London, 1729, Appendix, p. 12).   [85] Staal (see n. 81) is the best contemporary authority. [86] Radhakrishnan, II, 430–44; 466–70. See also the same author's Introduction to his translation of *The Brahma Sutra* (London, 1960), Colebrooke, like Radhakrishnan, places Sankara (as does Sankara himself) in a tradition which can be traced back via Badarayana to the older Upanishads (I, 350–401).

Basic to the metaphysics of the *Enneads* is the theory of the three hypostases, and a parallel to this can be found both in the Vedantin theory of the three *kosas* and in the Mahayana Buddhist theory of the *kayas* (or successively more aethereal 'bodies', equivalent to progressively more enlightened states of consciousness).[87] What is uncertain is the extent to which these similarities (both in images and ideas) are an outgrowth of mystical experience or of an inherited philosophical tradition—and if of a single philosophical tradition whether that of Greece or of India. If of India, nothing indicates how the mystical and therefore guarded (if not exclusive) doctrines of the Upanishads could have become known to Plotinus so much as the story, composed and made public in his own lifetime, of Apollonius making the journey to India he himself wanted to make; nor does anything indicate better how it is that any assertion about such a journey, including that it has been made, is immediately implicated in controversy.

Central to the perception which apprehends an Indian influence on Plotinus is the idea that ultimately metaphysics, and indeed thought itself, is subordinate to mystical experience. By the very nature of that philosophical position an *Advaitin* or a neo-Platonist will tend to discover identities rather than differences. What Plotinus has most in common with his Indian counterparts is a commitment to the mystical state as superseding metaphysics, even knowledge itself: 'Abandon even the word: It'.[88] The closer the mystic is to the suprarational state which Plotinus conceives as *ekstasis* in the One the less possible is it to see any distinction between this and *samadhi* in *Brahman* or *nirvana* in *Tathata*. The point, however, is that an awareness of such an identity is to be discovered within—through contemplation and meditation. The passage to India is a passage to the Self and India is a valid image for the abstract mystical state only in so far as the Indian cultural tradition insists on its own unexclusiveness. By this token the only admissible evidence of Indian 'influence' will be an awareness in the Mediterranean that such a philosophical theory and the practice conformable with it exists in India. It will then be no less—though no more—conclusive evidence of Indian 'influence' if Plotinus, being attracted to mysticism, desired to go to India (as well as Persia) than if, having gone to India, he was attracted to mystical practice.

---

[87] Colebrooke, I, 257–8; 395–6; Monier-Williams, pp. 246–7; Radhakrishnan, I, 598–600. H.H. Wilson supposed that Plotinus was indebted to India for his theory (VI, 13–14nn).   [88] *Enn.*, VI.viii.21 (as rendered by Staal, p. 179).

THE MEANING OF MAGIC

The full significance of the *Life of Apollonius of Tyana* becomes apparent when it is understood that for the neo-Platonists and neo-Pythagoreans, as for the Hindus and Buddhists, there is not only no incongruity between philosophy and magic but an actual identity. The Christian attack on the *Life* was based on a denial not of miraculous powers *per se* but of the belief that those powers were invested in anyone other than Jesus Christ. Those philosophical traditions which do not limit divine immanence to the person of Jesus will necessarily permit the belief that the possibility of miracles exists wherever the body and its senses are not permitted to obstruct the process of Self-realization.

Apollonius himself derides magicians whose 'whole art lies in the deluded fancies of the spectators'. These men—'pseudo-sophists' he calls them—are not to be confounded with real philosophers.[89] To Euphrates, the Ethiopian sage, he writes: 'You think it your duty to call philosophers who follow Pythagoras magicians, and likewise also those who follow Orpheus. For my own part I think that those who follow no matter whom, ought to be called magicians, if only they are determined to be divine and just men'. A further letter, in which he denounces Euphrates, elaborates on this: 'The Persians give the name of *magi* to divine beings. A *magus* then is either a worshipper of the gods or one who is by nature divine'.[90] Likewise Iamblichus says that when the daemonically-inspired soul has innate knowledge of God, the senses are suspended, normal life is interrupted and a man has the ability to do wonders since he is living a divine life. Plotinus had said that 'the true magic is internal to the All'. The magician draws on the patterns of spiritual power which, as in Love, are mutually attractive and 'by ranging himself also into the pattern is able tranquilly to possess himself of these forces with whose nature and purpose he has become identified'. It is only the man who understands the true nature of magic who can escape falling under its spell: 'What we look to, draws us magically. Only the self-intent go free of magic. Hence every action has magic as its source and the entire life of the practical man is a bewitchment'.[91]

The need to give magic a more philosophical definition is pointed out by Apuleius, another disciple of Pythagoras and Plato, who, when put on trial for magic, argues that if he were a magician in the sense the authorities claim they would not be able to hold

[89] Berwick, VIII.vii.438.   [90] Epistles XVI–XVII, Conybeare, II, 422–3.
[91] *Enn.*, IV.vi.40,43.

him in custody. Like Apollonius in a similar situation, Apuleius feels that it is philosophy itself which is on trial and, furthermore, the sort of philosophy which holds that a wise man will free himself of all possessions so as not to be enslaved by the phenomenal world. In his *Defence* Apuleius notes that the charge of being a magician is invariably brought against philosophers who inquire into 'the pure and primary causes of matter'. They are accused of bringing about what they simply know to take place.[92] To the ordinary perception the abstract Good of Plato, no less than the purification of Empedocles or the daemon of Socrates, can become an object of suspicion.

Persia was often regarded by the Greeks as the home of magic (Zoroaster was sometimes said to be its inventor),[93] although when a later Platonist such as Ammianus Marcellinus comes to consider the subject he adds that Zoroaster was taught his philosophy by the Brahmins in their forests in north-west India. Ammianus also mentions the Brahmins whom Apollonius saw walk through the air among their altars,[94] and as far back as Vedic times there were said to be *munis* who as a result of their sanctity could rise on the wind and, resembling the sun, fly in the paths of the gods.[95] In late Vedic times the magical power called *brahman* was thought to be invested in the priest and in the verses he chanted, but increasingly asceticism tended to displace sacrifice as the chief means by which magical powers were attained, culminating for the truly spiritual in full mystical insight.[96] It is the contribution of the Upanishads to discover a psychological root for the older religious concepts and rites. *Brahman* is immanent not only in the person of the priest but in every person and thing, in every form of consciousness. It is but two sides of the same truth to suggest that our own ignorance or nescience—*avidya*—prevents our realization of this and to say that the One by his magic assumes manifold forms.[97] Much of the teaching in the Upanishads is given over to establishing those correspondences between macrocosm and microcosm which are basic to the performance of magic: but while the premise is familiar that control over the parts of the self is *per se* control over the universe, it is tempered by the proviso that the parts of the self have to be perceived as undifferentiated Self.

[92] 'The Defence of Apuleius', *The Works of Apuleius*, Bohn edition (London, 1853), pp. 247–9, 265, 273–4.   [93] Apuleius cites Plato (*Alcibiades* I, 122A).   [94] Ammianus Marcellinus, XXIII, 6, 19 and 33; XXVIII, 1, 13.   [95] *RV*, X.136.   [96] Basham, pp. 241, 246–8.   [97] e.g. *Svetasvatara Upanishad*, 4.9–10, Hume, p. 404. The term *maya*, suggesting magic powers, is used as early as *RV*, 6.47.18 (see *BA*, 2.5.19).

Bernier, a sceptical pupil of Gassendi's, makes a distinction about magicians in the seventeenth century curiously similar to that made by Apollonius. There are the *yogis*, he says, who experience religious ecstasy after practising austerities surpassing anything known in Europe and there are the *yogis* who perform magic tricks.[98] Another European traveller, Mandelslo, had earlier made a nice distinction when he observed that the real *yogis* do not believe in transmigration of souls but in *immediate* salvation.[99] At such a point the only magic being practised by the mystic, presumably, is that whereby the spirit is freed from bondage to matter, specifically to the body. Both Mahayana Buddhism and the Vedanta assert that in order to speak about existence at all it is necessary to elaborate a theory of two truths—i.e. of an ultimate Reality and of a relative reality. The ultimate Reality is indescribable and unimaginable: the relative reality is the Ultimate as it is apprehended at the level of description and imagination. One could say that in the *Enneads* Plotinus performs *his* magic by turning language inside out and the world upside down. In a story such as that of Apollonius of Tyana visiting sages in India the inner life of the sages, their freedom from magic, can (ironically) be depicted or imagined only in terms of *their* possessing magical powers.

A fuller understanding of the meaning of magic may be arrived at by a look at the metamorphosis undergone by the Sanskrit word *maya*. Ananda Coomaraswamy has written: '*Maya* is precisely the maker's power or art', 'magic' in Jacob Boehme's sense:

It is a mother in all three worlds, and makes each thing after the model of that thing's will. It is not the understanding, but it is a creatrix according to the understanding, and lends itself to good or to evil. . . from eternity a ground and support of all things . . . In sum: Magic is the activity of the Will-Spirit.

Zimmer comments:

the *maya* of the gods is their power to assume diverse shapes by displaying at will various aspects of their subtle essence. But the gods are themselves

[98] 'On the Gentils of Indostan', IV, 130–9, Bernier (1672). Bernier's contemporary, Pietro della Valle, not only sees the *yogis* as successors to the gymnosophists encountered by the Greeks; he also makes reference to Apollonius when he writes about a book in the *nagari* script apparently written by Pythagoras. He is perceptive about the understandable confusion of Brahmin and Pythagorean doctrines (*The Travels of Pietro della Valle*, trans., Edward Grey, 1664, 2 vols, London, 1892, I, Letter I, XIII, 75–7; XV, 99–101; XVII, 105–8).   [99] 'Mandelslo's Travels into the Indies', Bk. I, p. 57, Olearius, *The Voyages and Travels of the Ambassadors*, 2nd ed., trans. John Davies (London, 1669).

the productions of a greater *maya*: the spontaneous self-transformation of an originally undifferentiated, all-generating divine Substance. And this greater *maya* produces, not the gods alone, but the universe in which they operate.

As the dynamic aspect of both the universal substance and the cosmic flux, *maya* is at once the cause and effect of existence and on account of its ability to wrap the ego in a cocoon it appears to be ultimate reality.[100] In the *Vishnu Purana* Vishnu is hymned by Aditi, the visible Infinite as Mother Goddess, with the words: 'The notions that "I am—this is mine", which influence mankind are but the delusions of the mother of the world, originating in thy active agency'.[101] The ego and the phenomenal world are identical. It is as true for Plotinus as for the Hindus that Nature is a sorcery which loses its tangibility as soon as it is seen to depend for its distinct existence on the organs of perception. The enlightened sage appears as a magician not because he controls the natural world but because he is no longer controlled by it.

There is a modern account of a visit to a Hill of Sages in India which raises some of the same questions raised by the visit of Apollonius to Iarchas. In his book *A Search in Secret India*, Paul Brunton tells of how on his way to question the holy man of Arunchala, who like Iarchas lived on an Indian hilltop, he sensed that his questions had been answered telepathically.[102] To the questioner this would appear to be magic. The logic of non-dualism suggests another way of perceiving what had happened. Assuming the holy man of Arunchala, Ramana Maharishi, to be a genuinely enlightened mystic, a disciple approaching would automatically sense the *ahamkara*, or egoity, implicit in the very act of questioning, the dialectical method of question and answer being by its nature part of the world of duality: while the questioner might get the impression his question had been answered what would have happened rather is that in an ambience of quietude or quiescence he had realized the question need never be framed. The Upanishads indicate that the mystical transcends thought itself: it is not that a genuine mystic reads thought—it is that thought itself dissolves in the mystical atmosphere.[103] From an idealist viewpoint it is not inconceivable that a mystic should have magical powers; what is inconceivable is that he should wish to use them. Perhaps it is, as Apuleius and Apollonius both suggest, that other people force on metaphysicians the epithet of magicians. It is a popular way—and

[100] Heinrich Zimmer, *Myths and Symbols in Indian Art and Civilization*, ed. Joseph Campbell (New York, 1962), pp. 24–6 and 24n.   [101] *VP*, v. v. xxx, 95.
[102] (London, 1934), pp. 141–2.   [103] Radhakrishnan, I, 173–81.

in fiction perhaps the only way—of according recognition to those who are *not* enslaved by the world's magic. It is this philosophical conception of magic which accounts for the high reputation Apollonius enjoyed among the neo-Platonists.

THE INDIA OF APOLLONIUS: OTHER ALLUSIONS

By a curious irony the view of India as the home of philosophy purveyed by Apollonius is widely diffused by two writers who would be the last to give any credit to the miraculous powers of Apollonius: namely, the Epicurean Lucian and the Christian Eusebius. Since he pre-dates Philostratus, Lucian is instrumental in establishing the historicity of Apollonius, although it is in a reference where he pours scorn on one of the disciples of the Tyanean.[104] For this very reason his attitude to India is the more revealing, although the import of his remarks is sometimes made as obscure by his facetious sense of humour as that of Apollonius by his lack of it.

Lucian's awareness of Indian influences on the Mediterranean is most clearly seen in 'The Passing of Peregrinus'. Lucian does not underrate the fame of Peregrinus. He is at some pains to show that the man was held in esteem among the Christians of Palestine as 'a new Socrates' second only to Christ himself and was compared by the poor to Diogenes and Crates. On the other hand his decision to immolate himself at the conclusion of the Olympic Games in 165 AD Lucian ascribes to an attachment not to verity but to publicity:

But for what reason does this man throw himself bodily into the fire? Oh, yes! to demonstrate his fortitude, like the Brahmans, for Theagenes thought fit to compare him with them, just as if there could not be fools and notoriety-seekers even among the Indians. Well, then, let him at least imitate them. They do not leap into the fire (so Onesicritus says, Alexander's navigator, who saw Calanus burning), but when they have built their pyre, they stand close beside it motionless and endure being toasted; then, mounting upon it, they cremate themselves decorously, without the slightest alteration of the position in which they are lying.

Whatever the motives of Peregrinus, there is no doubt be conceived of himself as performing an act in the Hindu tradition. In the last days of his life he 'changed his name to Phoenix, because the phoenix, the Indian bird, is said to mount a pyre when it is very

---

[104] 'Alexander the False Prophet', IV, 174–253, *Lucian*, trans. A.M. Harmon, K. Kilburn and M.D. Macleod, 8 vols (Cambridge, Mass., 1913–67). The reference to Apollonius is in § 6. See Phillimore, Introduction, I, xlvi–lvi.

far advanced in age'. Although, in the event, he immolates himself at night under a full moon, it had alternatively 'been given out that he would greet the rising sun, as, in fact, they say the Brahmans do, before mounting the pyre. . .'. Before he does mount the pyre Peregrinus invokes the *manes* to the south ('even the south, too, had to do with the show'), a practice which a note to a recent edition of Lucian properly indicates is a rite of Yama, the Hindu god of the underworld, as prescribed in the *Atharva Veda*.[105]

Nothing about India seized the imagination of the Hellenistic world so much as the indifference with which a philosopher would face death through self-immolation, a rite described in the *Mimamsa Sutras*.[106] The best and most widely-known example, as Lucian suggests, is that of Calanus in the presence of Alexander the Great at Susa.[107] Another story disseminated by Diodorus was that of the two widows of Keteus striving for the honour of which should die with their husband on the funeral pyre—a story which may have been borrowed from Indian literature, although that would by no means preclude its being realized also in Indian life.[108] Furthermore, the custom of self-immolation, in India dating from the time of the Vedic sacrifice (designed to recreate the world anew) and periodically referred to in literature, had been carried into the very home of Western philosophy when, in the presence of Emperor Augustus and after initiation into the local mysteries, Zarmanochegas (probably Sramanacharya), on an embassy from India, had committed himself to the flames in Athens in 25 BC.[109] Possibly this is the event referred to by St Paul in the passage in his first Epistle to the Corinthians when he speaks of the valuelessness, without love, of giving the body to be burned.[110] Whether or not this is so, the manner in which Peregrinus chose to end his life testifies to the extent the active Indian contempt for death had impressed itself on the Greek mind.[111]

In a further dialogue written by Lucian to deprecate Peregrinus

[105] Ibid., v, 2–51 and 40n. The phoenix is declared to be an Indian bird not only by Apollonius but by Nicolo di Conti; this recurs in some versions of Prester John's letter and some of the Alexander Romances, This may reflect on the story of the sacrificial golden bird in the Vedas. [106] Colebrooke, I.346–7. The immolation of an ascetic, Sarabhanga, is recorded in the *Ramayana*, III.9. [107] Strabo, xv.i.68. [108] Diodorus Siculus, xix.33.1–34.6. See also Plutarch, 'Whether Vice Be Sufficient to Cause Unhappiness', § 3, *Moralia*, 499C. Advancing their respective claims with similar arguments, the two wives of Pandu, Madri and Kunti, dispute who should ascend his funeral pyre (*MH*, Section cxxv in the Sambhava of the Adi Parva, pp. 367–9). [109] Strabo, xv.i.73. See also Dio Cassius, LIV.9.10. [110] *Eastern Religions and Western Thought*, p. 157, n. 1. [111] Plutarch suggests that in austerities the Indians out-do even the Cynics, 'On the Fortune or the Virtue of Alexander', I, § 10, *Moralia*, 332B. Dion Chrysostom

(some indication of the furore which the self-immolation must have created), Philosophy in Heaven is made to remind Zeus of how he had first sent her to Earth:

When I sped off, father, I did not head for the Greeks straight-way . . . Making for the Indians to begin with, the most numerous population in the world, I had no difficulty about persuading them to come down off their elephants and associate with me. Consequently, a whole tribe, the Brahmans, who border upon the Nechraei and the Oxyd-racae, are all enlisted under my command and not only live in accordance with my tenets, honoured by all their neighbours, but die a marvellous kind of death.

Zeus takes it that this is a reference to the gymnosophists who immolate themselves without flinching. Philosophy, after a further exchange, continues:

After the Brahmans I went direct to Ethiopia, and then down to Egypt; and after associating with their priests and prophets and instructing them in religion, I departed for Babylon to initiate Chaldeans and Magi; then from there to Scythia and then to Thrace, where I conversed with Eumol-pus and Orpheus, whom I sent in advance to Greece, one of them Eumol-pus, to give them the mysteries, as he had learned all about religion from me, and the other to win them over by the witchery of his music.[112]

It is a basic premise of the *Life of Apollonius* that philosophy was known first in India and thence travelled to Egypt by way of Ethiopia. While Lucian's comic fantasy is not historical evidence for an Indian priority in philosophical speculation any more than is the mystical assertion of Apollonius, it is indicative of the image India could evoke in the Hellenistic mind that it should be accorded this primacy in two such disparate contexts.

The idea that India was the original home of pagan philosophy received ecclesiastical sanction when Eusebius, whatever else he rejected about the *Life of Apollonius*, recorded in his *Chronicon* that the Ethiopian emigration from India took place in the fortieth year of the Jewish captivity in Egypt. Eusebius may not have wished to give Apollonius much credit, but the reputation of the Brahmins in the early centuries AD stood high—not only among the pagans who polemicized with the Christians but also with the Christians who often found it preferable not to repudiate the

---

remarks not only on the discipline of the Brahmins but also on the prescience which depends on their devotion to the divine (Oration, XLIX.7). An Indian fable which demonstrates the love and self-fulfilment which may lie behind asceticism is that of king Sivi and the dove (*MH*, Section CCXLVII of the Markandeya-samyasya of the Vana Parva, pp. 596–9).

Brahmins but to appropriate them for their own dialectical purposes. Clement of Alexandria, sympathetic both to the Pythagoreans on account of their belief that God is One and immanent in the universe, and to the Brahmins whom (on the authority of Alexander Polyhistor's book on the Pythagorean symbols) he says Pythagoras had heard, includes among the polemical chapters of the *Stromata* one suggests that Greek philosophy was in great part derived from, among others, the Indians, and another which specifies a Greek debt for their philosophical tenets to the Egyptian and Indian gymnosophists.

Clement not only provides the West with its first recorded references to Buddha and to Buddhists; he is also interested enough in the accounts of the lives of the Indian ascetics (perhaps Buddhist, though more probably Brahmin or Jain) whom the Greeks called *Hylobii*. These he compares to the Christian Encratites. Furthermore, Clement reports with approval the remark attributed to Zeno that he would prefer to see one Indian burn on the pyre than to hear all the arguments about the value of bearing pain.[113] While Clement was drawing off Classical literary sources, he was also the foremost pupil of and successor to Pantaenus, the first principal of the Christian College in Alexandria. According to Eusebius Pantaenus had previously led a Christian mission to India, his education as a Stoic philosopher, according to the further gloss of Jerome, being decisive in his selection to preach Christianity among the Brahmins and philosophers of that nation.[114]

It is Eusebius who records the most curious of all the Classical references made to India. He has preserved from Aristoxenus, a contemporary of Alexander the Great, a report concerning a confrontation in Classical Athens between Socrates and some Indian philosophers. One Indian was said to have asked Socrates the scope of his philosophy and to have burst out laughing when Socrates replied that it was an enquiry into human phenomena. The Indian is reported to have replied that there was no point in inquiring into human phenomena unless the divine was first understood.[115] The authenticity of this story might reasonably be disputed on the grounds that Aristoxenus, who wrote a treatise on the Pythagorean way of life,[116] was habitually critical of Socrates,[117] perhaps because he felt Socrates had founded a tradition antithetical to the Pythagorean. Whether Socrates did in fact do so or whether as some claim he was really a Pythagorean cannot here be considered, especially as we have yet to consider whether Pythagoras himself was a Pythagorean. What is pertinent is that Aristoxenus should tell the story at all. Had Indian philosophers been seen and heard in the Athens of Socrates and Plato? Or was Aristoxenus (as I think more likely) using the new knowledge of Indian philosophy acquired by Alexander's men to invent a plausible fiction? Whatever the truth, the myth that India represents a spiritual dimension beyond that known to the West does not *originate* with Apollonius of Tyana but is at least as old as the fourth century BC.

Pythagoras: The Esoteric Doctrines of the *Brihad Aranyaka*

in which the myth of a passage to
India by Pythagoras is juxtaposed
to the teachings of his Indian
contemporary, Yajnavalkya.

The Master of the Law had, in the best of spirit, opposed the
Prajnamula and *Sata-Sastra*, and approved of the *Yoga*, with the
opinion that the illustrious (holy) men, who founded these
doctrines, each followed one thought, and were not mutually at
variance, or opposed; and if they cannot be quite reconciled, he
said, yet these are not contradictory, and the fault is with their
successors, but this cannot bar the truth of the Law.

The Life of Hiuen-Tsiang.

Egypt and Greece, good-bye, and good-bye, Rome!
Hermits upon Mount Meru or Everest,
Caverned in night under the drifted snow,
Or where that snow and winter's dreadful blast
Beat down upon their naked bodies, know
That day brings round the night, that before dawn
[Man's] glory and his monuments are gone.

W.B. Yeats, 'Meru'.

CHAPTER FOUR

Pythagoras: The Esoteric Doctrines of the *Brihad Aranyaka*

PYTHAGORAS IN INDIA: APULEIUS

Did Pythagoras ever actually visit India? That the 'passage to India' is a *return* passage, a return to the original source of wisdom, would have been established long ago could it have been shown that the more mystical aspects of neo-Pythagoreanism and neo-Platonism were the outcome of a decisive Indian influence either on the Hellenistic world or on Pythagoras and Plato themselves. Pythagoras, Plato and Plotinus are seminal names in an intellectual tradition within which the whole literary conception of the Romantic Imagination has been elaborated, and if India were a decisive influence on them it would be a *sine qua non* for an understanding of what is meant by the Imagination.

The story that Pythagoras had travelled to India and learnt the greater part of his philosophy from the Brahmins receives its most influential literary accreditation from Apuleius.[1] The admiration of Apuleius for Indian philosophy is the more important because, as Cudworth adduces authorities to show, Apuleius was the man the pagans named along with Apollonius of Tyana as a thaumaturge whose miracles were comparable to those of Jesus.[2] For Apuleius Pythagoras is a 'man of surpassingly mighty genius, and of more than human grandeur of soul, the first name and founder of philosophy'. Apuleius mentions the belief that Pythagoras was instructed by Zoroaster but says it is 'the more generally received story' that he travelled of his own accord to Egypt and that, not satisfied with what he had learnt there of the power of ceremonies,

---

[1] 'The Florida of Apuleius', xv, *Works of Apuleius*, pp. 388–9. For remarks on the Indian gymnosophists, see ibid., vi, 377–8.   [2] Cudworth, i, 265–74. See especially Lactantius, *Divinae Institutiones*, v. 3.

of numbers and of geometry, 'he afterwards visited the Chaldeans and the Brahmins, and among the latter the Gymnosophists'. Apuleius is even more precise about the respective influences of the Chaldeans and the Indians on Pythagoras than St Augustine will be about their influences on Porphyry.[3] The Chaldeans taught Pythagoras about the stars and, for a price, about medicine. 'But the Brahmins taught him the greater part of his philosophy; what are the rules and principles of the understanding: what the functions of the body; how many are the faculties of the soul, how many the mutations of life; what torments and rewards devolve upon the souls of the dead according to their respective deserts. . . '. This is a clear attribution of an original debt to India for Pythagorean ideas on the nature of the soul, its relationship to the body and its fate after death; furthermore, it comes from a Platonist who at this very point asserts that Plato imitates Pythagoras, differing in little or no degree from the Pythagoreans.

What are we to conclude from this? Did Pythagoras go to India? Was he in touch with Indian philosophers? Or is it that the prestige of Indian philosophy was great enough in Hellenistic times for Apuleius to say it is 'the more generally received story', disseminated further in one of (what are almost certainly) the orations of a widely-known philosopher, that not only is there an identity between the Pythagorean and Platonic tradition and Brahminical philosophy but that the Greeks are actually indebted to the Indians for the very foundations of their philosophy? The fact is that this story of Pythagoras going to India was never 'generally received' even among the neo-Platonists. While they are sometimes quoted to that effect,[4] neither Porphyry nor Iamblichus does in fact have Pythagoras venture so far as India. But then neither does Apollonius, who insists that Pythagoras was indebted to the Brahmins not directly but by way of Egypt. None the less, the idea that Pythagoras had actually made a literal, rather than a metaphorical, passage to India received fresh support from European travellers to India in the seventeenth and eighteenth centuries. These, like their Greek predecessors, were frequently struck by the similarity to the Pythagorean of Indian beliefs and manners. That Pythagoras was the debtor was an assumption which increasingly gained credibility as the antiquity of Indian civilization was rediscovered.

[3] See, chapter 3, p. 101.   [4] E.g. H.G. Rawlinson, 'India in European Literature and Thought', *The Legacy of India*, ed. G.T. Garratt (Oxford, 1937), p. 4; *Eastern Religions and Western Thought*, p. 142. These works, being seminal, serve to illustrate how persistent the error has been (e.g. in *IA*, v, 816; *The Life of H.T. Colebrooke*, p. 363).

In 1799 there appeared in Paris a six-volume account of the travels of Pythagoras, conceived in the style of Pausanias, a Classical author who asserted that the Chaldeans and the Indians had been the first to preach the immortality of the soul and had in this preceded Plato.[5] The French book, *Voyages de Pythagore*, is avowedly an attempt to reconstruct from literary sources the debt owed by Pythagoras to other nations.[6] The parts dealing with India represent the superimposition of a prevalent image of India in the 1790s—the decade when modern Europe was most sympathetic to Indian culture—upon the *Life of Apollonius*, the work which constitutes the most sympathetic apprehension of India in Hellenistic times. Both Lardner and the editors of the new *Biographical Dictionary* had expressed the opinion that the voyage to India of Apollonius was really that of Pythagoras.[7] In the French work the Brahmin Yarbas, by whom Pythagoras is instructed, is unmistakably the Iarchas of the *Life of Apollonius*. Contemporary writers like Huet, D'Herbelot and Mignot, themselves drawing off Classical sources, are cited as authority for the belief, then enjoying some currency, that India was the legislator for the nations of the Earth: the sacred letters of the Ethiopians, the Hermetic books at Thebes, the wisdom of Zoroaster and even of the Chinese, are all said to be derived from India. In a passage which foreshadows the theosophy of Madame Blavatsky, Yarbas tells Pythagoras that the Brahmins are the last link in an older chain of philosophers who were guardians of the secrets of the universe. This accords with a Hindu view which regards the Brahmins as the last guardians of *Satya Yuga*, the perfect era in the degenerate Age of Kali; with a Christian view which saw the Brahmin way of life as the last remaining manifestation of the pristine revelation of the Garden of Eden; and with a more general Hellenistic view which perceived the Brahmins as practising philosophy as it had been practised in the Golden Age.

From the Brahmins Pythagoras, said to be the first Greek to visit India, learns the truth central to his philosophy: 'The soul is God'. From them he also learns how to establish a community of philosophers: potential initiates have their character told from their physiognomy, they are enjoined to a vow of silence, they must renounce their goods and have no slaves or servants. The wisdom into which they are initiated has its esoteric and exoteric aspects, the exoteric comprised of fictions about the immortality of

---

[5] *Messenia*, XXXII. 4.   [6] Pierre-Sylvain Maréchal, *Voyages de Pythagore en Égypte, dans la Chaldée, dans l'Inde*, 6 vols (Paris, 1799). The Indian travels are in Tome III.   [7] Berwick, preface, iv–v.

the soul and about punishments in hell. The Brahmins tell Pythagoras that they are more concerned with the perfectibility of the human race than with its multiplication but that they are not wholly continent and regard sexual conjunction as the marriage of sun and earth. Pythagoras is taught why the androgynous statues (*ardhanarisvari*) in Indian temples are symbolic of creation and the triangle within the circle (*Sri Yantra*), of God. Yarbas admits that the Indians are easily conquered but adds that their ways outlast those of their conquerors.

The journey made by Apollonius has even been attributed to Plato, although Apuleius himself suggested that war had prevented Plato from carrying out his intention of visiting the Magi and the Indians.[8] In the *Historia de la Aethiopia* by Friar Luys de Urreta, as recorded by Purchas,[9] a description is given of the Ethiopian Table of the Sun, first mentioned by Herodotus:[10] a king has so arranged food to be laid out in the open air for travellers that they will assume it is the miraculous work of God. The reference touches off in the mind of the friar an association with Iarchas, representative as he is of the Indian tradition whereby sages are accorded the miraculous power, denied to kings, of producing food at will: 'Plato the Prince of Philosophers having travelled through Asia as farre as Caucasus and gone also to the Brachmanes, to see and heare Hiarchas in a Throne of Gold, amongst a few disciples, disputing of Natures Mysteries, and discoursing of the Starres and Planets, returned . . . to see this renowned Table'. In this instance the friar has in fact transposed a passage on Apollonius from Jerome's *Letters*,[11] just as the author of the *Voyages de Pythagore* has projected his Pythagoras out of the *Life of Apollonius*.

Whether Plato and Pythagoras ever actually did get to India is in one sense no more material than whether Apollonius did. What is pertinent is that in associating these philosophers with the passage to India, imaginative fiction, bodying out the metaphors through which the Imagination is revealed, suggests that the tradition of which they are the protagonists owes India some sort of debt of recognition or acknowledgment.

---

[8] *De Platone et Eius Dogmate*, I.iii.186–7. Woodcock reports that in Alexandria in the second century AD there were some who claimed that Plato, as well as Pythagoras and Democritus, had visited the Brahmins (p. 150).   [9] Purchas, v.vii.728–9. The history was published in Valencia, 1610.   [10] Herodotus, III.17–18.   [11] Letter LIII, §1.

PYTHAGORAS IN INDIA: COLERIDGE AND SCHROEDER

The question of whether Pythagoras did actually travel to India continued to be discussed seriously well into the nineteenth century. It was a subject which Coleridge considered important enough to include in his seminal Philosophical Lectures of 1818–19 and, although this was part of what was essentially a Christian polemic, he none the less counted India, along with Egypt, Palestine and Greece, as one of four civilizations imaginative enough to be pantheistic. He concluded that it was extremely probable Pythagoras had been in India, which he assumed (not unreasonably in view of the evidence then available) had originally been Buddhist, and had derived thence the doctrine of metempsychosis, the taboo on beans and other foods, and the cosmology that there are ten bodies in the universe, including the *antichthon* or counter-earth. In one essential respect, however, he says that Pythagoras was not indebted to the great men of India any more than to those of Egypt or of his own country. He alone went back into the human reason to discover the laws of the universe: 'He found a something that was above time, above accident, it was drawn from the fountain of truth that was inexhaustible, and this was in man'. He discovered that the human reason was capable of apprehending its own likeness to the Deity and, at the same time, recognized that the Creator, being distinct from (though the ground for) Number, was distinct from creation. Classical Indian civilization was incapable of making such a distinction, and on this account Coleridge recants an earlier enthusiasm and rejects the claims of 'some of our modern contenders for Indian wisdom'.[12]

In spite of the argument made by Coleridge the contenders for Indian wisdom remained, further evidence continuing to be discovered in support of their claims. Writing as a Sanskritist, with the added tradition of nineteenth century scholarship behind him and with a far greater range of Vedic texts at his disposal, Leopold von Schroeder, in a long pamphlet which remains a standard work on the subject, renewed the claim that Pythagoras was wholly indebted to India for this knowledge of the laws of the universe. With Coleridge, and many others before and since, Schroeder shares the conviction that Pythagoras derived his belief in metempsychosis not, as Herodotus had asserted, from Egypt but from India. Schroeder's special contribution to the subject is to make as complete a case for Indian influence as has yet been

[12] *PL*, II, 91–110.

made. The doctrine that the soul makes a repeated return to the body until it finds ultimate release, he suggests, certainly did not originate with Pythagoras. All accounts of Pythagoras, however varied, agree that he was eager for knowledge of other cultures, and while the doctrine of metempsychosis remains peripheral to Greek thought and is unknown in Egypt, in India it is not only known before the time of Pythagoras, arising out of a world-view which is developed in the *Yajur Veda* and in the Brahmanas, but its central importance may be deduced from the fact that it is virtually the only Vedic doctrine which Buddha did not question. Schroeder also adduces evidence from the *Yajur Veda* to demonstrate an Indian priority for the Pythagorean prohibitions (like metempsychosis, dependent on a conviction about the unity of Being) on animal sacrifice and on the eating of meat, as well as on the less easily explicable eating of beans. The most vivid argument in favour of Pythagoras having quite literally made a passage to India is that, long before his own time, as the *Sulva Sutras* make clear, the Indians used the Pythagoras theorem (not as it was later to be elucidated by Euclid but as Pythagoras explained it) to establish a common area for the four-sided, the circular and the semi-circular figures of their sacrificial altars.[13]

Schroeder's argument has not been refuted. But in spite of further evidence that lines of communication between India and Greece may have been open in the sixth century BC, and even though it is undisputed that the Pythagorean world-view which remained peripheral to Greek culture was both previously known and all-pervasive in India, there is a disposition to prefer the theory of independent development. Three reasons for this disposition may be considered here. The first—evident in the way so many Western intellectuals have assumed without question that the most favourable images of India are not derived from India but are projections upon it—is a reluctance to consider that the foundations of Europe's Classical culture, no less than England's modern material prosperity,[14] may owe something to a place which Europe finds as difficult of approach on account of its traditional metaphysical abstruseness as on account of its contemporary material impoverishment.

The second reservation arises from the possibility that both India and Greece may be indebted to a common source, for example Babylon. Filliozat keeps this possibility in mind during his exposition of similarities between Indian and Greek medical doctrines of

[13] Leopold von Schroeder, *Pythagoras und die Inder* (Leipzig, 1884), chaps I–III, pp. 5–59.   [14] R. Palme Dutt, *India Today* (London, 1940), pp. 105–33.

pneumatism, both of which later developed mystical overtones in their respective cultures, and the relation of which to metaphysics is evident from the way the *Timaeus* (thought of as Pythagorean by the Old Academy) may be considered in terms of Indian pathology.[15] While the influence of Babylon undoubtedly was felt in India as well as in the eastern Mediterranean, and while, also, the invasion of (conceivably) similar matrilineal societies by (conceivably) similar patriarchal societies from the north could have produced the independent rise of similar philosophical beliefs,[16] the available evidence points to the following conclusions: namely, that it was in India that there first arose a concern for mystical experience and teaching; that it was in India alone that this concern came to dominate a culture; and that this growth is both original and native to India in that it clearly develops out of the older Vedic forms of hymn and sacrifice.

The third reservation arises from the application of the Jungian theory of archetypes to diverse cultures. The Pythagoras theorem, for example, could presumably materialize independently out of a common state of consciousness; furthermore, this could conceivably happen within an individual, irrespective of a hostile social or natural evironment. What is interesting here is that Jung himself, in elaborating his conception of the Collective Unconscious, reveals himself to be part of this very same neo-Platonist tradition which overtly acknowledges the importance to itself of its Indian equivalents.[17] Jung, whose conception of the archetypes is taken from the neo-Platonists, has written that the few manifestations of Indian influence on the surface of European intellectual life are not simply the 'tiny scattered islands' they seem to be but 'the peaks of submarine mountain ranges of considerable size'.[18] Jung's image is not only graphic but suggestive. Perhaps questions of Indian influence are to be resolved only deep in the ocean of the Collective Unconscious? Perhaps Europe will not fully understand the more imaginative productions of its own culture until it has first discovered the imaginative depths of the Indian? Indian culture, as a result of the central importance it accords to mystical experience, reveals through its myths a constant awareness that archetypal images—be they isles of the blest or paradises on the

---

[15] 'Communications between Greece and India before Alexander', chap. 9, J. Filliozat, *The Classical Doctrine of Indian Medicine*, trans. Dev Raj Chanana (Delhi, 1964), pp. 196–257.   [16] See chapter 7, p. 275 and n. 196.   [17] See chapter 1, n. 166.   [18] C.G. Jung, *Modern Man in Search of a Soul* (London, 1933), pp. 242–3. Jung suggests that theosophical ideas from India are considered 'unacademic' and are more likely to touch those lower social classes who respond to the unconscious levels of the psyche.

mountain-sides—are not ultimate. It is precisely this Indian insistence that no image is ultimately potent which paradoxically lends special potency to the image of India.

THE LOST FIGURE OF PYTHAGORAS

The discrepancy which adheres to any attempt to define Indian influence in terms of history and geography, and which is so invariable that (like the irrational number) it suggests it is itself part of the law, is evident even in the two foremost literary sources which ascribe an Indian origin to the philosophy of Pythagoras. While Apollonius supposes that Pythagoras was subject to Indian influences coming to him by way of Ethiopia and Egypt, Apuleius countenances the tradition that Pythagoras actually journeyed to India by way of Egypt and Chaldea. What both men share, besides an overwhelming admiration for Pythagoras as a divine being and founder of Greek philosophy, is the conviction that he was indebted for this to the Brahmins. Yet, here again, a further discrepancy, slighter but still distinct, appears to arise. According to Apollonius, what Pythagoras learnt was a way to reach the source of all divine knowledge in the soul, that is, he learnt a practical, mystical path; Apuleius, on the other hand, stresses his debt to India for philosophy in the theoretical sense. The discrepancy is probably illusory: the tradition of an exoteric and an esoteric doctrine supports the logical supposition that Pythagoras would first have to be taught the philosophical theory of the repeated return of the soul before he could be, or could even wish to be, initiated into the mystical practice which would ensure its release from the cycle.

None the less, an unexplained, perhaps inexplicable, residue remains. Schroeder cites evidence from Aristotle and Theophrastus to suggest that God originally played little or no part in the system of Pythagoras and that in this he is indebted to the old pre-Buddhist Samkhya school of philosophy, itself perhaps an outgrowth of pre-Vedic matrilineal forms of society. The Samkhya is concerned with the release during the transmigratory state of purely passive (if pluralistic) spirit from an active material universe. Furthermore, Schroeder believes that Buddha, as well as his contemporary Pythagoras, was indebted to the Samkhya for this world-view.[19] Coleridge adopts a position close to this when, in his Philosophical Lectures, he argues that the original inhabitants of India practised a Buddhism which elsewhere he refers to as 'reli-

[19] Schroeder, v, 66–76.

gious Atheism': 'God is only universal Matter considered abstractedly from all particular forms'.[20] But while Schroeder and Coleridge may largely agree about the particular sort of India which influenced Pythagoras, they have a diametrically opposed view of Pythagoras himself.

The basic problem is that, as Coleridge himself says, the figure of Pythagoras was obscure even by the time of Plato and Aristotle. He is therefore subject to diverse reconstructions. Since the whole purpose of the Philosophical Lectures is to demonstrate that with the coming of Christ 'philosophy received at once its object and completion', Coleridge is at some pains to see Pythagoras and Plato through the hindsight of Christianity. The compulsion to do this is the greater because Coleridge is also trying to square his own neo-Platonism with Christianity; and since the neo-Platonists are to be castigated on account of their active opposition to Christianity it becomes doubly important to argue (as, paradoxically, so does Plotinus) that all that is valuable in neo-Platonism was essentially present in the pre-Christian Pythagoras and Plato. The one critical difference is that while the neo-Platonists represent Pythagoras as having discovered within himself the immanent god common to all, Coleridge, as Christian polemicist, must argue that he had discovered the necessity for a transcendent deity—who would only *later* materialize in the person of Jesus Christ.[21]

Long before Coleridge, Clement of Alexandria also suggested that Christianity had been foreshadowed by the teachings of Pythagoras, that Pythagoras had listened to the Brahmins and that all previous divine inspiration had been superseded by the revelation of Christ.[22] Coleridge might have done better to have left it at that. Instead, he not only aruges that Pythagoras was aware of a distinction between Creator and creation; he argues that the Indians were *not*. In making this particular distinction Coleridge appears to be dissociating Pythagoras not so much from Buddhism as from Brahminism—which for him is synonymous with pantheism (or, what he calls in relation to the Hindus, cosmotheism). Pantheists do not, he argues in his second Philosophical Lecture, make a distinction, as some modern thinkers have supposed, between All-things-God and All-things-in-God. In the following lecture he quotes an extensive passage from Wilkins' translation of the *Bhagavad Gita* to show that the Brahmins did not make such a distinction. Had Coleridge chosen a passage from the *Gita* on

[20] S.T. Coleridge, *Aids to Reflection* (London, 1825), pp. 276–7.   [21] Aside from those to Lecture II, there are references here to Lectures IV, 165–166; V, 187; VI, 220; VII, 241–2; X, 295; XIV, 393.   [22] See chapter 3, p. 112.

either side of the one he did it would have included verses which demonstrate precisely the reverse. Had he cared to put the whole section in context he would have seen that it is the record of a vision vouchsafed by just such an *avatar* (Krishna) as he admits elsewhere constitutes a glimpse of the true revelation.[23] The truth may be that, much as he tried, Coleridge never did free himself of the original debt of homage he paid to the Indian scriptures and that to the end he was forced to conclude there was more to Brahminism than 'the Mist of Pantheism'.[24] Even in the Philosophical Lectures themselves he associates the pantheism of India with that of Spinoza who, as he is aware, recognizes an independent deity and a dependent creation.[25]

In rejecting the neo-Platonist position that Pythagoras was a god in favour of the claim that Pythagoras affirmed the existence of God, what Coleridge does force us to enquire is whether Schroeder is right in regarding Pythagoras as an atheist and in specifying the Samkhya as the particular Indian source to which he is indebted. It is of course possible that Pythagoras was indebted to the Samkhya and that Pythagoreanism—like the Samkhya and the Buddhism whose atheistical denial is, according to Coleridge, a form of religious acknowledgement—only later developed some sort of theistical aspect. On the other hand Pythagoras may never have been an atheist in the sense of denying or ignoring the concept of godhead. If Schroeder deduces an atheistical Pythagoras from Aristotle, it is also Aristotle who suggests how closely Plato followed Pythagoras, and he too who reports how surprised the Pythagoreans were at anyone who had not seen a divine being.[26] It is an alternative possibility, at least as viable as Schroeder's, that Pythagoras was the divinely-inspired mystic he was perceived to be by his later disciples.

---

[23] *PL*, III, 127–9. Coleridge cites Lecture XI, *BGW*, pp. 91–3. Arjuna is describing his limited apprehension of a vision of the Divine Nature in the form of the universe. By way of introduction, both Krishna and Sanjaya make clear it is a vision *within* the body of God (pp. 89–90). Furthermore, the point of the following lecture is to stress that 'the greater labour' for corporeal beings is to apprehend God in his *invisible* nature. This reiterates the conclusion of Lecture II, 43.   [24] *Aids to Reflection*, pp. 276–7; Muirhead, p. 284.   [25] *PL*, XIII, 385. Coleridge *is* prepared to be sympathetic to the mystical pantheism of Spinoza in spite of its possible ambivalence (*BL*, I, pt. II, 153–4; II, 158, 307). Jones had suggested that the Vedanta differed from the pantheism of Spinoza precisely because it was grounded 'on the doctrine of an immaterial creator supremely wise, and a constant preserver supremely benevolent' (*AR*, IV, 173).   [26] *Metaphysica*, I.vi.1, 987a. 29–30; Fragment R² 188, 'On the God of Socrates', *Works of Apuleius*, p. 370. See also Iamblichus, VI, 14–15.

If we do accept such a late conception of Pythagoras, we shall be doing no more than Schroeder himself has done in dealing with classical Indian philosophy in terms of two later systematizations of it, the Samkhya and the Vedanta. As Schroeder is himelf aware, his source for knowledge of the Samkhya, Isvara Krishna, flourished a whole millennium after the time of Pythagoras. Both the Samkhya and the Vedanta accept the Vedic tradition as *sruti*, or divine revelation, and appeal to it for their authority; it is therefore an anachronism to suggest that any one or more of the Upanishads be interpreted exclusively in terms of either, or any other, school. Schroeder is perhaps aware of this. At the outset of his argument that Pythagoras is influenced by the Samkhya he explicitly denies that he is influenced by the Vedanta. Yet previous to this he has argued that the theory of metempsychosis is an outgrowth of the Vedantic identity of *atman* and *Brahman*, the One immanent and transcendent, and it is not surprising that soon after this he asserts that the Samkhya also accepts the proposition *atman=Brahman*, though much more obliquely than the Vedanta.[27] The point is that both schools frequently derive differing conclusions from the same Upanishads.

One possible influence of the Samkhya on Pythagoras which Schroeder does not mention is that of the theory of the three *gunas*, or constituents or qualities, of *sattvas*, *rajas* and *tamas*, or purity, passion and darkness, which combine to obstruct the release of the soul.[28] Yet this theory need not (and in the Upanishads, the *Bhagavad Gita* and even in Sankara does not) conflict, any more than the theory of metempsychosis, with the Vedanta position that that which permits the release of the soul is knowledge of its identity with the Absolute, or God. In the *Republic*—a book which in consonance with Indian *smriti* or law argues the value to spiritual and political life of a stratified and static society, and which concludes with an exposition of the theory of metempsychosis in the myth of Er—a position concurrent with the Samkhya is evident when Socrates speaks of the three constituents (correspondent to the three *gunas*) which hinder the release of the soul as well as a position concurrent with the Vedanta when he speaks of the soul, united with the First Principle, going free.[29] As Guthrie has expressly argued, these two positions are not mutually exclusive.[30]

---

[27] Schroeder, pp. 26, 67–70.   [28] Radhakrishnan, II, 262–5. For the Pythagorean concept of the tripartite soul, see Diogenes Laertius VIII. 30.   [29] *Republic*, 439D–443B; 611B–612A.   [30] W.K.C. Guthrie, *A History of Greek Philosophy*, 4 vols to date (Cambridge, 1961–), IV, 476–8. Likewise, the *Gita* does not find

Furthermore, as Schroeder is again aware, Empedocles, who was in a position to know, connects the Pythagorean way of life with the mystical theology of Parmenides, whose philosophy Schroeder, like others besides him, identifies with what he terms the orthodox Brahmin Vedanta.[31] This provides all the more reason to suppose that Pythagoras is just as likely to be indebted to India for the rather more positively mystical approach Schroeder associates with the Vedanta as for the conversely 'negative' approach of the Samkhya. It would not be necessary to depart from the tradition of the *Yajur Veda*, so frequently cited by Schroeder, to show that it can support—not as an alternative but as complementary to Schroeder's view of Pythagoras—the view of Pythagoras suggested by the neo-Platonists, if not by Coleridge. None the less, this conclusion is necessarily speculative. Pythagoras remains as elusive of approach as the India to which he is said to have made passage and that passage—according to Forster's proviso (itself consistent both with the *Enneads* and with the Vedanta concept of *brahmavidya*)—entails a jump beyond ratiocination. In that case, science and history never could establish the existence of the passage to India of Pythagoras, though philosophy and literature might suggest the possibility of it. While it could never be validated, the least unreliable approach would be through the Imagination.

YAJNAVALKYA: THE INDIAN PYTHAGORAS?

Whether or not Pythagoras ever did get to India, the curious fact remains that had he done so there were sages there who could well have instructed him in the way of life we have come to call Pythagorean. In his introduction to an English translation of Patanjali's *Yoga Sutras*, Yeats writes of the Vedic sage Yajnavalkya:

Like Pythagoras, who occupied the same place in Greek civilization, he substituted philosophic reason for custom and mythology, put an end to the Golden Age and began that of the Sophists, an intellectual anarchy that found its Socrates in Buddha. He had substituted the eternal Self for all the gods.

Yeats goes on to express his regret that the humanism of the Euro-

---

these diverse aspects of the Samkhya and the Vedanta irreconcilable.   [31] Schroeder, pp. 62, 90. Empedocles is variously supposed to have been a pupil of Pythagoras and of Parmenides (Diogenes Laertius, VIII. 54–6). Parmenides is frequently associated with the Vedanta (e.g. Staal, p. 226).

pean Renaissance, ready for a follower of Yajnavalkya or Pythagoras, became engaged instead with mechanical science, and that
in such a cultural milieu the trances of men such as Boehme,
Swedenborg and of the Mesmerists could never attain to that
sovereign condition which accepts no limits.[32]

While Pythagoras, the Orphic rites notwithstanding, appears as
a lone and original figure in the Greek tradition, Yajnavalkya Va-
jasaneya is only one, if a notable one, of a number of Vedic sages.
There is no particular reason to doubt his historical existence:
there are extensive records of his discourses at the court of King
Janaka of Videha (perhaps in the seventh or sixth century BC) and
there is a compelling authenticity about his teaching to his wife,
Maitreyi, as well as to Janaka, which deservedly warrants the Hindu appellation of *sruti*, or revelation.[33] These teachings compose a
section of one of the oldest Upanishads, the *Brihad Aranyaka*, or
great forest book, itself only part of the fourteenth and last book
of the *Satapatha Brahmana*, itself only a part of the White, or revised, *Yajur Veda*, one of the three original Vedas. Yajnavalkya is
frequently cited by Sankara at crucial points of his commentary on
the Vedanta doctrine of Badarayana.[34] The continuing authority
of his name was such that in times contemporaneous with the Hellenistic a law book, second in importance only to that of Manu,
was ascribed to him and his name taken on by one founder of the
later system of Yoga, Yogi-Yajnavalkya.[35] It is similarly a mark of
his authority (rather than his authorship) that in later times, as in
the *Satapatha Brahmana* itself, was attributed to him the whole of
the White *Yajur Veda*.[36] Given the mystical symbolism attached to
the sun in this, as in the Pythagorean, tradition, it may be significant that the Veda was said to have been revealed to him by the sun
after he had been forced to disgorge it as he had traditionally received
it from his teacher, with whom he had had a dispute.[37] In contrast
to the original Black *Yajur Veda*, the White puts much greater
emphasis on the exact measurements of its sacrificial altars

[32] *Aphorisms of Yoga*, trans. Purohit Swami (London, 1938), Introduction, pp.
14–21. The comparison of Buddha to Socrates is fairly common (e.g. Radhakrishnan, I, 359).   [33] Janaka is treated as a pre-Buddhist historical figure by Basham
(p. 41). A later date *is* usually assigned to the verse part of the teaching (4.4.8–21)
and to the passage where Yajnavalkya denies the soul any greater reality than
the organs of sense (Radhakrishnan, I, 142).   [34] Colebrooke, I, 366, 371–2, 384,
386–93.   [35] See chapter 3, p. 93.   [36] *Satapatha Brahmana*, trans. Julius
Eggeling, 5 pts (Oxford, 1882–1900), pt. I, Introduction, xxx–xxxi, xlii–xliii; M.
Winternitz, *A History of Indian Literature*, rev. ed., trans. S. Ketkar, 2 vols
(Calcutta, 1927–33), I, 192–3, 245 n.4.   [37] Winternitz, 171 n.1.; *VP*, II, III, V,
52–7. Cf. Iamblichus, xxxv.132. The sun was associated with the *munis* as early as
RV, VIII.17.14; x.136.

and on the proper enunciation of words, and as such could have been the Indian school which, if any, influenced Pythagoras.

It is the constant theme of Yajnavalkya's philosophical teaching that the unity which underlies the correspondences between the macrocosm and the microcosm is to be apprehended in and by the *atman* (or Self) immanent within the heart. In a discourse which not only opens but is also repeated to close out his teaching in the *Brihad Aranyaka*,[38] he tells his wife Maitreyi that all things are dear not in and for themselves but for the common identity which subsists in all, That which, once known, makes all known. After death, when one returns whence one came, there is a cessation of consciousness in the sense that duality, the distinction between subject and object, ceases: 'Whereby and whom would one understand? Whereby would one understand him by whom one understands this All? Lo, whereby would one understand the understander'? Yajnavalkya asserts that the Knower of all knowledge can be known through Self-realization: that state which to an outsider confronting the yogic trance or *samadhi* so often appears, because he is disjoined from it, as self-delusion. As an answer this may shed light on that given by the Pythagoreans when they begged the rational question with an identical appeal to authority: *autos epha*. The context of Yajnavalkya's teaching is his departure from home in order to become a hermit; his wife Maitreyi refuses a settlement of wealth upon her lest this deny her immortality. The belief that desire for wealth and possessions is inimical to a knowledge of immortality—like the respect given to a woman seeking sacred knowledge and even the use of salt and water as an image for ultimate inseparability—is common to the Pythagoreans, as is the doctrine of the immanent Self, which Iamblichus ascribes to Pythagoras himself.[39]

The context of Yajnavalkya's next teaching is equally congenial with the Pythagorean view: Janaka, the king of Videha, in accordance with the laws governing the Indian social system of *varnas*, or 'caste', seeks an adviser from among the Brahmin philosophers.[40] The various arguments of his rivals concerning the nature of the universe are dismissed as partial apprehensions by Yajnavalkya, who in turn offers a complete set of concordances between all the organs of sense (including among such the soul) and the elements in the macrocosm, as well as between the cardinal virtues (*jnana-kanda*) and outward ceremonies (*karma-kanda*). So perfect is the concordance between the physical and the metaphysical that it is

[38] *BA*, 2.4.1–14; 4.5.1–15.   [39] *Enn.*, II.ix.9; Iamblichus, XXIX, 85. See also Iamblichus, XVI, 35–7; XXXI, 99–110.   [40] *BA*, 3.1.1–3.9.26.

easy to see why Indian idealism has been charged with being at best pantheistic and at worst materialist: Yajnavalkya teaches that only direct knowledge of the Self immanent in the human heart and all things unites the phenomenal, the noumenal and the spiritual in a single identity. This teaching, implicit in the answers given by Yajnavalkya to the Brahmins, is equally central to his own direct teaching when he resorts to the use of myth—a custom so congenial to the Platonist that it may explain why this is one of the few passages from the Vedas which Sir William Jones translated into English.[41] Man is compared to a tree but, while a felled tree can spring up anew from the root, a man, once hewn down by death, cannot spring up again from seed. Even a tree cannot sprout afresh from seed if it is totally uprooted. What root, then, would permit a man to rise again? The text indicates that Yajnavalkya intends as answer Brahma or the One: the physical universe has a metaphysical base which may be made known to him who stands still and knows it.

The myth is perhaps paradoxical: a man can only discover the difference between his nature and that of a tree by becoming like a tree. Bernier gives expression to a common European opinion that the *yogis* (whose tradition Yajnavalkya is sometimes said to have founded) resemble nothing so much as the trees whose vicinity they frequent.[42] The image, the most natural that could appear in an *aranyaka* or forest book, is first used to similar effect in the *Rig Veda* and Yajnavalkya's teaching, as well as being evident in the Buddhist *Dhammapada*, is developed centrally to the Hindu tradition both in the *Katha Upanishad* and in the *Bhagavad Gita*:[43] Man is approximated to a tree in such a way as to suggest that spiritual rebirth must be actively sought by cutting down the tree of ordinary life—and hence the renewed cycle of rebirths. Plato also suggests that man is a plant whose roots are in Heaven.[44] It is Plotinus, however, whose language and meaning are unequivocally close to the Indian tradition:

When shoots or topmost boughs are lopped from some growing thing, where goes the soul that was present in them? Simply, whence it came: soul never knew spatial separation and therefore is always within the source. If you cut the root to pieces, or burn it, where is the life that was present there? In the soul, which never went outside of itself.

---

[41] Ibid., 3.9.27–8; *WWJ*, XIII, 378–9.   [42] *A Classical Dictionary of Hindu Mythology*, 11th ed., ed. John Dowson (London, 1968), s.v. Yajnavalkya, p. 372; see chapter 3, nn. 47, 98.   [43] *RV*, I.24.7; x.31.7; x.81.4; *The Dhammapada*, trans. Irving Babbitt (New York, 1936), xx. 283; xxiv. 33; *Katha Upanishad*, 6.1; *BG*, 15, 1–6.   [44] *Timaeus*, 90A.

Later Plotinus again resorts to the image: 'The Supreme is the Term of all; it is like the principle and ground of some vast tree of rational life; itself unchanging, it gives reasoned being to the growth into which it enters'.[45]

Thereafter begins Yajnavalkya's teaching to Janaka, the king. In a passage which could almost be the origin of the most famous of all Indian philosophical fables (used alike by the greatest metaphysicians of Buddhism, Hinduism and Islam)[46]—that of the six blind men and the elephant—Janaka recounts the six partial definitions he has been given of Brahma.[47] Yajnavalkya points out the limitations of these definitions but himself says no more than that Brahma is to be identified with the heart which is the seat of all things. The king is forced to confess that though his soul were prepared with this teaching, as he might prepare a chariot or a ship for a journey (imagery which recurs in the *Enneads*),[48] he would still not know where to go. For further explanation Yajnavalkya resorts to a theory of vision, similar to that Diogenes Laertius attributed to Pythagoras,[49] whereby the identity of sun and eye, like other such pairings, is a manifestation of, as well as an image for, enlightenment. This is part of the cosmology of Viraj, wherein creation is conceived as a consequence of a spontaneous emanation or bifurcation of the Creator followed by copulation.[50] Telling Janaka that the gods prefer the cryptic to the evident (something germane to the Pythagorean *Golden Verses*), Yajnavalkya says that the androgynous soul, divided into male and female in the two eyes but united when they withdraw into the heart, will undertake a journey through metaphysical channels up and out of the body to that ultimate reality which is describable only in terms of negatives—not this, not that (*neti, neti*), unseizable, indestructible, unbound and fearless. This so-called negative theology, implying infinite possibility, will recur in Plotinus as well as Sankara.[51]

In the *Florida*, where Apuleius speaks of a decisive Brahminical influence on Pythagoras, he suggests there was an equally decisive influence of Pythagoras on the Platonists, from whom he says he learned in academic meditations the value both of remaining silent and of speaking with all his might when speech was required.[52]

---

[45] *Enn.*, v.ii.2; vi.viii.15. In the medieval schools, the different categories of Being were depicted in terms of what was known as Porphyry's Tree.   [46] R.C. Zaehner, *Hindu and Muslim Mysticism* (London, 1960), pp. 100–1.   [47] *BA*, 4.1.1–7. See also the story of the six householders, *Chandogya Upanishad*, 5.11.1–5.18.2.   [48] *Enn.*, i.vi.8.   [49] Diogenes Laertius, viii. 29–30.   [50] *BA*, 1.4.3.   [51] *Enn.*, v.v.6; vi.viii.11; vi.ix.3; Colebrooke, i, 383.   [52] The value of silence for the Pythagoreans is stressed also by Iamblichus, xvi, 36; xxx, 99 and

Yajnavalkya's most powerful evocation of the One is achieved on an occasion when, we are told, the philosopher would have preferred to remain silent.[53] He is lured out of his silence by Janaka's asking what light it is that a man has to guide him. In turn are rejected each of the lights that are useful to man: the sun sets, the moon sets, the fire goes out, speech is hushed. The only light that remains is the light of the soul. The soul is then described in terms congenial to the neo-Platonist: it appears to be part of this world of appearance and thought; in fact it exists in the world of Reality. In an intermediate third state of dreaming sleep, the soul allows us to see the phenomenal world in terms of Reality. This is the state that Forster's Adela Quested ultimately experiences when she penetrates the queer cocoon which has surrounded her from the time of hearing Godbole's song until she gives evidence during the Marabar trial; the cocoon surrounding phenomenal existence which Zimmer says Indian civilization has ever sought to break through; 'the membranous integument' which, in Greek and Egyptian symbolism (as Thomas Maurice points out), surrounds Psyche before the discovery of her destiny as a butterfly.[54]

Yajnavalkya elaborates on these various stages of consciousness towards enlightenment: waking, sleeping and dreaming and dreamless sleep.[55] In the illuminated dream state a man still has with him images of the phenomenal world but these are there subject to the Absolute within him. The soul, like a wild goose (*hamsa*), is free to leave the body and roam the universe, able to fashion or project any form at will:

> People see his pleasure-ground;
> Him no one sees at all.

Yajnavalkya adds that on a man's return from this state he is not followed by the vision. This dream state, where the Self is suspended between waking and sleeping, is compared to a fish slipping along between the two banks of a river. An image from Nature is also used to evoke the sleeping state, that where the soul is free of desires and dreams: it is compared to an eagle dropping to its nest to rest, an image suggestive not of escape but of penetration and possession. The metaphysical channels of the heart contain colours (white, blue, yellow, green, red) and the imagination still operates: bad dreams, such as of being chased by an elephant (the image and its context may have given rise to a later story ab-

---

Diogenes Laertius, VIII.10. See also *Enn.*, III.viii.4.   [53] *BA*, 4.3.1.   [54] *PI*, XIV, 133; XXIV, 228–30; Zimmer, p. 26; *IA*, V, 1018–22.   [55] *BA*, 4.3.14–32.

out Sankara) are a projection of waking fears and horrors.[56] A man who assimilates himself to the universal Self is free of these disturbances: in an image basic to the mystical poetry of India, he is compared to a man who in the embrace of his wife is conscious of nothing within or without.[57] Here the whole world of differentiation, personal and social, ceases to exist since Difference itself ceases to exist. Asceticism is superseded or, rather, absorbed, by mysticism: there is no duality. Whereas the seer can see, the Seer cannot because there remains nothing outside to be seen. The image of the Seer, recurrent as it is in the *Enneads* and congenial to the Western mind since Socrates in the *Phaedrus* singled out vision as the keenest of the physical perceptions,[58] is extended by Yajnavalkya so that we are made aware of the control enjoyed by the sage over the other four senses, as well as over speech, thought and knowledge. This principle of consciousness which persists through all states of being, including even death and liberation, is the universal ground present in every individual.

King Janaka, however, senses that the highest truth is being withheld from him, that the highest conceivable paradise, the Brahma-world on Mount Meru, does not represent the ultimate liberation. From this state, as from the others, the visionary returns to the world of ordinary consciousness. Yajnavalkya is forced to deal with the ultimate release of the soul—when it leaves the body without returning, like a fruit detaching itself from a stalk. At death the soul, in terms of a cosmology elaborated earlier, withdraws to the heart and, as the Person in the eye returns to its cosmic counterpart in the sun, all sense of form is lost. As the senses cease to be able to differentiate, one becomes One, there is a concentration of light in the heart and from there the Self makes an exit by way of the head, the eye or other bodily parts, pursued by the vital breaths and the faculties which seek to lay hold of it.[59] According to the old Vedic belief—reflected in the rights practised by Peregrinus at his self-immolation[60]—there are two paths which can be followed at death, that of the gods and that of the fathers or, as Yajnavalkya puts it, that of release or of return.

Using the image of a caterpillar or grasshopper reaching the end of a piece of grass, and that—used to the same effect in the *Timaeus*[61]—of a goldsmith refashioning gold, Yajnavalkya speaks

[56] Iamblichus names both music and a controlled diet as a means of forestalling phantasms during sleep (xv, 32; xxiv, 57).   [57] Cf. *Enn.*, vi.vii.34.   [58] Ibid., iii.viii.6; *Phaedrus*, 250D.   [59] *BA*, 4.3.33–4.4.2. Sankara follows this passage for his conception of the soul at death (Colebrooke, i, 388–93).   [60] See chapter 3, p. 110.   [61] *BA*, 4.4.3–6; *Timaeus*, 50A–C.

of the metamorphosis of the Self—the way the self itself fashions the form it will assume in the next incarnation. The *karma* (or accumulated actions) attached to the Self are critical since action is determined by resolve, or will, and resolve by desire: hence, whatever a man desires, through his actions he obtains for himself. This is the rationale behind the theory of metempsychosis. While Yajnavalkya himself never explicitly refers to the doctrine of transmigration through animal or other forms, possibly because like other Hindus and Pythagoreans he regarded it as an exoteric doctrine, it is taught in the same Upanishad,[62] belonging to the same school of thought (of which Yajnavalkya is a foremost exponent, if not actually the founder). This teaching lends clarity to Plato's apologue of Er: while the mind is attached, desires remain, actions are performed and the Self, imprisoned thereby by *karma*, returns to the world of action.

The man who has freed himself of all desires bar that for the Self, obtains the Self. For him there is immortality and no return to the world of action. The body lies like the slough of a snake. In what is probably a later interpolation, Yajnavalkya is made to celebrate this state by reciting a poem about the path to Brahma: on the path is the multi-coloured world (the colours earlier associated with the diverse channels of the heart), the world of darkness, 'void of bliss', entered by the ignorant, and the world of greater darkness entered by those who delight in knowledge—that is, either those who erroneously assume knowledge is its own end or, more probably in this context, those who in experiencing the disillusionment attendant upon enlightenment have lost all desire to remain mortal. All depends on Brahma, Brahma depends on nothing—very much the philosophical position Coleridge attributes to Pythagoras and denies to his potential Indian sources. The state of consciousness determines this realization: the man who perceives diversity on Earth repeatedly dies and is reborn, while he who apprehends the underlying unity is enlightened. This truth (discoverable within the metaphorical space within the heart which, supporting the microcosm, is identical with the space which supports the macrocosm) is the Self, untouched by good or evil or by any sort of dualism. It is the search for the Self which has led holy men to abandon the desire for wealth, for sons, or even for paradises. Yajnavalkya, aware of how easily he could be misunderstood, makes it clear that the superman who achieves this state is beyond good and evil in the sense that he is wholly quiescent: evil is overcome because he has learned that contemplation

[62] Ibid., 6.2.1-2, 15-16.

or knowledge of the Self is not achieved by action, either good or bad, since it is itself free of any attribute.[63] The state is 'good' only in the same sense that Plato and Plotinus refer to it as The Good.

The part of the *Brihad Aranyaka* given over to Yajnavalkya concludes with a repetition of the teaching which the philosopher had given to Maitreyi, his wife, though with the addition of the important proviso that the Self can be indicated only in terms of negation. Appended to this is a list of the teachers of this doctrine who constitute its living tradition, referable as it is and, on its own terms, can only be to Brahma, or the Self-existent (*Svayambhu*).[64] The importance of the living teacher is emphasized not only because the transmission of an *aranyaka* is part of an oral tradition practised, as the Greeks quickly recognized,[65] in the forests of India, but also because, as Yajnavalkya teaches, it is better not to meditate too much on words but to concentrate on direct knowledge—or what, to maintain the image, may be called the Word (in the sense it was used by Philo, yet another 'Pythagorean' admirer of Indian philosophical practice).[66]

This apprehension of the limits of language is something which, as we saw, Apuleius had also learned from a teacher in what he conceived of as the same tradition originating in India. It is now perhaps worth repeating exactly what Apuleius said constituted the greater part of the philosophy Pythagoras learned from the Brahmins: 'what are the rules and principles of the understanding; what the functions of the body; how many are the faculties of the soul, how many the mutations of life; what torments and rewards devolve upon the souls of the dead according to their respective deserts. . . '. It would be hard to find a more exact index of the teachings contained in the *Brihad Aranyaka*, and while other schools have dwelt on the same topics the ideas Yajnavalkya has about the body and soul—and some of the imagery he uses to express those ideas—are found both in the fragmented Pythagorean tradition and in that part of the Platonic tradition which Plato is traditionally thought to have inherited from Pythagoras and which flowers again in Plotinus.

The principal doctrines in common assert:

that man has an immortal soul which returns in diverse bodies to the sublunary realm until such time as it has attained liberation;

---

[63] Ibid., 4.4.6–25.   [64] Ibid., 4.6.1.   [65] Strabo, *Geographia*, xv.i.60; F.W. Thomas, 'Language and Early Literature', *The Legacy of India*, p. 60.   [66] See chapter 5, p. 166 and n. 78. It is Clement who calls Philo a Pythagorean.

that the soul's return is necessarily determined by a triad of qualities which attach to it as a result of deeds;

that a man may realize the liberation of the soul within himself and, knowing the Self, will discover the empathy between all things which makes the universe a single, living organism;

that, on account of such an empathy, man should learn to live simply, without attachment to possessions or to family and with respect for the animal and vegetable worlds;

that all things are enlivened by the principle of heat epitomized by the sun, the divine significance of which is as apprehensible to the divine eye in man as its ordinary significance is apprehensible to the ordinary eye;

that the faculties of the soul are winds as invisible as the aether, the air of the uppermost of three worlds, that of the gods, supported by the Imperishable to which the soul, escaping through the sutures of the skull, returns at the time of its liberation;

and that in their esoteric form these doctrines should not be disclosed publicly but should only be transmitted orally to such initiates as show they are fit to receive them and live according to them.

Neither the historical debt of Pythagoras to the Brahmins asserted by Apuleius nor the philosophical concordance of Pythagoras and Yajnavalkya apprehended by Yeats provides grounds for drawing historical conclusions. Taken together, and assuming a date for Yajnavalkya no later than the time of Pythagoras, the two do serve, however, to raise the question of whether there was ever an important Indian philosophical influence on Classical Greece. It has been shown that during the sixth century BC a Greek could be open to Indian influence by way of Persia, that Indian philosophical speculation flourished prior to the rise of Greek thought congenial with it, and that Pythagoras is the founder of a distinct school while Yajnavalkya is part of a general and older trend in Indian thought. On the face of it influence; as Platonic tradition again suggests, is more likely to have passed from East to West. Moreover, it seems unlikely that fairly detailed philosophical ideas and manners, unlike archetypal images, should have arisen independently in Greece shortly after they had happened to arise in India. Nor is a common origin elsewhere likely, since on available evidence philosophical speculation based on mystical experience— again as opposed to, say, archetypal myths of Paradise such as are found in the Babylonian story of Gilgamesh—is a late Vedic growth on Indian soil posterior to the divergence of the old Indo-Iranian peoples. This would be the historical ground for suggesting that the Perennial Philosophy—for that is what Yajnavalkya's teaching constitutes—originated in India.

As a case for historical influence this is as unsatisfactory as it is inconclusive, being highly circumstantial and unsupported by Greek recognition before the time of Alexander the Great. Furthermore, even after Alexander's conquest, just as after the modern British conquest, when there were those who not only acknowledged the value of Indian philosophy but even accorded it a priority to the Greek, there were many more who did not. This may be accounted for in a number of ways, some dependent on the extent to which India failed to realize its own idealist tradition, some on the extent to which other cultures confronting India had either absorbed Indian influences as their own or, alternatively, had not absorbed them and so, either way, were consequently blinded to aspects of Indian civilization.

What has to be understood, however, is not simply that the historical evidence is inconclusive but that any conceivable historical evidence which suggested that the Perennial Philosophy originated in India would necessarily be inconclusive. The Indian tradition itself attributes its origin to the immanent Self which is to be discovered deep within the consciousness. Paradoxically, the more Indian scripture argues that this realization is universally accessible, the more do men outside India imaginative enough to break out of their cultural milieux—idealist religions exclusive of other religions or materialist sciences dependent on analysis and differentiation—identify the Perennial Philosophy with India. But the Perennial Philosophy is an intellectual tradition only in the sense that it is an imaginative re-discovery or recognition made possible by intellectual traditions which, phoenix-like, make their own destruction a prerequisite of their realization: the Imagination rises out of the ashes of the intellect.

It may be that the visits to India of Greek philosophers, like those of the Persian *sufis* and the Chinese Buddhist pilgrims, mark a return passage of the Perennial Philosophy. But for the mystic, whether within India or outside it—passing into a state not contained by, though containing, time and space—the question of whether or when there was a decisive Indian influence on Greece is immaterial. A new mode of perception becomes operative: influence (being external) is superseded when identity (being internal) is apprehended. None the less, India may continue to be a valid image of this state for the *literary* man who, however much he may approach or experience the visionary state in the Imagination, remains, as he writes, among images—Yajnavalkya's dream state. According to the tradition which we have now traced as far back as the Vedic sage, the literary consciousness—expressed or embodied in imaginative fiction—is real only to the extent that it indicates the greater Reality or Unity, outside which it has no reality or unity of its own.

PART II
THE PASSAGE BACK

Alexander the Great: Indian Ascetics and the Christian Image of Paradise

*in which Alexander's confrontation with
the Indian ascetics is traced through
various literary transformations and
questions are raised about the nature
of Indian influence.*

He wanted not to convert but to harmonize, and conceived himself
as the divine and impartial ruler beneath whom harmony shall proceed. That way lies madness. Persia fell. Then it was the turn of
India.

> E.M. Forster on Alexander, 'The Return from Siwa'.

Ye Brachmans old, whom purer aeras bore,
Ere Western Science lisped her ancient lore!
How will your wonders flush the Athenian Sage?
How ray with glory my historic page?

> Alexander in *Alexander's Expedition* (1792), by Thomas Beddoes.

Every Place is a Paradise, which a Man fancies to be so; and nothing can beat me off from the Conceit I have of the Indies.

> Mahmut in *Letters Writ by a Turkish Spy*.

CHAPTER FIVE

Alexander the Great: Indian Ascetics and the Christian Image of Paradise

Alexander the Great's invasion of India marks the beginning of extensive and long-standing contact between India and the West. This contact was consolidated by the construction of Alexandria, destined to be the principal market for trade between East and West. It was in Alexandria in the second century BC that the compilers of the *Septuagint* confused time and place and recorded that Eden was established by God not in the beginning but in the East, thereby providing a scriptural basis for those who would locate Paradise in or about India.[1] It was from Alexandria that the first recorded Christian mission left for India. Not only is it the Alexandrian Clement who provides the first reference in the West to Buddha[2] but it was in Alexandria that Terebinthus, the disciple of Scythianus (who had acquired a knowledge of Indian philosophy in India), established himself as a living *buddha*, his books, according to the Church historian Socrates, providing a doctrinal basis for Mani.[3] Apollonius of Tyana is associated with the city not only by Philostratus and Jerome, who have him return to Alexandria after his visit to Iarchas, but also by the Muslims in their tradition.[4] Ptolemy appears to have been indebted for information

---

[1] Granville Penn, 'Remarks on the Eastern Origination of Mankind', *The Oriental Collections*, vol. II, no. I (Jan–Mar, 1798), pp. 74–7. In the Middle Ages Peter Lombard had noticed this confusion (Kirtland Wright, p. 261). It is frequently discussed in books concerned with the origins of civilization (e.g. Sir Walter Ralegh, *The History of the World*, London, 1614, I, I, 3, § 3, pp. 35–7; Thomas Burnet, *The Sacred Theory of the Earth*, 5th ed., 2 vols, London, 1722, I, 347). [2] See chapter 3, p. 112. [3] Socrates, *Historia Ecclesiastica*, I, xxii. [4] Berwick, v.xxiv–xliii.272–299; Letter LIII, §1; last paragraph of this chapter, p. 189.

about India to Indians he met in Alexandria, Dion Chrysostom noticed Indians among his audience in the same city, and it was from Alexandria that Lucian, in one of his dialogues, has a Cynic philosopher, Demetrius, relinquish all his money and go away to India to join the Brahmins.[5] An Alexandrian novel, *Kleitophon and Leukippe*, by Achilles Tatius, incorporated the first description to reach the West of Indian sculpture.[6] Brahmins living an abstemious life are reported to have lodged in the house of Severus in Alexandria shortly before AD 470. Not long after, Cosmas Indicopleustes, who was almost certainly an Alexandrian, traded with India first in merchandise and then in ideas.[7]

The most lasting monument to Alexander and his contact with the East, however, is the Romance of his life composed probably by a native of Alexandria sometime after 200 BC and generally referred to as the *Pseudo-Callisthenes*.[8] This romance history, in one form or another, was extremely popular in medieval Europe and a very great deal of what was then known about the East was derived from it. It was also popular throughout the East itself and underwent far-reaching transformations in the literatures of various Oriental countries. In fact the treatment of one very crucial Indian incident in the (so-called) Oriental Alexander throws an interesting light on the treatment of the same incident in the (so-called) Medieval Alexander. The various ways the story is re-told raises a number of questions about the workings of the Imagination and the place of India within it.

THE INDIAN ASCETICS IN HISTORY AND IN ROMANCE

(i) *Alexander and the Indian Ascetics*

While much is made of Alexander's conquest of the Indian king, Porus, it is clear he turned back in the Punjab and never reached the Jumna or the Ganges, even by then the heartland of India.[9] The real limit of his conquest is denoted by a small anecdote which has not only touched the literary imagination but epitomizes (as it originates) the long-standing and popular antithesis between a

---

[5] 'Geography', I, 17, §§ 4–5, *Ancient India as described by Ptolemy*, trans. J.W. McCrindle (London, 1885), p. 29; *Oration*, XXXII.40; 'Toxaris', § 34, Lucian, V, 159.   [6] Drijvers, pp. 174–5.   [7] Damascius, cited in 'Origin and Decline of the Christian Religion in India', Francis Wilford, *AR*, X, 111; Priaulx, pp. 189–90; *The Christian Topography of Cosmas*, trans. J.W. McCrindle (London, 1897), Introduction, pp. iv–viii. Cosmas is familiar with the Brahmins and what is apparently their theory of the meridian (Bk. II, p. 48).   [8] George Cary, *The Medieval Alexander*, ed. D.J.A. Ross (Cambridge, 1956), p. 9.   [9] Woodcock, chap. II.

spiritual India and a materialist West. After he had occupied Taxila, Alexander wished to acquaint himself with the beliefs and practices of the Indian philosophers, about whose hardy mode of life he had already heard.[10] There are two apparently independent accounts of the meeting between Alexander's emissaries and the Indian philosophers, and since the story has been as greatly embellished as it has been widely diffused it is important to establish the original facts of the story. Strabo, writing at the turn of the Christian era, includes both versions, one derived from Onesicritus—the Cynic philosopher who accompanied Alexander to India—and the other from Megasthenes, who, as the ambassador of Seleucus Nicator at the court of Chandragupta, was the first known European long resident in India.

According to Onesicritus[11] he was himself sent to approach the gymnosophists and found them living some way out of the city, as Europeans have ever since invariably found Indian *yogis*, naked and in diverse motionless postures in the unendurable heat. One gymnosophist, Calanus, who was later to accompany Alexander on his return journey and immolate himself, berates Onesicritus for being clothed and eulogizes the Golden Age when men lived simply and Earth satisfied their needs, which were few. The oldest of the group, Mandanis, however, rebukes Calanus and praises Alexander for being a king interested in philosophy. As for his own beliefs, he accounts the best philosophy that which removes pleasure and pain from the soul and toughens the body through discipline. Onesicritus tells him that Pythagoras had taught such doctrines among the Greeks, as well as advocating a vegetarian diet, and had been followed in this by Socrates and by Diogenes, his own teacher.

The account given by Strabo from Megasthenes may be clarified by reference to Arrian, who also cites Megasthenes.[12] Once again it is the fame of the gymnosophists which causes Alexander, while at Taxila, to send for one, though his messengers are not here named. By this account, Mandanis, again said to be the master and oldest of the group, combines the qualities of both the Indian gymnosophists portrayed by Onesicritus. He denies that Alexander is the son of Zeus any more than he himself is and says that neither he nor his disciples have cause either to go to Alexander or to

[10] It is now generally assumed these men were Jains, all of whom in Alexander's time went as naked as the Digambara sect still do. Previously, they had been thought to be Buddhists. Their reported belief in God and in the immortality of the soul does not rule out the possibility that they were, as was traditionally supposed, Brahmins.   [11] Strabo, *Geographia*, xv.i.63–5.   [12] Ibid., xv.i.59; Arrian, *Anabasis*, vii.ii.2–4.

receive gifts from him. Contrasting their way of life with that of
Alexander, he says that they are free of desire while the desire to
conquer the world is one which can never be satisfied. Nor do
they fear the consequences that such a reply might bring; if they
live it is simply on whatever fruits the Indian seasons afford, and if
they die they go to a better state of existence. According to this
version Calanus, though admired by the Greeks for his fearless
death, is condemned by the Indians for choosing to serve Alexander. Common to both accounts is the resistance to Alexander and
the way of life his great conquests represent and the exposition of
an alternative way of life entailing self-discipline and simplicity
based on belief in the soul's immortality. Common to both also is
the approval expressed by the Greek commentator for Alexander's interest in and tolerance of philosophy and its practitioners.

It is important to establish the authenticity of this incident.
While details differ, the general impression of the gymnosophists'
beliefs and practices given by Onesicritus is corroborated by
Megasthenes. The latter version, as it is taken up by other writers,
is seen by Plutarch, for example, as an alternative and independent variation.[13] Furthermore, not only Megasthenes but virtually
all succeeding accounts of Indian philosophers, many of them
indicative of renewed contact with India, corroborate Onesicritus.
If this were not enough, it is clear that the life and thought of
the gymnosophists accords closely with that of the Vedic *rishis* and
expounders of the Upanishads. In the *Vishnu Purana*, the *muni*
Asita communicates to King Janaka the following stanzas chanted
by Earth:

How great is the folly of princes, who are endowed with the faculty of
reason, to cherish the confidence of ambition, when they themselves are
but foam upon the wave! . . . 'Thus', say they, 'will we conquer the
ocean-encircled earth', and, intent upon their project, behold not death,
which is not far off. But what mighty matter is the subjugation of the sea-
girt earth to one who can subdue himself? Emancipation from existence is
the fruit of self control . . .[14]

These verses, 'by listening to which, ambition fades away, like
snow before the sun', though written late, embody a far older
sentiment intrinsic to the relationship between, for example,
Vasistha and Visvamitra or Yajnavalkya and Janaka.

As it happens, it is less the version according to Onesicritus than
that of Megasthenes which forms the basis for the development in
literatures farther West of the story of Alexander's confrontation

---

[13] *Life of Alexander*, LXV, 3.   [14] *VP*, IV, IV, XXIV, 238–9.

with the Indian philosopher. Calanus is usually remembered as the first Indian whom the Greeks saw immolate himself without any sign of fear—though Megasthenes makes clear that the Indians considered this a sign of too ardent a temper.[15] It is Mandanis (later more frequently called Dandamis) as he is depicted by Megasthenes who remains the embodiment of Indian philosophical life. This philosophical life is described more fully by Megasthenes. In a reference to the *brahmacarin* stage of life, he tells how the young Brahmin is removed from his family to be put in the care of philosophers whose simple life includes philosophical discourse, sexual continence and a vegetarian diet. That Megasthenes provides an authentic account of a Brahminical education may be confirmed by a perusal of the *Manu Smriti*, especially the second chapter, the one detail missing from Manu—an injunction against coughing and spitting as well as talking—being evident in another law code.[16] In the next stage of life, as householders, the Brahmins may live less rigorous lives, though they do not divulge the forbidden mysteries to their wives. They discipline themselves as a preparation for death, about which they speak much and which they regard as birth into a happier state. They consider nothing that befalls mankind to be either good or bad, to suppose otherwise being a dream-like illusion, since some are grieved and others delighted by the very same things, and the same individuals are affected by the same things at different times with opposite emotions.[17]

When Mandanis had said something of similar import to Onesicritus, namely that the best teaching was that which removed pleasure and pain from the soul, the Cynic philosopher had been reminded especially of Pythagoras, though also of Socrates and Diogenes. Megasthenes, with a more extensive knowledge of the Brahmins at his command, sees a similar identity. He notes that, like the Greeks, the Indians believe the universe to be subject to periodical cycles, to be spherical in shape and to be pervaded by the Deity who gave rise to it. Both peoples hold that while various primal elements operate in the universe, water was the principle employed in the making of the world. Both assert that there is a fifth element from which the heavens and the stars were produced. 'Concerning generation, and the nature of the soul, and many other subjects, they express views like those maintained by the Greeks. They wrap up their doctrines about immortality and future judgement, and kindred topics, in allegories, after the manner

[15] Strabo, xv.i.68.   [16] H.T. Colebrooke, 'On the Religious Ceremonies of the Hindus', *AR*, v, 347–8.   [17] Strabo, xv.i.59.

of Plato'. If Megasthenes is reminded of Plato, it is of those aspects of Plato traditionally considered Pythagorean.

(ii) *From History to Romance*

The confrontation between Alexander's messenger and Dandamis (as Mandanis now becomes) is cleverly put into direct speech and thus dramatized in a fragment attributed to Palladius, Bishop of Helenopolis (AD *c.*363–*c.*430) and incorporated into the *Pseudo-Callisthenes*.[18] Although this fragment names Onesicritus as the messenger sent to the Brahmins by Alexander, it is squarely based on the account originally given by Megasthenes. Dandamis points out that Alexander, being mortal, is not God, nor even master of the world. He rejects offers of gifts on the grounds that Earth supplies all his wants and that possessions cause sorrow and vexation. At the outset of his monologue Dandamis asserts that God is the creator of light, the author of body, soul and all else. When he adds that if Alexander has him killed he will leave his body behind like a torn garment and, becoming spirit, will ascend to God, this is consistent with the Vedanta philosophy of the Brahmins previously recorded by Bishop Hippolytus. While Hippolytus noted that in India Dandamis was spoken of as a god, Arrian reported that Calanus, presumably by way of contrast to Dandamis, was seen as a man who, in following Alexander, had chosen to serve a master other than God.[19] The extra theistic stress evident in (the so-called) 'Palladius' need not, therefore, be read as a projection onto India of Christian theism. It *can* equally well be read as a Christian acknowledgement of Indian theism.

The 'Palladius' fragment is sympathetic to the philosophical beliefs and practices of the Brahmins: although Alexander has conquered many nations he has met more than his match in the old and naked Dandamis. At the farthest extreme of his conquest of the world, Alexander is confronted with the truth that he would

---

[18] 'Pseudo-Callisthenes Historiam Fabulosam', III.7–16, *Arriani Anabasis et Indica*, ed. C. Muller (Paris, 1846), pp. 102–20. George Cary has noted that, although the whole passage is traditionally ascribed to Palladius, probably only 7–10 was his work (p. 13). Apart from the reference to the marital customs of the Indians, all the information regarding them can be found in earlier accounts. N.B.: Pseudo-Callisthenes was widely available in England in the edition of Sir Edward Bysshe, *Palladius de Gentibus Indiae* (London, 1665), pp. 1–54. It is followed by *De Moribus Brachmanorum*, a condensed version of 'Palladius' once attributed to St Ambrose (pp. 57–84).   [19] See chapter 3, pp. 102–3; this chapter, n. 12. The passage by Hippolytus was long attributed to Origen (see *Contra Haereses*, I. 44–5).

have done better to have conquered himself. That this account remains authentic to India is the more important since it is especially influential on the medieval image of India and, later, on the eighteenth century European view of the Brahmins.

Following the refusal of Dandamis to go to him, Alexander, according to this version, is the more eager to meet Dandamis. The report of Aristobulus, who accompanied Alexander to India, that two Brahmin ascetics did meet Alexander at Taxila[20] provided historical ground, were it needed, to ensure that, as a dramatic sense demands, Alexander was eventually brought face to face with the most eloquent of the Brahmins. It is interesting that even in the historical accounts Alexander's character (the authorial comment on his tolerance excepted) is wholly to be inferred from the contrast provided by the way of life and the remarks of the Brahmins. In the *Pseudo-Callisthenes*, having been lectured face to face by Dandamis, Alexander is permitted to speak for himself; in another literary version, perhaps equally ancient, he defends his way of life in a lengthy exchange of letters. The point to be made is that, however more elaborate these later literary accounts and whatever the sympathies of their authors, Alexander still conforms to the original Indian perception of him.

While it is true—as Abelard, writing in the twelfth century, remarks—that Dindimus (his name again slightly altered) is a figure highly regarded by Christian commentators,[21] even those descriptions of the confrontation which are more sympathetic to Alexander do not give him characteristics which are foreign to the original accounts. Thus the most conclusive argument put into the mouth of Alexander (used, for example, in the *Historia de Preliis* but cut out of the *exempla*),[22] namely, that he makes war because he is fated by God to be a soldier, is consistent with the position originally adopted by Mandanis. The latter, as reported by Onesicritus, far from seeking to convert Alexander, simply accepted that Alexander was destined to be a ruler, just as the Brahmins were destined to live a simple, philosophical life. This attitude, which is also that of the Brahmins in the *Pseudo-Callisthenes*, is perfectly in accordance with the Indian social order, the *varnasramadharma*, whereby a hereditary social division is made between the Brahmins, or philosophers, and the *ksatriyas*, or warriors, from among whom kings are drawn. The duty of a soldier to be true to his particular destiny is the theme of one of the central passages of Hindu scripture—the teaching of Krishna to Arjuna in the *Bhagavad Gita*. The implication (explicit in Megas-

---

[20] Strabo, xv.i.61. [21] *Introductio ad Theologiam*, I, xxii–xxiii, cited in Cary, p. 93. [22] Cary, p. 148.

thenes) does, of course, remain that the Brahmins, temporarily at least, enjoy a superior destiny and by virtue of their profession as philosophers—as both Onesicritus and Nearchus report—are consulted by kings.

The furthest stage in the evolution of the confrontation between Alexander and Dindimus as a distinct story is reached in the epistolary version, the *Collatio*, the Indian tractate best known in medieval Europe.[23] Dindimus stresses the divergence between their ways of life, elaborating on the simplicity, purity, pacifism and godliness of the life of the Brahmins. While Alexander turns his attention to externals, the Brahmins turn inwards, seeking to overcome fear and desire or acquisitiveness. An exchange of letters ensures that there will be not only an implied superiority of the Brahmin way of life but an overt condemnation of Alexander's. Alexander rejects the Brahminical life on the grounds that it is static, being based on a denial of the senses and dishonouring the Creator in that it fails to enjoy his creation. Dindimus replies that this life is only a temporary state and men merely pilgrims in a world where it is futile to acquire riches. These remarks by Dindimus are consistent with the portrait drawn by Megasthenes. It *is* a departure from the original account when Dindimus deplores the killing and sacrifice of animals (implicit though this is in the original account of his vegetarian diet), and when he attacks the morality of the Greek gods, as well as their naturalism and anthropomorphic character and the construction of idols. None the less, even these interpolated views are consistent with aspects of Indian culture that could have been deduced from other Greek accounts of India.

(iii) *A Passage from India*

This story of Alexander's confrontation with the Indian ascetics is well known. Why, then, has time been taken here to show that in the transformation it undergoes in the Romance tradition it does not depart in any of its essentials from the historical accounts? The reason is that it has been widely assumed that the Indian ascetics are simply a convenient device used for polemical purposes. W.W. Skeat, who edited and translated into modern English a Middle English version of the correspondence between Alexander and

---

[23] 'Collatio Alexandri cum Dindimo, Rege Bragmanorum, per Litteras Facta', *Juli Valeri Alexandri Polemi Res Gestae Alexandri Macedonis*, ed. Bernard Kuebler (Leipzig, 1888), pp. 169–89. This is Collatio I of Cary (pp. 13–14) and the 'Anonymus de Bragmanibus' of Bysshe, pp. 85–103.

Dindimus, wrote that though it 'deals with India, and attempts an account of the life of the Brahmans, there is little that is eastern about it'.[24] That assumption is questionable. While it is true that the Indian ascetics have been appropriated as part of a Christian dialectic, we have seen that it is arguably an authentic part of Indian culture that the Christians have appropriated. Like Skeat, George Cary also arrived at the conclusion that Dindimus had been used as a mouthpiece for Christian values (originally, he thought, Cynic). Unlike Skeat, however, he observed that the choice of mouthpiece was peculiarly suitable on account of the 'strange' similarity of Brahminical and Christian asceticism.[25] The strangeness is there only so long as we neglect or refuse to consider a hypothesis as simple as it is obvious: namely, that the medieval Christian image of India was based on a tradition which was authentic to India and had perennially commanded the respect of Christians.

One reason why more attention has not been paid to the remarkable coincidence between the ideal images of India found in European literature and those in Indian literature lies in the tacit assumption that European idealization of India is just one more example of the widespread habit of attributing wisdom to any people in the East: *ex oriente lux*. In his book, *Utopias of the Classical World*, John Ferguson writes of Onesicritus 'idealizing' remote peoples such as the Indians.[26] But the main difference between the idealization of India and the idealization of other cultures is that the idealization of India happens to accord with Indian conceptions. In other cases, the projections are fanciful; in the case of India, authentic. Instead of assuming that the conception of *ex oriente lux* gave rise to the idealization of India it might be wiser to consider whether it is not rather that Alexander's contact with the Indian ascetics gave a powerful stimulus to the conception of *ex oriente lux*. It is certainly misleading to say that the neo-Pythagoreans and Platonists sought to lend dignity or mystique to their philosophy by associating it with the Indians in the East. It was the neo-Pythagoreans and Platonists who, following the re-

---

[24] Walter Skeat, ed. and trans., *Alexander and Dindimus* (London, 1878), Introduction, p. xviii. [25] Cary, p. 91. Woodcock, who is prepared to concede the possibility of Indian influence on Greek philosophy, none the less repeats this assumption of a Cynic projection (p. 33). That the Greeks superimposed their own Cynicism is the less plausible since the Greeks themselves quickly recognized that the Indians were even *more* frugal than Diogenes (e.g. Plutarch, *Moralia*, 332B). [26] London, 1975, p. 122. This, even though Ferguson believes that Pythagoras and, through him, Plato moulded their thought to Indian ideas (pp. 46–7).

ports of Onesicritus and Megasthenes, themselves first gave Indian philosophy the dignity or mystique they are supposed to have derived from it.

This argument against treating the idealized image of Indian asceticism as merely fanciful is even more pertinent to the Christian idealization of the Brahmins. Although the Christians borrowed extensively from their pagan predecessors, George Boas has made the point that, unlike the pagans, the Christians were *not* given to idealizing the ancient peoples of remote places.[27] Such peoples had been denied the revelation of Christ. Boas can find only one substantial exception to this comprehensive anathema: the Brahmins—especially as they had appeared in their confrontation with Alexander. Why did the Christians make this single exception? An obvious answer is that initial Greek contact had shown the Brahmins to be a philosophical people whose practice of asceticism was exemplary. Further contact with India had confirmed this impression.

An immediate objection to this argument may be made on the grounds that certain sentences in the letters attributed to Dindimus are directly derived from the *Apologeticus* of Tertullian.[28] Of course, a medieval European monk wishing to embellish (by extending in a series of letters or speeches) the words or sentiments of an Indian Brahmin had little choice but to resort to equivalents within his own tradition. At least two English novelists in the twentieth century, notwithstanding the incomparably greater wealth of information at their disposal, have done precisely the same thing.[29] The consequent distortion is not necessarily fatal to my argument. A medieval monk may flesh out the remarks of an Indian ascetic by reference to the writings of the Church Fathers. But then the Church Fathers themselves, including Tertullian, were also familiar with the Brahmins and frequently expressed admiration for them. Moreover, they did so shortly before, as well as during, the rise of a cult of Christian asceticism in the third century AD.[30] Clement of Alexandria provides details of the auster-

---

[27] *Essays on Primitivism and Related Ideas in the Middle Ages* (Baltimore, 1948), pp. 137–51. Boas concurs with Skeat in the opinion that the episode of the Indian ascetics, 'it goes without saying, is no part of serious history' (p. 146, n. 37). He is influenced by the fact that Quintus Curtius does not mention the ascetics.   [28] Cary, citing Liénard (n. 11, p. 280). Cary notices that, whatever the intention of the 'Collatio', Christians read it as a vindication of the Brahmin point of view.   [29] E.M. Forster and L.H. Myers (see chapter 1, pp. 15–17, nn. 15–24).   [30] The likelihood of an actual influence is considered by Sir Charles Eliot, *Hinduism and Buddhism*, 3 vols (London, 1921), III, 429–48. Extensive similarities between Christian and Buddhist asceticism are noticed in W.Y. Evans-Wentz, ed. and trans., *Tibet's Great Yogi Milarepa*, 2nd ed. (London, 1951), Introduction.

ities endured by Indian ascetics and St Augustine shows familiarity with the life of the gymnosophists. St Ambrose, in a letter in which he borrows from Philo a version of the Indian confrontation with Alexander, actually uses Indian asceticism as a standard against which to measure Christian ascetics. St Jerome, perhaps the epitome of Christian asceticism, expresses his admiration for the asceticism of the Indians.[31]

As we have seen, knowledge of Indian asceticism was not confined to the accounts of Alexander's meeting with the ascetics nor even to ensuing accounts that came in by way of Bardaisan, Porphyry and the *Life of Apollonius of Tyana*: Indian ascetic practice was carried into the Mediterranean itself.[32] For the same reason that we cannot say definitely whether or not neo-Platonic idealism was influenced by Indian philosophy, we cannot say whether Christian asceticism was influenced by Indian asceticism. Given the high esteem in which Indian ascetics were held by the Christians, however, it remains a distinct possibility that, even if Indian asceticism did not give rise to its Christian counterpart, it gave it valuable impetus. Why else should the 'Brahmins' enjoy such unique prestige?

INDIA IN THE ETHIOPIC ALEXANDER: THE CHRISTIAN IMAGE OF PARADISE

We have seen that there is at least some reason for taking Dandamis at face value and regarding him, as did medieval monks, as an Indian ideal held up to Christians as worthy of their emulation. This episode from the Alexander Romances provides an example of Indian influence, by way of an authentic image of India, reaching the English literary tradition in an overtly recognizable form. Yet the recognizable has not hitherto been recognized. Dandamis has been regarded *simply* as a Christian ideal projected onto a pre-Christian past. It has been necessary to argue at this late date that the image of the Indian ascetics is not merely fanciful but genuinely imaginative. Obviously, it would be even more hazardous to argue for the possibility of an Indian origin for an image which has few, if any, intimations of India about it. None the less, it has been successfully demonstrated that the Roman Catholic saints Barlaam and Josaphat (to whose story Shakespeare was indebted

---

[31] Clement (*Stromata*, I.xv; III.vii); Augustine (*De Civitate Dei*, X.xxxii, XIV.xvii; XV.xx); Ambrose (Letter XXXVII, § 35, *The Letters of St Ambrose*, trans. anon., Oxford, 1881, p. 246 = Philo, see this chapter, n. 78); and Jerome (*Contra Jovinianum*, II.14; Letter CVII, §8). Jerome refers to Buddha in I.42. [32] See chapter 3, pp. 109–10.

for his parable of the three caskets in *The Merchant of Venice*) were originally Buddhist;[33] that the faithful dog Gellert in the popular Welsh folk-tale was originally, like Kipling's Rikki-tikki-tavi, a domestic Indian mongoose;[34] that the Arabic numbers as they reached Europe might more properly be termed Indian;[35] and that the gypsies are not ultimately, as their name suggests, from Egypt but from India.[36]

Bearing in mind the sort of metamorphoses undergone by these Indian images on their way West, it may prove instructive to consider how the image of Indian asceticism which, as we have seen, made such an impression on early Christians may be related to something as apparently un-Indian as the Christian image of the earthly paradise. One thing the account of Alexander's meeting with the Indian ascetics does is show us that Indian idealism is intimately related both to the practice of asceticism and to the belief in a golden age. In their realms of, respectively, thought, practice and story, it is possible to see the idealism, asceticism and mythology of the Indians as interchangeable expressions of the same philosophy. It is the identification by Onesicritus of Indian philosophy with the Pythagorean which first gave rise to the idea that Greek *idealism* had been influenced by the Indian. We have now seen that the popularity of this same story about the gymnosophists may indicate that *asceticism* in the Middle East was reinforced or refined as a result of contact with India. It remains to take a close look at the way the Alexander tradition developed in the Middle East and see that from the story of the Indian ascetics Christians may even have derived support for their conception of paradise as a place to which the enlightened saints go in preparation for immortality.

(i) *The Ethiopic Romances*

As part of the myth of *ex oriente lux*, two countries besides India which have engaged the attention of Europeans as a source of wisdom and a site of Paradise are Ethiopia and Persia. Of all the cultures of the East, however, it is only the Indian which permits or encourages this rather sweeping and volatile European projection.

[33] Joseph Jacobs, ed., *Barlaam and Josaphat* (London, 1896); David Marshall Lang, ed. and trans., *The Wisdom of Balhavar* (London and New York, 1957), pp. 11–65.   [34] S. Baring-Gould, *Curious Myths of the Middle Ages* (London, 1866), pp. 126–36; *The Panchatantra*, trans. Franklin Edgerton (London, 1965), Introduction, pp. 16–19; Rudyard Kipling, *The Jungle Book* (London, 1894), pp. 123–51.   [35] See chapter 3, nn. 38, 40. Note a reservation against attributing an Indian origin to the most ancient form of Arabic numerals (Smith and Karpinski, p. 14).   [36] Basham, pp. 514–17.

It is the more interesting, then, that both Ethiopian and Persian literatures, in their versions of the Alexander Romances, confirm or acknowledge (if obliquely) the importance of India as an image of the ideal. If the study of the Ethiopic Romances which now follows is somewhat lengthy and apparently discursive, it is because it provides an opportunity for us to speculate simultaneously about the nature both of Indian influence and of the literary imagination.

Ethiopia is a country which has frequently been associated with India. According to Buddhist as well as neo-Pythagorean tradition, Ethiopia was once subject to Indian religious influence.[37] Whether or not this was so, Ethiopia and India were so hopelessly confused in the Classical mind that Alexander mistook the Indus for the source of the Nile, a confusion still abroad in medieval times when Marco Polo referred to Ethiopia as Middle India.[38]

The Ethiopic version of the *Pseudo-Callisthenes* is a Christian one, apparently based on Arabic texts derived from the Greek original.[39] Relative to India, it records Alexander's meeting with a group of Brahmins to whom he puts questions, an account in which the respect accorded to the Brahmins may be measured by the fact that the Eastern Christians, like Christians farther West who were interested in India—men such as Marignolli and Ralegh and Thomas Maurice[40]—felt compelled to reconcile the Indian tradition with Old Testament history. Hence the Brahmins are the 70,000 men whom the Lord God told Elijah had not acknowledged Baal nor any god but himself; they are the Children of Seth covered over during the Flood in a hidden place of the Earth. The Ethiopic *Pseudo-Callisthenes*, however, does not make specific mention of Dandamis since, unlike the earlier Greek version, it includes neither the interpolation ascribed to Palladius (where the speech of Dandamis is authentically dramatized) nor does it name Dandamis as the leader of the group of Brahmins interrogated by Alexander. The Ethiopic text does follow the Greek in incorporating the person, practices and sentiments of Dandamis as he is represented by Megasthenes into the description of the Brahmins to whom Alexander puts ten questions.[41] Thus, in the Ethiopian

---

[37] Karl Jahn, *Rashid al-Din's 'History of India': Collected Essays* (Hague, 1965), p. lx; see chapter 3, p. 95. This assumption was still current in the time of Sir William Jones, see Chapter 6, p. 200.   [38] Strabo, xv.i.25; Yule II, III, xxxv, pp. 427 and n. 1., 431–2. See also Arrian, *Anabasis*, vi.i; Virgil, *Georgics*, iv. 293 and the Church histories of Socrates (I.19) and Sozomen (II.24).   [39] *The Life and Exploits of Alexander the Great: from the Ethiopic Histories*, trans. E.A. Wallis Budge (London, 1896), Preface, pp. x–xi, xix, xxiv–xxv.   [40] See this chapter, p. 175 and n. 116; chap. 6, p. 190 & n.21, p. 204 & n. 67.   [41] Wallis Budge, pp. 126–37.

tradition, Dandamis disappears from the scene as a distinct character, though a full exposition of his way of life remains.

Instead of including the passage ascribed to Palladius, the
Ethiopic *Pseudo-Callisthenes* goes straight on to reproduce
Alexander's letter to Aristotle on the Wonders of India.[42] This
mythical letter, which had considerable influence on the element
of the fabulous in European literature,[43] contains accounts of
many marvellous hybrid creatures, strange things and places ultimately derived, perhaps, from the Indian epics. The climax to Alexander's adventures in India as he relates them to Aristotle is to
find himself on the borders of Paradise. He climbs to a garden on
the highest among a range of mountains which, on account both of
its situation and the sweet scent of its flowers, he assumes must be
Paradise. Of this assumption he is disabused by a voice from within a golden temple. Enoch—a figure the Christians substitute for
Dionysus as the founder of civilization in the East—warns Alexander that he should neither expect to attain knowledge nor pry into
the mysteries of God the Eternal. His guides from India, he is told,
can neither make him 'ascend above the air nor above the lofty
mountains to the place where existeth Paradise.' Returned again
to the plains, Alexander meets other Indians who inform him—as
both St Athanasius and Mas'udi also report[44]—that there is no
country beyond India except the region adjacent to Paradise, the
proximity of which accounts for the sweet scent of the flowers and
the crystal clarity of the streams. Journeying in that direction Alexander reaches the Trees of the Sun and the Moon which give him
prescience of his death.

While the Ethiopic version of Alexander's quest for Paradise
owes at least something to Babylonian sources,[45] the association of
this quest with the Indian part of Alexander's adventures in the
older Greek version[46] indicates that the original pattern for it
might reasonably be sought in the historical accounts of Alexander
in India. Only once, and that at the farthest extent of his journey,
is the historical Alexander confronted with the limitations of his

---

[42] Ibid., 142–65. The Ethiopic version continues in the first person for some
pages and there is no clear termination of the letter. In the late eighteenth century
Jones speculated whether Aristotle, by way of Callisthenes, had been influenced by
the Nyaya school (*WWJ*, III, 237–8).   [43] Rudolf Wittkower, 'Marvels of the East',
Journal of the Warburg and Courtauld Institutes, v (1942), 159–97 (see esp. p.
179).   [44] *Cathay and the Way Thither*, trans. Sir Henry Yule, rev. ed. Henri
Cordier, 4 vols (London, 1913–16), III, 226, n. 3. For a comparison with
neo-Pythagorean and Buddhist conceptions of an abstract paradise. see chapter 3,
p. 88.   [45] Wallis Budge, Introduction, pp. xl–xliii.   [46] Alexander writes his
letter to Aristotle from India itself, Pseudo-Callisthenes, III.17, Muller, p. 120.

ambition and that is when Dandamis taxes him with his failure to consider his mortality, undertake an inner spiritual quest, know God and attain peace on Earth. At the comparable point in the narrative, the Ethiopic *Pseudo-Callisthenes* tells the story of Alexander's forestalled approach to Paradise. That this fable, no less than the interrogation of the Brahmins or the interpolation of 'Palladius', could be an imaginative re-rendering of Alexander's confrontation with the ascetic Dandamis takes on greater credibility when it is recalled that a book on the lives of Christian ascetics compiled by Palladius is entitled *Paradise*.[47] The simple ascetic life, as Dandamis tells Alexander, *is* the Golden Age: it *is* Paradise.

A similar approach to Alexander's journey East is evident in a further Christian legend inserted in the Ethiopic *Pseudo-Callisthenes*.[48] According to this legend and the sequel (or rather repeated variation) of his journey across the Ocean, the whole purpose of Alexander's expedition is less one of military conquest (though he is to shut up the wicked tribes of Gog and Magog) than an essentially spiritual quest for the Water of Life which flows out of Paradise. India is no longer mentioned as the land beyond which an approach to Paradise may be made among the mountaintops and the legend appears to derive its imaginative geography solely from Semitic sources.[49] Bearing in mind, however, that the Arabs may have derived something of their cosmology—among other sciences—from the Hindus, certain features of this Paradise point to a possible Indian constituent. It is approached by way of some mountains inhabited by men with faces like dogs. Like a mighty city it stands between heaven and earth, above the tops of lofty mountains and the four winds. Four great rivers come forth from Paradise by way of the earth and flow to the four cardinal points. The gate of Paradise is a mountain which encompasses the whole world and, but for the Water of Life, is shrouded in darkness lest the heavenly light consumes those who approach it. It is 80,000 *stadia* high, its top reaching to the first heaven, the heaven of this world, and its base to the seventh earth.

Hindus and Buddhists alike situate Paradise, the *svarga* of Indra or Brahmapura, the heavenly city of Brahma, on top of the cosmic mountain Meru, the navel of the earth.[50] Furthermore, while Mount Meru, according to the Indian texts, is said to be 84,000 *yo-*

---

[47] *The Paradise of the Holy Fathers*, trans. E.A. Wallis Budge, 2 vols (London, 1907).   [48] Wallis Budge, pp. 216 seq. (esp. pp. 234–5).   [49] Ibid., Introduction, pp. xxxiii–xxxv.   [50] Francis Wilford, 'Of the Geographical Systems of the Hindus', *AR*, VIII, 267–339 *passim*; *VP*, II, II, II, 109–26; Waddell, pp. 77–81. See also this chapter, pp. 168–9 and n. 89.

janas high, it so happens that accounts of the Buddhist concept of
Meru as it reached the Islamic world (as, incidentally, one report
which reached Europe)[51] rounded out the figure to 80,000
yojanas.[52] The Indian world-mountain is said to extend as high as
the first (though sometimes second) of the seven (or, later, more)
heavens and to have its base in the lowest earth.[53] From Meru,
having first gone underground, four rivers flow to the cardinal
points. In so far as it has an earthly geography, Meru is invariably
located amongst the highest mountains in the world, the Himalayas, near the sources of four great rivers—the one running to the
south, through the territory of tribes referred to by the so-called
Aryans as dog-faced,[54] being the sacred Ganges. In the early
eighteenth century when the intelligent Jesuit student of Tibetan
Buddhism, Ippolyte Desideri, rediscovered this cosmology he
made the usual European assumption that it derived from Christian sources and had been introduced into India in the sixth century
by the Egyptian monk, Cosmas Indicopleustes.[55] In fact, since the
development of the cosmology of Mount Meru and its association
with the Himalayas pre-dates Cosmas—and Arab science—the
debt, if any, is more likely to be owed to, and not by, India.

Some light on this reading of the legend is shed by a metrical
Syriac version attributed to Mar Jacob of Serugh.[56] According to
Mar Jacob, who also wrote about St Thomas in India,[57] India is
the country to which Alexander journeys in order to undertake his
search for the fountain of life. It would not be wise to set too much
store by Mar Jacob's physical geography since his India has a Persian king. It is worth remarking, however, that Dandamis was said
by 'Palladius' to have at hand a fountain of peace from which he
drank. The image of Alexander going in quest of the waters of immortality (an image which, in the eighteenth century, fascinated,
among others, William Beckford)[58] follows naturally upon the way
Mandanis, according to Megasthenes, confronted Alexander with
his mortality. The Alexander of Mar Jacob's version appears to be
precisely the sort of man the Indian ascetic, by implication, might

---

[51] A.A. Giorgi, *Alphabetum Tibetanum* (Rome, 1762), p. 472.   [52] Sachau, I,
249.   [53] Monier-Williams, pp. 206–8. Cf. *Corinthians*, XII.2–3.   [54] McCrindle
(Ktesias), pp. 21–5 and Lassen's review, pp. 84–7; Wittkower, p.
163.   [55] Ippolyte Desideri, *An Account of Tibet*, trans. Filippo de Filippe
(London, 1932), pp. 229–30.   [56] *The History of Alexander the Great: from the
Syriac Histories*, trans. E.A. Wallis Budge (Cambridge, 1889), pp. 163–
200.   [57] Vsevolod Slessarev, *Prester John: the Letter and the Legend* (Minneapo-
lis, 1959), p. 90.   [58] Letter of William Beckford to Lady Hamilton, 20 Feb. 1781,
The Life and Letters of William Beckford, ed. Lewis Melville (London, 1910), p.
103. Beckford may have read Bysshe, pp. 20–1.

wish him to be. He arrives in India proclaiming peace and seeks the advice of the old men who know the secrets of the country. This is by way of preparation for his journey to the Land of Darkness in search of just that immortality which Dandamis, according to the Romance tradition, requested of him in order to demonstrate to him that it was not his to give. However, Alexander's quest still takes the external form of a journey to India— Dandamis, according to Arrian, comments on the futility of undertaking such travels—and thus in the mountains which extend to the north of India immortality is denied him.

There is a later Ethiopian history of Alexander, described as a Christian Romance, which, while repeating this story of a journey in search of the Water of Life, has as its point precisely the added dimension that the secret of immortality is really to be found deep within the heart.[59] Like the Pariksitas referred to by Yajnavalkya,[60] Alexander is transported across the Ocean to the Country of the Living. Here he finds the City of the Saints (the Brahmins are described by Pseudo-Josephus, also known in an Ethiopic translation, as living in the City of the Blessed)[61] where the climate is equable and the water sweet, where *manna* falls from heaven, the cisterns are full of honey and the beasts filled with milk. This description, as Wallis Budge indicated,[62] is based on that given in 'Palladius' of the *macrobioi* living on their island Taprobane (quite possibly the mythical Jambudvipa of Indian cosmology).[63] From there Alexander makes his journey to the spiritual tabernacle on a high place in the desert, this time occupied not only by Enoch but also by Elijah: they too live an idyllic life without sickness or pain, receiving food and drink from Paradise.

Alexander is told he has been able to reach the Country of the Living because, on account of his celibacy, he is pure in heart. He is advised by the Holy Spirit to make of his heart a royal palace for God to inhabit and to regard the senses (and motion) as doors of the palace through which God within can perceive the good. Alexander abandons his earthly palace and all therein to the poor and becomes an ascetic, living on green herbs and offering advice, especially to kings. Ultimately, when the Holy Spirit informs him he is about to die, Alexander asks his mother to make a feast for

---

[59] Wallis Budge, pp. 437–553.   [60] *BA*, III.4.2.   [61] Wallis Budge, pp. 421–2; see also this chapter, p. 159.   [62] Ibid., Introduction, pp. lii, liv. Wallis Budge here gives it as his opinion that Ethiopian accounts of Alexander's travels to an idyllic place were based on his Indian travels; earlier he had thought only in terms of Middle Eastern sources.   [63] See chapter 3, p. 91 n. 34; this chapter, pp. 168–9.

him and tells her that if at the feast she serves water taken from a house wherein no man has ever died he will become immortal. His mother, eager to save him from death, hurries out, but failing to find such a house realizes her son has sent her that she may understand hers is a universal experience. This story would appear to be a variation on a well-known Buddhist story, that in which Buddha promises a woman he will restore her son to life if she will bring him a mustard-seed from a house which has never known the sorrow of death.[64]

The Alexander of this Romance bears some resemblance to the single archetypal figure of Buddha who stands behind the legends both of Nagasena and Milinda and of Barlaam and Josaphat, as well possibly as that of Thomas and Gundafor, in all of which stories an Indian prince exchanges an earthly palace for the life of an ascetic. These stories all gained some currency outside India.[65] A less decided though possible indication of Buddhist influence may be seen in the reference Alexander makes to cold hells (of ice and snow) as well as to hot (of fire and brimstone). The Buddhist images of Hell are based on an old Brahminical concept, and older than Buddhism, too, is the doctrine, derived from the Upanishads, that God dwells in the palace of the heart, pervasive in the senses though unaffected by them.[66] Whether or not an Indian influence is at work in these particulars, what is undeniable is that Alexander has been developed by Christian authors into precisely that alternative image of a man with which he was confronted in India by the person of Dandamis. The nature of his passage to India in the Ethiopic Romances is such that he has *become* Dandamis. In Europe, Peter Abelard makes Dindimus an Indian king who foresaw the coming of Christ;[67] in the Ethiopic Christian Romance Alexander is accorded the same prescience of Christ's coming because his life is identical with that of the Indian sage.

The possibility that Alexander could conceivably have been remade by Christians in the image of an Indian holy man (unlikely as that may seem) receives peculiar and unexpected support from the last Ethiopic Romance of Alexander included by Wallis Budge in his series of translations: 'The History of the Blessed Men Who

---

[64] *Buddhist Legends translated from the Dhammapada Commentary*, trans. E.W. Burlingame, 3 Pts. (Cambridge, Mass., 1921), Pt. II, Bk. VIII, Story 13, pp. 257–60. See also Pt. III, XX, 11. That the story in the Romance has an Indian original is the likelier since it is put in the same context: namely, that death is inevitable, the dead are more in number than the living.   [65] VII.7.21, *The Questions of King Milinda*, II, 374; Lang, pp. 13–14; 'The Acts of Judas Thomas', *Apocryphal Acts of the Apostles*, trans. W. Wright, 2 vols (London, 1871), II, 164–7; Woodcock, pp. 94–5.   [66] Waddell, pp. 89–100; see this chapter, p. 167.   [67] Cary, p. 93.

lived in the Days of Jeremiah the Prophet'.[68] This book records that in Jeremiah's time goodly men of Israel, who, like the Alexander of the Christian Romance and the Dandamis of the 'Collatio', refused to worship idols, were carried by angels to a mountain on an island in the sea where they could live in peace and love, free from heat or cold, pain or sorrow or any other discomfort or vice. Alexander, following his slaughter of the priests in Jerusalem, comes to this Island of the Blessed, and having questioned the inhabitants about their way of life concludes that it is blessed to be free of the lusts of the world. Wallis Budge pointed out that the Island of the Blessed is either India or Sri Lanka, though the need, on account of the reference to an island, to shift the Brahmins to Sri Lanka is obviated once one is aware that both Hindu and Buddhist cosmology conceive of India as Jambudvipa or the rose-apple island.[69] The Christian monk Gerasimas, a Greek, who, in the fifth century, lived in a cave beyond the Jordan and there founded a monastery of strict rule, read of this story of the Island of the Blessed in the *Book of Alexander*. Vouchsafed a vision as a result of his strict penances, Gerasimas is transported to the Island of the Blessed.

Like Dandamis and his fellow Brahmins, the Blessed receive their food from the trees and drink the pure water of the stream, as well as having sexual intercourse with their wives only at a specified time each year. Like the Brahmins, too, they know no pain or sorrow, though they do know death. They have foreknowledge of the time of their death and dig their own graves (in India *yogis* are still buried in the lotus posture).[70] They had prescience also of Christ's coming and all the events of his life, including the journey from the East of the Magi (one of whom, Gaspar, is sometimes identified as the Indian king Gundafor, or Gondophares).[71] Gerasimas, like the companions of Alexander in the Christian Romance before him, wishes to remain among the saints in such an idyllic place (and, by a trick, tries to do so) but is told he must return. While the monk assures us that the saints he has met are Christians and, furthermore, Christians who were Christians

---

[68] Wallis Budge, pp. 555–84. [69] See this chapter pp. 168–9. Most classical accounts of India are clearly a compound of Indian life and Indian literature. One example is the account of Iambulus (Diodorus Siculus II.55.1–II.60.3). Much of his information is consistent with what is known of social life in south India, especially Malabar; and the suggestion that before he makes his way by sea to the Ganges valley he is on a Utopian island (which is one of seven) is explicable in terms of the Indian cosmology of the *dvipas*. No doubt he recorded what he was told by local people. [70] Mircea Eliadé, *Yoga: Immortality and Freedom*, trans. Willard R. Trask (London, 1958), Note VIII, 4, pp. 422–3. [71] Slessarev. pp. 29–30.

before the birth of Christ, we know that they are in fact Brahmins. In the history of Abba Gerasimas we are confronted, therefore, with a passage to India made by a Christian monk who, as a result of his penances, is vouchsafed a vision of the Hindu way of life.

It may be that the vision of Gerasimas will bear comparison with that of the Chinese Buddhist monk, Hiuen-Tsiang, who prior to his departure from China for India had a vision of himself transported to Mount Meru in the middle of the Ocean.[72] In the case of Hiuen-Tsiang's vision, there is further historical evidence available which permits us to conclude that it constitutes, among other things, an implicit acknowledgement of an Indian influence on China. His visionary passage to India presupposes an imaginative passage *from* India. The similar vision of Gerasimas may similarly be an acknowledgement of an historical Indian influence. Be that as it may, it is at least indicative of the sort of imaginative potency India has within the Christian tradition that for a monk such as Gerasimas, India—and specifically the asceticism of India—is, as it is here, a paradise.

(ii) *Medieval Europe and the Indian River of Paradise*

The Ethiopic Alexander, and in particular the vision of Abba Gerasimas, illustrates the way an image original to India may have infiltrated, been transformed and absorbed into the Christian tradition. This is pertinent since in medieval Europe we are faced with what otherwise seems to be a purely fanciful or fantastic association of India with the terrestrial paradise. To say that the Christian search for Paradise, on account of Alexander's contact with the Brahmins, becomes particularly associated with India, as it often does in the Middle Ages,[73] is not to say that it becomes associated *only* with India—any more than that the image of Paradise is either original or exclusive to India. None the less, without the contact in Alexander's time whereby the West becomes familiar with figures such as Dandamis and Calanus and with the philosophy which sustains them—namely, that paradise is a psychological state realizable during one's physical existence—it would be inexplicable why India, in Europe no less than Ethiopia, should figure at all in a Christian cosmology otherwise almost wholly determined by the Old Testament.

A work as historically early and geographically remote from India as the Icelandic *Rymbegla* reported that the Ganges took its

---

[72] *The Life of Hiuen-Tsiang*, new ed., trans. Samuel Beal (London, 1911), p. 11.   [73] Wittkower, p. 181; Kirtland Wright, p. 273.

rise in the mountains of Eden.[74] The map of Andrea Bianchi at Venice puts the terrestrial paradise adjoining Kanya Kumari, with the four rivers of Paradise flowing up the centre of India.[75] Such a location of Paradise is frequently seen as an understandable attempt to remove it to the farthest known place, preferably eastward on account of the sun and civilization taking their rise in that quarter. Other, less fanciful, factors may, however, account for an association being made between India and Paradise.

The imaginative place that India could come to occupy within the Judaeo-Christian tradition is evident in the *Iter ad Paradisum*, a Jewish story derived from an original common also to a story dating from before AD 500 in the Babylonian *Talmud*. The *Iter ad Paradisum* was universally popular in medieval Europe, both as an independent story and as it was incorporated into the Alexander saga as a whole.[76] The association of Paradise with India is particularly noticeable in a story drawn from the tradition whence we have the Garden of Eden. Alexander sails up the Ganges in search of Paradise and reaches a long city wall in which, eventually, a window is discovered. This city, it transpires, is the abode of the blessed on earth and an old man gives Alexander's companions, who speak of him as Lord of the World, a stone with a mystic meaning as a present for Alexander. The stone outweighs any gold put in the balance against it but if dust is put on the stone even a feather will outweigh it. Symbolic of the nature of human existence, it is an ultimate comment on both the cupidity and mortality of Alexander. Just such a comment was made by the Brahmins in India following Alexander's subjugation of the country: the stone in the fable occupies precisely the place occupied in the histories and the romances by Dandamis. That such an identification may be made between the Indian ascetic and the stone is further suggested by an additional detail included in a retelling of the story in the *Thesaurus Novus*. There the old man who gives Alexander's men the mystic stone after being captured by them near Paradise says, in words reminiscent of Dandamis: 'Go and announce to Alexander that it is in vain he seeks Paradise, his efforts will be perfectly fruitless, for the way of Paradise is the way of humility, a way of which he knows nothing'.[77] There is a close correlation here between Indian asceticism and Paradise.

[74] Baring-Gould, p. 240. Another (fourteenth century) Icelandic narrative mentioned here tells how Eirek, like Alexander, travels to India in search of Paradise and finds it quite literally in the dragon's mouth across the river P(h)ison (Ibid., pp. 236–41).   [75] Yule (Cathay), III, 197–8.   [76] *Alexandri Magni Iter ad Paradisum*, ed. Julius Zacher (Konigsberg, 1859), pp. 19–32; Cary, pp. 19–20.   [77] Baring-Gould, p. 233. Cf. Pseudo-Callisthenes, III.13, Muller, pp.

Among Rabbinical writers, Philo and Josephus, who are both familiar with Megasthenes, show a respect for Indian philosophy. Philo reads the story of Alexander's confrontation in India to mean that Indian philosophers are actually superior to the Greeks[78] and Josephus associates Indian asceticism with the sort of mysticism which receives its classic statement in the *Mandukya Upanishad*.[79] It is Josephus who first establishes the tradition that one of the four rivers of Paradise, the Phison, is the Ganges.[80] This tradition is sometimes countenanced by the Church Fathers. St Jerome, for example, hears that merchants are prepared to brave great dangers in quest of bright pigments which the Ganges is said to bring down from its source in Paradise. He suggests that the story be read allegorically: Christ's merchants should be equally assiduous in their search for a pearl of great price and their desire to buy eternal treasure.[81] The curious possibility exists that Jerome is simply restoring to an Indian story a dimension it had in the Indian epics before it began to be taken literally, either by Indians who told the story or by travellers listening to them.

Something very similar happens when the Europeans renew their contact with India in modern times. At the end of the sixteenth century Jan van Linschoten reported the Bengalis as saying that the Ganges came from Paradise, a place of pleasant air, still water and fragrant earth. This description, as we shall see, accords perfectly with Indian cosmology.[82] Even the information that the King of Bengal had sent an expedition up river to discover Paradise is not inconsistent with the Indian custom of making a pilgrimage to the sacred source of the Ganges in the mountains. Half a century later, Bernier imagined Kashmiri poets claiming a Himalayan source for the four rivers of Paradise,[83] and after a further half-century had passed Desideri discovered that this was in fact the Buddhist belief.[84] Christian ministers like Henry Lord and Abraham Roger familiarized themselves and Europe with the *puranas* during the seventeenth century, but it remained for the successors of Sir William Jones, most notably Wilford and H.H.

110–11. *Thesaurus Novus* is a vulgar appellation for the *Sermones* attributed to Petrus de Palude, Patriarch of Jerusalem.   [78] 'Quod Omnis Probus Liber Sit', XIV.92–7. See also Ibid., XI.74; 'De Somniis', II.viii.56; 'De Abrahamo', XXXIII.177–83.   [79] *Jewish War*, VII.343–57 (part of which = 'On Abstinence', Bk. IV, § 18, *SWP*); see Afterword, pp. 285–8, 292.   [80] *Jewish Antiquities*, I.38. At I.147 he speaks of the descendants of Shem inhabiting India.   [81] Letter CXXV, § 3.   [82] *The Voyage of John Huyghen van Linschoten*, Bk. I, ed. and trans. A.C. Burnell and P.A. Tiele, 2 vols (London, 1885), I, 92.   [83] 'The Paradise of Indostan', III, 92–3, Bernier (1672). See chapter 6, p. 201 and n. 62.   [84] See this chapter, n. 55.

Wilson, to complete the gradual rediscovery of a cosmology which, the similar nature of the scattered references suggests, had been known to the West in Hellenistic times in equally fragmented forms.

INDIAN COSMOLOGY IN INDIA AND IN THE CLASSICAL HERITAGE

(i) *Indian Cosmology*

The scattered references to India's river of Paradise in the Judaeo-Christian tradition, in addition to the references to India in the Ethiopic Alexander, raise the possibility that the Christian concept of Paradise was informed not only by the image of Indian ascetics enjoying a paradisal state of enlightenment but also by the descriptions of paradises which pervade Indian mythology. The earliest elaboration in Indian scripture of Paradise—Brahmapura, the city of Brahma, or *svarga-loka*, the heavenly place—such as it is later to be represented atop Mount Meru, appears in the *Chandogya Upanishad*. It is immediately emphasized that the real paradise is the small space within a lotus-flower within Paradise. This space within the lotus-heart, once known, is exclusive of nothing in the micro- or macrocosm: it is immortality itself. Immortality, by this account, is inclusive of mortality, two worlds kept apart by the bridge of the soul until such time as it has been traversed by a *brahmacarin*, or ascetic student of sacred knowledge.[85]

This passage in the *Chandogya Upanishad* is especially pertinent to the iconography of Hinduism and Buddhism. It suggests how the lotus becomes a symbol of spiritual rebirth (or immaterial birth) and why Mount Meru is frequently represented as the calyx of a lotus. The same part of the Upanishad also mentions the lake of paradise, which affords refreshment and ecstasy, the sacred fig-tree, which yields the nectarous *soma*, and the golden, unconquered citadel of the Lord. The context makes it clear that this account of the pilgrimage to Paradise is a chart of abstract spiritual states. This is a development on the old Vedic concept of *svarga* as the home of the gods in the firmament and it suggests a spiritual geography or cosmology which is further developed in the Indian epics, the *puranas* and the *mahatmyas*.

In the account Onesicritus gives of his meeting with the two Brahmin ascetics, Calanus is reported as saying that in olden times when the world was full of barley-meal and wheat-meal there were fountains of water, milk, honey, wine and olive oil. The context of

---

[85] *Chandogya Upanishad*, 8.1.1–6; 8.4.1–3; 8.5.1–4, Hume.

this description is a warning by Calanus that, on account of man's gluttony, luxury and arrogance, all this was destroyed by Zeus and man condemned to a life of toil and that, although the original blessed state was restored when self-control and other virtues were exercised, the world is again in danger of destruction.[86] If we allow that Zeus is a generic name for God and that Onesicritus (or one of the two or more interpreters involved), in relaying this story, substituted the cooking agent of the Greeks for that more likely to be used in India, the passage need not be read (as it commonly has been) as a Cynic interpolation. The words of Calanus are absolutely consistent with Indian tradition.

We have already seen that belief in the periodicity of the universe is as common to the Indian as it is to the Pythagorean tradition, as is the belief that within the present cycle we are living in *Kali Yuga*, or the age which is a total debasement of an original Golden Age of natural simplicity and spiritual harmony—*Satya Yuga*. The earliest Indian reference to the rivers of Paradise is in the *Atharva Veda*, a context which makes clear their origin as libations in a sacrifice designed to obtain *svarga*:

> Full lakes of butter with their banks of honey,
> flowing with wine, and milk and curds and water—
> Abundant with their overflow of sweetness, these
> streams shall reach thee in the world of *Svarga*,
> whole lakes with lotus-blossom shall approach thee.[87]

Earlier still, in the *Rig Veda*, Indians had desired that the *soma* sacrifice would obtain for them immortality in the 'deathless, undecaying world wherein the light of heaven is set, and everlasting lustre shines', where 'waters are young and fresh', where 'lucid worlds are full of light', 'the region of the golden Sun, where food and full delight are found', where 'happiness and transports, where joys and felicities combine, and longing wishes are fulfilled'.[88]

The development of this aspiration into a spiritual geography is especially evident in the epics and in the *puranas*, among which the *Bhagavata Purana* and the *Vishnu Purana* have been best known in the West.[89] While variations abound, the puranic cosmology is basically consistent. The earth was levelled at first and then divided into portions by the eruption of mountains. Seven continents (eight according to the Indian Buddhists), separated by seas of

[86] Strabo, xv.i.64.   [87] Bk. iv, Hymn 34, v.6, *The Hymns of the Atharva-Veda*, trans. R.T.H. Griffith, 2 vols (Benares, 1895–6), i, 177.   [88] *RV*. ix.113.7–11.   [89] S.M. Ali, *The Geography of the Puranas*, 2nd ed. (Delhi, 1973), pp. 15–25.

milk, honey, etc. radiate in concentric circles from a central circular island, Jambudvipa, out of the middle of which rises the sacred mountain Meru—a cosmology also expressed in terms of a lotus and its pericarp. Much exact detail is given, but it is necessary here to mention only that Meru is composed of gold and precious stones and that the paradises of diverse aetherial beings ascend its four sides until the paradises of Vishnu, Brahma and Siva are reached on its peaks. After falling from Heaven, through the circle of the moon, the Ganges—so sacred that even the sound of its name has power to purify sin—divides into four on reaching Meru's summit (the three peaks, like the three gods, tend to coalesce into one) and, forming lakes (of milk, honey, etc.) on four adjacent hills which contain paradisal gardens, assumes diverse names and flows to the points of the compass.

The relationship of this cosmology to the philosophy of the Upanishads is not lost sight of by the Indians. One fable within the *Mahabharata* which makes this abundantly clear is that where the sage Mudgala, offered the reward of Paradise, inquires further about it. He is told of the paradise garden on top of the golden mountain Meru where one's body is determined not by physical birth but by *karma*. But he is also told of other, higher regions where dwell, respectively, the *rishis*, the *ribhus*, the gods of the gods. The limitation of the paradise on Meru (and this view is equally applicable to the paradise on the Buddhist Wheel of Life) is that it is neither eternal nor is there the opportunity there to accumulate the merit which would win for the sage a higher heaven. Mudgala opts to stay on earth and strive for the highest heaven, a region of eternal light, higher than Brahmaloka, the highest paradise on Meru:

Thither none can proceed who are devoted to objects of sense, or who are the slaves of dishonesty, avarice, anger, delusion, or malice; but only the unselfish, the humble, those who are indifferent to pain and pleasure, those whose senses are under restraint, and those who practise contemplation and fix their minds on the deity.

Hearing this,

the sage then dismissed the messenger of the gods, began to practice ascetic virtues, becoming indifferent to praise and blame, regarding clods, stones, and gold as alike. Pure knowledge led to fixed contemplation; and that again imparted strength and complete comprehension, whereby he attained supreme eternal perfection, in the nature of quietude (*nirvana*).[90]

---

[90] *MH*, Sections CCLIX–CCLX of the Ghosha-yatra of the Vana Parva, pp. 768–75. I have here preferred the translation in *Original Sanskrit Texts*, trans. J. Muir, 5 Pts

By this reckoning the ascent of Mount Meru is a popular metaphor for the stages of enlightenment to be realized through *dhyana*, or mystical abstract meditation. According to Buddhist cosmology—and Hiuen-Tsiang, about to be put to death by religious *thugs* on the Ganges, actually records having such an experience[91]—the adept in *dhyana* ascends far above the sensual paradises of the gods on Mount Meru to the heavens of True-Form, if not, ultimately, to the heavens of No-Form.[92]

Indian cosmology is not only to be identified with metaphysical states of consciousness; it may also be identified with the physical geography of north-west India. The cosmology developed as the so-called Aryan invaders moved eastwards from the Indus to the Ganges (both names meaning simply *the river*). These Vedic peoples shared with their Iranian kinsmen a reverence for a sacred river (or lake), the Sarasvati, situated in the mountains, and since the land adjacent to it was regarded as holy successive Indian rivers to the East probably bore this name until the Ganges assimilated the properties previously associated with it.[93] Referring to the sanctity accorded to the Himalayas in the *Ramayana*, C.A. Sherring, in a book on this region, wrote: 'Mount Meru is described with a wonderful fulness and detail, but there is apparently little doubt that there is a mingling of facts true of the country to the north of Cashmere with facts true of the country north of Kumaon'.[94] The mountains of these ranges alone can claim to contain a central source for four great rivers flowing to diverse points of the compass, just as the lands about the Indus can account, if an account is to be rendered in physical terms, for the earlier Vedic conception of seven sacred rivers.

It is not, however, because the Hindus can lay claim to the highest mountains in the world (a physical fact only established as late as the nineteenth century)[95] or to the existence of four great rivers issuing from them that peoples to the West have been drawn outside the topographical confines of their own cultures to locate Paradise in the mountains beyond India. That is dependent on the fact that for 3000 years or more in the forests in the foothills of the Himalayas, and along the banks of the rivers leading out of them,

---

(London, 1858–70), v, 326. For a similar picture of the abstracted sage, see *BG*, xiv, 22–5.   [91] Beal, pp. 86–9.   [92] Waddell, pp. 84–6, 110–22.   [93] Zénaide A. Ragozin, *Vedic India*, 2nd ed. (London, 1899), pp. 106–9, 265–9.   [94] Charles A. Sherring, *Western Tibet and the British Borderland* (London, 1906), p. 40; Ali, pp. 47–59.   [95] As late as his article 'On the Sources of the Ganges', written a decade into the nineteenth century, Colebrooke still cannot say whether or not the Himalaya is higher than the Andes (*AR*, xi, 445).

Indian ascetics such as Alexander encountered have sought to realize a state of mystical enlightenment for which the image of Mount Meru and its sacred river is a metaphor so perfectly congenial with the environment as to be quite literally true. This close identity of physical geography, mystical philosophy and graphic mythology may demonstrate how successfully Indian culture has realized the proposition that to the properly refined consciousness the physical is indistinguishable from the metaphysical.

It was not until recently that Western scholarship, in its apprehension of India, differentiated this identity into component parts. A discourse by Dion Chrysostom, the contemporary of Apollonius of Tyana, includes a typical example of how the Hellenistic world could absorb from India India's own perception of itself in what we would now categorize as literary terms. Dion evokes the image from Indian mythology of India as a paradise, its rivers flowing with wine, honey and oil. These rivers like the lakes in the pertinent passage on Paradise in the *Atharva Veda*, abound with lotuses. The meadows are full of flowers, the birds more melodious than musical instruments, the wind gentle, the temperature equable, the sky clear and the people ignorant of both old age and disease. But, says Dion, the Brahmins—whose behaviour here resembles that of Sage Mudgala—actually turn away from this idyllic life to lead a life of philosophic contemplation, subjecting their bodies to the most severe hardships. These men possess the most remarkable fountain of all—that of Truth—from which none who has drunk can ever be satiated.[96]

(ii) *The Classical Heritage and the Holy Mountain of India*

Before Alexander's invasion, the Greeks do not appear to have had much reliable information about India. It is possible, however, that some fragments of Indian mythology (though not presented as such) were transmitted by way of the *Indika* of Ktesias. The *Indika*, preserved in the paraphrase of Photius and in countless references in Classical and medieval writings, is the oldest extensive record to shape the Western view of India. A physician at the Persian royal court at the end of the fifth century BC, Ktesias is familiar with the Indians, whom he describes as just, devoted to their king, and, in a phrase which will recur, contemptuous of death. It is Ktesias who first refers to the wonderful fountain from which Dion says the Brahmins drink and from which 'Palladius' also reports that Dandamis drank. It seems likely that Ktesias had some

[96] *Oration*, xxxv.18–22.

knowledge of Indian legend.[97] Mount Meru is mentioned as early as the *Tattiriya Aranyaka*[98] and is described in the *Mahabharata*,[99] and it may be that the mountains of gold Ktesias had heard about are Meru and its adjacent ranges. Ktesias does seem to be acquainted with the *henotiktontes*, or once-bearing people (literally the Sanskrit: *ekagarbha*), who, according to the *Bhagavata Purana*, inhabit the eight *varsas* or terrestrial heavens. He also seems to be acquainted with the Uttarakurus, a people (perhaps an atavistic memory for the Aryans) who live free of pain and sorrow in a land of perpetual spring on the north side of Meru. From the latter—who appear in their own form as *Attacorae* in Pliny and as *Ottorokorrhai* in Ptolemy—it has been argued the Greeks derived their concept of the Hyperboreans.[100]

The image of Mount Meru was certainly prevalent in Indian mythology by the time Alexander reached India: there is a clear reference to it in the story the Greeks retailed of Dionysus retreating to a place in the mountains above India called *Meros* where fresh breezes and cooling fountains healed the sickness of his soldiers.[101] Polyaenus, retelling the story, actually refers to the mountain, as the Hindus (on account of their three great gods) sometimes do, as three-peaked. But the explanation that the name *Meros* was bestowed on it by Dionysus in memory of his birth from his father's thigh (*meros*) is less likely than that the name of the mountain sacred to an Indian god—probably Siva, with whom Alexander's men identified Dionysus—gave rise to the association with the story of the thigh.[102] Diodorus Siculus goes further and suggests that the story of the thigh, through linguistic confusion, is actually derived (as it could well be) from the name of the Indian sacred mountain. It is Diodorus, too, who reports the view of mythographers that the most ancient Dionysus was in fact born in India.[103] The idea that the Bacchic rites in their Orphic form were common to India has persisted into our own time. Whilst unproven historically this might account, if true, for the perennial

[97] McCrindle (Ktesias), Introduction, pp. 1–6; § 14, pp. 17–18. For fountains, see also ibid., § 4, pp. 8–9; § 30, p. 31. Herodotus does not show much coherent knowledge of India but he had heard of Indian ascetics who refused to take life and lived on herbs (III.100).   [99] *The Taittiriya Aranyaka*, ed. Rajendralala Mitra (Calcutta, 1872), Introduction, pp. 14–15, Bk. I, Section 7, Mantra 8 *et seq.*, pp. 43ff.   [99] *MH*, Section XVII in the Astika of the Adi Parva, p. 78.   [100] McCrindle (Ktesias), § 31, pp. 31–2 and Lassen's review, pp. 82–4 and n. 47; *Naturalis Historia*, VI.xx.55; *Geography*, Bk. VI, chap. 16, §§ 2, 5, 8, McCrindle (Ptolemy), pp. 298–300, 305; *Ancient India as described by Megasthenes and Arrian*, trans. J.W. McCrindle (London, 1877), p. 77n.   [101] Diodorus, II.38.3–4.   [102] *VP*, II, II, II, p. 110n; Fragment LVII, McCrindle (Megasthenes), pp. 111n; 157.   [103] Diodorus, III.63.3–5.

fascination with the mirror image (given a poetic form by Nonnus which Coleridge also wanted to give it) of an invasion of India by Bacchus.[104] Orosius fostered the idea of India as a place of original innocence by asserting that it was quiet and content until polluted by Bacchus.[105] The obverse view, that Dionysus was an Orphic figure original to India, appearing as a god made visible to civilize mankind and make people gentle (*hemeros*) by the vine (*hemeris*) he planted, was held by the neo-Platonist Emperor Julian.[106]

Ktesias is only the first of a long line of writers, including Isidore, Solinus and Pliny, whose Indian material was incorporated into the maps of medieval Europe which were committed neither, like Eratosthenes and Ptolemy, to depicting only a physical geography nor, like the Hindus and Buddhists, to representing only a spiritual cosmology. On the medieval maps there are some curious coincidences with Indian mythology. For example, the discrepancy whereby in medieval times Paradise is variously located in India itself, on the mountains beyond India, to the north of the mountains or beyond the ultimate Ocean, coincides with similar variations within the Indian tradition itself. The Osma Beatus map, for example, depicts four rivers flowing from a central circle in a Paradise which dominates the East. The Hereford map shows Paradise surrounded not by the flames of *Genesis* but situated on a circular island at the edge of India.[107] This is agreeable to the puranic concept of the paradisal regions of Meru dominating the central island of Jambudvipa, or India. Martianus Capella prefers to locate Paradise farther north among the Hyperboreans and if it is true that the Hyperboreans are the Uttarakurus Hellenized (Pliny notices the perfect identity) this is a direct representation of the Hindu belief that, as their name indicates, the Uttarakurus live their idyllic life somewhere to the north of the mountains.[108] The Jerome map, following Ptolemy, actually locates the Uttarakurus in the Hindu Kush—but converts them, as perhaps the story of the Sarasvati once had, into a river.[109]

Other medieval accounts place Paradise not in India itself but farther east beyond the Ocean, that is at the top of most medieval maps. Not only does a Vedic sage such as Yajnavalkya do much

---

[104]*Eastern Religions and Western Thought*, pp. 135–43; Gladys M.N. Davis, *Asiatic Dionysos* (London, 1914), *passim*; *Dionysiaca*, trans. W.H.D. Rouse, 3 vols (London, 1962–3); *Specimens of the Table Talk of Samuel Taylor Coleridge*, 2nd ed. (London, 1836), p. 274.   [105] *Against the Pagans*, I.9.   [106] *Oration*, VII, 221 A–C.   [107] Konrad Miller, ed., *Mappaemundi*, 6 vols (Stuttgart, 1895–8), II, Table 3b; IV, map attached to back cover.   [108] Kirtland Wright, p. 71; see this chapter, p. 172 and n. 100.   [109] *Mappaemundi*, II, Table 11.

the same thing[110] but it was the practice of Hindu astronomers, making a compromise with Hindu cosmology, to shift Mount Meru out from the centre of their charts to the circumference at the top, directly under the north pole. It has even been suggested that as a result of this displacement of Meru as a world centre by Ujjain and the consequent representation of a prime meridian by a cupola, Columbus could have been inspired, by way of a medieval map which depicted the concept the Arabs had derived from the Hindus, to seek India by a westward route.[111] This would not be more curious than the way medieval Europe absorbed Hindu influences by means of an Arabic treatise ascribed to Aristotle.[112]

Col. Yule, who more than anyone has charted the medieval imagination on its Eastern marches, observes: 'It may be said with general truth that the world-maps current up to the end of the 13th century had more analogy to the mythical cosmology of the Hindus than anything purely geographical'.[113] Arguably, it could be more than a case of analogy. Many of the illustrations on medieval maps have been traced, especially by way of the Romances of Alexander, to sources in the Indian epics. To account satisfactorily for the location of Paradise in India it may be necessary to seek out similar sources. A solution to this problem would apparently demand as extensive a knowledge as John Donne conceives of as being sought by Mr S.B.:

> O thou which to search out the secret parts
> Of the India, or rather paradise
> Of knowledge, hast with courage and advise
> Lately launched into the vast Sea of Arts . . .[114]

India and Paradise are interchangeable images for a search for knowledge best represented, perhaps, in terms not of history but of imaginative literature.

SPIRITUAL CONQUERORS OF INDIA IN MEDIEVAL LEGEND AND IN PERSIAN LITERATURE

(i) *Medieval Legend and the Loss of Paradise*

Medieval Christianity had the authority of the Church Fathers for expressing admiration for the Indian ascetics and this, together

---

[110] *BA*, 3.4.2.   [111] C. Raymond Beazley, *The Dawn of Modern Geography*, 3 vols (London, 1897–1906), I, 405. Beazley follows al-Biruni for his ideas concerning an Indian origin for *Arim* (ibid., I, 339, 395, 488).   [112] Kirtland Wright, p. 82.   [113] Yule, Introduction, p. 132.   [114] *Poetical Works*, ed. Herbert J.C. Grierson (Oxford, 1971), p. 186.

with information derived from the 'pagan' encyclopaedists, ensured that India would have a special place in the medieval mind. A writer such as Mandeville is content to say that the Brahmins on their island live a truly Christian life[115]—but many Christians were not so comfortable with this idyllic image. The Ethiopic Romances have illustrated how some Christians got over the problem of Hindus who out-Christian the Christians. One expedient was to identify them with the sons of Seth, who had retained a knowledge of the pristine life in Eden. In medieval Europe the friar Marignolli, who had direct experience of Buddhist monks in Sri Lanka living in Adamite simplicity (as he supposed within forty Italian miles of Paradise), speaks of both Brahmins and Buddhists as following the discipline of Enoch, son of Seth.[116] Another expedient, evident in the story of Gerasimas, is to retain the description of the way of life of the Indians but to conceal the name of their homeland and their religion. A third possibility is to retain the name of India but only so that India's role in the story can be reversed and India made to appear the recipient of something original to its own culture. This happens most obviously in the story of Barlaam and Josaphat where Christians in effect convert Buddha, and thereby India, to Christianity by means of teaching original to Buddha. In this instance the passage to India is manifestly a cryptic acknowledgement of a passage *from* India. The Persian Romances of Alexander provide examples of this happening, as we shall see shortly. It may be that this happens also in two other stories given much prominence in the Middle Ages: those of St Thomas and Prester John.

The story of St Thomas has him convert the Indian king, Gundafor or Gondophares (whose historicity in the first century AD numismatics has established), by constructing for him a heavenly palace through bestowing on the poor the money the king had given him to build an earthly palace. The story, recorded in the apocryphal *Acts of St Thomas*, a Syriac work of the third or fourth century AD, is part of a polemic in favour of the celibate life which at least one historian of Christianity in India has found more congenial to Indian religion than to Christianity.[117] Be that as it may, the story of St Thomas shares with *Barlaam and Josaphat*, for which a Buddhist origin is beyond doubt, a plot where India is con-

---

[115] *Mandeville's Travels*, ed. Malcolm Letts, 2 vols (London, 1953), I, xxxii, 204–6.   [116] Yule (Cathay), III, 234–5. Yule suspects that Marignolli is being familiarized with Buddhist cosmology via a Muslim interpreter.   [117] The first two Acts of Judas Thomas, W. Wright, II, 146–69 (see this chapter, p. 162, n. 65); J.N. Ogilvie, *The Apostles of India* (London, 1915), pp. 26–8. Robert Sencourt suggests that the phrases the seventeenth century antiquarian John Marshall put into the

verted by means of its king, who learns from an ascetic saint the worthlessness of having an earthly palace. V. Slessarev has suggested the likelihood of a common source for the legends of St Thomas and Prester John. Basic to this suggestion is the fact that the story of Prester John, otherwise largely compounded of material from the Alexander Romances, incorporates the heavenly palace St Thomas built for the Indian king, Gundafor.[118] The idea is the more interesting in the light of the Ethiopic Christian Romance of Alexander where, as we have seen, Alexander, like the Indian ruler in the *Acts of St Thomas*, rejects his earthly palace in favour of the heaven to be won by a pure and ascetic life.

A most important medieval image of India is to be found in the story of Prester John. There are diverse versions of the letter of Prester John, ostensibly sent to the Emperor Manuel in the twelfth century, but the chief features are recurrent. Prester John is king of the three Indias, a land flowing with milk and honey. The geography is generally agreeable to that of the *puranas*. Through John's dominions flows the river Ydonis, a river most obviously identified with the Indus, though more perceptively with the Ganges. Like the Ganges of Indian cosmology, this river encircles Paradise before issuing into the plains, through which it then winds. In one version there is report of a Mount Olympus and a fountain at its foot which rejuvenates all who drink of it—for which Mount Meru with the terrestrial spring of the Jambu, or Ganges, river at its foot provides an exact equivalent native to India. Another version, congenial with the Buddhist account, makes the four rivers of Paradise flow from this spring.[119] These are ingredients which, if they are of Indian provenance, could have filtered into the Western imagination at any time after Ktesias.

The description of Prester John's India as an ideal state is attributed by Slessarev to the view of India provided by the correspondence of Dindimus and Alexander. Several further details sup-

---

mouth of a Brahmin by way of introduction to the *Bhagavata Purana* were 'an echo of St Thomas' (*India in English Literature*, London, 1925, pp. 168–9). This could be another example of the way a debt to India may be expressed as the converse.   [118] 'Two Eastern Legends', Slessarev, pp. 9–31.   [119] Ibid., pp. 32–54; Sir E. Denison Ross, 'Prester John and the Empire of Ethiopia', *Travellers in the Middle Ages*, ed. Arthur Percival Newton (1926; reissued London 1968), pp. 174–8; Kirtland Wright, pp. 265, 273; Baring-Gould, pp. 38, 42. Baring-Gould notes that St Basil and St Ambrose have been cited in support of the assertion that Paradise was situated on top of a mountain higher than Ararat, from which four rivers fall in cascade to a lake at its foot (p. 234). Some acquaintance with the cosmology of Meru is at least possible.

port this view. The wives of Prester John—who prefers to be considered a priest rather than a king—can approach him, as 'Palladius' reported their wives could approach the Brahmins, only on specified occasions during the year. In one telling, the wine served in Prester John's palace deprives any who drink of it of the desire for worldly things.[120] Here the palace, likewise without windows and doors (allegorically, of the senses), resembles the walled city of the Ganges from which Alexander, with the mystic stone in his hand, was turned back on his way to Paradise. The palace, which has walls of crystal, like the heavenly palace of Gundafor, might conceivably find its original in the inaccessible crystal dome through which, in one legend, Buddha, who had rejected his earthly palace, ascended into heaven.[121]

Slessarev has traced the Prester John story to two distinct sources: the life of a Buddhist ruler in Central Asia and the legend of St Thomas in India. The only conceivable common prototype for these disparate sources is the legendary life of Lord Buddha.[122] While such origins remain obscure, it is still possible to assert that Prester John, in the celestial palace of St Thomas, is yet another image for an ultimate ideal state, fabled in the West but central to Indian culture. As such he has something in common with the figure of Dandamis, to whom he is at least partly indebted for his existence. Olschki has read the letter of Prester John as a piece of utopian literature.[123] This view, like that which assumes Dandamis to be a Cynic or a Christian creation, fails to consider whether the vision projected on to India has features so recognizably Indian that it could have originated there.

The search for Prester John, combined as this was with the search for the terrestrial Paradise, led the Europeans eventually to conquer the world in a much more far-reaching way than Alexander had been able to do. India remained central to this conquest and no imperial possession played about the imagination so much as India. The world the Europeans conquered, however, was a physical one, the geography of which was to be accurately mapped and the history of which was to be carefully compiled. It is true that the old cosmology died hard. In 1807 Thomas Legge walked into the tent of James Tod outside Jaipur and claimed to have found the Garden of Eden in a cave in the Hindu Kush. Significantly, in view of all that we have said, Legge followed up this announcement by adopting the life of a naked Indian ascetic.[124] At

---

[120] Slessarev, p. 78.   [121] Jahn, p. xlviii.   [122] Best known in Europe have been the *Buddha-Carita* of Asvaghosa and the *Lalita-Vistara*.   [123] Cited in Slessarev, p. 39.   [124] James Tod, 'Sketches of Remarkable Characters in India', *The Asiatic*

the same time, European explorers were still using the cosmography of the *puranas* in their search to find in Lake Manasa the terrestrial source of the sacred Ganges.[125] They ended by discrediting the *puranas*. Lord Macaulay, in his 'Minute on Education' of 1835, expressed the prevalent European mood of his time when he said it was no longer possible to countenance 'History, abounding with kings thirty feet high, and reigns thirty thousand years long,—and Geography, made up of seas of treacle and seas of butter'.[126] Sacred geography was no longer acceptable to the European mind and, it may be argued, the price the West paid for its conquest of the world was precisely that indicated so long before by Dandamis in his reply to Alexander—the loss of Paradise itself.

(ii) *The Persian Alexander*

There remains the Persian Alexander. Persia's association with India is more intimate than Ethiopia's. The early Vedic hymns are the common property of an Indo-Iranian people before their split. Zoroaster, living in the mountains of Eastern Persia, according to the myth put about both by the Platonist Ammianus Marcellinus and by Parsee tradition, made contact with the Brahmins.[127] Mahayana Buddhism, itself not free of Zoroastrian influence, penetrated Eastern Persia.[128] Mani probably absorbed Indian thought in Persia as well as in India.[129] Plotinus nearly lost his life trying to do the same. As late as the Sassanids, the Persian rulers were still sending to India to learn its secrets, as perhaps they were already doing when the Greek doctor Ktesias acquired his knowledge of Indian lore while at the Persian court.[130] Moreover, since Persia is (culturally) India's western neighbour, it is perhaps not surprising that the imaginative approach to India made by the English has frequently been by way of the poetry of Persia. For this reason it is interesting to see how, in its treatment of the story of Alexander and the Brahmins, the Persian Alexander provides

---

Journal, N.S., XVI (Jan.–April, 1835), 268–70. Tod suggests this may reflect an acquaintance with Hindu cosmology and on the legend of the Cave of Prometheus. See chapter 7, pp. 231–2.   [125] Instruction 2, Capt. F.V. Raper 'Survey of the Ganges', *AR*, XI, 447; H.T. Colebrooke in ibid., XI, 438–40.   [126] Minute of 2 Feb. 1835, *Macaulay's Minutes on Education in India*, coll. H. Woodrow (Calcutta, 1862), p. 109.   [127] See chapter 3, p. 106; *Dabistan*, I, 276–7, 280–3.   [128] Ernst Herzfeld, *Zoroaster and his World*, 2 vols (Princeton, 1947), II, 754–6; Sachau, I, 21.   [129] Jairazbhoy, p. 88; Lang, pp. 24–5.   [130] 'A Fable from the *Anwar e Soheily*', trans. William Chambers, *AM*, I, 343–51; *The Heetopades* (Wilkins), Preface, pp. vii–xiv.

examples both of the image of India being obscured altogether and of its significance being turned inside out so that a debt to India is concealed.

The Alexander legend is made the subject of poems by, among others, poets as central to the Persian tradition as Firdausi, Nizami, Jami and Ashraf. The attitude Dandamis adopted towards Alexander reflects on an Indian social ideal which, no doubt because it is an ideal shared by Plato, the early Greek commentators frequently notice: namely, that in India kings subordinate themselves to the philosophers. Alexander's refusal to take umbrage at the attitude of Dandamis, along with his education under Aristotle and his broad vision of a multi-racial empire, encouraged the idea that he was himself as much philosopher as king.[131] Conversely, Dandamis, having shown himself more than a match for Alexander, becomes in the eyes of the Persian poets, no less than in Abelard's, a king. In Firdausi's *Shah-Nama* Dandamis becomes the pacifist Indian king, Kaid, who refuses to fight Alexander and instead sends Alexander a sage, Mihran, who by way of an interchange of riddling-symbols (incidentally, engaged in earlier by the Chinese Buddhist Hiuen-Tsiang) indicates that his values, too, are precisely those of Dandamis. Firdausi is so impressed by the Indian philosopher that he actually takes his Alexander back to India a second time to meet the sages, this time in a version closely based on the *Pseudo-Callisthenes*.[132]

Nizami is overtly more attracted to Alexander and the Indians are of little consequence in the Romance where he depicts Alexander as a world-conqueror. However, having written one *Alexandriad*, Nizami composed another, spiritual in tone rather than conventionally heroic, in which Alexander is portrayed as a prophet and philosopher. This second book, especially concerned with philosophy and its practitioners, is unlike anything else in the Romance tradition except in the (by now) familiar tendency to transform an Indian original. Socrates, as Brahminical as the Brahmins who confront him in the Aristoxenus story, is described as an Oriental hermit living a life of contemplation and abstemiousness in the wilderness. When Alexander sends messengers commanding his presence, Socrates refuses to move. Thereupon Alexander goes to see him and, for his pains, is told that he is a slave of passion while Socrates is its master. Furthermore, Socrates

---

[131] e.g. Plutarch, 'De Alexandri Magni Fortuna aut Virtute', I, § 5, *Moralia*, 329 D–F.   [132] 'Sikandar', VI, 60–190, Firdausi, *The Shahnama*, trans, Arthur George Warner and Edmond Warner, 9 vols (London, 1905–25). See esp. VI, 61–3, 67–8, 91–110 (Firdausi C 1290–C 1304), 143–7 (Firdausi C 1327–C 1330).

refuses the offer of a boon, saying he has no wants.[133] While the English explicator of this text supposes the story to be derived from that where Alexander confronts Diogenes and is asked to move out of the sun, it has far more in common—even if we were to ignore the Islamic generalization of Indian into Oriental—with the story of Alexander's confrontation with Dandamis.[134]

Nor is this all. Instructed by Socrates, as well as by his encounter with him, Alexander is approached by an Indian, a sun-worshipper and evidently a Brahmin, who asks him a number of questions about the nature of God and the universe. This is a direct reversal of the tradition, common not only to Plutarch and the Romances but also to the *Shah-Nama* of Firdausi (a work constantly in Nizami's mind as he wrote), where it is Alexander who questions a group of Brahmin philosophers.[135] In Firdausi's version these Brahmins, like those in the *Pseudo-Callisthenes*, have all the characteristics of Dandamis, living a simple, pacifist, abstemious life and asking Alexander why, if he cannot close the door of death, he bothers to conquer the world. In Nizami's second *Alexandriad*, on the other hand, if Alexander is to adopt the spiritual vocation the Brahmins indicated he lacked, it is a literary device, as logical as it is simple, to reverse the roles. The need to reckon with, conceal and absorb the existence of the Hindu Brahmins is as great for an Islamic Persian as it is for a Christian Ethiopic account of Alexander. The subsequent transposition illustrates once again how a story ostensibly about Indian indebtedness may conceal a debt to India.

Eventually, after travelling to the other quarters of the world, Nizami's spiritual Alexander comes to a place in the north which is considered as Paradise less on account of its natural beauties than on account of the virtuous life of its people, who are peaceful, honest and content. Alexander says that seeing the life of this community he has no further desire to conquer the world, and that had he met these people before he would never have undertaken his journey and instead would have become a religious hermit. The way of life in this paradise is that attributed by the Greeks to the Brahmins and by the Brahmins, in their mythology, to a people of the north—the Uttarakurus. Having met these people Alexander is left, as he is left in Plutarch's *Life of Alexander* after meeting

---

[133] Nizami, *The Sikandar Nama*, trans. H. Wilberforce Clarke (London, 1881), cantos XLV–XLVI, pp. 562–83; Wilhelm Bacher, *Memoir of the Life and Writings of the Persian Poet Nizami*, trans. Samuel Robinson (London, 1873), pp. 89–171 (see esp. pp. 116–22). [134] For earliest commentary on *both* stories, see Arrian, *Anabasis*, VII.ii; Plutarch, *Moralia*, 331F, 332B. [135] For variations, see Wallis Budge, p. 131, n. 2. Clement lists the questions (*Stromata*, VI.vi). So does Plutarch in his *Life of Alexander* (chap. LXIV).

Dandamis and Calanus, with nothing to do but turn for home, Babylon and death.

By the end of Nizami's second book, Alexander, who set out to convert the world to Islam, has rejected the role of orthodox missionary warrior for that of *sufi* mystic. That a Brahmin analogue should underwrite his conversion to sufism is not incongruous: R.C. Zaehner suggests sufism only withstood the orthodox monotheism of Islam on account of the proximity and influence of the Indian Vedanta.[136] If this is true—and, like all arguments in favour of Indian mystical influence, it is necessarily bitterly contested—it is worth considering the idea that, in accordance with the zone maps which India adopted and adapted to its own cosmography, there is a geography of mysticism whereby the importance accorded to it diminishes the farther the concentric circles radiate from their centre at Mount Meru in the continent of India. This chart is applicable in the Far East, where a mystical brand of Buddhism spread to Tibet, China and Japan. Something of the same Indian influence was felt in South East Asia and Indonesia. A similar diminishing field of force exists to the West. Just as it was the more Eastern forms of Christianity which were readier to adapt to neo-Platonist and other mystical ideas, so too did Islamic orthodoxy have to accommodate itself more to mysticism the closer it was to India; so much so that in India itself, especially in the time of Akbar and of Dara Shikoh, Islam was actually threatened with absorption into a mystical Hindu ethos.[137]

One further image, already familiar to us, will illustrate this Persian propensity for mysticism. In both of Nizami's *Alexandriads*, Alexander is accompanied on his journey to the East by Apollonius of Tyana, whose miraculous powers are generally acknowledged in the Islamic tradition and to whom many works in Arabic are ascribed.[138] In Nizami's first *Alexandriad* Aristotle recommends Apollonius as the man with the magic necessary to remove any obstacles which stand in Alexander's way, and it is he who is sent to the Indian king. In Ashraf's version of the Alexander Romance it is the magic of Apollonius in Sri Lanka that enables Alexander to scale the mountain peak which Islam, in transposing a Buddhist legend original to India, denominated the spot where Adam had alighted after his fall from Paradise. That the

---

[136] Zaehner (1960), pp. 86–109.   [137] See chapter 2, pp. 53–4 and n. 67.   [138] 'Apollonius of Tyana in the Alexander-Saga', Bacher, pp. 97–101; William Ouseley, *Travels in Various Countries of the East*, 3 vols (London, 1819–23), I, 54–63. Ouseley notes that it was Selden who first identified Balinas as Apollonius.

magic of Apollonius has a spiritual dimension is indicated in Niza-mi's work, as it was in his letter to Valerius, when, at the time of his death, he speaks of his mastery over Nature and of his convic-tion that his real being is the soul which will be liberated.

The earliest literary acknowledgement in the Islamic tradition of the spiritual powers of Apollonius comes in the *Mujmal-al-Tawarikh*, where he is said to have set in the Pharos at Alexandria a magic mirror which reflected all that happened in the world.[139] It is equally a recognition of his stature that he should be associated with Alexander the Great, an association which is anachronistic, of course, but which for that very reason demonstrates how history may be transformed in the literary imagination, and, freed from the lineality of chronology, become mythopoeic. Not that historic-al details cannot provide some piquant ironies. In the same cen-tury when Nizami in Persia associated Apollonius with Alexander, John of Salisbury in Europe compared Alexander with Pythagoras.[140] Only one image, however ambiguously, has ever emerged in literature to indicate what Apollonius, Alexander and Pythagoras had in common: all three are said to have made the passage to India.

[139] *Mujmal-al-Tawarikh-wa-al-Qisas: written about 520. A.H.*, ed. Muhammad Taqi Bahar (Tehran, 1318 Shamsi era), p. 489. See also *The Itinerary of Benjamin of Tudela*, trans. Marcus Nathan Adler (London, 1907), p. 75.   [140] *Policraticus* v. 12, *Ioannis Saresberiensis Episcopi Carnotensis Policratici*, ed. Clemens C.I. Webb, 2 vols (Oxford, 1909), I, 335. Elsewhere John takes a 'Gandhian' view of the relationship between Alexander and the Brahmins (ibid., IV.11, Webb, I, 270–1). He also tells the story of Anaxarchus telling Alexander that there is no end to the conquest of worlds (ibid., VIII.5, Webb, II, 247). Anaxarchus accompanied Alexander on his expedition to India and, according to Diogenes Laertius, something of Pyrrho's Scepticism was fostered by hearing an Indian tell Anaxarchus that he was in no position to philosophize on goodness while he danced attendance on kings (IX.61–3). Is it another example of European inversion when Max Müller refers to one Buddhist philosophical position as 'extreme Pyrrhonism'? Once again, the antiquity of both Greek and Indian traditions probably precludes a conclusive answer.

CHAPTER SIX

Coleridge: 'Kubla Khan' and the Rise of Tantric Buddhism

in which the poem is read in terms first
of the new Orientalism inspired by Jones
and then of the Tantric imagery with
which Kublai Khan was familiar.

What are
These Potentates of inmost Ind?

S.T. Coleridge.

Were Hindu literature better known to us, it is possible that we should find that we have borrowed from it the romantic style of our days, which some find so beautiful and others so silly.

Abbe Dubois, *Hindu Manners, Customs and Ceremonies*.

CHAPTER SIX

Coleridge: 'Kubla Khan' and the Rise of Tantric Buddhism

COLERIDGE AND INDIA

In an issue of *The Friend*, Coleridge takes up a complaint made by Schelling in 1815 that 'now we hear of nothing but the language and wisdom of India'.[1] The complaint is typical of a general reaction which set in after an initially enthusiastic response to the earliest translations of Indian texts.[2] In the 'Opus Maximum', Coleridge recalls how he had originally regarded classical Sanskrit texts on philosophy and religion with an almost superstitious awe but adds that later he confronted himself with the sceptical question:

> What are
> These Potentates of inmost Ind?

Upon reflection, he thought that the rarity and difficulty of their achievement had erroneously if understandably led Jones and Wilkins—and thereby himself—to treat as awesome Indian works thought to be so ancient they were regarded as antiquity itself.[3]

Whatever Coleridge's change of attitude, the image of India's sacred books as 'Potentates of inmost Ind' is not only vivid but peculiarly appropriate. India and that part of the Orient which came under its influence has known many kings and emperors who sought not merely temporal power but also that spiritual power which is the subject of these old Sanskrit texts. There are a considerable number of references to India scattered through Col-

---

[1] *The Friend*, ed. H.N. Coleridge, 4th ed., 3 vols (London, 1850), II, 245. Schelling had originally been responsive to the classical culture of India as Jones had evoked it.   [2] See chapter 2, n. 192.   [3] Muirhead, pp. 283–4.

eridge's work, and two things may be said about them. First, Coleridge is usually at some pains to disparage or dismantle an idealized view of India, invariably in the context of an apologia for Christianity and increasingly to the accompaniment of a dismissive attitude towards neo-Platonism. Second, the references often include imaginative images highly evocative of India. I mention this because the fierceness with which Coleridge later attacks Indian culture and the vividness of the metaphors he uses indicate as surely as do more favourable references that there had once been a time when, as he himself says, he had been excited to awe and 'paid this debt of homage' to the very thought of these sacred Indian texts.[4]

It is not that, as time went on, Coleridge asked a different sort of question, such as that concerning the potentates of inmost Ind. It is that the state of mind or consciousness in which he asked it was increasingly sceptical rather than speculative. The tone had changed. In spite of this change, Coleridge's intellectual approach to India remained the traditional Platonist one revived by the Orientalists in the 1790s. In the Philosophical Lectures of 1818–19, Coleridge not only considers and accepts the story that Pythagoras had been to India;[5] he also shows he is familiar with the other two Classical passages to India which brought the Greeks into contact with Indian philosophy—those of Apollonius of Tyana and Alexander the Great. Of Apollonius, Coleridge has an unusual awareness in that he attributes to him not so much miraculous powers as a great morality.[6] Even more interestingly, as the measure for a judgement on Socrates Coleridge uses Calanus, the Indian gymnosophist who confronted Alexander with an alternative and simple way of life evocative of the Golden Age.[7] A further re-

---

[4] Coleridge objects that *avatars*, metamorphoses and incarnations are incompatible with 'the doctrines of omneity and infinity, which are the constant theme and the philosophic import of the Indian theology'.   [5] See chapter 4, pp. 121, 124–6 and nn. 12, 20–1, 23–5.   [6] See chapter 3, p. 86 and n. 10. Apollonius lends a fictional colour to the rather abstract mystical philosophy of Plotinus and in the 1790s William Enfield (*The History of Philosophy*, 2 vols, London, 1791, II, 66) supposed that the interest of Plotinus in India had been fostered by the visit of Apollonius. Enfield also noticed that the association between the two men is the greater because Apollonius appeared to subscribe to a similar non-dualist philosophy (ibid., II, 49). Coleridge took the first volume of Enfield out of the Bristol Library and, like Southey, may have read both volumes before taking out Brucker's German original.   [7] *PL*, IV, 154. Cf. Purchas, v.v.479. See also chapter 5, pp. 147–9, 167–80. It is also likely to be Calanus whom Coleridge has in mind when he pairs the gymnosophist with the naked savage as an example of extremes meeting (*CNB*, I, 1725). This conception of Alexander being confronted by an idyllic India was the subject of *Alexander's Expedition* (London, 1792), a poem by Thomas Beddoes, whose biography Coleridge said he would like to have written

ference in the Philosophical Lectures, which almost certainly reveals an acquaintance with Porphyry's eulogy on the Indians, quite categorically states that the philosophical practices of the neo-Platonists are perfectly like those of the Brahmins.[8] In a later lecture Coleridge associates the pantheism of India with that of Spinoza,[9] and it really does show how immersed he could be in Indian thought that, in the marginalia to the book on the Hindus by the Abbé Dubois, he not only compares the Advaita to the Eleatic school but actually writes of Spinoza as 'the sternest and most consistent of Adwitamists' (i.e. *Advaitins*).[10] Already Thomas Maurice, whom Coleridge had read, had referred to Plato as 'the Vyasa of Greece'.[11] It says something about the regard in which India was held at this time that Coleridge, like Maurice, was prepared to conceive of a leading European idealist philosopher in terms of Indian tradition.

It would be foolish to ignore how severely Coleridge eventually rejected the conception of India as some sort of source of ultimate wisdom. What is interesting is that this *is* the conception with which he is struggling. The Philosophical Lectures are a great Christian polemic and in them even neo-Platonism has to be interred. Yet Coleridge never does finally lay to rest his view of Indian thought as purely pantheistic. In *Aids to Reflection*—a book in which he suggests that because the Indians put exertion into penances rather than into reflection they should be considered 'highly civilized, though fearfully uncultivated'—he qualifies his earlier (rather partial) reading of the *Gita* when he concedes that in 'the most ancient Books of the Brahmins' the deep sense of Original Sin and doctrines grounded on obscure traditions of 'the promised Remedy, are seen struggling, and now gleaming, and now flashing, through the Mist of Pantheism'.[12] In the *Biographia Literaria*, India is named as one of four countries where Coleridge believes 'the analysis of the mind had reached its noon and manhood while experimental research was still in its dawn and infancy'.[13] Passing as these references are and made as they are at a time when Coleridge is a committed apologist for Christianity,

---

(*CLSTC*, Letter 742, III, 171).   [8] Ibid., x, 296. I suspect that the missing reference in this passage is to the *Samanaeans* (Buddhists or Jains) mentioned by Porphyry in conjunction with the Brahmins (see chapter 3, p. 101 and n. 78). Two contemporary reviewers of *BGW* noticed that the Indian conception of a sage was close to that of the Platonists (*MR*, LXXVI, March 1787, 208–10; *BC*, III, Feb. 1794, 154).   [9] See chapter 4, n. 25.   [10] British Library copy of Abbé J.A. Dubois, *Description of the Character, Manners and Customs of the People of India*, trans. unnamed (London, 1817), pp. 323–4.   [11] *IA*, v, 1001.   [12] *Aids to Reflection*, pp. 10–11, 276–7.   [13] *BL*, I, Pt 1, 89.

they are none the less suggestive of an intimate concern with Indian culture and raise the possibility that, in earlier years when (to use Muirhead's distinction) philosophical doctrine was not subordinate to theological dogma,[14] Coleridge may have been more open to (what he later calls) 'the interesting Deformities of ancient Greece and India'.[15]

COLERIDGE AS VISHNU

Many of Coleridge's references to India are made comparatively late in his poetic career and we can do little more than speculate what might have been the effect had his initial awe of classical Indian civilization been combined with an actual experience of those mental and imaginative states advocated by the neo-Platonism which had once attracted him. The earlier period of the 1790s does include at least one important reference to Indian mythology: if Coleridge has not yet portrayed Spinoza as an *Advaitin* he has, even more graphically, depicted himself as the Indian god 'Vishna'. Furthermore, the reference comes in a letter where he is explaining how in certain states of consciousness his whole being can become transfigured.

It is in a letter to Thelwall of 14 October 1797 that the image of the Indian god is used by Coleridge as a metaphor for his own meditative state:

I can at times feel strongly the beauties, you describe, in themselves, and for themselves—but more frequently all things appear little—all the knowledge, that can be acquired, child's play—the universe itself—what but an immense heap of little things?—I can contemplate nothing but parts, and parts are all little— ! —My mind feels as if it ached to behold and know something great—something one and indivisible—and it is only in the faith of this that rocks or waterfalls, mountains or caverns give me the sense of sublimity or majesty! — But in this faith all things counterfeit infinity! . . . It is but seldom that I raise and spiritualize my intellect to this height—and at other times I adopt the Brahman Creed, and say—It is better to sit than to stand, it is better to lie than to sit, it is better to sleep than to wake—but Death is the best of all! —I should much wish, like the Indian Vishna, to float along an infinite ocean cradled in the flower of the Lotos, and wake once in a million years for a few minutes—just to know that I was going to sleep for a million years more.

Coleridge goes on to say that he has put this sensation into the mouth of the 'Moorish Woman' Alhadra in his play *Osorio*:

[14] Muirhead, pp. 114–15. Writing of Coleridge, Shelley refers to 'the better and holier aspirations of his youth' ('Note on the Early Poems', *PWPBS*, p. 528). [15] *The Friend*, No. 1, June 1st, 1809, p. 7.

> O would to Alla,
> The Raven and the Seamew were appointed
> To bring me food—or rather that my Soul
> Could drink in life from the universal air!
> It were a lot divine in some small skiff
> Along some Ocean's boundless solitude
> To float for ever with a careless course,
> And think myself the only Being alive.[16]

The prose passage is remarkable for the way it takes us through several shifts of consciousness. Coleridge begins by suggesting he has an objective sense of beauty. He regrets, however, that this is not always sustained: too often all possible knowledge, and the universe itself, appears fragmented, partial and therefore insignificant. This leads him to aspire towards a coherent vision in which natural scenery appears sublime. In such a state, he says, all things counterfeit infinity. Since he refers to this rare state as one where the intellect is spiritualized we may assume that the word 'counterfeit' is only as minimally ambiguous as the word 'finite' is for Plotinus when he says that the finite beauty of the world indicates the existence of infinite beauty. At this point, however, Coleridge makes reference not to neo-Platonism but to Indian culture. He regrets that by way of contrast to the spiritualized state of intellect he more frequently falls into a state of lassitude where the more supine the posture and the more insensate the consciousness the better. At such times, he says, he has become a Brahmin in his attitude. This is, of course, a travesty of the significance of traditional yogic teaching and it is an extraordinary (and possibly double) irony that Coleridge, having rather idly postulated a Brahmin predilection for a series of living states which successively assimilate themselves to death, slips—just like a *yogi*—into a vision of himself as an archetypal Indian god in the cosmic interval before the recreation of the universe.[17]

Perhaps no single image 'counterfeits infinity' quite so well as that of the Indian god as the One only Being afloat on the cosmic ocean.[18] That Coleridge continues to be attracted to this image as one for a state which is potentially divine rather than dangerous, creative rather than enervating, can be seen when he takes it up again three years later in his play, *The Triumph of Loyalty*:

> Oh! there is Joy above the name of Pleasure,
> Deep self-possession, an intense Repose.

[16] *CLSTC*, Letter 209, I, 349–51. See also ibid., Letter 484, II, 916; *CNB*, I, 191. See *Osorio*, v.i.49–56 and *Remorse*, IV.iii.13–20, respectively in *CPW*, II, 584, 868.   [17] Zimmer, pp. 36–8.   [18] In a note made in 1796 Coleridge follows Cudworth in referring to 'great things that on the ocean counterfeit infinity' (*CNB*, I, 273).

No other than as Eastern Sages feign,
The God, who floats upon a Lotos Leaf,
Dreams for a thousand ages; then awaking,
Creates a world, and smiling at the bubble,
Relapses into bliss . . .

The passage concludes:

Ah was that bliss
Fear'd as an alien, and too vast for man?

When in 1813 Coleridge salvaged a fragment of this play as a dramatic dialogue, 'The Night Scene', this was the passage central to it.[19] By then, however, the intellectual danger of such a speculative state had impressed itself on Coleridge. He was also becoming increasingly sceptical of the beneficence both of mysticism and the systems of thought that aspire to it and makes a sharp division in the passage so that the evocation of the god upon the lotus leaf by Earl Henry can be made subject to the dry sarcasm of Sandoval.

It is curious to discover that there are several literary contexts in the 1790s in which Coleridge might have had (what in retrospect may seem) an unlikely encounter with the image of Vishnu. On 16 October 1797, two days after writing to Thelwall, for example, he wrote to ask Bowles for a copy of his poem: *The Spirit of Discovery by Sea.*[20] In this poem the Indian Caucasus (as the Hindu Kush was then known) is taken, as it had been by Ralegh,[21] as the world-centre on which Noah's ark came to rest and from which Alexander, as though from Paradise, was turned back by a Brahmin.[22] It is typical of the mental shift towards the Indian Orient taking place in the 1790s that a clergyman such as Bowles has Noah's ark protected by 'the great Vishnu'. A month earlier, when Coleridge went to see Bowles,[23] they might well have discussed the Indian god in the context of the poems both of them were then completing. We have already mentioned how, shortly after this, William Taylor was to suggest that Southey incorporate Vishnu into a poem about India, and with Southey also Coleridge may have discussed the same image in the context of *Osorio.*[24] Resuming his correspondence with Coleridge two years later, Southey

---

[19] I.i.311–318, *CPW*, II, 1071 and nn (showing variants); 11.50–8, *CPW*, I, 422. [20] *CLSTC*, Letter 211, I, 356. [21] Ralegh, Pt I, Bk I, chap. 7, § 10, xiii–xiiii, pp. 125–6. [22] *The Poetical Works of William Lisle Bowles*, ed. Rev. George Gilfillan, 2 vols (Edinburgh, 1855), I, Introduction, pp. 228–9; Canto III, 11.140–272, pp. 262–6. For the origins of this conception, see chapter 5, pp. 166–7, 174–5. [23] *CLSTC*, Letter 205, I, 344 and n. [24] Curry (*New Letters*), I, 152. See chapter 2, p. 50.

likens himself to yet another Indian image of a meditative 'deity'—
that of a self-sufficient Buddha.[25]

While Coleridge is indebted to an intelligent article in the
Annual Register for his idea about Brahmin belief,[26] the single
most important literary source for his conception of the god on the
lotus is almost certainly the first volume of Thomas Maurice's *History of Hindostan*. In this volume there is a most graphic plate of
Vishnu 'reposing during . . . a thousand Ages'. Lowes suggests
that Coleridge read this book especially closely[27] and it may not
therefore be a coincidence that nowhere else is to be found the uncommon phrase 'the Indian Veeshnu' which finds a direct echo in
Coleridge. The plate depicting Vishnu is used by way of illustration to verses (reproduced by Maurice) from the *Bhagavata Purana* describing the birth of Brahma out of the flower of the lotus. At
the outset of his book, Maurice had already noted that, according
to the Hindus, the creation of the present world is called the lotus
creation since it took place when Brahma, gliding on the surface of
the waters, awoke from his slumber of a thousand years upon the
leafy bed of the lotus.[28] Virtually the same phrases, the same image and a similar significance attached to it appear in the conception evoked by Coleridge, whose transliteration of the final letter
of Vishnu's name also might reflect on the way that in Maurice (as
in the Vaishnavite *puranas*) Vishnu not only takes on the attributes of Krishna but absorbs those of Brahma.

As we have already noted, Jones was Maurice's mentor and inspired him not only to centre his literary projects on India but to
use Indian culture as a means of interpreting other ancient civilizations. Like Jones before him, Maurice associates Vishnu with,
among other Asian gods, Osiris, an identification repeated in, for

[25] Ibid., I, 201. In view of Coleridge's image of Vishnu cradled in the lotus, it is
worth noting that Southey's (more flippant) image of Sommona-Codom was
derived from passages in Picart, one of which records how the child was set within
the bud of a flower which enclosed him as it were in a cradle (*SCB*. Ser, 4, pp.
40–1). That Sommona-Codom was Sramana Gautam or Buddha was first reported
in England in *CR*, N. A., VII (April 1793), 434.   [26] Dr Munir Ahmad of Aligarh
University noticed the sympathetic and intelligent account of the Brahmins
reprinted in the *Annual Register* for 1782 (Characters, pp. 31–9), which Coleridge
borrowed from the Bristol Library, 26 Feb.–10 March 1796 (Whalley, p. 122). A
reference to Halhed's *Code of Gentoo Laws* suggests that the author of this
account, like Beddoes in a footnote to *Alexander's Expedition* (p. 55), may have
been thinking of the stages of consciousness—waking, sleeping and absorbed
trance—enumerated by Halhed in his Preface (p. xxxv and §) and central to Indian
thought at least since the time of Yajnavalkya.   [27] John Livingston Lowes, *The
Road to Xanadu* (London, 1927), pp. 33–4, 379–84.   [28] *HH*, I, Plate VI (facing p.
401). See also pp. 65–6, 407, 566.

example, the *Monthly Magazine* for September 1797.[29] Coleridge had certainly read Jones's translation, the *Ordinances of Menu*, previous to this. In the first chapter, which Coleridge thought the most sublime,[30] 'the great sages' are told how Brahma, having created the universe, was reabsorbed into the Supreme Spirit, exchanging energy for repose, the world expanding when he awakes and fading away when he slumbers.[31] From Coleridge's own later complimentary reference to Jones it seems likely that he had read more of his works than this one translation. As early as 1792 people very closely associated with Jones were among those most solicitous about Coleridge when his military escapade proved so disastrous and, more importantly, Coleridge's earliest work as a writer was included or reviewed in periodicals which were paying tribute to and disseminating the work of Jones and his 'disciples'.[32]

---

[29] Ibid., I, 359–61; *MM*, I (Sept. 1797), 189.   [30] *CLSTC*, Letter 152, I, 252.   [31] *Menu*, I 51–57. *BGW*, which Coleridge had also almost certainly read previous to this (Muirhead, pp. 283–4) not only makes the sight of Brahma on his lotus-throne part of the mystic vision of Krishna as Vishnu afforded to Arjuna (XI, 90–1) but also suggests that the man who entrusts his life to the Supreme 'remaineth like the leaf of the lotus unaffected by the waters' (V, 58). A reference to the flower, rather than the leaf, of the lotus is made in the review of Kindersley's *Specimens of Hindoo Literature* (London, 1794) in *MR*, Appendix to XVI (1795), 566. Coleridge's image of Vishnu as the supreme God afloat on a lotus on the cosmic ocean is the more interesting because the texts he had, or could have, read invariably depict Vishnu on the cosmic snake and Brahma on the lotus. It does so happen, however, that, like Coleridge, the Vaishnavas, in their *puranas*, not only attribute to Vishnu his customary power of preserving creation but also appropriate to him the power of creation usually associated with Brahma, and, most important of all, Brahme's (or Narayana's) supreme power (evoked so powerfully in poetry by Jones) to exist free of the laws of flux pertinent to matter (*VP*, I, II, 39–54). Such is the henotheistic atmosphere of Indian religion that the Buddhists also appropriated to Avalokita Buddha attributes of both Brahma and Vishnu, and, while the Vaishnavas returned the compliment and made Buddha an *avatar* of Vishnu (*HH*, I, 398–400; II, 480–502), the image of the God on the lotus, as well as in the lotus posture, is even more evident, where Southey encountered it, in the Buddhist tradition (Curry, I, 201).   [32] *CR*, N.A., XII (Nov. 1794) includes favourable reviews of *The Fall of Robespierre* (260–2) and *Specimens of Hindoo Literature* (326–37). *BC*, V (May 1795), which in a review of Maurice's elegy on Jones (510–14) speaks as highly as it had always done of both men, makes favourable mention of *The Fall of Robespierre* (539–40) and, commending Coleridge as a poet, reproduces 'The Sigh' (549–50). *MR*, N.S., XX (June 1796) extracts Ouseley's tribute to Jones from the *Persian Miscellanies* there under review (121–7) and treats Coleridge's *Poems* of 1796 in a very complimentary way (194–9). All three magazines in these years paid sympathetic attention both to Jones and the claims he and other Orientalists were making for India and to the works of the young Coleridge and his friends. Additionally, *MM*, which published a sonnet in commemoration of Jones (I, June 1796, 404), printed poems by Coleridge in Sept. and Oct. (II, 647, 732). The *Annual Register*, 1796, includes a letter from Jones to Gibbon (Characters, pp. 378–9), and a poem by Coleridge (Poetry, pp. 494–5). For the personal link, see chapter 2, p. 77 and n. 191.

It seems reasonable to suppose, therefore, that Coleridge may have been familiar with Jones's best and most popular Indian ode, the 'Hymn to Narayena'. In the *History of Hindostan* Maurice notes that the way all the *Dii Majores* of Asia are represented sitting upon the sacred lotus is symbolic of 'the incumbent deity' originally moving or brooding upon the waters. Jones's poem—the argument to which specifies that Vishnu is the name for the spirit which moves on the waters in its capacity as preserver—not only follows *Menu* and verses from the *Bhagavata Purana* (reproduced in the *History of Hindostan*) in describing the birth from 'a lucid bubble' of the God 'heav'nly-pensive on the lotus', but, like the *Gita*, which Coleridge had also almost certainly read prior to this, associates the apprehension of the Supreme with the refinement of consciousness to a state where the soul is wholly absorbed in 'the One only Being'.[33] Whether Coleridge is directly or indirectly indebted to the most imaginative Orientalist of the time, he certainly invests one very central Indian mythological figure with much the same sort of psychological significance it has in its own culture.

It might seem somewhat pedantic to spend so much time elucidating sources for a single image used in a letter, even though the image is a significant one and recurs in the poetry. That Coleridge discovered the figure of an Indian god to be the most appropriate image for his own most abstruse meditative states in the intervals between creation could be seen as no more than a reflection of the passing fashion—were it not that in one of those same meditative states and quite possibly at the very same time he first referred to the image (in mid October 1797) he produced (what is by common consent) one of the great Oriental poems in the language, 'Kubla Khan'.[34] That poem, whatever its exact date of composition, was written at a time when Coleridge was still 'all afloat' in his ideas about the Supreme Being.[35] Perhaps no myth better than that of the supreme Hindu god (whether in the form of Brahma, Vishnu or Siva) conveys precisely the ambiguity that attaches to the relationship between an infinite, wholly self-absorbed and passive state of meditation, and the paradoxically active manifestation of this state in the creation of a finite (if infinitely repetitive) cosmos. This riddle, central to the philosophy of both the Vedanta and

---

[33] *BGW*, v, 58; xi, 90–1.   [34] That is, allowing the argument of E.K. Chambers (*Samuel Taylor Coleridge*, Oxford, 1938, pp. 100–3), E.L. Griggs (*CLSTC*, i, 348–349) *et al*. that the poem was written in mid October 1797. For present purposes it is sufficient to accept the testimony of the Crewe manuscript that it was composed sometime in the fall of that year. My basic argument would not be materially affected even if the poem was, in fact, written as late as 1798.   [35] *BL*, i (Pt ii), 204.

neo-Platonism, Jones had made clear was expressed in Indian mythology in terms of the relationship of the figure of a passive god to that of his active consort or *sakti*, the goddess. As we shall see later, it is possible to read 'Kubla Khan' in terms of this basic *mythos*.

COLERIDGE AND MARCO POLO'S ORIENT

Whatever other reading went into the making of Coleridge's response to the Orient by the time 'Kubla Khan' was composed, we can be sure at least that his most immediate interest was in Marco Polo's account of his Eastern travels, a document which the eighteenth century had begun to discover was as accurate as it was marvellous. If Coleridge had never extended his reading beyond Purchas (and assuming that he knew the *Pilgrimes* as well as the *Pilgrimage* prior to the Fall of 1797)[36] his mind would have been left with a reasonably accurate impression of the Tartar court. William de Rubruquis, for example, does justice to the theology of the Buddhists (or idolators as both he and Marco Polo call them): 'God is everywhere, and ruleth all things, and yet is he invisible, being understanding and wisedome it selfe'. He writes particularly of the eclecticism of Kublai's predecessor, Mangu (Möngke) Khan, as well as of the paradisal silver tree he has had constructed with its pipes of milk, whey, wine and honey and of the soothsayers and religious rites of the Tartars. From Marco Polo alone, however, Coleridge would have absorbed a fair impression of Kublai's world.

Marco Polo's approach to the court of Kublai includes an account of the Tartar sack of India and the acquisition there of magical arts, an account of an Islamic paradise in the Persian mountains (which also contains pipes of wine, milk, honey and water) and, from hearsay, an account of Kashmir as the original home of magic and idolatry (or Buddhism). Kublai, the greatest of the Khans, has added the rest of the world to the conquests of his ancestors and has constructed two great palaces—the winter palace at Taidu and the summer palace at Xandu. It is Xandu that has the goodly house of pleasure in a fair wood where, at the time of Kublai's departure in August, there is a special lunar festival when maresmilk is sprinkled on the earth. However, it is at the winter site, which (as the result of a prophecy of rebellion against Kublai's empire) is built across the river ('famous from antiquity')

---

[36] Lowes, pp. 360–1.

from the old capital, that there is a Green Mountain where the trees are always in leaf (a universal token of Paradise) and a palace where, to the strains of music, Kublai is ceremoniously served his drink by a fair Damosell. Nor is this the only way Kublai receives his drink. Marco Polo speaks of the *bakshis*, or *bhiksus*, the king's magicians as Purchas terms them, who protect the pleasure-house at Xandu from rain and storm. These take their names from the countries of their origin, Tibet and Kashmir. Their most notable magic is to make cups of wine or milk appear and pass through the air into Kublai's hand and they believe in metempsychosis.[37]

Marco Polo's account, which, as he circles Asia, shows his knowledge both of Indian philosophical practice and of the seminal story of Buddha's life, is the great medieval passage to the East. For the first time, Europe is made aware of the extent of civilization in the Far East.[38] In effect China is added to the map. In spite of this, India remains the original and better-known reference point for dealing with Asia. Purchas's *Pilgrimes*, for example—a collection of voyages theoretically designed to illustrate how man lost Paradise and is doomed to wander the world because he preferred the creature to the Creator (a theme congenial to Coleridge)—is so arranged as to first turn attention to India as the source and object of the European desire to travel and thereafter circumnavigate the globe in such a way as to conclude with those relations which deal with the attempt to find India by a westward route. Purchas writes: 'India doth now with us signifie all the Easterne World in vulgar appellation'. This reflects the view of a commercial nation seeking trading privileges with the Great Mughal (whose kinship with the Mongols Purchas is quick to notice in his marginalia). Behind that stands the medieval view of the crusading Europeans who sought in India the salvation, both spiritual and temporal, promised by the figure of Prester John. And behind that again is the Hellenistic view, expressed by Purchas near the outset of his collection, when a reference to Pythagoras leads him to speak of India as a place where philosophy is practised with a continuity and vigour surpassing that of the Greeks, who, like the Persian Magi, are said to be indebted for their philosophy to India.[39]

[37] Purchas, III.i.22–88, *passim*. See also the informative notes in Yule, I, I, xxxi.   [38] Reading Marco Polo, Ralegh was confirmed in his impression that it was to the nations of the East that the West was indebted for its knowledge and its civilization (Pt I. Bk I, chap. 7, § 10, iii, p. 116). Marco Polo, in turn, had been largely inspired by the Alexander Romances (Yule, I, Introduction, 113–15).   [39] Purchas, I.i.44, 76.

COLERIDGE AND JONES'S INDIAN ORIENT: TARTARY TO ABYSSINIA

What I am suggesting is that whereas Coleridge is indebted for several of the images in 'Kubla Khan' to a particular passage in Purchas about Kublai's court, the context of that passage is quite likely to have evoked India and whatever associations India had for Coleridge. Not only was the medieval concept of the farther East prior to Marco Polo confined, like the classical, exclusively to India but in Coleridge's own younger days the newer investigations into classical Asian civilizations were largely being done by British scholars based in India and publishing their findings in Jones's *Asiatic Researches*. The need to re-examine yet again Coleridge's reading and what it meant to him exists not only because Marco Polo's description does not account for many of the images in 'Kubla Khan' but also, much more importantly, because it does not account for the highly-charged magical tone or mystical spirit which invests the poem.

Of course, on the face of it, India has no more to do with the Xanadu of 'Kubla Khan' than with the Abyssinia of the maid with her dulcimer. In fact, in the 1790s India was closely associated with both. The difference is that whereas the supposition of an Abyssinian debt to India for its philosophy was of long standing, knowledge of a similar debt owed by the Tartars was only then freshly established. Accounts of both these links, then widely accepted as authoritative throughout Europe, are to be found in the essays on the peoples of Asia written by Jones in India.

In November 1802 Coleridge wrote in his notebook: 'Kublai Khan ordered letters to be invented for his people—'. It is curious to have to record (since, such is the neglect of Jones, it has not hitherto been recorded) that the passage is taken from Jones's essay on the Tartars.[40] Jones uses the word 'nation' rather than 'people'and concludes the sentence: '. . . by a Tibetian, whom he rewarded with the dignity of chief Lama'.[41] What is not known, unfortunately, is whether Coleridge made the note because the information was new to him or, as may be the case, because he wanted to put in writing what was already familiar to him. Obviously, one asks the question because the concept of Kublai Khan ordering letters to be invented for his people and thus being the fountainhead of a civilization might very well underlie the ini-

[40] *CNB*, I, 1281; 'On the Tartars', *AR*, II, 19–41.   [41] Ibid., II, 27. For further information about the fate of this alphabet see Yule, I, 28, n. 1; Henry H. Howorth, *History of the Mongols*, 4 pts in 5 vols (London, 1876–1927), IV, 129–30; Helmuth Hoffman, *The Religions of Tibet*, trans. Edward Fitzgerald (London, 1961), p. 139.

tial image in Coleridge's poem of Kubla ordering an artistically miraculous dome to be built at a place where (as it seems) Alph has its source.[42] The impression that Coleridge may already have been familiar with Jones's essay in 1797 is strengthened by the fact that, as Jones says, the holy lama who invented the alphabet was, as a reward, invested with the highest sacred office in the land. Not only is Coleridge's Alph a sacred river but also apparently the control of it bears some relation to the existence of the mystical figure at the end of the poem.[43]

There is one further reason for thinking Coleridge may have read Jones's essay on the Tartars prior to the composition of 'Kubla Khan'. In the essay Jones says he could find no better way to depict Tartary than in 'a magnificent image' used by Joseph de Guignes in his monumental *Histoire Générale des Huns*,[44]

describing it as a stupendous edifice, the beams and pillars of which are many ranges of lofty hills, and the dome one prodigious mountain, to which the Chinese give the epithet of Celestial, with a considerable number of broad rivers flowing down its sides. If the mansion be so amazingly sublime, the land around it is proportionably extended, but more wonderfully diversified; for some parts of it are encrusted with ice, others parched with inflamed air, and covered with a kind of lava; here we meet with immense tracts of sandy deserts, and forests, almost impenetrable; there, with gardens, groves, and meadows, perfumed with musk, watered by numberless rivulets, and abounding in fruits and flowers; and, from east to west, lie many considerable provinces, which appear as valleys in comparison of the hills towering above them, but in truth are the flat summits of the highest mountains in the world, or at least the highest in Asia.[45]

---

[42] See Beer, pp. 207–10.   [43] In view of the significance sometimes attached to the letter Aleph or Alpha in cultures further West it is perhaps worth noting that an important section of the *Kanjur* which Kublai had translated by the lamas at Sakya deals with transcendental wisdom. The full text is in twelve volumes but there are various abridgements of decreasingly fewer volumes and fewer leaves until the whole is mystically condensed into the letter A, 'considered in Buddhistic works as the mother of all Wisdom; and therefore, all men of genius, all Bodhisatwas and Buddhas, are said to have been produced by 'A', since this is the first element for forming syllables, words, sentences, and a whole discourse; and the means for acquiring knowledge and wisdom' (Waddell, pp. 160–1). The mystical importance given 'A' in India is made clear both in Kindersley (reprinted in *MR*, App. to XVI, 1795, 566) and *BGW*, x.87.   [44] 4 vols in 5 (Paris, 1756–8), I (Pt II), iv–v. Jones mentions other authorities he was using. For information about Kublai Khan Visdelou's Supplement to d'Herbelot's *Bibliothèque Orientale* is of little importance beside Antoine Gaubil, *Histoire de Gentchiscan et de toute la Dinastie de Mongous* (Paris, 1739), pp. 132–222, and J.A.M. de Moyriac de Mailla, *Histoire Générale de la Chine*, 13 vols (Paris, 1777–85), IX, 275–461.   [45] *AR*, II, 20. N.B.: This passage was reprinted in *MR* Appendix to VII (1792), 565.

Jones's description is, in fact, far more memorable than that of de Guignes, whose work, Jones notes, abounds more in solid learning than in rhetorical ornaments and invariably trails away like the rivers he mentions, one of which loses itself in the desert while others drop into a subterranean abyss.[46]

Jones not only evokes a Tartar landscape which is quite extraordinary for the richness of its contrasts, he also depicts it as a single garden surrounding a domed edifice, the dome itself being a mountain considered celestial. The landscape in Coleridge's poem, being an interior landscape, has been partially identified with so many landscapes from all over the world that to suggest it owes something to a description of the actual Tartar landscape over which Kublai ruled may sound curiously eccentric. However, the inclination to add this landscape to the others is the greater not only on account of the particular imagery of dome and garden used to give coherence to the natural contrasts, but also because of the tightness of the syntax which expresses these antitheses. At the outset of his poem when Coleridge repeats the demonstrative adverb—'And here were gardens . . . And here were forests . . .'[47]—one might well be catching an echo of Jones's description of Tartary where he introduces similar images in a similar way and, more importantly, to similar effect. More indicative than whether or not Coleridge's 'sinuous rills' were derived from Jones's 'numberless rivulets' and his 'forests ancient as the hills' from Jones's impenetrable forests among the worlds highest hills is the shared sense that the Oriental landscape is a magical one.

Given his catholic reading habits it is unlikely that Coleridge would have delayed reading something as central as Jones's essays on Asian civilization until 1802.[48] It may be that he was then re-reading Jones in the edition of his works published in 1799. Any man who claimed, as Coleridge did, to have been awed by Jones's work was more likely to have been awed by it a full decade earlier—before a reaction set in. And if Coleridge did read the essay on the Tartars in the 1790s it would not have been in order to acquire the few images I have mentioned, evocative as they may be. Jones's essay is essentially concerned with the theory of the French writer, J.S. Bailly, who in the late eighteenth century drew the attention of European intellectuals to Tartary when, in a series of letters to Voltaire, be argued that the region was the original home of the arts and sciences, whence civilization, remnants of

---

[46] De Guignes, I (Pt II), v.   [47] 11.8, 10, *CPW*, I, 297.   [48] E.S. Shaffer has suggested the possible importance (and significance) of Jones to Coleridge in *'Kubla Khan' and the Fall of Jerusalem* (Cambridge, 1975), pp. 105–6, 116–19.

which still existed in India, had spread to the rest of the world.[49]
While Jones goes to some lengths to demolish Bailly's theory, we
may be struck in retrospect, as was Coleridge some years later,[50]
by the way both men share the assumption, as did Voltaire, that
civilization had a single source, that this source was in Asia (Voltaire had suggested India, Jones was to suggest Iran), and that the
language and literature of the Brahmins was the only surviving key
to knowledge of this original state of mankind.[51] The point of difference between them is that Jones argues, quite accurately, that
the arts and sciences flourished among the Tartars not from the be-
ginnings of time but only from the time of Kublai Khan. In this
process, he says, Buddhism had played a part which suggested
Tartary was indebted to India for its learning and not India to Tartary.

Jones's conclusion depended on, among other things, an intelligent reading of de Guignes, who concluded that Kublai Khan, on
account of his patronage of the arts and sciences and the grandness
of his projects, deserved to be regarded as one of the greatest
princes who ever reigned. Coleridge was aware of this prevailing
image of Kublai Khan as an archetypal emperor.[52] However, the
most striking thing about Jones's piece is its concern to establish in
historical and geographical terms the truth about mankind's
monogenesis. The opening up of the ancient civilizations of the
East had led to a good deal of speculation about the single source
of civilization, or, as the religious sometimes saw it, the location of
Paradise. I have suggested that Jones was continually on the edge
of a realization that India was the key to this question not because
the common source of mankind was to be found within its boundaries, but because the culture which developed within those
boundaries had made central to itself an inner search for the common source of mankind. This apprehension (which, if it existed,
remained residual) found expression in Jones's essays in terms of
the historical influence of Indian philosophy on other cultures. In
determining that Tartary was indebted to India through Kublai's
adoption of Buddhism, Jones was pioneering a new field. In
another of his essays on Asia, however, where he considers

[49] Bailly traces our descent to an ancient race, from whom all civilization has
come like a river from the mountains. He locates that primaeval race in Tartary by
means of an argument involving the theory of an interplay between the sun and the
earth when it was still glacierized.   [50] *The Friend* (1850), III, Section II, Essay vii
p. 145n.   [51] See chapter 2, p. 68 and nn. 123–4, 206; *AR*, II, 22–3ff.   [52] De
Guignes, III, 188–90; *CNB*, I, 1840. The reference is again late (January 1804) but
Coleridge was clearly familiar with it earlier through Purchas. Howorth also
suggests Europe may have been much indebted to Kublai's civilization (I, 277–8).

whether Abyssinia was ever subject to a similar Indian influence, he is dealing with a very ancient tradition.

In his remarks on the Abyssinians in an essay on 'The Borderers . . . of Asia', Jones inclines to the opinion that the Ethiops of Meroe were not only the first Egyptians but also the same people as the original Hindus.[53] Following Bruce and Bryant, he bases this identification on the convertibility the names Ethiopian and Indian enjoyed in the Greek mind, a confusion which persisted so long that even Marco Polo (Coleridge's primary 'source') still refers to Ethiopia as Middle India. However, unlike the Abbé Mignot, who had been as sympathetic as his friend Voltaire to claims for the superior antiquity of Indian civilization, Jones was not prepared to conclude so definitely that the Ethiopians, like the Tartars, had imported their sacred letters from India. None the less, he does leave us with a reminder that the gymnosophists of Ethiopia seem to have professed the doctrines of Buddha.

The story that Abyssinia was once subject to a decisive Indian influence has its original reference point in the biography of Apollonius of Tyana. The two older authorities who otherwise deprecate Apollonius, Lucian and Eusebius, both accept his assertion that the Ethiopians derived their philosophy from India. If, in the 1790s, when theories of a monogenesis still prevailed, there were men such as Bowles who continued to adhere to the idea that, even if it was India which had been settled first after the Flood it was Egypt where the mind had first been developed,[54] there were others such as George Dyer (through whom Coleridge may have come to read the *Ordinances of Menu*)[55] who accepted the renewed conception of India as the cradle of the arts and sciences, whence Egypt and the West had received its philosophy and poetry.[56] Coleridge's use of the word Abyssinian in relation to the maid in his poem could indicate merely that she has a dark complexion, although in this context the word is obviously more evocative than that. Bruce's *Travels*, with its account of the sacred river Nile and the Mountains of the Moon, clearly played an important part in the reading that stands behind the writing of 'Kubla Khan'.[57] Once more, however, it is typical of the Orientalism of the decade that the first independent confirmation of the authenticity of Bruce's travels came from Jones in India, a fact which the

[53] *AR*, III, 4–5. See also ibid., I, 427–8. Mignot is cited in the introduction to *The Dabistan*, I, cvi–cvii. [54] *Hermes Britannicus* (London, 1828), p. 51n. [55] *CLSTC*, Letter 152, I, 252. [56] George Dyer, *Poems* (London, 1801), p. 245n. Other notes show that Dyer had read both Jones and Maurice. [57] Lowes, pp. 370–9; Beer, p. 63.

Gentleman's Magazine reiterated as late as August 1797.[58] Moreover, while Isis, the goddess of the Nile playing her sistrum to Lucius Apuleius, has been canvassed as the prototype for the Abyssinian maid,[59] her story does not in itself explain the significance of the maid.

Jones's speculation that the awesome landscape of Tartary and the sacred landscape of Abyssinia might originally have been subject to an Indian Buddhist influence seemed important enough to an Orientalist such as Quintin Craufurd to write two essays concerning the subject and make them the occasion (as they were to be the object of the reviews) of a new, enlarged edition of his book, *Sketches of the Hindoos*.[60] For all this, our demonstration of the importance of India to the Orientalism of the last decade of the eighteenth century might seem somewhat tangential to the composition of 'Kubla Khan' were it not that a description of the most scenic and mystical of all Indian landscapes appears to have been as important a literary 'source' as any for the images in the poem. In *The Road to Xanadu* Lowes suggests that the two central images in 'Kubla Khan'—the sunny pleasure-dome and the caves of ice—are immediately determined by Bernier's description of Kashmir.[61]

THE IMAGE OF KASHMIR IN THE 1790s

Bernier, the first European to visit Kashmir, borrows from the Mughal emperors their conception of it as 'the terrestrial Paradise of the Indies'. He tells us that after Akbar had established his pleasure-grounds among the waters of a place designed by nature to be the capital of an empire extending from Tartary to Sri Lanka, his son Jahangir had gone so far as to say he would prefer to lose the rest of his empire rather than Kashmir. Bernier follows this remark by describing a contest between poets and suggests that one poet, who had written about the low wooded hills of Kashmir and the snow mountains beyond, should have concluded his poem by asserting that the Ganges, the Indus, the Chenab and the Jumna were the four rivers of Eden and Kashmir, the true terrestrial Paradise.[62]

---

[58] 'A Conversation with Abram, an Abyssinian', *AR*, I, 383–6; *CR*, LXIX, (June 1790), 616; *GM*, LXVII, Pt. II (August 1797), 642–3.   [59] Beer, pp. 254–5. See also Thomas Taylor's poem on this subject, which may be relevant if 'Kubla Khan' was composed later than October 1797 (*MM*, IV, Nov. 1797, 375–6).   [60] London, 1792, 2 vols. The first, one volume, edition had been published in London only two years earlier.   [61] Lowes, pp. 379–87. Maurice strongly commends Bernier (*HH*, I, 36–7).   [62] 'Mr F. Bernier's Voyage to Surat etc.', *A Collection of Voyages and*

Initially Bernier had spoken of the legend which suggested that Kashmir had once been a lake and himself expresses the opinion that the waters were released not 'miraculously' by a saint but by an earthquake which had opened 'some cavern underground, which the mountain did sink into . . .'. The river which winds its way gently through the kingdom now flows out there, having been formed from the fountains which gush forth from the low wooded hills. Beyond these hills are the high snow mountains, likened to Olympus, calm and clear above the clouds and mist. The kingdom is like 'some evergreen garden'; its innocent mountains are 'flowing with milk and honey, as were those of the land of promise'. The houses of the capital, which is specifically said to be 'without walls', stand upon the river, and behind the capital is a hill called the Verdant Mountain, crowned with fine green trees, while on the lake are gardens of pleasure with fruit-bearing trees and arbours. Most notable of the gardens is 'Shalamar', whose summerhouses 'are in a manner made like domes, situate in the middle of the canal . . .'.

Bernier approaches 'the terrestrial Paradise of the Indies' by way of 'the infernal regions' of the Punjab before scaling, in the language of the Alexander Romances, 'the dreadful wall of the world'. As he ascends the wall he passes a cascade he believes is unparalleled, and trees perhaps coeval with the creation of the world, before encountering the strange, savage hermit of the Pir Pantsal who sits at the pass into Kashmir and can not only raise storms and thunders (like the Kashmiri at Kublai's court) but can bring destruction on passing emperors whose armies make any noise. The pass also marks the place where, within the same hour, is to be felt the opposition of summer and winter, of burning sun and icy snow. This peculiar opposition, Bernier suggests, is also responsible for the first of the natural 'wonders' of Kashmir which he journeys to investigate. This is a sacred fountain in a hillside which, for a month in spring, ebbs and flows thrice a day. Bernier concludes that an explanation for this phenomenon is to be found in an interplay between the heat of the sun and the frozen waters within the hillside. Thereafter he visits other fountains ornamented by formal gardens and a lake where a hermitage is said to 'miraculously float upon the water'. Eventually he

---

Travels, eds A. and John Churchill, 8 vols (London, 1704–52), VIII, 227–34, 236. This edition, based on the translation of 1671–2, is preferred in this chapter as one readily available in the eighteenth century. The association of India with the four rivers of Paradise is also evident in Baldeus (Churchill's *Voyages*, III, 661–2) and in Giorgi (p. 186).

has to turn back from a journey into the mountains, where he had hoped to see a lake which even in summer is heaped with ice and near which there is a grotto full of odd congelations. It is perhaps worth noting also that he meets a Tibetan lama whom he asks to write down his alphabet. The lama tells him he believes in metempsychosis, recounts the story of the reincarnations of the Dalai Lama and speaks of war with the Tartars.

It will be clear that a good many of the principal images of 'Kubla Khan' are to be found also in Bernier, not simply scattered about but held together by a similar underlying sense of Paradise so crucial to the poem. However, notwithstanding the savage hermit on the Pir Pantsal, Bernier's account lacks an overriding sense of the daemonic and potentially destructive, nor does it evoke, in spite of his predilection for Kashmiri women, the Abyssinian maid and her celestial music. This deficiency in Bernier might easily have been supplied by Kashmiri legends and myths, but Bernier was a pupil of Gassendi's and was intent on discovering natural explanations for what the natives regarded as supernatural phenomena: he was therefore careful to exclude all superstitious legends. As George Forster, in 1783 the first Englishman to visit Kashmir, pointed out, Bernier was limited to a Muslim apprehension of the place and this tended to obscure the Hindu aspect.[63]

Something of the Hindu aspect which gives to the physical beauty of Kashmir a metaphysical dimension was known to Akbar's minister, Abu-l-Fazl, whose *Ain-i-Akbari*, including a description of the Kashmiri landscape and legends, was translated by Gladwin in the 1780s and was, like Forster's account, read by both Rennell and Maurice.[64] Rennell dilates upon the 'romantic beauties' of the Valley[65] but Maurice, whose first volume of the *History of Hindostan* Coleridge read closely,[66] has an even live-

---

[63] *A Journey from Bengal to England*, 2 vols in 1 (London, 1798), II, 30–1. This work incorporates Forster's *Sketches of the Mythology and Customs of the Hindoos* (London, 1785). Forster was read by Jones as early as 1786 (*LWJ*, Letter 433, II, 697) and later by both Rennell and Maurice.   [64] Gladwin, II, 152–92.   [65] James Rennell, *A Memoir on a Map of Hindostan*, 2nd ed. (London, 1788), pp. 104–7. Incidentally, Rennell also speaks of Bernier's *Travels* as being 'in everybody's hands' (p. 57). His own work, which Coleridge noted down to read (*CNB*, I, 241), is eloquent only on the subject of 'romantic' Kashmir.   [66] Coleridge may have borrowed more than the image of Vishnu and the material for his projected Hymns to the Sun and Moon from *HH*, I. Through reading it he could have acquired a fair knowledge of the work of Jones and Wilkins, of theories like Bailly's concerning the Asiatic origin of civilization and of the Indian myths of the Fall of Man, the Flood and the successive incarnations of a Saviour which were causing concern to Christians. From this book he might also have derived his concept of atheistical

lier awareness of the potential importance of Kashmir since ne regards it as the earliest residence of the Brahmins and the place where theological rites were purest.[67]

In spite of Maurice's concern to defend the claim of the Euphrates valley to being the site of Eden—no less than that of Chaldea to being the parent country of the arts and sciences—he is tempted to concede the alternative claims of Kashmir. This is because it is in India, where the lunar zodiac was perhaps first invented and where Pythagoras learnt that the sun was the centre of the universe, that the clearest traces remain of the one great primaeval Family of Man. While Indian chronology is quite literally astronomical and thus, like the visionary system which traces the descent of India's kings from the Sun and Moon, 'airbuilt', in India is to be found an alphabet probably superior in antiquity to the Mosaic and possibly a remnant of the grand primaeval alphabet perhaps bequeathed to the Indians through the line of Shem. Besides this, the Indians have a concept of the Golden Age preserved from the patriarchal tradition and fables of Vishnu's earlier *avatars* which reflect not only on the Flood but on antediluvian periods. Although Maurice refers only infrequently to Kashmir, when he does so it is to conceive of it as standing in the same relation to India as India does to the rest of Asia, that is as the place which probably holds the key to many unanswered questions about the human race in its infancy and which would, therefore, best help him to penetrate to that fountainhead of human knowledge, the most appropriate image for which he finds in the mountain-source of the sacred Ganges.[68]

Maurice, in his turgid and obscure way, is following Jones in his supposition that Kashmir could be critical to an understanding of mankind's origins. Kashmir had long been regarded as a centre of mystical religion. On his way to Kublai's court Macro Polo had heard that it was the home of magic and idolatry (or Buddhism). An article on the Brahmins which Coleridge is thought to have

---

Buddhism and of the similarity between Indian pantheism and Spinozism. It might well have aroused his interest in the question of what Pythagoras had learnt in India. Had he read *HH*, ii, it could have extended his knowledge of these subjects and fostered his desire to write about the invasion of India by Bacchus.   [67] *HH*, i, 106. This image of Kashmir as 'the holy land of superstition' is evident in *IA* (v, 861), where it is regarded as the place in the East settled by the Sethites (iv, 462) from which Zoroaster derived the theology and theurgy which formed the basis of Mithraism (ii, 125–30).   [68] Ibid., i, esp. 56–123, 160–9, 207–73, 364–72, 403–14, 497–521. For the misspelt name of the mountain, Kentaissi (or Kanteshan), see J.B. Du Halde, *The General History of China*, trans. R. Brookes, 4 vols (London, 1736), iv, 452.

read reports that in the hills of Kashmir there were men who lived some hundreds of years and who, by holding their breaths, could lie in trances for several years together so long as they were kept warm.[69] This more mysterious aspect of Kashmir Coleridge might also have encountered in the portrait of 'the Brahmin of Cashmire' drawn by the Turkish Spy, who dramatises the hermit on Pir Pantsal as 'the Oracle of the Indies' with powers so great that from every part of Asia men make pilgrimage to this 'Apollo of the East'.[70]

When interest in the Orient became centred on India in the 1790s, Kashmir was inevitably to rise in the English consciousness as an Oriental paradise. Already before the turn of the century Southey (who worked closely with Coleridge in 1795) planned to make use of 'the delightful realm of Cashmeer' in *Thalaba*[71] and, while this plan was not realized, descriptions of Kashmir almost certainly inform his conceptions of the paradises of the Hindu gods in *The Curse of Kehama*.[72] Not long afterwards, Kashmir was to receive its most popular poetic celebration in Moore's *Lalla Rookh*, the culminating book of which shows a prince, disguised as a poet, making a journey to the valley.[73] But that a poetic mind of a different order could make something more of descriptions of Kashmir is evident from the way that, after being named in several of Shelley's poems, the valley becomes the setting for the highly-charged events of *Prometheus Unbound*,[74] though it is there unnamed, perhaps because the interior landscape of the psyche necessarily resists confinement to a particular geographical location.

That Kashmir might be an unnamed objective correlative for the highly-charged interior landscape of 'Kubla Khan' Coleridge's reading of Bernier or Maurice gives us some reason for believing.

[69] *Philosophical Transactions*, XXII (1700–1), 735. A.H. Nethercot (*The Road to Tryermaine*, Chicago, 1939, pp. 134–5) suggests that this article on the Brahmins was known to Coleridge through the abridged edition, V, Pt II (1700–20), 169. It was the work of John Marshall (see chapter 3, p. 86 and n. 6).   [70] *Turkish Spy*, VII.III.vi. Lowes suggests Coleridge may have read the *Turkish Spy* (p. 244).   [71] *SCB*, Ser. 4, p. 182; *MWTN*, Southey to Taylor Letter 5, I, 248.   [72] *The Curse of Kehama* (London, 1810), Canto VII, stanzas 9–10, pp. 64–6; x.2–4, 94–6. Southey had read Gladwin's translation of Abu-l-Fazl's description of Kashmir by this time (see chapter 7, n. 31). It is very possible Southey and Coleridge had in the mid 1790s read and discussed at least Bernier, Gladwin and Maurice on India in general and on Kashmir in particular.   [73] 'The Light of the Haram', *Lalla Rookh*, 2nd ed. (London, 1817), pp. 295–335. Moore had read Bernier. G.T. Vigne (*Travels in Kashmir, Ladakh, Iskardo*, 2 vols, London, 1842, II, 75) suggests that the Kashmir of *Lalla Rookh* is essentially that of the time of Jahangir, who repeatedly proclaimed it to be 'paradise on earth'.   [74] See chapter 7, n. 18 and pp. 254–6, 262–3, 273.

In both those writers, however, one catches only something of that mystical spirit which the Mughals to some extent and the Hindus and Buddhists to a greater extent share with the author of 'Kubla Khan'. All we can fairly conclude about Coleridge at this point is that he could hardly avoid taking an intelligent interest in the Orientalism of the 1790s, that this Orientalism, largely under the aegis of Jones, centred on India, and that the new knowledge of ancient Indian culture was used to speculate about man's origins and the single primaeval source of his civilization. Only in so far as India holds out so much promise in the 1790s can we look upon it as pertinent to the Orientalism of a man whose reading was not only much more diverse, but whose way of reading was such that a discussion of man's origins was liable to leave him not located in some temporal Eden but, like an Indian god, afloat on a cosmic lotus before the creation of a world.

THE BUDDHIST KUBLAI KHAN

So far we have been intent on recreating the intellectual milieu within which an Oriental poem like 'Kubla Khan' might have been written. If that milieu, fostered by Jones, did one thing, it encouraged the literary (in keeping with a long Platonist tradition) to search amid the scenic grandeur of the Indianized Orient for original and authoritative knowledge lost or withheld from modern civilization. Jones and his protégés undoubtedly left behind them a sense of the unexplored potential of a potentate like Kublai and of a paradise like Kashmir. Any extensive information about either of these, however, was not forthcoming until rather later. It is this later information which I wish to use to offer a coherent reading of 'Kubla Khan', suggested by (but by no means fully explicable in terms of) what Coleridge himself read in the 1790s. I undertake this somewhat arcane pursuit for two related reasons. The first is that 'Kubla Khan' apparently provides yet another example of an imaginative projection on the East by a Platonist happening to accord with the Oriental reality it represents.[75] The second is that an examination of such a peculiar coincidence may allow us to speculate further about the nature of the poetic imagination.

Of all the knowledge about the Orient acquired since the poem was written which suggests it is anything but the fragment it purports to be, the most important concerns Kublai Khan. Jorge Luis Borges used some of this later information to surmise that in

[75] See chapter 3, pp. 95–6; chapter 4, p. 128; chapter 5, pp. 153–5.

a sense Coleridge's soul had been penetrated by that of the historical Kublai. Ironically enough, his argument is based on (what is) a mistranslation of Rashid-al-din.[76] Other Oriental texts, however, indicate that Borges was probably quite right in thinking that Kublai had more in common with Coleridge than is usually realized. The daemonic figure of the fourth section of 'Kubla Khan' can be identified with the Kubla of the first section, and indeed if the title of the poem is comprehensive it is not unreasonable to suppose that the emperor who builds a paradise garden is susceptible also to a rather more refined mystical experience. This imaginative conception of Kubla, as opposed to that which regards him as an Oriental despot concerned only with temporal power, happens to agree very closely with the figure portrayed in the Buddhist chronicles of his own people. The names in the first line of Coleridge's poem have always seemed peculiarly charged, no doubt on account of their exotic flavour. Among Mongolian Buddhists 'Xanadu' was still being venerated in recent times on account of its spiritual associations with the emperor 'Kubla Khan'.[77]

Even in the late eighteenth century it was possible to know that the historical Kublai was strongly under the influence of the great lama Pakpa, and (as Coleridge himself noticed) was a patron of sacred learning as well as of art. In 1796, in a review of the *Ordinances of Menu* which Coleridge might well have read, the reviewer, considering Asia as the cradle of civilization, wrote that a belief in an immediate intercourse between heaven and earth was the grand foundation of the Tartar religion.[78] Given the interest Coleridge had in the relationship of transcendental to transcendent states,[79] such a reference could easily have led him to speculate whether there had been a Tartar Khan who, like Timur, 'with a sort of wild grandeur, not ungratifying to the imagination',[80] but with a better claim than Timur, pretended to godhead.

Be that as it may, the historical Kublai occupies a very special

---

[76] Jorge Luis Borges, 'The Dream of Coleridge', *Other Inquisitions*, trans. Ruth L.C. Simms (London, 1973), pp. 14–17; Rashid-al-din, *The Successors of Genghis Khan*, trans. J.A. Boyle (New York, 1971), pp. 274–7. It was in consequence of a dream that Kublai *abandoned* the alternative building site at Lang-Ten (Cool Pavilion). Jones was aware that the histories of the Tartars by Muslim historians available in translation in eighteenth-century Europe were based on Rashid-al-din (*AR*, II, 24, 39).   [77] Bushell's account cited in Yule, I, 304–5, n. 2; Howorth, I, 278–9.   [78] *BC*, VIII (Nov. 1796), 541. *Menu* engaged the attention of Coleridge at this time (see this chapter, p. 200 and n. 55).   [79] *BL*, I (Pt II), 245.   [80] *The Friend*, No. 12 (9 Nov. 1809), p. 180n.

place in the Buddhist tradition. The first Mongolian history of the Khans, written in the seventeenth century, not only acknowledges Kublai as the founder of Buddhism among his people but depicts the last of the Chingizides, Toghon Timur, being told by a lama (whom he had asked to interpret a dream) how in Kublai's time the lama Pakpa had wept for three days because, as he told Kublai, he had foreseen the destruction in war of both his dynasty and his religion. Toghon remembers this when, driven from his throne, he laments the loss not only of his capital (the great work of art of the Immortal Kublai, as he calls it) but also of the cool, delicious summer-seat of Shang-tu (Marco Polo's Xandu), the delight of his god-like sires. He bewails that, falling into a dream, he has lost these seats of perfection where, in the days of his glory as Lord of the Earth, the breezes had been full of fragrance and he had looked on nothing that was not beautiful.[81]

This sense of imperial loss, said to have been foreseen by the wife[82] who (perhaps on account of it) insisted on Kublai's conversion to Buddhism, is evoked not *per se* but because when the dynasty fell Buddhism lapsed in Mongolia. The history reports that when, three centuries later, the religion was permanently revived, it was done so by a Tibetan lama who claimed that the Mongolian emperor he approached was an incarnation of Kublai Khan while he himself was an incarnation of Pakpa. In return the honours heaped on him were designed to match those Kublai had showered upon Pakpa and he became the first Dalai Lama, a title which has since remained the epitome of belief in reincarnation.[83] The lama he left behind as his representative the Mongolians regarded as their first incarnate lama, equivalent of the Tibetan 'seer with bright eyes'. They called such a person a *khubilighan*.[84]

The Mongolian chronicle provides some indication of the sort of Buddhism into which Pakpa would have initiated Kublai. The

[81] Reproduced in Howorth, I, 332–5. Setzen's *History of the Mongol Khans* (1662) was translated by Isaac Jacob Schmidt, *Geschichte der Ost-Mongolen und Ihres Fürstenhauses* (St Petersburg, 1829). See also Yule, I, 305, n. 2.   [82] De Guignes, III, 167–8.   [83] Howorth, I, 420–3. Pakpa had been the first lama to be given effective control over large parts of Tibet (ibid., IV, 129; Hoffman, pp. 137–9).   [84] L.A. Waddell, 'The Indian Buddhist Cult of Avalokita', *JRAS*, N.S., XXVI (1894), 51–89; Hoffman, p. 172. According to Howorth's account (IV, 141), the first evocation of a *khubilgana* descent, the term itself being Mongolian, would have to be that involving Kublai Khan. It is, however, an etymological coincidence that the name and the term associated with re-incarnation should sound so much alike. In a letter to me of 15 March 1977 Prof. C.R. Bawden, of SOAS, writes that, although there is no scholarly derivation, he thinks there just may have been a folk etymology connecting the Mongol emperor with the idea of change. In Waddell's index the Mongol term for incarnation is given as *kublaighan*.

Indian influence is very strong and Pakpa himself was endowed with Indian titles.[85] On one occasion Kublai is said to have given Pakpa a dish with a representation upon it of Mount Meru,[86] the holy mountain of Hindu and Buddhist mythology, which initiates must ascend and, if a material conception of Paradise is to be superseded for something more abstract (the Heavens of No-Form), surmount. This mystical cosmology, where imagery is used to indicate the limitations of imagery, is consistent with the warning given by Buddha that those who imagine they are already in Paradise sitting enlightened on a lotus amid palaces and gardens are still trapped within the calyx of the lotus[87] (that is, within the cycle of metempsychosis).[88] But Kublai almost certainly also learned to conceive of Paradise in terms of Shamba-la, that ideal conception of the esoteric Tantric tradition of the *Kalacakra* (or Wheel of Time).[89] At the outset of his reign Kublai had bestowed upon him 'the four consecrations of the exalted Kei Wadshra' (or Hevajra) after an intriguing incident when, upon first meeting Pakpa, he had surprised him by showing a superior knowledge of the *Tantras* of the Hevajra. Pakpa was able to secure Kublai's submission and full initiation next day only after being visited in a dream and given understanding of the *Tantras*

[85] Sir Charles Bell, *The Religion of Tibet*, (Oxford, 1931), p. 66. Cf. Gaubil, p. 189, n. 2 and de Mailla, IX, p. 403n. The first detailed biographies of Pakpa available in Europe were in Schmidt, pp. 15–19, 395–8 and in Georg Huth, ed. and trans., *Geschichte de Buddhismus in der Mongolei*, 2 vols (Strassburg, 1892–6), II, 139ff.   [86] Howorth, I, 508. See also Hoffman, p. 137. For the widespread influence of Indian cosmology, see Waddell, pp. 77–81. That the Tibetans used this Indian cosmology was made known in the eighteenth century by the Jesuits and is reported by Desideri (see chapter 5, n. 55) and Giorgi (p. 472). Giorgi's book, which includes the first European reproduction of the Buddhist Wheel of Life (with its paradises and hells), was known to Jones (*LWJ* Letter 433, II, 698; *AR*, III, 10–11) and, since it makes reference to itself as *Alph. Tib.* could just perhaps have had some bearing on Coleridge's river Alph? In 1795 it was the subject of an important attack which took the form of a defence of the antiquity of Indian letters (Paulinus a S. Bartholomaeo, *De Veteribus Indis Dissertatio in qua Cavillationes Auctoris Alphabeti Tibetani Castigantur*, Rome, 1795), An earlier book on Indian religion by the same author, *Systema Bramanicum* (Rome, 1791), reviewed in *BC*, I (June 1793), 225, was later sought by Southey (*MWTN*, Southey to Taylor Letter 49. II, 116). Another, *Examen Historico-criticum Codicum Indicorum* (Rome, 1792), reviewed in *BC*, III (Jan. 1794), 99–102, argues in favour of both a Classical Greek and a northern Buddhist debt to India and notes the close similarity between passages in the (work of) Amarasimha and the Orphic hymns.   [87] *Buddhist Mahayana Sutras*, trans. E.B. Cowell *et al.* (London, 1894) Pt II, 60–5. For its derivation from the Brahmin, see ibid., Pt II, xxii.   [88] Waddell, pp. 86–8, 149. At this time the Sukhavati (Paradise) school was prevalent in the Mongol Court in Iran as well as in the Far East (Waddell, p. 139; Jahn, pp. xl, lxxi, lxxv).   [89] Hoffman, pp. 123–30.

by lordly Mahakala (Great Time, or Eternity) in the form of a Brahmin.[90]

Of Kublai's spiritual development following his initiation into the *Tantras* there is (and perhaps can be) no record beyond the association of his name with those processes whereby a man learns to control his incarnations and so transcend time. At Sakya, the Tibetan monastery where Pakpa received his training and to whose hierarch the *Tantras* of the Hevajra belonged, Kublai is still regarded as a *bodhisattva*. In Kublai's time, as now, Sakya was famous as a centre for the practice of both yogic meditation and magic rites designed to achieve for the initiate mastery over those demonic powers which stand between him and that state of enlightenment to which Buddhist art points by way of its paradisal images of Mount Meru and Shamba-la.[91] Through concentration, the *yogi* or *arhat* is believed to gain such mastery over matter that, as a by-product, he can perform magical or miraculous feats such as Marco Polo reports seeing at Kublai's court—the work, Friar Ricold further noted, of men of great wisdom and morality from India.[92] Compounded with the practice of yoga is the use of *mantras*, or spells, whereby words, invariably arranged in circles, are wholly identified with the things they denote. The initiate seeks to harness the fierce as well as the quiescent side of the self and assimilate the demonic to the bodhisattvic.[93] Lest the pertinence of all this to a reading of 'Kubla Khan' is obscure, one might add that, in Mahayana Buddhist art, the initiate who has achieved this demonified state (the *mahabhava* of Indian *bhakti*) is customarily depicted with flashing eyes and floating hair.[94] When he in turn inducts others into the same tradition, the initiates circle him thrice.

Sakya was also a stronghold of saktism which means that the lamas sought to become incarnate with Avalokita, or 'the seer with bright eyes', by way of the vision of his female embodiment or *sakti*, the active or demonic manifestation of his power.[95] In the (then current) tradition of the *Kalacakra*, the sensual is to be mastered by a sublimation (though not a repression) of the sex-

---

[90] Howorth, I, 421, 506–8. The Kei Wadshra (or Hevajra) is the most important Tantric tradition.   [91] Bell, p. 65; Waddell, pp. 13–15, 128, 141–2; Monier-Williams, p. 245.   [92] Purchas, III.i.81; Yule, I, 315.   [93] Waddell, pp. 15, 128, 142–3, 152–3. The most famous *mantra* of the Buddhists is first reported by Rubruquis (Purchas, III.i.21).   [94] e.g. ibid., p. 385.   [95] Bell, p. 68; Waddell, pp. 129–31. Although Waddell (in *JRAS*) asserts that Avalokita resembles Prajapati or Brahma more than Vishnu, the identity with Vishnu has been observed by Giorgi (p. 507), Howorth (IV, 139), Monier-Williams (pp. 196–200) and Zimmer (p. 97).

ual, and demon women or *yoginis* are invoked, through whom, as they appear singly or gathering in circles, powers are acquired which permit the god within to be approached by way of the goddess. According to the archetypal imagery of the *Kalacakra*, the adept is confronted with a vision of the goddess, Time is dislocated, and he is transported to the ideal mountain valley of the Collective Unconscious. In the Buddhist *tankas*, or paintings, which depict this psychological state, the goddess is frequently shown holding a musical instrument; in the *Tantras* initiates are said to hear her divine music.

THE MYTHOLOGY OF KASHMIR

It does seem, then, that the historical Kublai may have tried to make that transition from imperial to spiritual power which his namesake in the poem apparently aspires to make. If that is so, it may be worth considering also whether the imagery in the poem which marks the transition from one to the other can be understood in terms of the imagery of the Tantric tradition into which Kublai was initiated. From what particular geographical location, if any, the psychological imagery of Shamba-la was derived is uncertain. There are a number of beautiful central Asian valleys amid whose awesome scenery the Tantric rites were developed and practised. It seems that Marco Polo was misinformed and Kashmir was not the place where these rites originated. Yet Kashmir was the hub of Mahayana Buddhist activity in northern Asia and its reputation was such in eighteenth century Europe that Buddha himself was sometimes supposed to have been a Kashmiri.[96] In the East itself Buddha was reported as saying that no country would surpass Kashmir in the practice of yoga and *samadhi*, or religious trance.[97] Maurice was quite right in surmising that it had a high reputation among Indian Brahmins,[98] and it was revered also by Chinese Buddhists and Persian Muslims.[99]

Whatever intimations of Kashmir and its conceptions of immortality there may have been in the English mind at the end of the eighteenth century, much more was known and realized about them at the court of Kublai. Marco Polo mentions the prom-

[96] De Mailla, IX, 403n; *HH*, II, 491. See Comte de Volney, *The Ruins*, trans. unnamed, 2nd ed. (London, 1795), p. 206; Jones in *AR*, I, 425; II, 125.   [97] J.Ph. Vogel, *Indian Serpent Lore* (London, 1926), p. 234.   [98] Muir, II, 337–9. [99] Samuel Beal, trans. *Si-yu-ki: Buddhist Records of the Western World*, 2 vols (London, 1884), I, 151–6; *Kalhana's Rajatarangini*, trans. M.A. Stein, 2 vols (Westminster, 1890), II, 359–60 and nn. 46–7; Jahn, pp. xiii, xxxii.

inence of one Kashmiri there,[100] but apart from that Kashmiris had been the first Buddhists to be raised to honour at the Mongol court and Kashmiris were among those engaged by Kublai to collate and translate the Mahayana Buddhist canon.[101] The tradition within which Pakpa was trained at Sakya had been established by Sakyasribadya, popularly known as the Pandit of Kashmir,[102] and almost every important Tibetan Buddhist had either studied in Kashmir or under a Kashmiri how to practise the arts of the 'Mother' *Tantras* and so be able to 'convert the demonesses'.[103] Such powers were developed to free the initiate from the repetitious cycle of metempsychosis, of being bound to the body by time and place. It seems reasonable to assume that the scenery of Kashmir provided the imagery used by those who developed the Tantric rites in the midst of it. Be that as it may, what is certain is that the scenery so evocatively described by Bernier *is* arranged into a coherent mythology which images out those states of consciousness thought to be indicative of the very edge of enlightenment.

If we now turn to Kashmiri mythology to provide a coherent reading of 'Kubla Khan' it is not only because it belongs to a more general Oriental tradition to which Coleridge was attracted and for which he could find equivalents in his own intellectual tradition. It is also because that intellectual tradition (itself the one most open to Oriental equivalents) offers a metaphysical scheme which indicates that a proper arrangement of the Oriental images, if they were to be at once both imaginatively and historically true, could have been discovered by the poet only in the imaginative state whose comprehensive powers he, for one, did not doubt. Coleridge was not and did not have to be informed

[100] Purchas, III.i.81. His name was 'Qarantas Bakshi' (see Boyle, p. 302).   [101] Gaubil, pp. 105–6 and 105 n. 3. See also De Mailla, IX.253–4. For the perennial contribution of Kashmiris, see J.N. and P.N. Ganhar, *Buddhism in Kashmir and Ladakh* (New Delhi, n.d., *c.* 1956), pp. 127–42; Waddell, pp. 21n, 30n, 35n and in *JRAS* (XXVI), 68; Hoffman, pp. 46, 73.   [102] Hoffman, pp. 131, 136; Ganhar, pp. 138–9. From the earliest establishment of Buddhism in Tibet, the influence of the Sarvastivadins, who flourished in Kashmir, was strongly felt (Bell, p. 38; Ganhar, pp. 23–4; Basham, p. 266) and the extent of Kashmiri influence may be gauged from the fact that, just as the Mongolians were to have an alphabet invented for them based on the Tibetan to convey the new Buddhist learning, so had the Tibetans had an alphabet invented for them for the same purpose based on that prevalent in Kashmir (Hoffman, p. 37). Later, Tibetans were also to date their calendar from the arrival in their country of a Kashmiri teacher, Somanatha (Ganhar, p. 135; Hoffman, p. 129).   [103] For the links with Kashmir of Rin-chen and Atisha, see Hoffman, pp. 115–116; Bell, p. 51; Ganhar, pp. 134–5; of Chos-rab of Rva, Hoffman, pp. 129–30, 145–6; of Padma Sambhava, Waddell, p. 73 and Ganhar, p. 130.

about Kashmiri mythology for us to read his poem in terms of it. What he did have to be aware of was the great potential attributed in his day to Indian mythology (of which the Kashmiri is a variant). In his *Sketches of the Hindoos*, which Coleridge may have read,[104] Craufurd suggests that when an Egyptian image is compared with its Indian equivalent it always gives the idea of a copy in which some of the accessory parts of the original have been left out.[105] George Forster said the same thing.[106] The validity of this view of Indian mythology was shortly to be confirmed by H. H. Wilson, the first European to become thoroughly conversant with Indian cosmology, when he wrote that 'the Hindu account explains what is imperfect or contradictory in ancient tradition, as handed down from other and less carefully perpetuated sources'.[107] Wilson was saying this in the context of Burnet's cosmogony, one that is thought to have been influential on Coleridge and which Burnet himself recognized was similar to the Brahmin.[108] Whether or not we wish to concede the Hindus a priority in these matters, Craufurd as early as the 1790s leaves open the possibility that were we more fully informed about Indian mythology even so vivid a figure as Isis might pale into insignificance before her Indian prototype.

A digression into Kashmiri mythology is perhaps the more justified since it can provide us with a coherent reading of not only 'Kubla Khan' but also *Prometheus Unbound*. At the outset of this digression I should like to specify what seem to be the chief images of Coleridge's poem. The first section (11.1–11), set in Tartary, tells of a male figure (an emperor) who has attempted to build an earthly paradise, or at least a place of great beauty, centred on a river. The second section (11.12–30) deals with a fountain which seems to be the source of the river in the first section. Through its sheer natural force it threatens to destroy the paradise. The fountain is associated with a female figure and with the moon. The third section (11.31–6), however, suggests that the terrestrial dome central to the paradise is open to the sunlight, and far from being inevitably subject to destruction from the sun-

---

[104] Whalley, p. 127. *History of ye Hindoos* is the title under which Craufurd's book is bound in the Bristol Library (see this chapter, n. 126).   [105] Craufurd, pp. 322–3.   [106] George Forster, I, 54–6.   [107] Wilson, VI, cx–cxi n. See also ibid., VI, 14.   [108] Beer, pp. 242–4; Burnet, I, 381–8, 394–6; II, 20–5; *Reflections upon the Theory of the Earth* (London, 1712), p. 18. Burnet (II, 25) noticed a resemblance between his own and the Brahmin theory of the destruction and recreation of the earth. The Buddhist theory encountered in Siam was soon to be likened to Burnet's (Picart, IV, Supplement, Pt II, p. 48). For Burnet's further awareness of the similarity of his own to Indian theories, see chapter 3, n. 84.

less caves underground might actually be held in harmony with them. The fourth section (11.37–54), set in Abyssinia, tells of a female figure who sings of a mountain. The man who could revive within himself her music would be capable not only of containing the caves within the dome but of thereby building the dome in air, an aetherealization which is clearly to be valued since others who heard the same music would recognize him as a sacred or mystical figure. The recurring image of the dome may lead us to conjecture that this male figure represents a potential not realized by his counterpart (or other self) in the first section.

The dome, as we have seen, Coleridge may have associated directly with Kashmir. The historical Kublai is not said to have built a dome and the association is much more (and indeed highly) likely with the Mughal rulers of India. As it happens, Purchas, like the Mughals themselves, regarded them as direct descendants of the Mongols,[109] from whom they did, in fact, borrow the architecture of the dome. It was a late-eighteenth-century view, evident in the Indian writings of not only Maurice but also Hodges and Robertson, that domed architecture was a supraterrestrial expression of the cave as planisphere.[110] Maurice, especially, regarded the cave in Platonist terms as the world out of which the soul has to make its ascent.[111] This view happens to be congenial with the account given by a Kashmiri contemporary of Kublai's of how Buddha attained *parinirvana* by ascending through the top of a dome-shaped edifice of pure crystal, a symbol of the soul's final ascent through the sutures of the skull.[112] The domes built by the mystical Mughals decorated gardens deliberately conceived of as paradises, earthly expressions as those are of the state of spiritual enlightenment.[113]

[109] Yule, I, 348–9, n. 1. The relationship of the Mughals to the Tartars is discussed in Aziz Ahmad, p. 20. The association between them is made in the marginalia to Purchas, III.i.84, 88, 102. Kublai's religious eclecticism is noticed in Purchas, v.iv.420.   [110] *IA*, III, 346, 501–16; William Hodges, *Travels in India* (London, 1793), pp. 63–77; William Robertson, *An Historical Disquisition Concerning the Knowledge which the Ancients had of India* (London, 1791), pp. 278–81.   [111] Ibid., II, 112–14, 131–82. Cf. a contemporary account prefiguring Forster's Marabars in *AR*, I, 276–83. For Coleridge on Indian caves as the architectural form most typical of pantheistic Indian culture, see Beer, p. 247.   [112] Jahn, xlviii.   [113] As George Forster notes, it was Jahangir who especially endowed Kashmir with its decorative beauties (II, 12). In *Lalla Rookh*, Moore uses as a refrain the inscription carved by Jahangir at Shalamar: 'If there be a paradise on earth, it is this, it is this, it is this' (*Lalla Rookh*, pp. 328–30). Moore had read not only Bernier but also some of the memoirs of Jahangir, the *Tuzuki-i-Jahangiri*, trans by James Anderson, extracts of which, including some reference to Kashmir, appeared in *AM*, II, 71–85, 173–89.

The conception of the caves of ice (which in 'Kubla Khan' threaten the existence of the sunny pleasure-dome) has been traced to a reference Maurice makes to the cave at which Bernier hoped to conclude his tour of Kashmir.[114] Even Maurice was not fully aware of the significance of this cave. Situated high up in the mountains, it is the object of an important pilgrimage for Hindus on the full moon day of *Sravana* in late summer. Its name, Amarnath, literally means Lord of Immortality, and this refers to the block of ice within it which during that month first waxes and then decreases in size. It is an embodiment of the god Siva, the great *yogi* who practises asceticism in these mountains. The legend is that when the gods, threatened by Death, sought Siva's protection, he gave them here the *amrita*, or milk of immortality, before relapsing into his customary absorbed state of devotional abstraction. Those who similarly still seek him out may find him in the cave at Amarnath in the form of a *linga* of ice, for the Hindus a supernatural because self-created (*svayambhu*) wonder within (and not exclusive of) Nature. Porphyry could speak of a cave being symbolic not only of the material void but also of the intelligible essence, but Amarnath is a unique public expression of how a cave of ice can be transformed into the milk of paradise.[115]

The mythology of Kashmir which, it should be repeated, was unknown to Coleridge, encourages the identification of each and all of its sacred mountains with one or other of India's great male archetypal gods, although most frequently with Siva the ascetic. The corresponding goddesses are invariably identified with the rivers of Kashmir and the fountains by which they burst from underground. The first of the natural wonders of Kashmir whose legend Bernier preferred to discount was that of Sundabrar, a place where the effect of the sun on a fountain in the springtime forms a perfect complement to that of the moon on ice at Amarnath and is worshipped as a manifestation of the goddess.[116] The customary Kashmiri complement to Siva on his mountain, however, is Parvati, the goddess who surfaced as a river to water the desiccated land when it was first settled.[117] As we have seen from Jones's authentic 'Hymn to Durga', Parvati is regarded as the active, or female, manifestation of the passive, or male, Siva.

With Shelley's *Prometheus Unbound* in mind no less than 'Kub-

---

[114] Bernier, p. 234; Gladwin, II, 161; *HH*, I, 106–7; *CNB*, I, 240; *CPW*, I, 298 n. 1.   [115] Vigne, II, 7–11; Stein, II, 409.   [116] Bernier, pp. 232–3; Vigne, I, 339–41; Stein, I (i.33n).   [117] K. de Vreese, ed., *Nilamata or Teachings of Nila* (Leiden, 1936), 247–52; R.J. Kanjilal and J. Zadoo, eds., *Nilamatapuranam* (Lahore, 1924), 335–40. These works are variants of Kashmir's most important *purana*.

la Khan', it may be useful to record the Kashmiri cosmogony which Bernier ignored. Beneath the spring where Parvati surfaced at Vernag (literally Powerful Snake) is the underground residence of Nilanaga,[118] the Kashmiri version of the cosmic serpent of Indian mythology (itself graphically described by Maurice), the powerful *vahan*, or vehicle, on which Vishnu presides over the successive recreations of the universe. Nilanaga, whose progenitor was a sage, has been the sovereign power of Kashmir ever since the time the gods came down to 'the land in the womb of the Himalaya', previously a lifeless ocean, liberated it from a demon who had taken control after the Flood and made it possible for the goddesses to inhabit it in the shape of rivers.[119] Nilanaga granted the right of human settlement to a Brahmin on condition that humans followed certain rites to propitiate the *nagas*, or powerful daemonic forces, which continue to break out of the landscape in the shape of fountains. However, unlike the lesser Kashmiri *nagas* who leave their homes at the base of the mountains and emerge above ground at fountains to use their powers for good or ill,[120] the Nilanaga is archetypal and like Shelley's Demogorgon (who is similarly described and located) moves only at cosmic moments.[121]

The mythology of Kashmir is not simply metaphorical. The imagery drawn from the landscape is returned to it in such an idealized shape that it is only necessary to look at the pattern of a popular pilgrimage to understand the meaning of the mythology. The object of a pilgrimage is invariably a *tirtha*, or sacred watering-place.[122] The daemonic force, or *naga*, is propitiated and the sacred river, or active energy of the god, is followed back to its source on the sacred mountain, where it is reabsorbed in (as it originally emanated from) the passive god. Sages are actually thought to have such control over nature as to be able to make a river stand

[118] *Nilamata*, 329–31; *Nilamatapuranam*, Appendix A, pp. 429–32; Stein, I (i.28 and n).   [119] A fully elaborated account of the Flood myth of Kashmir extends up to *Nilamata*, 329; *Nilamatapuranam*, 429. The legend is told in English in Vogel, pp. 235–8. Although Buhler, in discussing the Nilamata legend (p. 38), notes that much of it may be derived from *MH*, *MH* itself probably drew many of its legends from this northern region. Buddhist accounts of the settlement of Kashmir are even more pertinent to our discussion of 'Kubla Khan' and *Prometheus Unbound* in that they make it dependent not on the transcendent powers of gods but on the immanent powers of a sage (Vogel, pp. 233–5; Beal, I, 149–50).   [120] Vogel, p. 232. Note that a *naga* (the serpent power) may become a pious ascetic or a self-denying saint (ibid., p. vii).   [121] See chapter 7, pp. 265–8. Cf. the description of Seshanaga in *VP*, II, v, 211–13 and that from the *Bhagavata Purana* in *HH*, II, 455–7 with *Nilamata*, 323–71; *Nilamatapuranam*, 424–75; Vogel, 238–9.   [122] Stein, II, 367, 381. Mythology *per se* assumes that *tirthas* exist in the mind as well as on earth; Hindu texts confirm this point (e.g. *MH*, Section CVIII of the Anuçasana Parva, pp. 538–40).

up in the form of a goddess and return to source.[123]

In the popular Kashmiri imagination the goddess (Maya, or Nature) invariably appears as Parvati the river-daughter of the mountains. For the *pandits*, however, and especially the Sarasvata Brahmins, she takes the form of Sarasvati, a mountain stream still but specifically a stream of learning and poetry. Kashmir is regarded as 'the abode of Sarasvati', a home of poetry, and the oldest alphabet in use in Kashmir is not only sacred to but actually regarded as *being* Sarasvati. One of the most famous of all Indian shrines was established in Kashmir when a sage who had practised great austerities was promised a vision of Sarasvati if he went on a pilgrimage to the northernmost part of the country. The vision he had of her before joining her on her sacred mountain was in her triple form as Sarada, as Sarasvati and as Vagdevi. In this form the goddess is, simultaneously, the sacred river born of the mountains, the inventor of the *vina*, or lyre, and divine speech.[124]

Sarasvati, in fact, is of very ancient lineage, being the name of India's oldest sacred river, far older than the Ganges.[125] While it is a reading (and not the writing) of 'Kubla Khan' which now occupies us, it is worth mentioning that Coleridge may have been aware of the existence of this Indian goddess. Jones wrote a hymn about her and an edited version of this was published in Craufurd's *Sketches*, a copy of which was available in the Bristol Library and, for example, taken out in Robert Lovell's name in September 1795.[126] Craufurd includes Jones's note which describes Sarasvati (the consort of the creative god, Brahma) as the patroness of imagination and invention, who is represented with a musical instrument in her hand and is said to have invented an alphabet and a language as a means of conveying divine laws to mankind. Another note refers to Sarasvati as a sacred river which joins other such rivers underground.[127] Whether or not Coleridge ever knew of her in her Indian *avatar*, the goddess of poetry in this form does have, as Craufurd suggests Indian images have, a lot of those accessory parts which her equivalents in other mytho-

---

[123] Ibid., I, (i.160–6); *MH*, Section XC in the Tirtha-yatra of the Vana Parva, pp. 294–6. This conception was carried to the Mongol court (Howorth, I, 420). The condition of control of the senses is described in the Buddhist *Dhammapada* as being 'bound upstream' (XVI, 218).   [124] G. Buhler, 'Detailed Report of a Tour in Search of Sanskrit Mss.'. *JRAS* (Bombay), Extra No. (1877), pp. 19, 29–31, 48; Stein, I, Introduction, 46, n. 5; i.37 and n; II, Note B, 279–89; Muir, II, 338–9; Vigne, I, 365; Sachau, I, 117.   [125] See chapter 5, p. 170 and n. 93.   [126] See this chapter, p. 213 and n. 104. This book was taken out on 21 Sept. 1795, shortly before Coleridge married Lovell's sister-in-law.   [127] Craufurd, pp. 150–5. See this chapter, n. 136.

logies lack.[128] The figure of Isis may encourage us to identify the sacred river of the first section of 'Kubla Khan' with the Abyssinian maid of the fourth, but her myth is not comprehensive enough to suggest the connection between all the main images in the poem.

To show that Sarasvati does have this capacity, there is one further Kashmiri legend which may be mentioned. As early as the *Aitereya Brahmana* it was said that Sarasvati could enable a man to 'see' a hymn and thus become a *rishi*.[129] According to Wilford in an early volume of *Asiatic Researches*,[130] it was Sarasvati who declared that the Kashmiri Samdhimati would be a king, a prophecy which caused the reigning monarch to have him impaled or crucified. As we have noted , Kashmir is famed for its Tantric rites, practised by Hindu and Buddhist alike[131] and designed to give the initiate control over nature, or supernatural powers. These rites include that centred on a *cakranayaka* within the circle of mothers, or goddesses. Samdhimati's corpse was subjected to this rite. Serpentine *yoginis* danced around and attracted his wandering spirit back to the body, procured for him a *membrum virile*, made him the master of their band and en-

[128] See Muir, v, 337–43. Sarasvati is the Goddess (or Maya) in her creative aspect as the *sakti* or dynamic form of Brahma, though also, according to the Vaishnava *puranas*, of Vishnu, as whose spouse she is depicted seated on a lotus playing a *vina*, or Indian lyre ('The Hymn to Saraswati', Arthur and Ellen Avalon, trans., *Hymns to the Goddess*, London, 1913, pp. 118–23 and 118n; *VP*, I, IX, 148; Zimmer, p. 89; Dowson, s.v. Saraswati). Sarasvati, whose names signifies 'watery' or 'flowing', is worshipped simultaneously as a river and as divinely-inspired speech. (Vasistha identifies the river with the goddess of speech in *MH*, Section XLII of the *Çalya* Parva, p. 166). In the Vedas she is the sacred river of heaven which flows uninterruptedly from the mountains to the sea but, according to the Brahmanas and the *Mahabharata*, in fulfilment of a curse on the surrounding land, thitherto holy, she goes underground and is lost in the desert—as indeed the river honoured as Sarasvati in Vedic times and still called by that name in India actually does (Ragozin, p. 108). In the *Mahabharata* this river goddess is identified, perhaps, as Muir has suggested, as a result of ceremonies celebrated within her margins, with Vach, the goddess of speech who in the *Rig Veda* (x.125.5) makes both terrible and intelligent the priests and sages whom she loves (Muir, II, 220). [129] *Aitereya Brahmana*, II, 19; Ragozin, p. 127. [130] 'Origin and Decline of the Christian Religion in India', *AR*, X, 53. [131] Buhler, pp. 23–24, 40–1; Stein, I (iii.444 and n). Bhattacharyya writes: 'The Saiva Agamas, the Vaishnava Samhitas and the Sakta Tantras [the three canons of modern Indian religion] agree on one point, namely, that the female principle representing the sakti must be associated with ultimate reality. This power is not only the cause of manifestation, but is also responsible for differentiation, and hence the diversified world in time and space, including finite individuals, comes into being because of the association of the male and the female. The universe, so originated, has a systematic process, inasmuch as the created world returns to its source in course of time, when Sakti comes to repose in Siva.' (p. 96)

joyed him as their demon lover.[132] As such he had the powers of Siva when, as Lord of the Demons, he dances his *tandava* dance amid the skulls of the dead, his hair afloat about his head, at once the sacred river fallen from heaven and the *nagas* who go out to hold it up, his eyes, like those of the *nagas* who hear music through them, flashing with the concentrated power of his third (divine) eye.[133] After this rite Samdhimati was acclaimed king but, consistently with the sublimated sexuality of the Tantric rites, he desired neither women nor music, devoting himself instead to the consecreation of *lingas* (divine embodiment as those are, to the Indian mind, of energy discovering through the physical its metaphysical reality), then abdicated and disappeared into the mountains, rejoicing 'in his heart like a beggar who builds himself kingdoms in his thoughts'.[134]

In terms of this Kashmiri mythology, how may 'Kubla Khan' be read? The Kubla of Coleridge's poem, almost certainly like the historical Kublai and beyond doubt like the Mughals, seeks to express his mystical aspiration by constructing a pleasure-dome in the midst of a paradise garden. This conception is limited because the rest of the landscape is walled out and natural forces which are excluded and unharnessed are bound to prove destructive. Unlike the ascetic Siva, Kubla has neither literally nor metaphorically sought to enter the caves of ice and his sunny pleasure-dome fails to incorporate them. The river runs away from its source, or fountain, active energy uncontrolled. Kubla has not sought to 'convert the demoness' and so the woman is left wailing for her demon lover. Or so it seems. For the possibility is then raised that in some way perhaps Kubla did contain this force and hold nature in harmony with his art. Many kings of Kashmir had tried to do so, most notably Zainu-l-'abidin, who made the hermitage which, Bernier reported, was said to miraculously float upon the water. It is pertinent that the same king was popularly believed to have found a way to let his soul go free of his body.[135] The ability to create a miracle of rare device is supposed to be possible only to a sage who has harnessed his active energies, at which point the interior and exterior landscapes (microcosm and macrocosm) becoming increasingly identical, he may, like the Kashmiri *rishis* make the sacred river stand up in the form

[132] Stein, I (ii.98–110).   [133] Zimmer, pp. 115, 151–6, 166–75; Ananda Coomaraswamy, *The Dance of Siva* (New York, 1918), pp. 56–66; Stein, I (v.1 and n.1).   [134] Stein, I (ii.158–71). According to Marco Polo this was also the fate of Buddha (Yule, II, III, xv, 316–20, 328–30, n. 6). For a story of this type in English literature, see Kipling's 'The Miracle of Purun Bhagat', *The Second Jungle Book* (London, 1895), pp. 26–46.   [135] Vigne, II, 153–4; Gladwin, II, 189–90.

of a goddess, or, to put it another way, be accorded a vision of the goddess Sarasvati. He is no longer subject to the material world, to the processes of nature embodied in a goddess figure. He has not rejected the material world but he has seen it aright and is therefore spiritually enlightened.

According to this reading the Abyssinian maid is just such an appearance of the goddess, who is no longer a river running away through the valley to be lost underground but a call to return to the holy mountain (Abora) where active energies are properly reabsorbed and concentrated in the passive. The emperor Kubla, like Samdhimati, has aspired to be an ascetic and, like Siva, can now be identified with the mountain in the same way that his counterpart, the maid, is identified with the river. Possibly, like Buddha himself, Kubla moves into a third condition beyond those of emperor or ascetic where images of dome and cave are alike transcended and—activity resolved in passivity, action in contemplation, actual in potential—the mystic builds indestructibly, because intangibly, 'in air'.

Still within the framework of Kashmiri mythology, it is possible to vary or elaborate on this reading of 'Kubla Khan' and take the second part of the poem (section four, or the Abyssinian maid section) as a reworking from a slightly different angle of the first (sections one to three, on Kubla). This second part of the poem can be read as a reflection on the first, a meditation on the loss of Vision which was perilously but ultimately achieved there by Kubla. The poet now is no longer inside the Vision, identifying with the threatened male archetype. Instead, he is distanced, the male has undergone metamorphosis into a remote mountain and it is the active river with whom the poet seeks to identify. The river is harnessed in that it has been made to 'stand up' in its archetypal female shape and as such is a call to Vision. Read in terms of the myth of Sarasvati that call involves not only Kubla but Coleridge and the reader. The Abyssinian maid may be regarded as the goddess who permitted Coleridge to 'see' a poem expressive of the divine laws. This can be apprehended in the way a multiplicity of disparate images from nature coexist harmoniously and the world recreated in the poem is in that sense supernatural or aethereal. Nature has been transformed by Imagination. Just as the song of Godbole impersonating the maid Radha is a call which extends to take in not just the other characters but the whole of *A Passage to India* (so that it, too, becomes a call to Vision), so is the singing of the Abyssinian maid a call which extends throughout—and out through—'Kubla Khan'.[136]

In the chapter on *A Passage to India* we noticed that *bhakta* dualism (through its very insistence on separation and distance) might be more evocative of mystical vision or union (and perhaps more apposite to art) than Sankara's non-dualism. So, too, in 'Kubla Khan', the sense of a mystical state is most powerfully evoked when the poet claims to have lost it and aspires to regain it. The fact that the Vision is here conceived in terms of its loss or absence might encourage a more sceptical reading of the poem. On the other hand, it is a mystical vision that is lost or absent. Towards the end of 'Kubla Khan' Coleridge makes a point about the mystical dance at its climax similar to that made by Forster about the corresponding dance at Mau: namely, that it is celebrated only by those who aspire to 'hear' the visionary music. By this token a reading in terms of mysticism, like mysticism itself, might seem impossibly solipsistic were it not that in the poem, as in the novel, it is the elusive mystical figure central to it who embodies a philosophy capable of providing a coherent explanation for the imagery of the whole.

THE APPROACH THROUGH NEO-PLATONISM

The final reference to *A Passage to India* in the context of 'Kubla Khan' might appear anachronistic and ahistorical were it not that a study of the intellectual background to Forster's novel has pointed up perennial problems about mysticism and India as old and as obscure as the origins of Hellenic idealism. It is not wholly gratuitous, therefore, to pose the question as to whether 'Kubla Khan' can be considered a passage to India. In an obvious sense the answer must be 'not at all'. In the first chapter of this book it was suggested that Forster's novel could be read more essentially as a passage to the Imagination than as a passage to India and that that passage might be charted in terms of neo-Platonism. It could not be denied, however, that Forster not only used Indian images but used India as a comprehensive, or ideal, image for the whole. In 'Kubla Khan' Coleridge does not resort to a single overtly Indian image, and if Forster's novel need not be read as a passage

---

[136] E.M. Forster invoked Sarasvati at the outset of his attempt to write a novel about India: 'I want something beyond the field of action and behaviour: the waters of the river that rises from the middle of the earth to join the Ganges and the Jumna where they join.' He continues 'India is full of such wonders, but she can't give them to me' (Letter to Forrest Reid of 2 Feb. 1913, cited in Furbank, I, 249).

to India it might seem to follow that 'Kubla Khan' simply can not be. Paradoxically, this does not follow. Once the possibility is established that the relationship of neo-Platonism to Indian idealism is ambiguous and Forster's novel can be read as a neo-Platonist work cloaked in Indian imagery, then it follows that, conversely, works ostensibly 'neo-Platonist' may absorb or conceal Indian influences behind a façade of Greek or other images. Neo-Platonism *itself* may be the prime example of this phenomenon. The possibility of Indian influence remains everlastingly open.

In Coleridge's poem we have a collection of Oriental images which could be explained in terms of the neo-Platonist philosophers who were up to the time of its composition his 'darling studies'.[137] We know that Coleridge, like many of his contemporaries, conceived of the Indian Orient in terms of Pythagoras and neo-Platonism and that he did so not only prosaically but also when he was speculating about those imaginative states in which neo-Platonism asserts that identities are discovered. It might appear odd to read even an avowedly Oriental poem in terms of the Indian concept of a *sakti* and her relationship to the god were it not clear that contemporaries such as Jones and Maurice quite consciously conceived of the Indian goddess in terms of the Psyche of neo-Platonism, whether depicted by Apuleius as the mistress who wanders the world in search of her immortal lover[138] or by Plotinus as the daughter who seeks her heavenly father.[139]

In a passage which is pertinent to the way we have read 'Kubla Khan', Plotinus writes that Soul is

a secondary, an image of the Intellectual-Principle . . . an *utterance* of the Intellectual-Principle; it is even the total of its activity, the entire *stream* of life sent forth by that Principle to the production of further being . . . for its perfecting it must look to that Divine Mind, which may be thought of as a father watching over the development of his child born imperfect in comparison with himself.

In a premise basic to neo-Platonism, Plotinus adds that the world of sense, however beautiful, is but an image of the Intellectual, or archetypal, world that is the true Golden Age. This conception

---

[137] *CLSTC*, Letter 156 (to Thelwall, 19 Nov. 1796), I, 260. Lowes (somewhat lightly) lists all the neo-Platonist influences (pp. 229–33). Beer's book treats them more seriously. In view of the Preface to 'Kubla Khan' concerning the person from Porlock, it may be worth recording that Porphyry writes of Plotinus that 'interrupted, perhaps, by someone entering on business, he never lost hold of his plan'. [138] The myth of Cupid and Psyche in *The Golden Ass*, IV.28–VI.24. [139] *Enn.*, III.v.8; VI.ix.9.

of the active female archetype as an 'utterance' or 'stream' is wholly consistent with all we have said about Sarasvatī—or the Abyssinian maid.[140]

I offer the example of Psyche simply to show how easily neo-Platonism may be, and in the 1790s was,[141] used as a mediating factor between English poetry and Indian mythology. Once more, however, it is necessary to repeat what the initial chapter on *A Passage to India* hoped to demonstrate: namely,that while we may make sense of Oriental images in terms of the neo-Platonist intellectual scheme, this does not necessarily assume on the part of the writer a conscious application of neo-Platonist thought so much as an attraction to neo-Platonism as the intellectual scheme which best mirrors his own imaginative experience. Much later in his life, in a passage in the *Biographia Literaria* where he was lifting himself towards the philosophic imagination of Plotinus, Coleridge said he was astounded that he had once conceived of rivers which, measured and sounded by a few in all ages, not only tell of a source far higher and farther inward than either the first range of hills or the mountains beyond, but, containing elements which neither vale nor mountains can supply, travel uphill to their source.[142] The task of unriddling the nature of that river, Coleridge left to 'Morpheus, the Dream-weaver', apologizing (ambiguously) for the passage just as he had apologized (ambiguously) for 'Kubla Khan', a poem similarly concerned about a magical river and similarly woven in a dream.

All this might encourage us to read 'Kubla Khan' as a European poem with a decorative Oriental surface, better read, perhaps, in terms of neo-Platonism. There is, of course, the fact that neo-Platonism itself is at least as Oriental as Alexandria, a port on the passage to, if not from, India. In spite of that it could be argued that even something so central as Jones's essays on Asia, like Forster's novel on India, are basically a Platonist conception decorated with Oriental images. Further than that the matter would not need to be taken were it not that the Platonist

---

[140] Ibid., v.i.3–4. Staal identifies the Indian *sakti* with the neo-Platonist *dynamis* (p. 177). Thomas Taylor had spoken of this conception of the goddess and the god as a feature of Orphism (Iamblichus, p. 18, n. 1).   [141] Thomas Taylor published his translation of this fable in 1795. A year earlier Thomas Maurice had already published an abridged version of it in *IA* (v, 1020–47), finding it congenial with Indian fictions and thus assuming it to be of Asiatic origin. It was Jones's favourite metaphysical fable and he not only associated it with the Indian concept of *maya* (*AR*, I, 223) but even conceived of the Indian philosophers mentioned by Clement of Alexandria as teaching in terms of it (*AR*, I, 424). The fable was attractive both to Coleridge (*Aids to Reflection*, p. 278) and to Shelley (*LPBS*, Letter 398, I, 542).   [142] *BL* (Pt II), 240–7 and 247 n. 3.

approach to India invariably elaborates images which accord with Indian reality. In composing 'Kubla Khan' Coleridge not only had the sort of imaginative experience which is valued in the Indian Orient, but during the experience he apprehended it in terms of images which that same Orient has associated with mysticism. It is this coincidence which has caused me to resort to the Indian cosmologies which the modern academic philosopher, J.N. Findlay, like the Turkish Spy,[143] considers not only congenial to the Pythagorean-Platonic but absolutely unmatched in their conceptions.[144]

A PSYCHOLOGICAL CURIOSITY

The information Coleridge did have about the historical Kublai does not in itself account for 'Kubla Khan' being written as it was any more than for how I have read the poem. The transformation of history into psychology is clearly as subtle an inner process as that of geography into mythology. We should not, however, underestimate Coleridge's conscious interest in the Orient. Not only did he share in the general contemporary interest in India but he was also aware, as few in his time were, of the influence of India on the Buddhist lamas of Tibet. In the same document where he refers to the awe with which in his younger days he regarded the earliest translations of Sanskrit religious texts, he uses the image of the Dalai Lama, 'the temple-throned infant of Thibet', as 'a pregnant symbol of the whole Brahman Theosophy'. In denouncing what he calls the languor, indistinction and unresolved riddles of the Hinduism which he had once so far fallen in with as to identify himself with their epitome—the god Vishnu—he here evokes the cognate image of the Dalai Lama (the incarnate Buddha, the basis of whose temporal power was first laid by Kublai Khan) sitting enthroned in the Himalayas, the Ganges cradled at his feet.[145] Coleridge had not always been so dogmatic. At the turn of the century, rehearsing the argument for having his sons christened, Coleridge admitted to times when he saw the superstitious customs of both lama and Brahmin as 'ever-

---

[143] *Turkish Spy*, VI.III xvii. [144] J.N. Findlay, *The Transcendence of the Cave* (London, 1967), pp. 165–7. 'I must here confess my immense debt to Indian cosmological ideas, both Hindu and Buddhist. Despite the many deficiencies of the Indian mind, it has undoubtedly been the recipient of an inspired spiritual geography and an inspired spiritual methodology of which no one else has possessed even the rudiments' (J.N. Findlay, *The Discipline of the Cave*, London, 1966, p. 39). [145] Muirhead, pp. 283–4. Shaffer remarks on the continuing attraction of this *topos* for Coleridge (p. 133).

varying incarnations of the eternal life . . . become sanctified and sublime by the feelings that cluster round them'.[146] He even spoke of his young son Hartley as having a 'Brahman love and awe of life'.[147] Wherever Coleridge first got his knowledge of the link between India and Tibet—and, in the 1790s, it could have been through Jones, Craufurd or, possibly, John Stewart[148]—the vividness of his later denunciation[149] is indicative of an imaginative grasp which, in a more speculative frame of mind, might rearrange with equal power and to greater effect his image of India's sacred river and mountains surmounted by a revered Buddhist figure whose temporal power was matched by his spiritual aspiration.

In his essay on 'Kubla Khan' Borges eventually concluded that, rather than speaking about the soul of Kublai penetrating that of Coleridge, it was preferable to think of two (among other) men being engaged in discovering what is essentially the same (Platonist concept of) archetype. In a similar though generalized context J.N. Findlay, conceiving of egos 'whose whole life is concentrated into pure pulses of thought, like the dwellers in the formless worlds of Buddhism', considers that even with them there may be a 'concrete carrying out of the content of their thought-intentions'. To say that Kublai and Coleridge met is a statement 'infected with a deep vein of the absurd'—such as Findlay admits 'the system of communicating egos' will be unless we 'remove that absurdity by rising above it altogether, perhaps to modes of conceiving and explaining not fully exemplified nor graspable in this present life'.[150] That an entranced Coleridge could discover

---

[146] *CLSTC*, Letter 352, I, 624–5.   [147] *CNB*, I, 959.   [148] The best English account of Tibet at this time, which stresses the affinity of the religion of the deified Dalai Lama with that of the Brahmins and their mutual respect for the waters of the Ganges, is in a letter from John Stewart to Sir John Pringle, pub. in *Philosophical Transactions*, LXVII, Pt 2 (1777), 465–92.   [149] Coleridge's objection that the Indians confuse greatness with bigness is identical with Southey's (*Kehama*, Note to XXIV, 254, p. 369. In this note on the *Siva Purana*, Southey writes: 'Throughout the Hindoo fables there is the constant mistake of bulk for sublimity').   [150] *The Discipline of the Cave*, pp. 197–8, 218. The context of Findlay's remarks is an argument that it is our participation in universal reason which makes the invisible accessible to us, precisely the philosophical position J.H. Muirhead claimed for Coleridge in asserting that he was not a mystic but a metaphysician ('Metaphysician or Mystic?', *Coleridge: Studies by Several Hands*, ed. Edmund Blunden and Earl Leslie Griggs, London, 1934, pp. 179–97). The very title of Muirhead's essay suggests the difficulty that exists and Findlay prefers to resort to Buddhist metaphysics to be coherent about what might otherwise be described as Platonist mysticism. The Buddhist position on 'communicating egos' is clearly stated by Asvaghosa. The pulsing of thought-intentions, of the individual out of the universal, is still an upheaval of *avidya*, or ignorance, out of the *Tathata*, or the

certain images arranged in an archetypal pattern is not surprising, but to find that the original of his own most dominant image, the emperor Kubla, may have done the same thing is certainly 'a psychological curiosity'. Since Coleridge did not have access to the more extensive information about the Orient which has now become available, we probably have to account for the coincidence in terms of the sort of imaginative experience for which the Indianized Orient, because of its adherence to mysticism, seemed in the imagination of Coleridge to provide the most appropriate imagery.

This is germane to our whole discussion of the place of India in the English Imagination. While insisting that it is in a *reading* of 'Kubla Khan' that India may prove an image useful to its interpretation, it will be clear that I do not rule out the possibility that it may have played about Coleridge's mind at the time of composition. The work of scholars such as J.L. Lowes and J.B. Beer, among others, has made it clear that Coleridge acquired his images from all over the world. Equally clearly there is a preponderance of Oriental references, but there is not a single specifically Indian image. Jones's essay on the Tartars may be important in establishing the atmosphere of the first section of the poem but that is not certain, and even then India stands hidden behind its own influence on Tartary. Bernier's description does seem to be a 'source' for images in the third section, but there again there is no overt reference to Kashmir in the way there is to Xanadu or to Abyssinia. The second section may owe something to several landscapes, and while the maid is denominated Abyssinian by the poet the male figure in the fourth section is sometimes thought to have been developed out of an Arabian or Persian original.[151] Only if the image of India took on a universal significance could it be said that the poem was in any sense Indian. But precisely what I have been arguing is that the intellectual milieu of the 1790s was particularly conducive to such an image of India as holding the key to man's origins. Was India the home

---

Absolute. It is, therefore, a *sakti*, or force of the Absolute which necessarily conceals Reality at the moment it manifests it (Radhakrishnan, I, 416–17, 592–6). Southey was fascinated by this Indian conception of the way Fate simultaneously reveals and blinds and used it centrally in *Kehama*, xx.4, 215. Kipling will make use of the same idea in an Indian context in 'The Finest Story in the World', *Many Inventions* (London, 1893), pp. 90–128. So (while acknowledging his debt to Kipling) will J.L. Borges in 'The Man on the Threshold', *The Aleph and Other Stories*, ed. and trans. Norman Thomas di Giovanni (London, 1971), pp. 129–35. [151] Lowes, pp. 361–2. Beer has suggested the possibility of an Indian original—the dance of Krishna (pp. 263–4).

of philosophy? Was Sanskrit the primaeval language of mankind? Did all civilization originate there? The Orientalism of the last decade of the eighteenth century gave promise and induced considerable speculation that further knowledge of ancient Indian civilization would lay bare secrets which man had lost when he came out of Paradise.

As time went on Coleridge became increasingly sceptical of the claims made for Indian wisdom, just as he became increasingly sceptical of neo-Platonist mysticism. This chapter has been written with the 1790s in view. Coleridge was then more open to these moods of abstruser musing which appear to have given rise to his most imaginative poetic work. He was acquainted with the work of Thomas Maurice, who uses the new researches into Indian civilization as a basis for speculating about the single terrestrial source of mankind both after the Fall and after the Flood. The space given in the leading periodicals of the day to Maurice's work and the effect it had on, for example, a fellow poet such as Bowles indicates something of the intellectual importance of the subject. The antiquity Jones claimed for Indian culture and the undoubted authority of his work on Indian mythology and the Sanskrit language forced Europe to conceive of its origins in terms of something more Oriental than Hellenism and Judaeism, and to create the sciences of comparative mythology and philology. Initially, however, it seemed as if the Indian might be not simply the key to its European equivalents but their source. The issue was always disputed, but the point is that this was the issue in dispute. Coleridge, in a speculative mood about imaginative states, could imagine himself as a meditative (and intermittently creative) Indian god. The real case for considering India to be the absent factor which none the less links the Far East of Kubla with the Near East of the Abyssinian maid rests on something quite abstract: namely, that it was renewed contact with India which in the last decade of the eighteenth century intensified religious speculation about man and his origins and that this, more than anything, made possible the mystical spirit as well as the Oriental location to be found in 'Kubla Khan'.

Shelley: *Prometheus Unbound* and a Vale in the Indian Caucasus

in which Shelley's poem is read in
terms of Kashmiri mythology and Jones
is shown to be the mediating factor
between them.

. . . Prometheus—that truly wonderful Fable, in which the characters of the rebellious Spirit and of the Divine Friend of Mankind
(*Theos Philanthropos*) are united in the same person.

Coleridge, *Aids to Reflection.*

This poem is the masterpiece of the Greece of my mind; read it
again and again: its strain is not easy.

Plunged in the wisdom of Greece, my mind rose again from the
deep in the land of Hind; be thou as if thou hadst fallen into this
deep abyss of my knowledge.

From a *Kasidah* by Faizi (Blochmann's translation)

CHAPTER SEVEN

Shelley: *Prometheus Unbound* and a Vale in the Indian Caucasus

SHELLEY AND THE INFLUENCE OF JONES

In the eighteenth century it had been supposed that the Pir Pantsal leading into Kashmir marked the spot in the Indian Caucasus where Alexander's men had come upon the cave of Prometheus and seen the rock to which he had been chained.[1] By the beginning of the nineteenth century, however, Sir William Jones's protégé, Francis Wilford had established that any such point had to be somewhat farther west.[2] In 1817 Shelley, at the very same time as he was reading Aeschylus,[3] was reading the first two chapters of Elphinstone's modern account of north-west India, in which he describes the Hindu Kush (for which he frequently uses the Greek term Indian Caucasus) as being of such stupendous height and awful and undisturbed solitude that the mind is astonished in a way language cannot express. Elphinstone also mentions that the eastern limit of the range is Kashmir, 'a high valley' he declines to describe since it has already been celebrated by Bernier and George Forster.[4]

Whether or not Shelley's undoubted interest in Kashmir caused

---

[1] Letter of 10 April 1716, *Lettres Edifiantes et Curieuses*, ed. J.B. Du Halde, xv (Paris, 1772), 185. This letter from Desideri was one of those further disseminated in the Abbé Lambert's collection. This passage from it is reproduced in Vigne, I, 262–63. [2] In the article already discussed, *AR*, VI, 512. In his 'Dissertation on the Orthography of Asiatic Words in Roman Letters' (*WWJ*, III, 254), Jones makes the point that D'Anville's map alone exists as an improvement on Ptolemy. In 'An Introduction to the History of Nader Shah' (ibid., XII, 345–46) he had previously lamented that there was no accurate map of Asia. [3] *Journal*, 26 July, 5 August 1817. [4] Mountstuart Elphinstone, *An Account of the Kingdom of Caubul*

him to look up these modern authorities, he had certainly been reading the Classical accounts of how Alexander's men crossed the Indian Caucasus. In Quintus Curtius, which he liked,[5] and also perhaps in Diodorus Siculus,[6] he would have read how the soldiers encountered the solitary place, icy and devoid of animal life, where Prometheus was supposed to have been tortured.[7] As Stuart Curran has pointed out,[8] Shelley may also have read in Faber's *The Origin of Pagan Idolatry* a condensed version of Wilford's thesis that in the Indian Caucasus is to be found not only the origin of the Promethean myth but of many of the diverse myths about the origins of mankind. Faber himself makes extensive use of Wilford's articles on the Hindus and spends some time considering Kashmir's claim to be the site of Paradise.[9]

In Shelley's day the effect of Jones's work was such that people continued to investigate the possibility that in India were to be found the originals for many of the myths and philosophies that we consider distinctively Greek (or Jewish). This phenomenon is pertinent here because neither the protagonist nor the total *mythos* of Shelley's *Prometheus Unbound* is wholly explicable in terms of the Greek tradition of which it appears to be a part. Both *are* explicable in terms of the Indian tradition. In considering 'Kubla Khan' we speculated about the way that Jones's conception of India might foster, as it had been fostered by, the sort of syncretism encouraged or discovered by neo-Platonist thought. The point might have seemed too fine to be worth pursuing were it not for the added dimension that it was only in terms of this

---

(London, 1815), pp. 83–5, 95, 506. For Elphinstone's use of the Greek names, see, e.g. ibid., Appendix C, pp. 617–30; ibid., pp. 42, 84–5 and 85n, 94; ibid., 15–25, 89 and Note on Rivers, pp. 646–63. The Classical ambience will be further evident from the fact that Elphinstone was searching for the descendants of Alexander's men.   [5] Shelley read Curtius between July and November 1816 and preferred it to Arrian, which he read the following summer (*Journal*, 4 August, 22–25 November 1816; 18, 20–24 June 1817; *LPBS*, Letter 400, I, 545. Shelley read Plutarch's *Life of Alexander* thereafter.   [6] The composition of 'Ozymandias' several months afterwards suggests this possibility (Diodorus, I.47). For Shelley's possession of Diodorus, see *LPBS*, Letter 218, I, 344. Diodorus (XVII. 82–3) and Arrian (*Anabasis*, III.28.4–7; v.3.1–4), but not Curtius, both mention the *cave* of Prometheus.   [7] Curtius, VII.iii.11–13, 22–3.   [8] Stuart Curran, *Shelley's Annus Mirabilis* (San Marino, 1975), p. 78. That the locale of *Prometheus Unbound* reflects a renewed interest in the Indian Caucasus as the home of civilization, see Joseph Raben, 'Shelley's *Prometheus Unbound*: Why the Indian Caucasus?', *Keats-Shelley Journal*, XII (1963), 95–106; Curran, pp. 60–7 *passim*. Curran reads *PU* as reflecting the dualism of Zoroastrianism, then of current interest. He does not refer to *The Missionary*, the novel which will here be considered the book most critical to Shelley's interest in the region.   [9] 3 vols (London, 1816), I, 314–56.

prevalent and perennial image of India that we could begin to account for the peculiar coincidence whereby Coleridge projects on to Kublai Khan a psychological or imaginative state which Kublai almost certainly did seek for himself. If we turn again now to the same Orientalist tradition fostered by Jones, it is to try to account for an equally peculiar coincidence. In *Prometheus Unbound* Shelley projects on to 'a Vale in the Indian Caucasus' a pattern of imaginative imagery which is perfectly identical with that elaborated in the mythology of Kashmir.

It was in December 1812 that Shelley ordered, among other books, the *Works* of Jones. At the same time he asked for Robertson's *Disquisition Concerning the Knowledge which the Ancients had of India* and a week earlier had ordered Moor's *Hindu Pantheon.*[10] Perhaps he had been re-reading Southey's *The Curse of Kehama*, since the notes to this poem cite both Robertson and Moor, as well as, on numerous occasions, Jones. If Shelley had encountered the work of Jones at Eton, where he might have seen Dr Lind's collection of Indian antiquities, or at Oxford where Jones as a distinguished *alumnus* of his own college may have been among the 'Eastern travellers' he read, there is no evidence of it.[11] *Queen Mab* seems to offer the first tangible proof of a reading of Jones. Koeppel has left little doubt that for the whole framework of the poem whereby Ianthe is taken up in an aerial car to Mab's celestial palace and there presented with a transcendent view of the past, the present and the future of the world, Shelley is indebted to Jones's poem, 'The Palace of Fortune'.[12] This story, as we have noticed, Jones got from the Brahmins by way of Inatulla of Delhi and Alexander Dow. Actually the fact that Ianthe, unlike Jones's heroine, is being rewarded for her struggle on Earth against evil betrays an additional debt to *The Curse of Kehama*, where Kailyal's assumption of immortality and her ascent into Heaven in a celestial car is described in closely identical terms. This, however, does not detract from the debt to Jones since Southey here, as elsewhere, is also indebted to Jones.[13] Be that as it may, Shelley, by 1821, regarded *Queen Mab* as 'crude and immature in moral and political spe-

[10] *LPBS*, Letter 216, I, 342; Letter 218, I, 344.   [11] Walter Edwin Peck, *Shelley: His Life and Work*, 2 vols (London, 1927), I, 23–5, 76.   [12] See chapter 2, pp. 63–4.   [13] *Kehama*, XXIV, 22–6, pp. 266–7. Peck (I, 303–11) notices this. Southey acknowledges his debt to Jones in the preface to the Collected Edition (see this chapter, p. 239). The importance of Jones in the conception of this poem is greater than the acknowledgement to specific works in the notes would suggest.

culation as well as in the subtler discriminations of metaphysical and religious doctrine',[14] and if the poem as a whole were to be considered in terms of the Oriental spirit which pervades Jones's work it would only go to show what little influence Jones had really had.[15]

A consideration of *Queen Mab* does illustrate how difficult it is to locate an Indian influence apart from the sort of structural debt noticed by Koeppel. An alternative approach to the same question was made by R.M. Hewitt when he suggested that Shelley's 'Hymn to Intellectual Beauty' betrayed a reading of Jones's 'Hymn to Narayena'.[16] He was less concerned to find a particular phrase or image in support of this than to identify a common tone and sensibility. Referring to the opening lines of the 'Hymn to Narayena', he asks: 'Who can fail to recognize in this exordium the style and measure of the "Hymn to Intellectual Beauty" '? Presumably he is also thinking of the way Shelley, like Jones, invokes the 'unseen Power', the shadow of whose awesome presence in all that is beautiful in art and nature is as unquestionable as the question of why the shadow of the presence should be transient is unanswerable. If that is so, Hewitt's own question must remain rhetorical. If it is true to say, as Jones does in his preface, that the 'Hymn to Narayena' is conceived as a poem where Platonism is absorbed by the Indian Vedanta tradition, that statement is itself made nonsense of by the imaginative experience to which both traditions point: namely, that at which a total synthesis has been achieved and neither tradition retains a separate identity. It might be expected then that, in a manner of speaking, Shelley's Platonism[17] could as easily re-absorb Jones's Orientalism as Jones's Platonism had been absorbed by the Vedanta. This may have happened in the 'Hymn to Intellectual Beauty'. What is interesting is that this does not always happen,

---

[14] *LPBS*, Letter 636, II, 304. Mary Shelley published this as part of a Note on *Queen Mab* in 1839 (*PWPBS*, p. 838).   [15] None the less, there are passages in *Queen Mab* where the 'Spirit of Nature' is addressed in much the same tone and to much the same effect as the 'Spirit of Spirits' in the 'Hymn to Narayena' (I.264–8; III.214–16, 226–9; VII.49–51). In *Queen Mab* Nature's health 'glows in the fruits, and mantles on the stream' (VIII.115). In the 'Hymn to Narayena', Nature 'glows in the rainbow, sparkles in the stream.'   [16] Hewitt, pp. 57–9.   [17] Shelley's Platonism is exhaustively considered in J.A. Notopoulos, *The Platonism of Shelley* (Durham, N.C., 1949). Notopoulos writes that '*Prometheus Unbound* marks the fruition of the development of Shelley's Platonism' (p. 232). He also says: 'It is in the alchemy of Shelley's mind, in its fusion of Platonic notions with its own "operations of the human mind", that there results a quality of poetry which, because of its general resemblances to Neoplatonism, is called Neoplatonism' (p. 241).

least of all in *Prometheus Unbound*, and that to the end of his life Shelley is drawn to India as an image for an apprehension Greece does not fully convey.[18]

SHELLEY'S IMAGE OF INDIA: 'THE CURSE OF KEHAMA'

Like Plotinus before him, Shelley expressed a desire to make an actual passage to India but, although in the last year of his life he made enquiries of Peacock at East India House about the prospects of obtaining employ in the court of a maharajah,[19] that particular experience was to be reserved for later English writers such as J.R. Ackerley and E.M. Forster. Referring to Peacock in his versified 'Letter to Maria Gisborne', Shelley wrote:

> have you not heard
> When a man marries, dies, or turns Hindoo
> His best friends hear no more of him?[20]

The jest depends on the remark having a more serious application and, from a number of references, we may deduce that Shelley had taken an interest in India long before Peacock moved into East India House or Thomas Medwin, asking Shelley if he should publish his poems on India, received the reply that there had been 'a strong demand in the imagination of our contemporaries for the scenery & situations which you have studied'.[21]

It is during the impressionable summer of 1811 that we have the earliest and clearest indication of India coming to the surface of Shelley's mind, at the same time, perhaps, as being absorbed into his psyche. In June of that year in a letter to his close correspondent Elizabeth Hitchener, he warns her that, beautiful as it is in poetry, she should not 'in the true style of Hindoostanish devotion' personify virtue as the Deity in the way war had once been personified as Mars, policy as Juno, etc. In a letter to his friend

---

[18] The homeland recalled by both the Indian youth and the Lady in 'Fragments of an Unfinished Drama' is an idyllic place of great natural beauty (11.61–74) replete with a pleasure-dome (11.89–92) situated in the Himalaya where the rivers of India rise (11.123, 150). As we shall see, this probably points to Kashmir.

[19] *LPBS*, Letter 667, II, 361 and n. 5. Possibly Shelley hoped an Indian state might furnish an opportunity to test out Plato's speculations on civil society which, in the same letter, he writes of with respect. Encouraged no doubt by Medwin (*LPBS*, Letter 591, II, 242) and stimulated perhaps by the songs of Mrs Williams (Thomas Medwin, *The Life of Percy Bysshe Shelley*, 2 vols, London, 1847, II, 126), Shelley's hopes of going to India were dashed by Peacock (*LPBS*, Letter 676, II, 374). At one time Southey also had thought of going to India (*MWTN*, Southey to Taylor Letter 19, I, 359). [20] 11.235–7, *PWPBS*, p. 368. [21] *LPBS*, Letter 559, II, 183.

Hogg in the same month, dissuading him from forming an attachment to his sister, Elizabeth Shelley, he speaks in terms of sacrificing at the altar and of becoming an unreflecting votary at the shrine of 'the Indian Camdeo, the god of mystic love'.[22] Since Jones had written a 'Hymn to Camdeo' and in this, as in his other hymns to the Hindu deities, had specifically associated 'Hindoostanish' devotion with Classical personification—and in the one form in which Shelley had said it might be beautiful, in poetry—anyone might be forgiven for assuming that Shelley had been reading Jones's hymns. It is possible that he had been. What is certain is that he had been reading two books directly inspired by Jones's works, the hymns among them, and, judging by his own reactions to these books, no others left such a powerful impression on him during the year. He mentions both in the same letter where he chides Elizabeth Hitchener for her Hindoostanish devotion. They are *The Curse of Kehama*, which he recommends to her as his favourite poem,[23] and *The Missionary, an Indian Tale*, by Sydney Owenson, Lady Morgan.[24]

The Curse of Kehama impressed Shelley so powerfully that he went to 'pay homage' to Southey in Keswick[25] and, however disillusioned he was to become with Southey's politics, this poem was still one of the first he read out to Mary when she came to live with him three years later.[26] He was, further, as ready to cite from it in 1821 as he had been ten years earlier.[27] When it is seen how highly both Shelley and Coleridge[28] regarded *Kehama*, it becomes apparent that Indian mythology was neither so unfamiliar nor such an impediment to a reading of the poem in its own time as it has invariably seemed since. It may be that Jones's hope that English poetry might be recharged by familiarity with the imagery of the Asiatics was not wholly vain and that an influence from the Orient was both felt and, at least by some, absorbed. If such an absorption did take place and if we are to argue that *Prometheus Unbound* as completely illustrates it as the 'Hymn to Narayena' initially indicated it, then *Kehama* plays an important part in the process.

The Curse of Kehama, like some of Jones's hymns to the Hindu deities, does sometimes labour among the images of Indian

[22] Ibid., Letter 82, I, 101; Letter, 87, I, 112.   [23] Miss Hitchener soon read this poem (*LPBS*, Letter 99, I, 126).   [24] 2nd ed., 3 vols (London, 1811). Shortly before her death, the author was working on a revised version of the novel, *Luxima, the Prophetess* (London, 1859).   [25] *LPBS*, Letter 142, I, 191. [26] *Journal*, 17 September 1814.   [27] *LPBS*, Letter 653, II, 330; Letter 144, I, 195. He also spoke about the poem with Southey (Letter 155, I, 212) and quoted its motto at him nine years later (Letter, 583, II, 232).   [28] *BL*, I (Pt I), 61.

mythology, but it is not on that account to be undervalued. There is considerable justification to Southey's later claim that, even if there was nothing Oriental in its style, 'the spirit of the poem was Indian',[29] derisory as that claim might appear to be in view of his opinion that Hinduism was 'of all false religions . . . the most monstrous in its fables,. and the most fatal in its effects'.[30] Besides being familiar with virtually every worthwhile modern authority on India, Southey had read not only the well-known translations of the *Bhagavad Gita* and *Sakuntala*, the *Manava Sastra* and the *Ain-i-Akbari*, but also that of *Nala Damayanti* and passages from the *Ramayana*, the *Mahabharata*, the *Yajur Veda*, the *Bhagavata Purana* and the *Siva Purana*.[31] Whatever his conscious prejudice, then, it did not prevent Southey from composing a narrative which had much that was authentically Indian about it and was firmly based on what he had (rightly) gathered was the essential, as also the peculiar, feature of Hinduism: namely, that 'prayers, penances, and sacrifices are supposed to possess an inherent and actual value, in no degree depending upon the disposition or motive of the person who performs them. They are drafts upon Heaven, for which the Gods cannot refuse payment'.[32]

In Southey's poem these powers are acquired by the villain, Kehama, and earn him the epithet 'Man Almighty', which Coleridge objected to as producing an effect like blasphemy.[33] In overruling this objection Southey remained faithful to his concept of an Indian villain made in the image of Ravana, the great antagonist of the *Ramayana*. Nor is the villain the only character derived from classical Hindu literature. Kailyal, the Hindu heroine, reflects Southey's acquaintance with such great prototypes as Sita, Sakuntala and Damayanti and her resemblance to the last in particular gives the lie to William Taylor's criticism that 'the pure loves of Eireenia and Kalyal . . . when translated into Tamul,

---

[29] Robert Southey, *The Poetical Works*, 10 vols (London, 1837–8), VIII, Preface, xvii.   [30] *Kehama*, Preface, p. vii. Southey had also written that it was inconceivable to him how the Hindu fables had ever appeared poetical to Jones (*MWTN*, Southey to Taylor Letter 13, I, 304).   [31] All these works are referred to in the notes to *Kehama* except the *Ain-i-Akbari*, Gladwin's translation of which had been cited in the notes to Bk V of *Thalaba*. In a note to *Kehama* in the Collected Edition, VIII, 227, note to V, p. 33, Southey expressed surprise that a passage in *Kehama* was identical to one in *Nala Damayanti*, not then translated by Milman. In fact, Southey had forgotten he had read this Indian work in Kindersley's translation (cited several times in notes to the original edition). The passage in question had even been reprinted in *MR*, Appendix to XVI (1795), 570–1.   [32] *Kehama*, Preface, p. vii. Cf. *BA*, 1.4.10.   [33] Curry, I, 382.

will surely not be thought at home'.[34] Moreover, quite apart from
the debt for characterization, the whole tenor and concern of *The
Curse of Kehama*, with its excursions into the *svargas*, or paradises of the gods, and into the dread depths of the *patalas*, or under-
worlds, has a great deal in common with stories from the Indian
epics and *puranas*.

With the hindsight provided by *Prometheus Unbound*, a work
which brought a demonstrably similar theme to greater perfection, it is possible to guess why the young Shelley had doted on
Southey's poem and regarded it as perfect.[35] Most obviously,
Shelley would have been attracted to the Indian belief that a man
through his own efforts might acquire a power the gods could not
withstand. What is more, Shelley could respond to this without
the basic lack of conviction in the belief which inhibits a Christian
like Southey. Thus Shelley's Prometheus (having first suffered
the fate of Kehama's son, Arvalan, frozen to an ice-rock on
Mount Meru, beyond the limits of the living world) is able to
combine the power of Kehama, 'the Almighty Man', which
brings down the king of the gods, with the goodness, endurance
and tenderness towards all living things of Ladurlad, who, condemned to live in pain without hope of sleep or death, remains patient and tranquil, though defiant.[36]

Furthermore, the ultimate triumph of good in *Kehama* is
achieved only after the paradisal regions of the highest Indian
mountains, both actual and mythical, have fallen under the blight
of evil and the faithful daughter of the protagonist, sustained by
love and revered by all living things, has had to penetrate to the
underworld in the depths of the ocean to drink from the cup of
immortality. This archetypal—and millennial—shape manifestly
recurs in *Prometheus Unbound*, where, as a result of the love and
endurance of Prometheus among the high mountains, Asia can
plumb the depths of the underworld for the immortality which
makes Earth a paradise. In Shelley's poem the pattern is less distended not only because Shelley is uninhibited by Christianity's
exclusiveness of other religions and its tendency, *vis-à-vis* good
and evil, towards dualism,[37] but also because he is too philosophical a poet to remain lost for a moment among the images of
a labyrinthine and localized mythology.[38] In Shelley's poem both

---

[34] *MWTN*, Taylor to Southey Letter 66, II, 351.   [35] Medwin, I, 61.
[36] *Kehama*, VI.4, p. 50; XI.15–17, pp. 122–3; XIII.9, pp. 137–8.   [37] Southey
conceived of *Kehama* in terms of 'the two families of light and darkness' (*MWTN*,
Southey to Taylor Letter 22, I, 386.   [38] Shelley warned Medwin against the
employment of Indian words in his work (*LPBS*, Letter 559, II, 183–4).

the monstrous sea-serpent (which long remained on his mind) and the superman Kehama are returned to the legitimate and harmonious place both have in a monistic—and, as we shall see, arguably *Vedantin*—cosmos.

The limitations (as they would appear to be from a monistic viewpoint) imposed on Southey by his Christianity should not be overstressed. His concept of Siva as the all-containing Mind, who cannot be found in his own, the highest, heaven, and whose voice can be heard only within, is perfectly consonant with the One of Plotinus. This conception is as unorthodox as anything Shelley was to write about the gods and their paradises.[39] It is in fact to support a Platonic belief in the pre-existence of the soul that Shelley cites lines from *Kehama* in a letter from Keswick in November 1811.[40] Southey may very well have been aware of this Platonic dimension to his Indian poem since, in one note to *Kehama*, he particularly notices a resemblance between the ways Manu, the Hindu law-giver, and Henry More, the Cambridge Platonist, conceive of the soul.[41] That, at the same time, he expresses his own reservations about this common conception may serve to suggest how, paradoxically, he could remain outside his poem when he wrote it in a way that Shelley, when he read it, did not. But then it was not to be long before Shelley would remark that Southey 'seldom or ever rises with his subject',[42] and Southey would denounce Shelley's work in much the same language he had used to denounce Hinduism.[43]

In the preface to *Kehama* written for the collected edition of his *Poetical Works*, Southey refers to its subject as 'that mythology which Sir William Jones had been the first to introduce into English poetry'. His notes to the poem acknowledge his extensive debt to Jones, both directly and by way of men like Maurice and Wilford who were inspired by him. Since Shelley increasingly becomes closer in spirit to Jones than to Southey, we may assume that much of the debt he owes to *The Curse of Kehama*—for the scope and even for some of the detail of his own later work—is really due, through the sensibility he exhibits as well as the in-

---

[39] *Kehama*, XIX.10–12, pp. 210–12.   [40] *LPBS*, Letter 144, I, 195. Southey had read Bouchet on Indo-Pythagorean-Platonic correspondences in Picart (see chapter 2, n. 203).   [41] *Kehama*, pp. 279–80 (note to II, p. 13). For More's interest in India, see chapter 3, p. 86 and nn. 6–7.   [42] Medwin, II, 33.   [43] Edward Dowden, ed., *The Correspondence of Robert Southey with Caroline Bowles* (Dublin and London, 1881), Correspondence with Shelley, Letter III, p. 359. Southey refers to Shelley's poems as being monstrous in their kind and pernicious in their tendency. Cf. the opening sentence of the Preface to *Kehama* (quoted this chapter, p. 237).

formation he supplies, to Jones. As far as details go it is typical,
for example, that either of the Indian references found in Shelley's letters of June 1811—that to the Hindu god of love, Camdeo, or that which considers the personification of virtue as being
in the style of Hindoostanish devotion—could as easily have been
derived from a reading of *Kehama* as from a reading of Jones.[44]
As it so happens, in this particular instance Shelley did not incur
his debt to Jones through reading Southey any more than through
reading Jones himself. The phraseology shows that it was incur-
red through reading *The Missionary*,[45] a novel by Sydney Owenson, where the influence of Jones is felt free of the inhibitions
which restrict it in *Kehama*.

SHELLEY'S IMAGE OF INDIA: 'THE MISSIONARY'

Shelley's first reference to *The Missionary*—in the letter to Elizabeth Hitchener where he borrows a phrase from it—is not flat-
tering. While admitting that 'when young' he had dwelt on the
same ideas with enthusiasm, he rejects these—which are mystical
and overtly Indian—on the grounds that they are subversive of
reason. It is likewise on account of her faith (presumably, like
Miss Hitchener's, in a deity) that, in the following sentence, he
qualifies his regard for 'the divine Kailyal', the heroine of
Kehama.[46] However, Shelley's reservations about *The Missionary*
do not survive this one letter (his second to an older woman
whom he wishes to impress) and for Luxima, its heroine—not
only, like Kailyal, a Hindu vestal but a Brahmin priestess
besides—he never expresses anything but unqualified
admiration.[47] The novel 'is a divine thing', he tells Hogg ten days
after his letter to Miss Hitchener, 'Luxima, the Indian Priestess,
were it possible to embody such a character, is perfect'. Hogg, who
is *thrice* asked if he has read the novel, is' first informed that since
reading it Shelley, his thoughts dwelling strangely on death and
heaven, has read nothing else and then, later, that having found a
copy in another house he has read it again.[48]

The physical setting of *The Missionary* is largely determined by
Bernier's picture of Kashmir as Paradise.[49] In the novel, howev-

[44] For a reference to Camdeo, see *Kehama*, x.19–22, pp. 106–8. Kailyal, is the
example of 'Hindoostanish devotion'.   [45] See this chapter, p. 236, n. 24.
[46] *LPBS*, Letter 82, I, 101.   [47] Towards the end of *TM* (III, 115) it is stressed
that Luxima does things 'less in faith than love'.   [48] Ibid., Letter 85, I, 107;
Letter 87, I, 112; Letter 101, I, 130. Harriet (*LPBS*, Letter 199, n. 6. I, 320) and,
later, Mary (*Journal*, 19 September 1817) also read the novel.   [49] Bernier is cited
in a number of footnotes and is the European philosopher referred to in the closing

er, the Kashmir landscape is so charged metaphysically that it is itself a critical factor in the development of the platonic relationship between an idealistic Christian missionary and a Kashmiri Brahmin girl. For this reason *The Missionary*, which on the surface lapses into what might justly be termed oriental gothic,[50] has like many other gothic novels an underlay of imaginative potential which might well excite a more powerful imagination than Miss Owenson's.

Hilarion, the missionary, is said to be a perfect model of Nature's power, his body so transfigured that it partakes of the immortality of a soul prepared to suffer and resist any vicissitude.[51] Like Robert de Nobili, on whom he is apparently modelled, Hilarion is an aristocrat turned *religieux* who, in order to make Brahmin converts, learns Sanskrit and Hindi and adopts the life of an Indian *sannyasin*.[52] The 'higher order of genius', which permits him to recognize that worldly conquest such as Alexander coveted is inferior to the perfect love of God in a heart where worldly ambition has ceased to linger and human passions have been exterminated, leads him to make straight for Kashmir, described as the birthplace of Brahma, the scene of his *avatars* and the model of Indra's heavenly Paradise.[53] On his way there he encounters the vestal Hindu priestess, Luxima, the tenets of whose religious belief are described to him by a Kashmiri *pandit*. The words used by the *pandit* are in fact those Jones had used to describe the postulates of the Vedanta: namely,

that matter has no essence, independent of mental perception; and that external sensation would vanish into nothing, if the divine energy for a moment subsided: that the soul differs in degree, but not in kind, from the creative spirit of which it is a particle, and into which it will be finally absorbed: that nothing has a pure and absolute existence, but spirit: and that a passionate and exclusive love of Heaven is that feeling only, which offers no illusion to the soul, and secures its eternal felicity.[54]

This description is a compound of phrases taken from passages

---

pages of the book who goes to Kashmir (*TM*, III, 219). See chapter 6, pp. 201–3. Miss Owenson collected the Indian material for her subject from the Oriental Library of Sir Charles Ormsby, which, she said, supplied her with rare books that gave the sanction of authority to her own wild and improbable visions (W. Hepworth Dixon, ed., *Lady Morgan's Memoirs* 2 vols, London, 1862, I, 388).

[50] Coleridge associates Gothic and Indian in *PL*, XIV, 398.   [51] *TM*, I, 9–11, 27–8, 35.   [52] Ibid., I, 60–3, 120, 138–9. Miss Owenson's familiarity with the story of the Jesuits in India, of whom de Nobili was the most notable, is displayed in the opening pages of the novel. For de Nobili's part in the Platonist approach to India see chapter 2, p. 79 and n. 202.   [53] Ibid., I, 39–42, 48–9, 58–9, 141.
[54] Ibid., I, 71.

in the essays, 'On the Philosophy of the Asiatics' and 'On the Mystical Poetry of the Persians and Hindus', where Jones's response to Asia is at its most intense.[55] The phrases themselves (and others recur throughout the novel) are only a superficial indication of what is, in fact, a total immersion in the work of Jones. How close Miss Owenson's reading of Jones was may be determined by the way she puts into the mouth of the Kashmiri *pandit* words which a hint in one of his essays suggests Jones· probably did have from a Kashmiri *pandit*, Goverdhan Caul.[56] The significance of Jones's influence for the novel is that Luxima is manifestly the embodiment of the mystical philosophy to which she adheres—from her it is said, as Jones said of Asiatic poetry, that 'the sublime but impassioned tenets of religious love flow with peculiar grace'[57]—and on her depends the realization of whatever is good and beautiful in the book. But there is even more to it than this. Hilarion's comment, on hearing the Vedanta doctrine of mystical love, that it is so pure and sublime that it wants only the holy impress of (Christian) revelation to stamp it as divine, is precisely the opinion of Jones.[58] Since the rest of the novel is given over to a study of the struggle between those two points of view, embodied in the uneasy if romantic platonic relationship between Hilarion and Luxima, the book may be read as a perfectly extraordinary fictionalization of the psyche of William Jones. This reading, far-fetched as it may sound, is lent further credibility by the fact that Hilarion and Luxima are brought together, both originally and ultimately, by the Kashmiri *pandit* who, personification of a third important aspect of Jones, is a deist with a belief in the Invisible.[59]

Guided by his genius, Hilarion is drawn on to the heartland of Hinduism, the valley of Kashmir, set 'in the majestic girdle of the Indian Caucasus', the 'cradle of infant Nature' where it is still possible to experience 'the venerable and touching simplicity of the patriarchal age'.[60] The landscape of Miss Owenson's book, unlike Bernier's, belongs to Hindu literature. Under the spiritual

---

[55] *WWJ*, III, 239; IV, 219–20. In her description of Indian religious sects at Lahore (I, 86–88), Miss Owenson is indebted for her conception of the misnamed Musnavis (confused with the Vaishnavas) to Jones's essay on Mystical Poetry and for the other sectaries to the essay on Asiatic philosophy (*WWJ*, III, 239–41, 246–7).   [56] Ibid., III, 322–3. See chapter 2, pp. 53 and n. 59; 60 and n. 88.
[57] *TM*, I, 104.   [58] Jones speaks of the purity and sublimity of the Vedanta in the essays already cited in this paragraph. In the second essay Jones reaffirms his belief in the necessity of a revealed religion (*WWJ*, III, 244–5).   [59] *TM*, I, 63–4, 68–70; III, 189–90. See chapter 2, pp. 47–8.   [60] Ibid., I, 130–42.

protection of her *guru*, Luxima, with two female attendants, lives as a devotee in a grove surrounded by trees and flowers bearing sonorous Sanskrit names.[61] It would be strange if this environment, combined with Luxima's concern for a wounded faun, did not reflect a reading of Jones's *Sacontala*.[62] It is certain, from her allusions alone, that the author, in addition to reading all of Jones's most seminal essays, read at least some of his hymns to the Hindu deities and the prefaces thereto. It is in the 'Hymn to Durga' that Jones explicitly makes his plea for the retention of the Sanskrit (as deserving to be considered the celestial) names for Indian flowers and trees.[63] Furthermore, it is only from a reading of the 'Hymn to Narayena' and the 'Hymn to Camdeo', combined with a reading of the *Gita Govinda*, to which the important essay 'On the Mystical Poetry of the Persians and Hindus' serves as introduction, that Miss Owenson could have derived the hybrid concept of *Vedantins* taking as an idol for their creed of mystic love the god Camdeo while worshipping in a temple dedicated to Krishna.[64] Moreover, Luxima herself certainly owes something to one or more of the various manifestations of the goddess as Jones conceives of her in these hymns, and this is entirely consistent with the suggestion that she is a personification of all that Jones said about the Asiatic imagination—not only in his later essays but as far back as 1772 in his essay 'On the Poetry of the Eastern Nations'.

The earliest confrontations between Hilarion and Luxima take place at the confluence of two rivers where, morning and evening, she recites the *Gayatri*, the hymn to the invisible power behind the sun, which, though translated by Jones, was also available to the English public in the translation used by Miss Owenson, that by Colebrooke. On the first occasion, at dawn, it is said of Hilarion and Luxima that 'they stood finely opposed, the noblest specimens of the human species, as it appears in the most opposite regions of the earth; she, like the East, lovely and luxuriant; he, like the West, lofty and commanding . . .'. Lux-

[61] Ibid., I, 158–60.   [62] *WWJ*, IX, *Sacontala*, Acts I, III, IV. The play contains each of the details here mentioned and in a very similar context.   [63] Ibid., XIII, 245; stanza III, 1, XIII, 252. From one reference Miss Owenson makes (III, 4) it is clear that she knows Jones's essays on the Spikenard of the Ancients (*WWJ*, v, 13–46) and her use of Sanskrit names elsewhere betokens a familiarity with his 'Botanical Observation on Select Indian Plants' (*WWJ*, v, 62–162).   [64] *TM*, I, 72, 77, 79, 82, 112. The first stanza of the 'Hymn to Narayena' suggests the Vedantin concept of 'mystick Love'; in both the 'Hymn to Camdeo' and the *Gita Govinda* Camdeo is represented as affecting the loves of Krishna.

ima, then, is symbolic of the East and Hilarion takes note of her characteristics:

The warm blush of sudden emotion, the playful smile of unrepressed pleasure, the low sigh of involuntary sadness, and all these simple and obvious expressions of strong and tender feelings, which, in an advanced state of society, are observed by ceremony, or concealed by affectation, betrayed to the Monk, a character, in which tenderness and enthusiasm, and genius and sensibility, mingled their attributes.[65]

This conception of the East almost certainly betrays a reading of Jones's early essays—'On the Poetry of the Eastern Nations' and 'On the Arts Commonly Called Imitative', where he argues that the power of Asiatic, like all good original, poetry consists in its being a natural expression of strong and tender passions.[66]

Jones's observation here, which he assumes has always been conceded, 'that the Asiaticks excel the inhabitants of our colder regions in the liveliness of their fancy, and the richness of their invention' leads on naturally to his later suggestion, made after he had actually got to India, that while reason and taste were the prerogatives of European minds the Asiatics had risen to loftier heights in the sphere of imagination. If it is to the later remark, made in the second anniversary discourse to the Asiatic Society, that Miss Owenson owes her presentation of Hilarion and Luxima as a distinct contrast between East and West, it is to the earlier essay on Eastern poetry, where Jones first began to evolve this theory, that she owes her further description of Luxima as being 'the emblem of that lovely region, whose mild and delicious climate had contributed to form the beauty of her person, the softness of her character, and the ardour of her imagination'.[67] It is the more interesting that, although in this context Miss Owenson is applying to Kashmir remarks Jones made about Arabia, already in that essay of 1772 Jones had noted that the one terrestrial paradise comparable to Arabia was Kashmir, a place destined to supersede Arabia in his imagination.[68]

Hilarion, having already chided Luxima for a failure to distinguish between created and Creator which he supposes is implicit in

---

[65] *TM*, I, 148–9; 193–4. For Colebrooke's translation of the *Gayatri*, see *AR*, V, 349; for Jones's translation, see *WWJ*, XIII, 367.   [66] WWJ, X, 338–60, 361–80. Jones's argument is made clear within the first few pages of each essay. The originality in contemporary poetic theory of the second of these essays was noted by M.H. Abrams, *The Mirror and the Lamp* (New York, 1953), pp. 87–8.

[67]*TM*, III, 6. It is the contention of Jones in his essay that it is the delightful climate of Asia which has given the people and their poetry characteristics like those here ascribed to Luxima.   [68]*WWJ*, X, 329.

the *Gayatri*,[69] is further shocked when he happens to observe her at her evening devotions to Camdeo. Drawn by strains of music which harmonize with the hour, the place and the peculiar tone of his own feelings and mind, to a mound rich with the odours of rare flowers and topped by a spring, he sees Luxima through the lattice of a pavilion, accompanying herself on the Indian lyre as she sings a hymn of mystic love. Initially abashed by the sensuousness of the hymn, addressed to the god of love, Camdeo, Hilarion hurries away. On reflection, however, he modifies his reaction:

Whatever glow of imagination warms the worship of the colder regions, he was aware that, in India, the ardent gratitude of created spirits was wont to ascend to the Creator in expressions of most fervid devotion; but the tender eloquence of mystic piety too frequently assumed the character of human feelings; and that the faint line, which sometimes separated the language of love from that of religion, was too delicate to be perceptible but to the pure in spirit and devout in mind.[70]

This conception of the nature of the Indian imagination is a paraphrase, largely in the phraseology there used, of the opening of Jones's essay, 'On the Mystical Poetry of the Persians and Hindus'.[71]

This scene at the pavilion—and it is one which impressed itself on Shelley's mind—reflects a most important influence of Indian literature. Jones's essay was written by way of introduction to his own translation of the *Gita Govinda*, the classical Sanskrit poem in which Radha, pierced by the arrows of the god of love, is depicted in a bower in a flowery forest in the spring season, awaiting the coming of the god Krishna. Luxima closely resembles Radha as she is described by Jayadeva as well as being invested with the mystical significance Jones suggests is attached to her.[72] Additionally, she almost certainly derives her name, as also something of her character, from the goddess who, as the spouse of Vishnu (of whom Krishna is an incarnation), is invoked at the end of Jayadeva's poem: Lakshmi, the subject of one of Jones's Hindu hymns.[73]

[69] *TM*, I, 163. If Hilarion here adopts an attitude to Indian pantheism similar to that taken by Coleridge in *PL*, so, too, does he share Coleridge's attitude towards the *avatars* (ibid., I, 90). [70] Ibid., I, 196–203. [71] *WWJ*, IV, 211–12. The first line is an echo of ibid., X, 338. [72] In the *Gita Govinda* (*WWJ*, IV, 236–268), Radha in her grove in a beautiful forest expresses her devotion to Krishna and at last goes to his bower. In his introduction to the poem Jones suggested that the sensual is allegorical of spiritual passion. Camdeo is also evoked. [73] *WWJ*, XIII, 289–99.

There is, however, more to Luxima even than this. In his prefaces to the Hindu hymns Jones made clear that just as the strength of Hindu music (for him the art in which the human passions received their truest, because most natural, expression) was based, through the modes, on 'an association of ideas',[74] so too do the Hindu goddesses, personifying particular attributes, coalesce. Hilarion likens Luxima as he has seen her at her music to one of the *raginis*, or female passions, 'which, in the poetical mythology of her religion, were supposed to preside over the harmony of the spheres, and to steal their power over the hearts of men by sounds which breathed of heaven'. The author had already prepared the way for such a conception of Luxima by describing Hilarion as being drawn to her by a musical mode which, in accordance with the allegory of the *ragas* and *raginis* related by Jones in his essay, 'On the Musical Modes of the Hindus', was appropriate to a particular hour, place and predominant sentiment.[75]

Nor is Luxima only a *ragini*, any more than she is only Radha or Lakshmi. When Hilarion next approaches Luxima at the time of the *Gayatri* on the evening of the following day, she appears to him to be the presiding deity of the stream.[76] Jones's most poetical evocation of the *raginis* is in his 'Hymn to Sereswaty', where these harmonious beings are depicted as attendant on the goddess who, as the active power of Brahma, is imagination and invention. In Jones's hymn, as in Indian mythology, she is represented both as a divine stream comparable to Ganga and as the inventor of the *vina*, or Indian lyre, which, Jones tells us, she is often portrayed as holding.[77] Thus Luxima, as she appears to Hilarion shortly before and shortly after he conceives of her as a *ragini*, resembles Sarasvati herself. One needs only to add that she also owes something to Parvati, from whose garland of flowers, in Jones's 'Hymn to Durga', Siva, like Hilarion, takes flight, believing that he has destroyed Camdeo,[78] to see that Luxima is the henotheistic

[74] Ibid., IV, 171–2, 191   [75] *TM*, I, 196, 202. Cf. *WWJ*, IV, 191–3, 204–6. The peculiar terminology used by Miss Owenson suggests that she may have read not only Jones but J.D. Paterson, 'On the Gramas or Musical Scales of the Hindus', *AR* IX, 454–9. This peculiarity of Indian music stressed by Paterson (pp. 455–6) was noticed also in *MR*, Appendix to LVIII (1809), 492–3. Jones had in fact read the manuscript to Paterson's *Odes to the Ragas*, not published until 1818, as early as 1785 (*LWJ*, Letter 405, II, 671–2). Miss Owenson may also have read Paterson's article, 'Of the Origin of the Hindu Religion' (*AR* VIII, 44–82; reviewed *MR*, Appendix to LII, 1807, 488–92) where he argues that Hinduism is 'founded on pure Deism, of which the Gayatri, translated by Sir William Jones, is a striking proof.'
[76] *TM*, I, 209–10.   [77] *WWJ*, XIII, 311–20. Jones makes a similar reference to her in the essay on Indian music (*WWJ*, IV, 184–5).   [78] Stanzas II.1–IV.1, *WWJ*, XIII, 251–3. Miss Owenson weaves a festival of Durga into her story (I, 109).

goddess celebrated in Jones's Hindu hymns in a variety of her manifestations.

The governing faculty of Hilarion's character is said to be 'his strong and powerful imagination',[79] and consequently he does not escape unscathed from his confrontation with the loftier heights of imagination scaled by Luxima in her invocation to the god of mystic love. At their second meeting at the stream Hilarion finds himself blessing her in the terminology of the *Gayatri* and she, in turn, again using phraseology borrowed from Jones, explains to him the symbolic meaning of the hymn[80]—which, as Hilarion had realized about the hymn to Camdeo, invests the physical with a metaphysical significance. The missionary observes that her belief combines the purest adoration of the Supreme Being and most sublime conceptions of his attributes with the wildest superstitions. This observation is again derived from a reading of Jones and if one wished to summarize in a single sentence the conclusions formed by Jones about Asia, as Asia crystallized for him around India, it would be hard to better the words used by Hilarion about Luxima:

He perceived that a pure system of natural religion was innate in her sublime and contemplative mind; but the images which personified the attributes of Deity, in her national faith, had powerfully fastened on her ardent imagination, and blended their influence with all the habits, the feelings and the expression of her life.[81]

Hilarion is dealing with a power which, as Jones found, is not always to be held at bay by such intellectual detachment. The missionary soon discovers that, in the interval that follows these encounters with Luxima, he is 'stunned by the revolution which had taken place in his mind and feeling, by the novelty of the images which occupied his fancy, by the association of ideas which linked themselves in his mind'.[82] Becoming half-aware that he has fallen in love with Luxima only when he speaks of relinquishing her, Hilarion has a vision of her in the moonlight in the same Kashmiri cave of ice which Coleridge apparently incorporated into 'Kubla Khan'.[83] The 'vision' is actually Luxima herself

---

[79] *TM*, II, 12.   [80] Ibid., I, 211–16. Luxima's words are derived from Jones's remarks on the *Gayatri* both in the Preface to *Menu* (*WWJ*, VII, 89) and in his translation of the verse itself (ibid., XIII, 367).   [81] Ibid., I, 227.   [82] Ibid., II, 4. The two phrases used here to describe the effect of Luxima on Hilarion are used by Jones to describe the effects of, respectively, an acquaintance with Asiatic poetry (*WWJ*, X, 204–5) and with Hindu music (ibid., IV, 191) as well as with an Indian play (ibid., IX, 372).   [83] ibid., II, 20–2. Hilarion took up residence in the cave of ice, Bernier's grotto of congelations, from the outset (ibid., I, 140–2).

who, having read the Bible in the light of the Veda, uses a passage from Jones's essay, 'On the Mystical Poetry of the Persians and Hindus', to demonstrate the identity of Christian with Vedantin concepts of mystic love.[84] Having realized this identity Luxima feels free to love Hilarion for the god in him, regarding him as a *sannyasin* in whom sensual passion is wholly sublimated.[85]

When, in return, Hilarion seeks to convince Luxima that she is confounding ideas which should be eternally distinct and separate,[86] it is the expression of a Christian sense of dualism between man and God seeking to suppress the recognition that it is he who has fallen in love with her:

He had brought with him into deserts, the virtues and the prejudices which belong to social life, in a certain stage of its progress; and in deserts, Nature, reclaiming her rights, unopposed by the immediate influence of the world, now taught him to feel her power through the medium of the most omnipotent of her passions.[87]

If Hilarion is overtaken here in precisely the way Jones was overtaken by Arabian poetry in 1772,[88] there is a further comment equally applicable to the Orientalist perception of India (and even, since he writes to her as if she were Kailyal or Luxima, to Shelley's apprehension of Miss Hitchener) when Hilarion, in suppressing the new and powerful emotion, 'by rendering the Indian more dangerous to his imagination than to his senses, invested her with that splendid, that touching ideal charm, which love, operating upon genius, in the absence of its object, can alone bestow'.[89]

A description of dawn breaking over the Indian Caucasus above the valley of Kashmir, in terms almost identical to those used in an earlier description when Hilarion first enters it, opens a chapter where the transformation which has been overcoming the man is complete. It is now misery and not bliss that he experiences as he awakes: 'He felt that the heart which once opens itself to the admission of a strong passion, is closed against every other impression, and that objects obtain, or lose their influence, only in proportion as they are connected with, or remote from, its interest'. Hilarion resolves to fly Kashmir. Kashmir would, in fact, become a correlative so perfect as to be identical with his inner state, did he not refuse to admit that his impersonal love of

[84] ibid., II, 28. Luxima's words are composed of a paraphrase of Barrow, followed by a phrase from him, followed by phrases drawn from Jones's remarks on him (*WWJ*, IV, 213–15; 215; 220).   [85] Ibid, II, 77.   [86] Ibid, II, 144.   [87] Ibid., II, 47–8.   [88] *WWJ*, X, 329–40.   [89] *TM*, II, 52.

God might be inclusive of his personal love for Luxima. He cannot resist the overwhelming awareness pressing upon him that a harmonious principle governs everything, but his own unnatural repression is projected into the generalization that man's preeminence in Nature consists in his experiencing a self-existing principle of intellectual pain.[90] When, by way of farewell, he chides Luxima with confounding ideas of divine and human love, Luxima expresses a readiness to die for him so that that part of him with which she feels an identity will have gone before him to the God of which they are both emanations.[91]

Symbolically, during the whole of the critical interview, Luxima's veil, which from the outset has been suggestive of religious mystery,[92] is drawn aside. Hilarion, like the Siva of Jones's 'Hymn to Durga', who also took flight from his crystal cave and a garland of blossoms made for him by a woman in holy love, is overcome by Camdeo, the god of love, just when he thinks he has destroyed him.[93] Like Siva confronted with Parvati's readiness to die for him, Hilarion, whose love has hitherto been for God alone, declares his love for Luxima, a vestal dedicated to God, and, no longer divided against himself, experiences the mystical vision of the *Vedantins*:

All external objects faded from his view for the moment; life was to him a series of ideas and feelings, of affections and emotions: he sought to retain no consciousness, but that of loving and being loved; and if he was absorbed in illusion, it was an illusion which, though reason condemned, innocence still ennobled and consecrated.[94]

The second half of the novel is quite deliberately conceived of as anti-climactic. If we have seen how, in the persons of Hilarion and Luxima, the finest idealism of Europe and of Asia might meet, we now see what forces within Europe and Asia act to pull them apart. If it is true that hitherto the novel might be read as an expression of the imaginative response to Asia in English letters at the time of, and by way of, William Jones, hereafter it may be read as a vision, as much prophetic as retrospective, of the way the English imagination, in its approach to India, more frequently failed to rise above a fanciful apprehension of Hindu images. The novel itself is the less sustained for having to turn its attention from imaginative harmony to disparate images; and the

[90] Ibid., II, 107–15. Cf. opening with ibid., I, 135–6.   [91] Ibid., II, 147.
[92] Ibid., I, 84.   [93] Stanzas VIII. 1–IX.1, *WWJ* XIII, 257–8. Jones's poem is a condensed re-creation of Kalidasa's *Cumara Sambhava*. Hilarion first betrays his sentiment for Luxima by picking up a wreath she has woven and taking it back to his cave of ice (*TM*, I, 152–5).   [94] *TM*, II, 153. See this chapter, p. 252 n. 107.

flight of Hilarion and Luxima from Kashmir is consciously depicted in terms of the loss of Paradise.[95]

The anticlimax is made necessary since the author wishes to show that the mystical passion of Hilarion and Luxima is not 'referable to any order, or any state of society'[96] On that account every order and state of society will use all its power to destroy it. Matured in a Kashmir which was the cradle of infant Nature before ever Brahma was born, the ideal love of Hilarion and Luxima is assaulted by the very religions which had originally distorted, even while they nursed, their idealism. Luxima's vision turns to nightmare when she is pursued by the Brahmins for polluting her caste and, in a cave resembling Elephanta, is excommunicated according to the laws of Manu—the single instance where Miss Owenson, in a footnote, acknowledges her debt to Jones.[97] Hilarion, ignorant, on account of Luxima's desire to protect him, of the forces which play on the superstitions they have engrafted on her imagination, is likewise subject to the religious prejudice inculcated in him and, thinking to save her, as well as himself, by baptizing her and taking her to a Dominican nunnery in Goa, destroys her.[98] Orthodox Christianity is no more ready to sanctify their platonic love than caste Hinduism and the counterpart of Brahmin excommunication is a Catholic *auto-da-fé*.

Hilarion and Luxima pass out of Kashmir by the rock of Bembhar. Following Bernier's description of this spot as steep, black and scorched, a veritable hell to be traversed on the way to paradise, the author stresses that there is no sound of Nature here, only silence resembling a primaeval world before human existence had given animation to the pathless wilds or human passions disturbed its calm.[99] The Kashmir left behind is overtly likened to Eden and their departure from it to the departure of Adam and Eve from Paradise. Since Luxima is herself said to be 'an emblem of that lovely region', in resigning Kashmir ('Heaven and Earth') for Hilarion, she resigns herself. In doing this she is fulfilled. When, after many misfortunes, Hilarion comes to regret ever taking her from 'an earthly paradise' like Kashmir, she explains to him that a woman's paradise is 'the presence of him she loves', an expression of love 'which resembles, in its singleness and simplicity, the primordial idea, which in the religion of my fathers, is supposed to have preceded time and worlds, and from which all

---

[95] Ibid., II, 252, III, 17, 22–3.   [96] Ibid., II, 188.   [97] Ibid., II, 212 and n. A curious reference to Brahma in 'his avatar of "the Destroyer"' (II, 157) also suggests a reading of Jones (*WWJ*, III, 351).   [98] Ibid., II, 225–6, 234–5.

[99] Ibid., III, 19–20. Miss Owenson has Bernier in mind, see ibid., I, 127–9 and nn.

created good has emanated'. In turn, Hilarion is her protector,
defiant of the literal, as he will be of the metaphorical, storm, 'his
brow fearlessly raised to meet the lightning's flash . . . looking
like one whose spirit, unsubdued by the mighty wreck of matter,
defied that threatened annihilation, which could not reach the
immortality it was created to inherit'. Luxima sees that Hilarion,
like Sakuntala's favourite plant, the Vasanti, which outgrows the
tree it climbs to point towards heaven, is strongest in adversity
and that, as soon as he comes again within the compass of civilized society, the purest feelings of his nature are stifled by
religion.[100]

Imprisoned and sentenced to death by the Inquisition, Hilarion
himself recognizes that 'the sufferings of man resulted less from
the constitution of his nature, than from the obstinacy with which
he abandons the dictates of Providence, and devotes himself to
those illusions which the law of human reason, and the impulse of
human affection, equally oppose'. Yet so ingrained is religious
prejudice that even then he is prepared to die in the belief that
his executioners are blind instruments of Heaven.[101] The sceptical Kashmiri deist who believes only in the Invisible intervenes
tangibly at this juncture and, in a dramatic scene where Luxima's
cry of 'Brahma' starts a revolution far less mystical than that
started by the utterance of a name at Forster's Chandrapore,
Hilarion and Luxima, attended by the Kashmiri *pandit*, realize
that, condemned alike by their religions and their countries,
there now remains nothing on earth for them but each other. In
spite of this Hilarion still tries to lose the man in the minister
and, on account of it, Luxima dies believing that he is already
dead and she is following his spirit, a final blissful illusion which
is no less divine for being misplaced.[102]

On leaving Kashmir Luxima had said that she, unlike those
who had been banished from Heaven for incurring the wrath of
Siva, had found 'communion, which images to the soul, in its
transient probation through time, the bliss which awaits it in
eternity'.[103] It is all the more interesting then that Hilarion's response to her final plea to teach toleration between Brahmins
and Christians is peculiarly Hindu: he returns to lead the solitary
life of a *rishi* in that cave of ice in Kashmir which, though Miss
Owenson did not know it, is consecrated to the absorption of the
phallic by the ascetic in the *svayambhu* image of Siva.[104] Kashmir
is as much an embodiment of Luxima as Luxima was of Kashmir,

[100] Ibid., III, 6, 22–3, 54–6, 68, 102, 105–6.   [101] Ibid., III, 142–4.   [102] Ibid.,
III, 159–215.   [103] Ibid., III, 30–1.   [104] See chapter 6, p. 215.   [105] *TM*, I, 213.

and Hilarion has learned at last to win Heaven and Earth by losing himself in Kashmir as Luxima had done by losing herself in
him.

The novel belongs to Luxima and it is Luxima who is especially
attractive to Shelley. Shelley's objection to Kailyal in *Kehama* is
that she is too governed by faith. While the two Hindu heroines
are not all that different—after all 'the boundless toleration' of
Luxima's religion is said to be united with 'the most obstinate
faith'[105]—Luxima is much more obviously sustained by love. Initially, however, Shelley discountenances Hindoostanish devotion
(such as it is practised by the *guru* in Lahore) on grounds similar
to those on which Coleridge, in response to an article in 'The
Morning Chronicle' on 22 May 1811, was objecting to
Hinduism—namely, that it demanded a suspension of human
reason.[106] Jones himself had said what *A Passage to India* also
indicates—that the doctrine of the Vedanta, 'a system wholly
built on the purest devotion . . . human reason alone could,
perhaps, neither fully demonstrate, nor fully disprove'.[107] Miss
Owenson leaves open, as she must, the possibility that the
Vedantin Luxima is living in an illusory world, even while the
whole thrust of her novel, like Forster's and like Jones's most
poetical work, suggests otherwise. The young Shelley did acknowledge that *in poetry* such devotion might be beautiful. When
in 1818–19 he attempted to discover in poetry what neither human reason nor social action had been able to discover for him,
Luxima, the Kashmiri *Vedantin*—difficult as Shelley had said it
would be to embody such a character—was at last free to rise
again to the surface as the Asia of *Prometheus Unbound*.[108] If
Luxima is herself a personification of Asia—as Asia was
apprehended by Jones as an image for the poetic imagination informed by the mystical metaphysics of the Vedanta—we may
conclude that Jones, by way of Miss Owenson's novel, played an
important part in Shelley's imaginative development.

V. de Sola Pinto, one critic who was certain, in spite of a lack

[106] *LPBS*, Letter 82, I, 101; *The Friend* (1850), General Introduction, Essay XIII,
I, 122–5. It is at Lahore that the religion of Camdeo is first shown to be devotional
and said to make 'no claim on the understanding' (*TM*, I, 93–95).   [107] *WWJ*, III,
239–40.   [108] In her Note on the Poems of 1817 (*PWPBS*, p. 551), Mary Shelley
comments that Shelley's life was 'now spent more in thought than action—he had
lost the eager spirit which believed it could achieve what it projected for the benefit
of mankind.' With due respect, what we might alternatively conclude is that the
eager spirit was more inward, trying to realize the One Life in ways more consistent
with the neo-Platonist tradition (see this chapter, p. 274).

of detailed evidence, that 'Shelley can be tracked everywhere in Jones's snow', suggested that 'there can be little doubt that Shelley's transition from the atheistic materialism of his early writings to the mystical pantheism of his mature works was largely due to his study of Sir William Jones's writings' [109] Although we have now discovered some evidence to justify Pinto's intuition, his conception of a poet *studying* another poet's writings is not a happy one. Poets, unlike scholars, do not necessarily 'study' the works they read. I mention this because it is germane to the whole argument of this book—that the more imaginative the state of the mind the greater is the mind's capacity for absorbing and rendering coherent. I have already argued that if Coleridge read Bernier, his greater imaginative powers might permit him to make a great deal more than Bernier himself had out of a description of the Kashmir landscape. The quality of his mind might permit him to read *through* Bernier to come closer, not only to the aesthetic Mughal perception of Kashmir which had clearly touched Bernier, but even beyond Bernier to the mystical Hindu perception which had touched the Mughals but found its fullest expression in the Hindu mythology of Kashmir.

Such a capacity for apprehending a potential which is suggested but barely realized by a work he was reading would similarly, I think, have been enjoyed by Shelley, who, like Coleridge, discerned in neo-Platonism the intellectual scheme which best mirrored his imaginative experience. A discriminating scholar might justly have reservations about Jones's scholarship, about Southey's poetry and about Miss Owenson's fiction, while a poet of Shelley's mentality might rather assimilate from them (possibly over a period of time) a common spirit more fully realized in his own poetry. If Shelley was not put out by (what to modern taste may seem) the effusive gothic romanticism of Miss Owenson's novel any more than by the erudite obscurity of Southey's poem, that may have been because he gathered from it something more essential.

Whether or not *The Missionary* is to be read, as I believe it can be read, as a perfectly extraordinary fictionalization of the psyche of William Jones, it is clear that Miss Owenson has taken from Jones's writings a poetic concept of the Indian Vedanta as a mys-

---

[109] Pinto, pp. 693–4. In *La Renaissance Orientale* (Paris, 1950), pp. 210–12, Raymond Schwab takes a similar (unsubstantiated) line. For a convincing defence of Shelley against the charge of atheistic materialism, see Medwin, I, 72–4, 139–40; II, 52. Medwin recognized that Shelley's pantheism, being founded on non-dualistic idealism, differed from that of Wordsworth and Coleridge (ibid., I, 275).

tical philosophy so all-encompassing that the finest type of plato-
nizing Christianity must eventually succumb to it. Following not
only Jones but an old Oriental—as well as a new Orientalist—
tradition, she uses Kashmir as a paradisal image for that ideal interior landscape of the fulfilled psyche. This idyllic valley in
(what was then called) the Indian Caucasus reappears in *Prometheus Unbound,* as does its personification in the form of an
ideal female figure. These images, as well as the basic shapes of
Indian mythology, were available to Shelley through his reading
of *Kehama,* but if Pinto is right and the mystical pantheism evident in Shelley's mature work is to be ascribed to the influence of
Jones, it was essentially through *The Missionary* that he absorbed
it and became aware of its association with India.

ALASTOR: THE KASHMIRI DIMENSION

One immediate effect of *The Missionary* on Shelley's work would
seem to be evident in a stanza from 'Zeinab and Kathema', written that same summer:

> Yet Albion's changeful skies and chilling wind
> The change from Cashmire's vale might well denote.
> There, Heaven and Earth are ever bright and kind;
> Here, blights and storms and damp forever float,
> Whilst hearts are more ungenial than the zone—
> Gross, spiritless, alive to no pangs but their own.

That a passage be made from England to Kashmir would seem to
be the recommendation implicit in this stanza and at the beginning of the next:

> There, flowers and fruits are ever fair and ripe;
> Autumn, there, mingles with the bloom of spring,
> And forms unpinched by frost or hunger's gripe
> A natural veil o'er natural spirits fling . . .[110]

The recommendation is, however, overshadowed by a bitter
attack on Christianity for having made such a passage and for
having so savagely disrupted the idyllic life of the people there.

[110] 11.91–100, *The Esdaile Notebook,* ed. Kenneth Neill Cameron (London,
1964), p. 51. See the commentary on the poem, ibid., pp. 276–8. Shelley follows
Miss Owenson in using an uncommon spelling of Kashmir and in the unhistorical
conception of a Christian assault on Kashmir. If stanzas II–III of 'The Solitary'
(*Esdaile,* p. 67) could be shown to reflect a reading of *TM* (III, 57–61) the poem
would have to be dated, as it was originally, 1811 instead of 1810 (*Esdaile,* note to
p. 67, p. 342). Later Shelley and Mary use the Indian term 'pariah' in application to
themselves (*LPBS,* Letter 545, II, 170; Letter 588, n. 4, II, 238).

Zeinab, the Kashmiri maiden, is but a cypher in Shelley's attack, the purpose of which is bluntly sociological.

Slight as the poem is, *The Missionary*, the book which apparently gave rise to it, as well as the poem itself, remained on Shelley's mind and in October 1814, a day after Mary Godwin had been described to Hogg in terms perhaps reminiscent of Luxima, Shelley requested the deserted Harriet to copy up and send him a poem called 'An Indian Tale'.[111] Whether or not this is, as is supposed, 'Zeinab and Kathema', it would seem to be associated, through its subtitle, with *The Missionary* and would, like it, no doubt reflect the dangers of permitting ideal love to be subverted by social or religious custom. The enduring effect of the novel is even more clearly evident a year later when, in spite of Shelley's immersion in the Classics at this time,[112] it is in the Vale of Kashmir that the young poet in *Alastor*, having scoured the ruins of all other ancient civilizations for 'the thrilling secrets of the birth of time', at last experiences a vision.

Alastor, Shelley's most important poem of these years, is the story of a youth who, nurtured by Nature, scours time and place for the secret of the universe. His search, like that of Jones, is satisfied neither by Classical learning nor by the sensual attractions of an Arab maiden. Instead, in a dell in Kashmir, the poet, in a trance, bodies forth 'a veiled maid' of his own imagining.[113] Shelley himself explains the significance of this vision: the youth's mind has been

suddenly awakened and thirsts for intercourse with an intelligence similar to itself. He images to himself the Being whom he loves. Conversant with speculations of the sublimest and most perfect natures, the vision in which he embodies his own imaginations unites all of wonderful, or wise, or beautiful, which the poet, the philosopher, or the lover could depicture.[114]

Unfortunately the young poet can neither sustain the vision nor revive it, can neither give it reality nor discover it in reality. While *Alastor* is not an autobiographical poem in any limited sense, it is a particular expression of the failure of creative power experienced by all poets who apprehend that there is a mystical power which their art, or life, fails to embody.

The maid envisioned in Kashmir whose music proves so elusive might well be thought to offer more than a passing echo of the

---

[111] *LPBS*, Letter 265, I, 402–3; Letter 266, I, 405 and n. 1.   [112] Note on the Early Poems, by Mrs Shelley, *PWPBS*, p. 528.   [113] *Alastor*, 11.107–91. [114] Preface to Alastor, *PWPBS*, p. 14; *Journal*, List of Books read in 1815, Shelley, pp. 49–50.

Abyssinian maid in 'Kubla Khan'. If she does, it is not in any superficial way since the Abyssinian maid had yet to make her public appearance,[115] and the echo (for there is one) may be traced instead to Miss Owenson's Luxima as she is observed at her devotions by Hilarion. Like Luxima, Shelley's maid is veiled and makes her visionary appearance in a dell in Kashmir replete with odorous plants and a rivulet.[116] Like Luxima heard at night in her pavilion, the music of her voice is not only solemn but harmonious with the mind and feelings of her hearer. She, like Luxima, accompanies herself while she sings a strange song of divine love whose numbers are both tender and wild.[117] In *Alastor*, however, the passion of the maid, who is, after all, a vision in the youth's mind, becomes immediately tumultuous, whereas in *The Missionary* a similar tumult arising within Hilarion is repeatedly repressed so that only after a time does Luxima develop a pale and disordered air.[118] What is essential is that the maid, like Luxima, is a sensuous embodiment of a 'pure mind' invested with 'the spirit of sweet human love'.[119] Moreover, her effect on the youth is close to that which Luxima has on Hilarion. Like Hilarion, similarly drawn by his genius to Kashmir,[120] the youth is stunned by the vision which floats on his imagination, uncertain of its reality though aware it images his soul. Like Hilarion, too, he loses the

---

[115] In 1816, Shelley, unlike Byron, had not apparently seen the poem in manuscript. Mary was later to refer to her imagination as 'my Kubla Khan, "my pleasure dome" ' (*Journal*, 2 December 1834). Possibly there are echoes of 'Kubla Khan' in *The Revolt of Islam* and in *The Triumph of Life*. For a landscape similar to that evoked in 'Kubla Khan', see *Kehama*, VII.9–10, pp. 64–6.   [116] *Alastor*, 11.145–52; *TM*, I, 135–55.   [117] *Alastor*, 11.153–68; *TM*, I, 196–201.
[118] *Alastor*, 11.174–80; *TM*, I, 188–9; II, 57–62, 117–18. The sense of a vision suddenly aborted pertains to the events detailed in ibid., II, 151–64.   [119] *Alastor*, 11.162, 203–5. Cf. a comment on the purity of Luxima's mind made at the close of *TM*, I (228). That she is a visionary representation of the spirit of sweet human love is evident throughout the novel. Echoes of *TM* persist to the end of the poem. Shortly before his death images of the past come to the youth like sweet music breathed through some dim latticed chamber (11.627–32); the sound of Luxima's music, heard likewise through a latticed chamber, leaves Hilarion in a similarly languid and imaginative state (*TM*, I, 197–201). The final images of the poet are as a vapour tinged by the sunset (11.663–5) and as a fragile lute on whose strings the breath of heaven wanders (11.667–8). At her most transfigured, Luxima is likened to a 'sun-ringed vapour' (*TM*, II, 115–18) and to one of the *raginis* of Indian music who steal their power over the hearts of men by sounds which breathe of heaven (*TM*, I, 202).   [120] *Alastor*, 1.145; *TM*, I, 48. The novel may also have helped to inspire the initial portrait of the poet as one who, nurtured by Mother Earth, has learned to love all living creatures. Luxima is first drawn to Hilarion on account of his tender treatment of her pet faun—he has acted, she says, 'as a Hindu would have acted' (*TM*, 1.87) and if in this detail she resembles Sakuntala (*WWJ*, 454, 473–4) no less than in that whereby she identifies human love with a luxuriant

vision through his own inadequacy and is haunted by it till his death.[121]

In *The Missionary*, Luxima, as we have seen, explains to Hilarion that her ideal love for him 'resembles, in its singleness and simplicity, the primordial idea, which in the religion of my fathers, is supposed to have preceded time and worlds, and from which all created good has emanated'.[122] She is referring here to the commonest of the creation (or, rather, as the Orientalists put it, emanation) myths of the Hindus. In his essay, 'On Mount Caucasus', Wilford recounts one version of it:

According to the Puranas, Swayambhuva, or Adima, Satyavrata, or Noah, lived in the north-west parts of India about Cashmir. There Brahma assumed a mortal shape according to the *Matsya-Purana*; and one half of his body springing out, without his experiencing any diminution whatsoever, he framed out of it Satarupa. She was so beautiful, that he fell in love with her. As he considered her as his daughter, being sprung from his body, he was ashamed.[123]

Brahma, torn between love and shame, at first simply produces extra faces to survey her in all four corners of the world but, we are told, 'having recovered his intellects, the other half of his body sprang from him and became Swayambhuva or Adima'. This is the most important Hindu concept of the creation and it is congenial to a similar neo-Platonist conception which recurs in Shelley's 'Adonais'.[124] Brahma is the Absolute (the One) in conceptual terms: Svayambhu-va literally means the appearance of the Self-Existent in assumed form and so provides a name for the Nameless One. Since we are, as part of creation, an emanation which cannot realize its true nature until it is reabsorbed in a state of total mystical love, we can at best project our origin in

Indian creeper it is because her whole sensibility and way of life in Kashmir is identical to that of Sakuntala in her hermitage. In *Alastor* not only do the animals, like those in Sakuntala's hermitage, take 'bloodless food' from the human hand and even the antelope lose its timidity (11.98–106; *WWJ*, IX, 380–5) but the creepers also entwine the trees in loving harmony, as responsive as they are to Sakuntala who, like the maid with 'her basket of Indian woof' in 'The Sensitive Plant' (*PWPBS*, pp. 589–96), tends them with sisterly care (*WWJ*, IX, 386–9).   [121] For Hilarion Kashmir is said to offer a repose which resembles a waking dream (*TM*, I, 132) and Luxima is said to appear as a brilliant vision on his imagination (ibid., I, 153). His soul is said to become identified with Luxima's at the moment of the vision (ibid., II, 151–3).   [122] Ibid., III, 56.   [123] *AR*, v, 472. This passage is summarized in Faber's *The Origin of Pagan Idolatry* (pp. 319–20) which Shelley may have read (see this chapter, p. 232). The Indian myth is first related in *BA*, 1.4.1–5. Colebrooke recounts it in his essay 'On the Vedas', *AR*, VIII, 440–1.
    [124] 'Adonais', stanza LII, 11.460–4, *PWPBS*, p. 443. Cf. *Enn.*, III.v.8; III.viii.8.

terms of imagery, neither wholly mystic nor wholly anthropomorphic, whereby Svayambhu first becomes manifest in Satarupa (literally, 'the hundred forms', or the Many) and then, falling in love with his own emanation, assumes tangible form. Thereafter, in spite of the fact that the female Many tries to elude the male One, the One and the Many, themselves but emanations of a Unity greater than either, together generate the diverse forms of creation (or emanation) until such time as they are reassimilated by a process the exact reverse of the original.

Miss Owenson, then, has Luxima conceive of her love in terms of the universal love ultimately reserved for Brahma by his consort. Clearly Miss Owenson herself identifies Luxima with the archetypal goddess since Hilarion's 'genius' draws him to Kashmir, the Indian paradise and 'birthplace of Brahma' precisely to be confronted by her. When, just before Hilarion attains the abstract mystical state, Luxima draws aside her veil, she is said to look 'like the tender vision which descends upon Passion's dream, like the splendid image, to whose creation Genius entrusts its own immortality'.[125] In the light of this it is possible to make sense of Shelley's curious and repeated comment after reading *The Missionary* that Luxima is perfect 'were it possible to embody such a character'.[126] Shelley clearly has intimations here of the difficulty experienced by the poet in *Alastor* of giving reality to his vision. He attributes the poet's failure to his 'self-centred seclusion' and this accords perfectly with the Hindu conception, relayed by Jones in the 'Hymn to Narayena' and from there taken up by Miss Owenson, that it is as the 'mystick Love' of the Absolute that the goddess, or Nature, has her being.[127] The poet in *Alastor* lacks this mystic love, or total going out of himself to all creation which Prometheus will realize, the vision of the maid dissolves and he is driven to fly the idyllic vale of Kashmir, as Prometheus is not.

PROMETHEUS UNBOUND, ACT I

In a footnote to his translation of the *Prometheus Bound* of Aeschylus, Thomas Medwin, Shelley's cousin and best biographer, noting that the name Prometheus means forewise or provident, cites the Hindu law-giver Manu as an authority for the doctrine that names should be prophetic of destinies.[128] Whatever other

[125] *TM*, II, 118.   [126] *LPBS*, Letter 85, I, 107; Letter 87, I, 112.   [127] Stanzas I–II, *WWJ*, XIII, 305–6.   [128] Thomas Medwin, trans., *Prometheus Bound* (London, 1832), p. 64. See also Medwin, I, 277. At the time of finishing Act I of

associations between Prometheus and India may have existed in Medwin's mind, any discussions he may have had with Shelley on either subject took place subsequent to the completion of *Prometheus Unbound*.[129] Prior to meeting Medwin, however, Shelley had reason to associate the *Prometheus* of Aeschylus with India.[130] What is distinct about Shelley's Prometheus is that, unlike the Prometheus of Alexander's men, he is not simply a defiant Greek figure who has been moved geographically east. His re-orientation, his re-location in the Orient, in Shelley's poem is indicative of an corresponding (and wholly appropriate) psychological shift in his character.

Before the first act of *Prometheus Unbound* is out, Prometheus has penetrated to an imaginative level unknown to his Greek original, and it is significant that the figure who in modern public life has come closest to practising the sort of positive non-violent passive resistance practised by Prometheus is Mahatma Gandhi. Europeans have associated passive resistance with India ever since Alexander's men were confronted by the Indian ascetics who preferred conquest of self to conquest of the world. Almost anyone reading about how Alexander's men encountered the rock in the Indian Caucasus where Prometheus remained defiant of Jupiter would also have gone on to read about how the Indian ascetics remained defiant of Alexander. At a deep imaginative level an association of these two images might be—and by Shelley might have been—made. Shelley's conception of Prometheus as a passive resister may also owe something to Southey's portrait of Ladurlad, who is ostensibly Indian. Perhaps the most critical factor in the indianization of Prometheus, however, is Hilarion, who, had he been responsive—rather than resistant—to his Vedantin counterpart, would have been as mythic as the Siva Jones (following Kalidasa) depicts in his cave in the Indian mountains.

In Shelley's most important note to *Queen Mab*, Prometheus is conceived of as the original corrupter of mankind who first used fire for culinary purposes and thus further encouraged the custom of eating flesh, to which Shelley, invoking 'the mythology of nearly all religions', believed all mankind's misfortunes might be

---

PU, Shelley asked Peacock (*LPBS*, Letter 483, II, 43) what Cicero had said about Aeschylus. Cicero had in fact cited the portrait of Prometheus as evidence that Aeschylus was a Pythagorean (*Tusc. Disput.*, II.x.23–5). Plato had once referred to Pythagoras as a new Prometheus (*Philebus*, 16 C). [129] Medwin (I, 337) rightly refers to Shelley's play as 'a bold and successful attempt, not so much to revive a lost play of Aeschylus, as to make the allegory a peg whereon to hand his abstruse and imaginative theories.' [130] See this chapter, p. 231.

traced. On account of this unnatural and (as Shelley believes) unique behaviour towards his fellow creatures, man's supereminence in an otherwise harmonious universe is, like Satan's, a supereminence of pain.[131] Shelley's words here betray a source of the idea. They are a close transcription of Hilarion's when, in perfect natural surroundings, he represses his love for Luxima and, as a result, deludes himself into believing that man's preeminence among creatures is denoted by the intellectual pain he suffers.[132] The reference to *The Missionary* is the more unmistakable since Shelley goes on to say that men whose passions were not perverted by an unnatural diet would not, among other things, look with coolness on an *auto-da-fé*.[133]

Shelley's explanation of why Paradise was lost is a development and refinement of Miss Owenson's. Shelley's redeemed Prometheus is precisely the man Miss Owenson indicates Hilarion would have been if, instead of submitting to the perverted image of a Creator taught by orthodox religion, he had submitted to the ideal love which was natural to his heart. Prometheus is able, as Hilarion was not, to realize within himself the total harmony of the universe embodied in the beauty of a vale in the In-

[131] *Queen Mab*, Note to VIII.211–12. *PWPBS*, pp. 826–7.   [132] *TM*, II, 114–15. Jones's *Sacontala*, with its elevation of the animal and the vegetable worlds, leaves a powerful impression on both *Kehama* and *The Missionary* and may well have had more to do than Shelley's comparatively late reading of Plutarch with his decision to lay aside his gun and adopt a vegetarian diet. Medwin (I, 108–11) reports that in 1810, as in 1809, Shelley was still shooting over his father's game reserves. At Oxford there was, perhaps, only 'a certain anticipation . . . of a vegetable diet' (ibid., I, 124), a propensity towards it such as Shelley was to show even after he no longer adhered to a strict 'Pythagorean system' (ibid., II, 240). Shelley was certainly a Pythagorean before he ordered his own copy of Plutarch's *Moralia* (*LPBS*, Letter 175, I, 274; Letter 216, I, 342; Letter 250, I, 380). In 1811 there had appeared John Frank Newton's *The Return to Nature; or, A Defence of the Vegetable Regimen*, a work which an important note on vegetarianism in *Queen Mab* reveals was influential on Shelley. In this (incomplete) work Newton makes only a couple of passing references to the Brahmins (pp. 10, 18 nn) but his later work, *Three Enigmas Attempted to be Explained* (London, 1821) demonstrates a considerable interest in Indian religion. I cannot trace any direct link but a seminal crusading vegetarian tract of the previous generation was J.Z. Holwell's *A Review of the Original Principles, Religious and Moral, of the Ancient Bramins* (London, 1779), reprint as this was of Pts II–III of *Interesting Historical Events* (see chapter 2, p. 79 and n. 205). Following the Turkish Spy, Holwell singles out the Indians as the only people who understand the dangers of killing animals for food. Holwell regards such a practice as Satanic and productive of disease, commerce and depravity (III, 149–75).   [133] *Queen Mab*, Note to VIII.211–12, *PWPBS*, p. 830; *TM*, III, 164–90. The *auto-da-fé* also figures prominently in Canto XII of *The Revolt of Islam*, significantly as a means by which the lovers regain Paradise.

dian Caucasus. At the conclusion of his note to *Queen Mab*, Shelley writes:

Every man forms, as it were, his god from his own character; to the divinity of one of simple habits no offering would be more acceptable than the happiness of his creatures. He would be incapable of hating or persecuting others for the love of God.

Shelley's Prometheus, loving and loved by Asia, can realize for himself and for all creation the Paradise Hilarion could have enjoyed had he not fought for so long against Nature and, in so doing, destroyed Luxima. Shelley's difficulty was never with Hilarion—from the first he concurred with Miss Owenson about the nature of Hilarion's error; it was Luxima, as he recognized immediately, who, though the very thought of her might thrill the soul, would be difficult to incorporate. It was not until he wrote *Prometheus Unbound* that mysticism, perhaps made possible by a growth of affection, so far overcame his reason as to permit him to surmount the difficulty.

The pain that Hilarion suffers as a result of his dislocation from the rest of creation and its harmony, Prometheus also endures. Unlike Hilarion, however, who only once accuses 'the Eternal Judge',[134] Prometheus is certain he can again realize the idyllic life he once enjoyed with Asia if he refuses to degrade creation in the name of a Creator. Prometheus stakes his whole defiance of Jupiter on the belief that he has within himself the 'One only Being' which, in Jones's 'Hymn to Narayena', is said not only to comprise through mystical love all creation but to be apprehensible in the absorbed soul.[135] This is his secret, and on account of it he refuses the advances of a Heaven he knows has no ultimate reality, in order to stay on Earth where alone the permanent paradise may be realized. Like Mudgala, a sage central to the Indian tradition, Prometheus realizes that images of gods and paradises are the creation of minds too limited to conceive of their end and origin in truly abstract terms, in terms of an imageless Imagination. If the reality of Jupiter's existence is not, out of fear or despair, acknowledged, both he and his agents, the Furies, which can cause pain to Prometheus (as they did to Hilarion) only if that acknowledgement is made, cease to exist.[136]

[134] *TM*, III, 38.   [135] *PU*, I.265; *WWJ*, XIII, 209.   [136] Medwin quite logically suggested to Shelley that the conscience of Prometheus being at rest there can be no place for the Furies (I.338-9). Their inclusion may be justified on the grounds that it comes at a point early enough in the play for a dramatic consideration to take precedence over a metaphysical one. For the story of Mudgala, see chapter 5, pp. 169-70.

If Prometheus is by implication an uncorrupted Hilarion, it is when the Spirits which, according to the mythology of *Prometheus Unbound*, are the alternative to the Furies, appear to Prometheus in Act I that Shelley's reading of *The Missionary* begins to obtrude more overtly. The Spirits, whose homes are 'the dim caves of human thought', inhabit as their objective correlative the world-surrounding aether. The last and most important pair of Spirits are 'shapes from the East and West', 'twin nurslings' who have both beheld the form of Love.[137] Miss Owenson, following Jones, refers to the Hindu image of Love, the god Camdeo, as the twin of Cupid,[138] and that this reference is behind Shelley's conception here is borne out by the fact that the 'planet-crested shape' of Love—described by the Fifth Spirit, or Spirit 'from the East', as sweeping by 'on lightning-braided pinions' and scattering 'liquid joy of life from his ambrosial tresses'—certainly does owe more, as Pinto suggests, to Jones's 'stary-crown'd' Camdeo than to any Classical deity.[139] The likelihood of this association is the greater since the impression the Spirits leave behind is likened to that left after an inspired voice and lute languish. It is the inspired voice and lyre of Luxima, singing her hymn to Camdeo, which first enervate Hilarion by their tender and impassioned languor,[140] and, lest this image should appear coincidental, Panthea, at this, the culminating point of Act I, reminds Prometheus of Asia in her far Indian vale

> invested with fair flowers and herbs,
> And haunted by sweet airs and sounds, which flow
> Among the woods and waters, from the aether
> Of her transforming presence . . .[141]

PROMETHEUS UNBOUND, ACT II

In August 1817 Shelley read *Lalla Rookh*, the fifth and final evocative section of which begins: 'Who has not heard of the

[137] *PU*, I.752–7, 763.   [138] *TM*, I, 199; *WWJ*, III, 367–8. See also *WWJ*, XIII, 236.   [139] Pinto, p. 693. In the 'Hymn to Camdeo' (*WWJ*, XIII, 237–9), the 'God of each lovely sight, each lovely sound' is depicted sweeping to Earth, his 'locks in braids ethereal streaming' (alternatively described as musky tresses gemmed with dew). There is said to be an azure fire blazing on his limbs and Miss Owenson (*TM*, II, 81n) speaks of his being armed with a flash of lightning, although in the 'Hymn to Durga' (stanza III, 2, *WWJ*, XIII, 252) he is said to be destroyed by a flame stronger than the keenest lightnings. In the 'Hymn to Indra' (*WWJ*, XIII, 274), where the word 'pinion' also occurs, Krishna, Camdeo's most important victim, is said to have 'looks ambrosial'.   [140] *TM*, I, 199–201.   [141] *PU*, I, 826–32. This vale is later envisaged as being covered by a lake, as Bernier reports Kashmir had once been (ibid., II.iii. 19–22).

Vale of Cashmere . . .?'[142] This poem may very well have served to remind him of those chapters in *The Missionary* which open with a description of sunrise over the perpetually Spring-like vale which Miss Owenson places in the Indian Caucasus.[143] Act II of *Prometheus Unbound* opens in a similar setting and with a similar sense of waking dream, and if Shelley does not here, as in *Alastor*, name Kashmir it is surely only because, in a mythological work, he does not want to localize paradise so specifically. Kashmir may be, as Miss Owenson asserts, the model for Indra's paradise in Indian fancy but Shelley, like Jones and Southey, is being consistent with Indian fancy in preferring a more generalized locale somewhere in the Indian mountains.

The passivity of Prometheus differs from that ultimately experienced by the poet in *Alastor* in that it is wholly creative. Prometheus, like Narayana, is incapable of any action except universal love and it is through the agency of Asia, who is, like Maya, the *sakti* or active embodiment of this, that the manifold forms of Nature both materialize and dissolve. As we have seen, the conception of a goddess, or female archetype, as the *sakti* of a god, or male archetype, informs not only the 'Hymn to Narayena' but many of Jones's Hindu hymns, which, along with his imaginative essays on Asia, seem to have been the most decisive intellectual influence in the creation of Shelley's Asia. As Jones noticed, this conception of the *sakti* is implicit, though rather more latent, in neo-Platonist mythology.[144] But Jones followed the neo-Platonists in using not only male and female as archetypes to indicate a progressive emanation of philosophic power, but also East and West.[145] Jones's assumption, derived from the neo-Platonists, that Platonism was indebted to India by way of Pythagoras is the accepted assumption of, among others, Thomas Medwin, who mentions it in reference to Shelley's ardent belief in pre-existence.[146] The Orientalism fostered by Jones is quite specific in that not only is Asia conceived in terms of the influence on it of the Indian Vedanta, but also the patterns of neo-Platonism receive a renewed or clearer definition.

In his preface to *Prometheus Unbound* Shelley argues that a

---

[142] *Journal*, 24 August 1817; *Lalla Rookh*, p. 295. For Shelley's request for this book, see *LPBS*, Letter 404, I, 549; Letter 407, I, 552.   [143] *TM*, I 135; II, 107–8. Mary was reading *TM* during her confinement a fortnight later (*Journal*, 19 September 1817). Possibly Shelley re-read the novel at this time since the culminating scene of the *auto-da-fé* in *Laon and Cythna*, then being written, is strongly reminiscent of the culminating scene in *TM*.   [144] *WWJ*, XIII, 302–3; see chapter 6, pp. 222–3.   [145] Iamblichus, VIII, 17.   [146] Medwin, I, 133. Coleridge and the *Phaedo* are cited here as immediate sources for Shelley's belief.

poet is not only a creator but a creation of his age.[147] It is possible that *Prometheus Unbound* accords with no intellectual current of its own day so much as with Jones's neo-Platonized Orientalism. This tradition does offer us a way of accounting not only for the existence of Shelley's Asia but also for her rather mysterious relationship with the other two daughters of Ocean, Panthea and Ione. The varying degrees of awareness or consciousness of these three female figures and their relationship to each other at the critical moment of mystical apprehension, when knowledge reaches Asia that Prometheus has realized love of the whole world, suggests a gradation like that represented not only by the *hypostases* of Plotinus but by their Indian equivalents.[148] Ione shows less response than Panthea while Panthea, having flown to Asia, finds that her very being is 'condensed' in that transfigured presence.[149] In terms of the prevailing Orientalism, Shelley's Asia may be seen as an embodiment of precisely the spirit of mystical love which according of Jones permitted the continent of Asia to rise to greater imaginative heights than Europe. If that is the case, Panthea may be taken to represent that pantheism which—though *through* it the truth of the soul may be glimpsed— can be fully apprehended only by the still greater power Asia embodies—the Imagination. Ione remains to epitomize the Ionic school of philosophy in which this imaginative power may 'glow and sparkle', but less strongly and only in dreams. If Ione does symbolize Greece, there is only one tradition that might encourage a Hellenist to assign Greece such a subordinate position. That is the Orientalist tradition at which we have been looking, and unless this tradition were working on Shelley at this time it is difficult to explain why the mountain regions of India should happen to be the place where the secrets of the death, as well as of the birth, of Time are laid bare.[150]

While Shelley, like Coleridge, did not know anything of Kashmiri mythology, he was certainly aware, through his reading of *The Missionary*, of the conception of Kashmir as Paradise. This conception carried with it images of a man and a woman who, on account of a mystical love (though flawed and obstructed), reflected their pristine archetypes. As we have seen, the similar pair of archetypal figures in Shelley's poem who reside in 'a vale in the Indian Caucasus' accord very closely with Kashmiri con-

---

[147] *PWPBS*, pp. 205–6.   [148] See chapter 3, p. 104, n. 87.   [149] *PU*, II.i.56–108.   [150] Ibid., IV.9–14; *Alastor*, 1.128. It is not to be explained by the *Dionysiaca* of Nonnus, ordered by Shelley in 1817 (*LPBS*, Letter 430, I, 575; Letter 438, I, 585), a book which, though it sets the scene of the battle between gods and Titans in India, is totally alien in spirit to Shelley's poem.

ceptions of the god and goddess, and there is actually a direct line of reading, via Owenson, Jones and Kalidasa which can account for that accordance. However, there is no image in *The Missionary* comparable to the third important figure in *Prometheus Unbound*—the Kashmiri deist with a belief in the Invisible pales into insignificance before the Invisible itself, Demogorgon. It is all the more ironic, then, that the best reason for returning to a Kashmiri mythology unknown to Shelley is that his conception of the mysterious and cataclysmic figure of Demogorgon dwelling deep beneath the Indian valley happens to coincide perfectly with a similar conception of the Kashmiris. If we again refer to Kashmiri mythology, it is to remove what some European readers have found to be a stumbling block to an understanding of Shelley's poem.

What is to be made of Demogorgon, to whose cave deep beneath the mountains Asia and Panthea, at the end of Act II, are drawn by spirits summoned by the universal love invested in Asia? If the note of the scholiast is to be trusted, Demogorgon is first mentioned by Statius, who in the *Thebaid* speaks of him as Lord of the Three Worlds. He is thought to be a spirit of the nether world invoked in magic, and in Alexandria was assumed to be of Oriental origin. When Demogorgon is named in the first of the supplementary cantos to *Orlando Furioso*, he is said to preside over the fairy world while inhabiting a gorgeous palace in the Himalayas.[151] Whether or not it is purely coincidence or (as it would otherwise have to be) some dim memory of an old Gnostic legend which accounts for it, this conception is identical with that of Nilanaga, the Cosmic Snake who, according to the Kashmiri mythology we have already mentioned, presides over the destiny of Kashmir in a cave deep beneath it.[152]

Nilanaga is described and his central place in the cosmic scheme made clear in Kashmir's most important *purana*, the *Nilamata*. When human beings first wanted to inhabit the valley permission to do so had to be sought from Nilanaga in his subterranean palace. Nila, the *purana* records,

resembling a mass of black antimony, shone forth by his earrings and by

[151] *Thebaid*, IV.516; *Oxford Companion to Classical Literature*, ed. Sir Paul Harvey (Oxford, 1937), s.v. Demogorgon; Lawrence John Zillman, ed., *Shelley's Prometheus Unbound*, Variorum ed. (Seattle, 1959), p. 315 and n. 8.   [152] If the ancient Gnostic conception of Demogorgon was originally derived from that of the Indian Serpent then the association with magic is explicable: the Snake presides over the greatest magic of all, God's *maya*, the successive recreations of the world. For the argument in favour of a Buddhist influence on Gnosticism, see esp. J. Kennedy, 'Buddhist Gnosticism, the System of Basilides' *JRAS*, N.S., XXXIV (1902), 377–415.

his diadem of sun-like splendour. He was adorned with a garment shining like lightning and with a silk upper garment. Being seated under a variegated canopy decorated all round with rows of little bells, he was distinguished by seven hundreds of terrible snake-hoods, radiant with jewels, and was surrounded by an effulgence spread by costly lamps.[153]

Popular *puranas* have a way of describing in ornate detail the trappings of immortal beings said to be indescribable but it will be clear that Nilanaga is a local variant of the more general Indian conception of the serpent of eternity, Seshanaga or Adi-Sesha.

If Shelley did have any conscious knowledge of the place the serpent has in the Indian cosmos, then it would have reached him through descriptions not on Nilanaga but of Seshanaga. In Indian mythology Seshanaga, like Nilanaga, is depicted as a serpent whose head sustains, while his eyes (jewels or mirrors) illuminate, all creation, including creation's most imaginative creations, the gods and their paradises, and the fire of whose mouth, at the end of each cycle, engulfs the Three Worlds beneath which he resides. It is said that his power, his glory, his nature and his form can neither be described nor comprehended by the gods themselves, but in a popular image he is represented as the couch of Vishnu (or Narayana) upon which the Preserver, invariably accompanied by his consort Lakshmi, 'sleeps during the intervals of creation'. In Shelley's time knowledge of Seshanaga was largely derived and made available by Halhed, Jones and Maurice from a Persian translation of the *Bhagavata Purana*, near the end of which the god Krishna (in the company of Arjuna) goes to propitiate Seshanaga so that a child can be brought back to life. In the *purana* Seshanaga is said to reside beyond the seven climates of the universe in a profound watery darkness where there is neither sun, moon or fire, and is described as 'the Being indescribable, who is pure and all-sufficient'.[154]

Jones, who quotes part of this description in his essay 'On the Gods of Greece, Italy and India', also depicts Seshanaga in his poetry, most graphically in his hymn to Lakshmi, the goddess who is the active form of Vishnu. It is in this hymn, if anywhere, that Shelley would have become familiar with Seshanaga as well as with the goddess who, I have argued, was the prototype, by way of Miss Owenson's Luxima, for his own Asia. Since Asia, just like Lakshmi, is born out of the Ocean, and like her is addressed as daughter of Ocean, Shelley may have been encouraged in his conception by learning directly from Jones that there

[153] See chapter 6, p. 216 and nn. 119–21.   [154] *HH*, II, 455–7.

was an Asian Aphrodite.[155] Be that as it may, the description of
Seshanaga immediately follows the account of Lakshmi's birth as
Vishnu hurries to claim her:

> Straight o'er the deep, then dimpling smooth, he rush'd;
> And tow'rd th'unmeasur'd snake, stupendous bed,
> The World's great mother, not reluctant, led:
> All nature glow'd, whene'er she smil'd or blush'd;
> The king of serpents hush'd
> His thousand heads, where diamond mirrors blaz'd,
> That multiplied her image, as he gaz'd.

> Thus multiplied, thus wedded, they pervade
> In varying myriads of ethereal forms,
> This pendent Egg by dovelike MAYA laid . . .[156]

In Shelley's poem, as in Indian mythology, the reabsorption of the
'myriads of ethereal forms' at the end of a cycle takes place
through a process the exact reverse of that by which they here
become manifest. The factor common to both is that the magical
cycle of creation within which we exist is ultimately reduced (or
expanded) to an archetypal pattern, or mythic triad, of male,
female and snake.

In a work published when Shelley was a child, George Forster
reported from Kashmir that this triad of god, goddess and serpent is symbolic of the union of strength, love and wisdom and
composes the Supreme Deity of the Hindus. This symbol, Forster
says, is never represented in temples in a material image, being
indivisible and of infinite space. In adjoining footnotes Forster
adds that Plato's mysterious triad might have been derived from
this conception of the Deity, which, he also tells us, first ani-
mated man at the time of creation with *akasa*, an aerial space

---

[155] Ibid., XIII, 291; *PU*, II.iv.168, 174.   [156] Ibid., XIII, 293. For the relationship
of Lakshmi to Vishnu as the goddess on the lotus who emerges at the time of the
Churning of the Ocean see *VP*, I, VIII–IX, 118–20, 144. In the usual henotheistic
Indian manner, she is also identified with Sarasvati (ibid., VI, 148). N.B. In an
appendix (F), 'Possible Indian Influence on Shelley', to an unpublished D.Phil.
thesis, 'Keats and Shelley: Comparative Studies in Two Types of Poetic Imagery'
(Oxford, 1957), pp. 634–54, S.R. Swaminathan, who finds in *PU* 'astonishingly
close and recurrent parallels to Indian images and ideas', reads Asia in terms of
Lakshmi (by way of Luxima) and Demogorgon in terms of Seshanaga. Like
previous scholars, including Amiyakumar Sen in an otherwise splendidly judicious
chapter in his *Studies in Shelley* (Calcutta, 1936), he assumes that *WWJ* and *TM*
both influenced Shelley but does not see the influence of *WWJ* through *TM*.
Although he also stresses an influence through Moor which I would discount,
nobody goes further than he towards making the sort of argument I make here.

equivalent to 'the Promethean fire'.[157] Given Shelley's interest in the region, it is possible he encountered this book which includes the first English description of it. But even if he didn't, it nevertheless offers a beautifully succinct paradigm in terms of which to read not only the relationship between the three main figures in *Prometheus Unbound* but also that of the poem itself to something as abstract and mystical as the deep and imageless truth.

India certainly provides an intellectual tradition in the light of which *Prometheus Unbound* can be *read*. It now seems that it reinforced the intellectual tradition in the light of which *Prometheus Unbound* was *written*. None the less, the poem is essentially conceived in Shelley's imagination. Demogorgon is a creature so imaginative, an immanent power so indescribable, that only once do we have the glimpse of an image, the hint of a description—Demogorgon is 'snake-like Doom' coiled beneath the throne of the Eternal.[158] Shelley's imagination is even more uncompromising than that evident in the *Bhagavata Purana*, which accommodates itself to the popular imagination and describes the Indescribable as having a thousand heads and resembling in magnitude Siva's sacred mountain. Jones's conception of Seshanaga is also fanciful. Though he might have been encouraged to do so by the *Vishnu Purana*, where Seshanaga is described as the form of Vishnu 'proceeding from the quality of darkness',[159] Jones never does conceive of the Serpent in the rather more abstract philosophical way he conceives of Narayana as being 'beyond the stretch of lab'ring thought sublime'.[160] The reason Seshanaga does not figure powerfully is that while Jones in his 'Hymn to Narayena' concedes that the 'One only Being' is to be apprehended immanently in the absorbed soul, that Being remains for him essentially transcendent. For Shelley transcendence is simply a condition or by-product of realized, or universal, immanence.

It is this intense consciousness of universal immanence—an awareness that the world is instinct with strength, love and wisdom—which allows us to identify Shelley with an Indian tradition older perhaps than Vedic times. The place of Demogorgon in Shelley's poem concurs not only with that occupied by Nilana-

---

[157] George Forster, p. 35 and nn* and §. See chapter 3, p. 91.   [158] *PU*, II.iii.95–98.   [159] *VP*, II, v, 211.   [160] Stanza I.3, 'Hymn to Narayena', *WWJ*, XIII, 305. Cf Jones's fanciful reference to 'the snake, that never dies' in the 'Hymn to Indra', ibid., XIII, 276.

ga or Seshanaga in Indian mythology but also with that accorded in the psychological system of yoga to the *kundalini* serpent which, if the sensual is to be spiritualized and the material aetherealized, must be raised from the nether parts of the body up through psychical centres into the crown of the head.[161] It is sometimes supposed that this system evolved out of a pre-Vedic serpent-worship with which the Vedic pantheon, led by Indra, a transcendent god of the firmament like Jupiter, had to make a compromise which is reflected in later Hindu mythology.[162] The Buddhists, in rejecting the authority of the Vedas, did not need to include transcendent gods in their versions of the same stories, but even where the Hindus refer, as in Kashmiri mythology, to gods on the mountain-tops, the mystical practices in Hinduism still convey the impression that, as R.C. Zaehner says, 'the immanent God is everything, the transcendent largely irrelevant'.[163] In a text central to Hinduism, the *Brihad Aranyaka*, Yajnavalkya describes the journey to the depths of the psyche, where, like the palace of Seshanaga, neither sun, moon nor fire shines.[164]

There has been a rather contrary emphasis in the Judaeo-Christian tradition—put crudely, God is transcendent and good, the Snake is immanent and bad—and because of this dualist conception, Southey, whatever else he got right about Hindu mythology, totally distorted the relationship of Seshanaga to Vishnu. In *Kehama* 'the rebel race' hope

> that the seven-headed Snake, whereon
> That strong Preserver sets his conquering feet,
> Will rise and shake him headlong from his throne.[165]

Shelley's imagination is wholly free of the Christian dualism which inhibits Southey and, to a lesser extent, Jones, and on account of it he can attribute to Demogorgon an immanent power which would have originally belonged to Demogorgon if it is true that Demogorgon was a Gnostic conception derived from India. But Shelley also goes beyond the Gnostics—giving to the Gnostic dualism deplored by Plotinus[166] a neo-Platonist gloss—

[161] Patanjali, Sutra III; Radhakrishnan, I, 366–8; Woodroffe, pp. 1–28.
[162] Radhakrishnan, II, 287–91; Hutton, Appendix B, pp. 224ff; *VP*, II, VI, 223–4.
[163] R.C. Zaehner, trans., *Hindu Scriptures* (London, 1966), Introduction, pp. xiv–xv. See also Zimmer, pp. 74–6.   [164] See chapter 4, p. 133. This passage (quoted by Jones following Caul) in *AR*, I, 349 is noted by Southey, *Kehama*, p. 364.
[165] *Kehama*, XXII, 5, p. 243. But note also ibid., XXIII.15, pp. 251–2. Southey recorded the description of Krishna's visit to Seshanaga from the *Bhagavata Purana* in *SCB*, Ser. 2, p. 482.   [166] *Enn.*, II.ix.10. Shelley's sense of Immanence is such that he rejects or supersedes even the beneficent, but transcendent Plotinian concept of Zeus (ibid., III.v.8; v.viii.10).

when he denies the very existence of a transcendent Demiurge such as the Gnostics elevated into a principle of evil. In denying the phantasm Jupiter—the cause of pain—any relative, let alone ultimate, reality, Shelley is not merely standing Milton on his head and suggesting that a transcendent God is satanic; he is saying that the very conception of such a God is indicative of an absence of universal love and as such is the *only* evil there is. Shelley's position here is identical with an Indian tradition of non-dualism which Sankara developed out of non-theistic Buddhism.

The descent into the imageless darkness in Act II of *Prometheus Unbound* is penultimate to the all-pervasiveness of imageless light. The power of wisdom Asia has invoked through love will now envelop all sublunary worlds and Asia herself ascends in a heavenly car.[167] In his rewriting of *Queen Mab* Shelley had begun to move closer to the spirit of *Prometheus Unbound* when he had had Ianthe bidden no longer by Mab but by the Daemon of the World with the words:

> Therefore from nature's inner shrine,
> Where gods and fiends in worship bend,
> Majestic spirit, be it thine
> The flame to seize, the veil to rend,
> Where the vast snake Eternity
> In charmèd sleep doth ever lie.[168]

The image of the ascending car, as we saw, was derived not only from 'The Palace of Fortune', Jones's poem based on an Indian tale, but also, in a context even more agreeable to Asia's, from the ascent of Southey's Kailyal after she drinks from the cup of immortality in Yama's court in the Ocean depths. Jones was later to find the image of the ascending car used by Kalidasa.[169] The ascending car is an image—since the poem, even where it depicts the dissolution of images, does so in images—for that state of utter transcendence or aetherealization which follows upon an apprehension of universal immanence. It is in Plotinian terms that Panthea now apprehends Asia:

> I feel but see thee not. I scarce endure
> The radiance of thy beauty . . .[170]

Asia stands revealed as did Luxima after Hilarion had taken that

[167] *PU*, II.iv.   [168] 'The Daemon of the World', Pt I, 96–101, *PWPBS*, p. 3.   [169] *Sacontala*, beginning of Act VII, *WWJ*, IX, 511ff.   [170] *PU*, II.v.17–18.

journey into the utter darkness of the psyche which, here in the image of Demogorgon unveiled, shows the deep truth to be imageless.[171]

PROMETHEUS UNBOUND, ACT III

The third Act of *Prometheus Unbound* sees the return of the Golden Age. The poem is, after all, Shelley's *Paradise Regained* or, rather, as his own preface suggests, his own resolution of the incongruous in *Paradise Lost*.[172] This is so because Shelley is free, on account of his rejection of Christian dualism, to combine in the single figure of Prometheus Satan's most heroic qualities together with the godhead Milton must necessarily as a Christian deny him. There is no conflict in *Prometheus Unbound*—since godhead is immanent, once love towards all things has been fully realized, the fear which bodies itself forth in images of a transcendent God evaporates and it is the terrestrial which is discovered to be the only celestial paradise. Notwithstanding Milton's theological commitment to the concept of a transcendent God, Shelley does respond to his poetic power and, in the preface to *Prometheus Unbound*, associates him with a tradition in England whereby the production of great literature is concomitant with a bold enquiry into the established institutions of morality and religion. From 'the peculiar style of intense and comprehensive imagery which distinguishes the modern literature of England' Shelley has no doubt that England is undergoing just such another outburst. If we see *Prometheus Unbound* as resolving the incongruities of a philosophy half–discovered by the imaginative power of *Paradise Lost*, then the new Orientalism centred on India may be a powerful factor in permitting such a resolution.

Jupiter suffers the same fate as Kehama. Having usurped Heaven, Kehama sought to dominate Earth (and Ladurlad, the one man who defied him) by usurping the throne of the underworld—only to find that, having reckoned without the im-

---

[171] Ibid., ii.iv.116; *TM*, ii, 147–53.   [172] Preface to *PU*, *PWPBS*, pp. 205–6. *Paradise Lost* includes half-a-dozen specific references to India and Milton's Eden has about it an Oriental ambience derived, perhaps, from Classical writers like Diodorus Siculus no less than from Renaissance accounts of the East. If Milton does not, like Dante, identify the Indian Fig with the Tree of the Knowledge of Good and Evil nor, like Ralegh, identify it with the Tree of Life, he does include an evocative description of the vegetable prodigy (ix.1001–1010) and it is indicative that men such as Wilkins and Hastings saw in Bk vi resemblances not only to the puranic accounts of the battle of the heavenly spirits but to Meru, the Mountain of God which, like Milton's, controls the alternation of night and day (vi.4–8).

mortal power of love possible to a man and woman, he had brought on himself his own destruction. Ravana in the *Ramayana* experienced a similar fate. In *Prometheus Unbound* there is no struggle, in spite of Jupiter's vain and dualistic image of himself as a vulture dragging the snake down with him into the darkness.[173] Both are mere images, but since that of the vulture derives what force it has only from fear, it follows logically that in this case it has nothing at all with which to resist the snake, Demogorgon being activated and invested by the universal love which eliminates all fear. The fall of Jupiter in *Prometheus Unbound* mirrors a supposition implicit in *The Missionary*, namely, that Christian theology is perverted and outmoded and ceases to be relevant in the light of the mystical philosophy of the Vedanta.[174]

Prometheus Unbound penetrates so deeply to the spirit which gave rise to the common archetypal images discovered in Indian mythology by Jones that the details of the imagery which might differentiate the Greek from the Indian are at times wholly absorbed. There is, for example, the veined shell from which Asia takes her birth out of the Ocean.[175] At this point in the poem the shell, like Lakshmi's conch described by Jones in the 'Hymn to Indra' as a 'breathing shell, that peals of conquest rang', is used to announce the fall of Jupiter.[176] The particular application of it and the fact that the shell is described as 'mystic' (the most distinctive adjective used in Jones's hymns), quite apart from the name of Asia herself, suggest that it is the Indian which has inspired the story common to both Lakshmi and Aphrodite (for Plotinus, as for Shelley, the 'female' soul attached to the 'male' Intellect).[177]

The poem penetrates to other identities common to both cultures. One example is provided by the joy Shelley's Earth expresses at her release from Jupiter's tyranny. A decade before *Prometheus Unbound* was written, Wilford, quoting from Virgil's Fourth Eclogue the Sibylline original for Shelley's celebrated song in *Hellas* about the renewal of the World's Great Age (*Mahayuga* in Sanskrit), commented: 'These are the very words of Vishnu to the Earth, when complaining to him and begging for redress'.[178] It is only with the use of Atlantis as a setting for the

---

[173] *PU*, III.i.70–83.   [174] Miss Owenson is no more sympathetic to Brahmin rites and to caste than she is to Christian dogma and intolerance. None the less, it is her response to the Vedanta which provides the novel with its idealistic ambience.   [175] *PU*, II.v.20–31. Asia also ascends from the underworld in an ivory shell (ibid., II.iv.157).   [176] *WWJ*, XIII, 273; *PU*, III.iii.69–83.   [177] See chapter 6. p. 222 and n. 139.   [178] *AR*, x, 31.

second scene, where Ocean and Sun dwell on the deeds that have been done between Earth and Moon,[179] that *Prometheus Unbound* might be thought to have escaped an Asian ambience. Yet even there it has not. Shelley had read the first volume of J.S. Bailly's series of letters to Voltaire devoted to the theory that, while the Brahmins held the key to the origins of civilization, the cradle of civilization was not in India itself but farther north in Asia. Since he liked the first volume enough to cite it as an authority,[180] it is unlikely that Shelley did not know at least the title of the second: *Lettres sur L'Atlantide de Platon et sur l'ancienne histoire de l'Asie.*[181] In the book, Atlantis is located in northern Asia.

The cave in which Prometheus and Asia take up their residence on the imparadised Earth is sometimes thought to be derived from the 'spontaneously produced cave, florid and having fountains', which Porphyry says Zoroaster reputedly consecrated in the mountains of Persia. Additionally, however, Shelley's Earth indicates quite specifically that the cave is in a vale beyond Bacchic Nysa and Indus and its tribute rivers,[182] precisely the approach to Kashmir which would be suggested by a reading of Elphinstone and Miss Owenson.[183] That Miss Owenson's Kashmir has again come to the surface is indicated by the vale being the place not only where, during Jupiter's tyranny, Shelley's Earth, like Asia, was sustained by the thought of Prometheus, but also from where the simplicity of the Golden Age will be restored. Furthermore, the cave is distinguished by more than its flowers and fountain:

> From its curved roof the mountain's frozen tears
> Like snow, or silver, or long diamond spires,
> Hang downward, raining forth a doubtful light.[184]

In this it resembles the cave of Hilarion, the chief feature of which is its 'pendant spars' that 'hung like glittering icicles from its shining roof' and which, on the night Luxima visits the cave, obliquely reflect the moon's light.[185] This cave Hilarion eventual-

---

[179] *PU*, III.ii.   [180] Note to VI.45, 46, Notes on *Queen Mab, PWPBS*, p. 809.
[181] See chapter 2, n. 206; chapter 6, pp. 198–9 and n. 49. English translations of Bailly's two volumes appeared in 1801 and 1804 respectively.   [182] *PU,* III.iii.152–75.   [183] Elphinstone (pp. 83–118) conceives of Kashmir as the eastern boundary of the Hindu Kush or Indian Caucasus, whence spring the rivers of the Punjab, the principal river being the Indus. To approach Kashmir Hilarion sails up the Indus and the Ravi to Lahore (*TM*, I, 55–9). The map attached to Volney's *Ruins* might suggest a similar approach.   [184] Ibid., III.iii.15–17.   [185] *TM*, I, 140–142, 179–83; II, 20–2.

ly dedicates to the Spirit of Love he had first encountered in the domed shrine of Camdeo nearby,[186] and the temple of Prometheus built by votaries close to the cave in *Prometheus Unbound* may also owe something to this temple of Camdeo.

By the end of Act III, in what can be read as a metaphorical acknowledgement of the prevailing importance of Orientalism, the Spirit of the Earth is shown to have become one with Asia, the Spirit of the Hour to have seen into the mysteries, and the painted veil which those who live call life to have been torn aside.[187] Like that of Jones, Shelley's republicanism has realized itself most fully in the republic of letters. Here he has discovered the means to the Golden Age which had eluded him in *Queen Mab*. The Earth will be transformed not through social, or any other, action, but only through that absolute quietus which is universal love in the heart.

The Missionary was not the only novel Shelley read which associated India with a way of life reminiscent of the Golden Age. In 1812 he read, and acknowledged his conversion to the doctrines of, *The Empire of the Nairs*, a novel by Sir James Lawrence subtitled 'an Utopian Romance' and frequently taken as such.[188] While the work, like Eliza Hamilton's *Letters of a Hindoo Rajah*, is a satire on English manners, it, too, is firmly grounded in Indian fact, here the way of life of the Nair caste of Malabar, whose *marumakkathayam*, or matrilineal, social system may once have been as widespread in India as Lawrence makes it in his novel.[189] In a rider to the title of a prefatory essay, 'On the Nair system of Gallantry and Inheritance', Lawrence declared his intention of 'shewing its advantages over marriage, in insuring an indubitable birth, and being favorable to population, to the rights of women, and to the active genius of men'.[190] Under the Nair system, with which Lawrence had become familiar through Buchanan and which had fascinated Europeans ever since Duarte Barbosa's classic account of it in the sixteenth century,[191] women were genuinely free to choose their own lovers, property being invested in them and their daughters, while sons, brought up by

---

[186] Ibid., III, 221–2.   [187] *PU*, III,iv.   [188] James Henry Lawrence, *The Empire of the Nairs*, An Utopian Romance, 4 vols (London, 1811); *LPBS*, Letter 201, I, 323; Letter 202, I, 325. Mary read the novel shortly after going to live with Shelley (*Journal*, 26–27 September 1814).   [189] Hutton, p. 160.   [190] Lawrence, I, Introductory Essay, i.   [191] *The Book of Duarte Barbosa . . . completed about the year 1518 A.D.*, trans. M.L. Dames, 2 vols (London, 1918–21). Francis Buchanan, *A Journey from Madras through Mysore, Canara and Malabar*, 3 vols (London, 1807). Barbosa's work appeared in a number of editions in the sixteenth century translated into Italian by G.B. Ramusio.

their maternal uncles, from whom they took their name, grew up as free to pursue their genius as, according to Bacon, only bachelors could.[192] If Shelley expressed his gratitude to Lawrence for the realization that in such a system prostitution, like bastardy, could not exist,[193] we can be sure that it was because he concurred with Lawrence's apprehension of its chief virtue: 'Love . . . would rekindle that open and generous fire that would make the world a paradise'.

In the novel, the Nair system becomes the given for a satire on English manners such as Shelley would find congenial: reviews of the German original recalled both 'the principles of Mrs Wolstonecraft' and the 'part of the republic of Plato, in which the community of women is in the same manner ennobled by moral and political syllogisms'.[194] Lawrence argued that the Nair system was not only the best system of society but the natural system and the original system. One of the European characters in the novel has to journey to Malabar itself to become convinced of the real existence of such a society: 'At first I considered it a kind of Utopia, a land existing only in a poet's brain'.[195] It is not only a character in Lawrence's book who is impressed. J.H. Hutton, a modern authority on caste in India, speaks of the system as 'perhaps the best in the world when taken by itself'. Furthermore, Hutton supports the contention of Lawrence that this was the original system:

It seems likely that the *marumakkathayam* was the ancient and civilized system, which was replaced in most countries of southern Europe and southern Asia by the *makkathayam* [or patrilineal system] under the stress of conquest by a ruder people from the steppes of southern Russia.

In coming to this conclusion, with modern archaeological findings at his disposal, Hutton concurs with an idea which has long haunted the literary imagination: namely, that prior to a patrilineal system introduced by invaders India and the Mediterranean shared a common culture, the principal features of which were a matrilineal system, a lunar cult and a worship of the goddess.[196]

In Shelley's day both Maurice and Wilford, extrapolating from

---

[192] This theme is indicated in a rider to the title of the essay. The reference to Bacon is on pp. xxxv–xxxvi. [193] *LPBS*, Letter 201, I, 323. [194] Lawrence, I, Advertisement, vii–viii. [195] Ibid., III, 85. It has been argued that the Second Book of More's *Utopia* was based on Indian, or indological, sources (J. Duncan M. Derrett, 'Thomas More and Joseph the Indian', *JRAS*, 1962, 18–34). [196] Hutton, pp. 149–69 (quote p. 160).

Classical sources, had already foreshadowed this conclusion.[197]
The question that remained to engage their attention was how
this common culture had been effected and for those who, with
Diodorus Siculus, doubted that Dionysus had really carried civilization into India, there was another legend, also told by
Diodorus, of the invasion of India by Semiramis.[198] It is Semiramis whom Lawrence, in *The Empire of the Nairs*, decides to
make the link between Biblos, Babylon and India. Her Syrian
followers leave Babylon determined to found a new society on
the other side of the Indus. This they succeed in doing. The first
Indian village they encounter 'lay at the foot of a mountain; a
brook tumbled down a rock, and bathed the earthly paradise: the
very elements favored this happy spot'.[199] The Syrians and Indians dance in natural love and Indostan becomes a paradise of
love which will be as antithetical to Islamic Persia as it will be bewildering to itinerants from Christian Europe.

While the literary imagination is, according to the neo-
Platonist scheme and its Indian equivalents, subject to the vagar-
ies of imagery, its potential for realizing the archetypes in the
Collective Unconscious make it a possible guide to an historical
reality which it cannot exclude even though it may supersede it.
The third act of *Prometheus Unbound* can be read as the imaginative discovery of an historical, no less than a prophetic,
truth since it is close in spirit to the type of pre-Vedic society
Hutton believes existed in India.[200] There is, of course, a converse and not necessarily exclusive alternative to this conclusion
and that is that Hutton, like Jones before him, has stated in terms
of earlier periods of history what are really penetrations of deeper levels of the psyche. A mythopoeic treatment of history of this
kind belongs to what J.N. Findlay denominated the Indo-
Pythagorean-Platonic, as opposed to the Judaeo-Christian, view
of the universe.[201] In terms of the Indo-Pythagorean view, which
holds that the universe is subject to periodical cycles, it would
matter little whether Shelley set his poem in the past or in the future: both past and future are equally a measure of distance from
an unrealized present.

It is, perhaps, a consciousness of this distance which led Shel-

<hr/>

[197] *IA*, v, 910ff; 'A Dissertation on Semiramis', *AR*, IV, 376–
400.   [198] Diodorus, II.16–19. At the beginning of this account, India is noticed as
a land of unusual beauty.   [199] Lawrence, I, 28.   [200] Hutton, Appendix B, pp.
222–61, esp. the earlier pages. That India is heir to a continuous tradition based on
yoga and a devotion to the Goddess is argued in Mircea Eliadé, pp. 348–58.
Bhattacharyya, among others, argues that the matrilineal system was once
widespread (pp. 110–11).   [201] See chapter 6, p. 224 and n. 144.

ley, some time later, to add a fourth act to *Prometheus Unbound.*[202] In *Queen Mab* Ianthe is taken up in a vision to a transcendent position from which the past, the present and the future may be apprehended. While this (incidentally) demonstrates how the actual structure of the Indian fable on which it is based has metaphysical implications, Shelley's use of it remains somewhat mechanical. *Prometheus Unbound* on the other hand discovers a form of expression appropriate to the experience of vision immanent in it. What was originally a dramatic poem becomes a wholly lyrical one. At the end of the third act, creation is still subject to Time: in Act IV three-fold Time is superseded by Eternity.

PROMETHEUS UNBOUND, ACT IV

As soon as Time, at the commencement of Act IV, is borne to his tomb in Eternity, the Spirits of the Hours, the true nature of which has long been suppressed, are free to rise from the deep. The psyche no longer takes on an appearance of either history or prophecy: it is seen to be an ever-present reality. The Hours, which

> weave the mystic measure
> Of music, and dance, and shapes of light,[203]

like those in *The Curse of Kehama*, which, 'in Brama's region'

> Weave the vast circle of his age-long day,[204]

are a re-creation, more total than Southey's, of the *raginis* of whom it is said in Jones's 'Hymn to Indra'

> Like shooting stars around his regal seat
> A veil of many-colour'd light they weave . . .
> With love of song and sacred beauty smit
> The mystic dance they knit;
> Pursuing, circling, whirling, twining, leading,
> Now chasing, now receding . . .[205]

In the 'Hymn to Sereswaty' they not only come

> With many a sparkling glance
> And knit the mazy dance
> Like yon bright orbs, that gird the solar flame,

---

[202] Note on *PU* by Mrs Shelley, *PWPBS*, p. 271.   [203] *PU*, IV, 77–8.   [204] *Kehama*, XXIII.5, p. 243.   [205] *WWJ*, XIII, 271.

> Now parted, now combin'd,
> Clear as thy speech and various as thy mind

but join 'the jocund hours' to sing 'the sweet return of Spring'. Because the aethereal *raginis*, each appropriate to a particular hour, season and predominant mood, combine to embody most beautifully the divine harmony of music and poetry, they were considered by Jones to be 'the most pleasing invention of the ancient Hindus'.[206] They come to the surface in *Prometheus Unbound* at this point not only as the Spirits of the Hours but as the Spirits who, 'wrapped in sweet sounds', rise from the human mind to explain their existence in terms of 'the Indian deep'.[207]

The human mind, like the Indian deep, contains a wondrous imagery of crystal caverns, skiey towers and azure isles. But marvellous imagery also points on towards the more abstract Imagination (what Coleridge once called 'the Vast') and so Shelley's human mind is also like the Indian deep in being

> an ocean
> of clear emotion,
> A heaven of serene and mighty motion.

The Spirits who rise from it join the Chorus of the Hours in dancing the mystic measure, calling in also Spirits

> From the depths of the sky and the ends of the Earth.

The release of the entire Chorus has been obtained by what the Spirits of the human mind acknowledge lies beyond their eyes: human love

> Which makes all its gazes on Paradise.

One semi-chorus of Spirits can assert

> We, beyond heaven, are driven along,

the other,

> Us the enchantments of earth retain.[208]

and, coming together again, eliminate that distinction between Heaven and Earth which, in its apprehension of India, attaches to Forster's novel as well as to Kipling's ballad. When Asia's conch-shell blew to signal the triumph of love and 'all things had put their evil nature off', that is, in neo-Platonist parlance, lost

---

[206] Ibid., XIII, 312, 315–16.   [207] *PU*, IV.81–8. A less imaginative portrait of the Indian deep is given in *Kehama*, XVI.5–6, pp. 172–4.   [208] Ibid., IV.93–162.

their materiality, the whole Earth had no choice but to be aetherealized (Shelley, like George Forster, conceiving of Promethean fire as aether, the element into which, by Indian and Pythagorean reckoning, the other four are absorbed). The Earth is Heaven, and to illustrate that the gross forms which, in both these traditions, are supposed to inhabit only the sublunary realms no longer exist, the frigid Moon, its 'void annihilation' filled with a love bursting in 'like light on caves', is impregnated by the Spirit of Earth.

The prologue to Jones's *Sacontala* tells us that 'the subtil Ether which is the vehicle of sound, pervades the universe'.[209] The process of aethereal absorption in *Prometheus Unbound* is apprehended by Panthea and Ione as 'a stream of sound',[210] the sensation which, for the Indians no less than the Pythagoreans, occupies the same ultimate position in relation to the others that aether does in relation to the elements.[211] If the poem is itself an experience of the Vision which is its subject, it follows that its imagery will be as aetherealized as its language is musical. To regard this as a poetic weakness would be to make a mistake the same in kind as Earth makes when Prometheus says that he wishes no living thing to suffer pain or to be blind to the fact that it is the meekness of Asia which alone can unleash the snake-like Doom coiled beneath the Eternal, the Immortal.[212] Shelley's imagery—of caves and fountains, mountains and ocean—is, paradoxically, intangible (in comparison to that of, say, Keats) only because his commitment to the Earth is so total that he penetrates brute matter in all its distinct forms to find where it is instinct with divinity. If Nature is a veil, then the natural images in the poem will point beyond themselves to the mystical power of which, though they take their beauty from it, they are but images.

That the natural imagery of the poem does in fact have scarcely any independent life of its own may be demonstrated by the way that, while Shelley himself says it was inspired by the Roman Campagna[213] (and Mary suggests an obvious additional debt both to the Apennines and the Alps),[214] it is equally evocative of the Himalayan scenery it purports to describe. The *Journal* entries which tell how Shelley had been reading Aeschylus concurrently with Elphinstone's *Travels in the Kingdom of Caubul* are suggestive, but once again it is Jones who really provides the clue to the

[209] *WWJ*, IX, 377.   [210] *PU*, IV.505–6.   [211] Colebrooke, I, 397. See also chapter 1, pp. 27–9.   [212] *PU*, I, 303–11; II.iii.93–8.   [213] Preface to *PU*, *PWPBS*, p. 205.   [214] *Journal*, 26 March 1818; 15 November 1818.

resolution of this apparent incongruity. By way of introduction to
'The Palace of Fortune', which Shelley had (it seems) read,
Jones remarks that the Italian poets, including Petrarch, have so
much in common with the Asiatic poets that he can only suppose
the Italians actually owe a debt to the East by way of the
Arabians.[215] Whether or not that is so, his own English transla-
tions of both dramatize the similarity of the sentiment and the
imagery. Later, in India, referring to *Satya Yuga*, the Golden
Age hymned in Indian literature, Jones says of Tasso (whose life
Shelley in the summer of 1818 was planning to dramatize)[216] that
'with a lyre strung in India' he would have delighted in it because
'Nature then reign'd, and Nature's laws'.[217]

These references may suggest that what permits the Italian and
Indian landscapes to merge in *Prometheus Unbound* is the sub-
ordination of the details which differentiate them to the archetypal shape and immensity they assume precisely because they are a
common image of paradise. As the poet in *Alastor* recognizes,
every aspect—fountain, course and gulfs—of the stream whose
source is inaccessibly profound has each its type in him.[218] The
claim that something so obviously universal as an interior landscape should be especially associated with India rests solely on
the supposition that, of all mythologies, it is the Indian which has
most deeply penetrated (as Indian philosophical tradition supposes mythology should) to the identities common to all, and
transformed Nature in the sense that it discovers the supernatural
(or unifying) principle within the (differentiating or diversifying)
natural. It can be read as a tacit acknowledgement of the primacy
or priority of the Indian imagination that *Prometheus Unbound*
attributes the power to transform Panthea to Asia as she resides
in an Indian vale.

While Shelley did not have to be influenced by Jones to be a
Platonist, only a familiarity with Jones and the ethos he fostered
could have led him to associate with a vale in the Indian Cau-

---

[215] See chapter 2, pp. 64–5 and n. 112. A more marginal, but intriguing, association
of East and West is to be found in the *Journal* entry for 12 February 1818: 'Go to the
Indian Library, and the Panorama of Rome.'   [216] *LPBS*, Letter 462, II, 8; Letter
465, II, 15. Shelley preferred the work of Petrarch (*LPBS*, Letter 470, II, 19–20;
Letter 517, II, 122).   [217] *WWJ*, XIII, 213–14. The opening of 'The Enchanted
Fruit' is conceived in terms of Tasso's 'Aminta'. Elsewhere Jones speaks of Sanskrit
as being the equal of Italian in şoftness and elegance (ibid., IV, 194). In *PI*, Fielding
is said to be in the habit of seeing India in terms of Italy (VII,
p. 59).   [218] *Alastor*, II.502–14. In a letter to Peacock (*LPBS*, Letter 354, I,
490) Shelley suggests that, unlike roads, which are the work of man, rivers imitate
mind in that they wander at will into places otherwise inaccessible.

casus the sort of imaginative experience valued by neo-Platonism. We cannot regard this association, persistently made by Shelley, as purely fanciful since, as Jones guessed and others suggested, India's own most imaginative conceptions, which we can best approach in terms of neo-Platonism, were formulated in these very mountains. For Shelley, then, Jones must have been something of a catalyst. However, the extent to which Shelley penetrates farther than Jones to India in the abstract may be measured by the degree to which the imagery in his work is absorbed in Imagination. Jones hoped that the new imagery to be found in Asiatic literature might permit an English poet to write with greater sublimity than Aeschylus. *Prometheus Unbound* has a unique claim to being the fulfilment of that hope. Jones's hope followed upon a recognition that the Classical pantheon had outworn its poetic use and *Prometheus Unbound* quite literally pulls the king of the pantheon down out of the sky. Furthermore, the Chorus of Spirits in Shelley's poem goes far towards supplying the deficiency which made Jones, writing on Indian music, regret that Shakespeare was not alive to give speech and form to the aerial beings which allegorize the Hindu melodies appropriate to particular human passions at specific hours and seasons.[219]

Shelley goes further than Jones, who could never fully realize even in his poetry the implications of what he said in prose about the Indian spirit. It could not be by displacing a set of outworn images with a set of unfamiliar, if novel, ones that a poet could attain to the musical power of a *raga* or achieve a sublimity comparable to Aeschylus. Jones himself must have been aware of this when he said that the principle by which art was created had to be sought for 'in the deepest recesses of the human mind'.[220] But his own poetry, like that of Southey after him, is frequently constrained by the same Indian imagery that he hoped would liberate it. The imaginative power simply did not operate intensely enough and it remained for Shelley, going further than Jones or Southey, to respond not to particular Hindu images but to the spirit behind them to which Jones, more than anyone, had pointed. The Indian setting of *Prometheus Unbound*, as faintly discernible as an ultimate veil, serves to indicate that what might pass for an Indian influence is a recognition within the Imagination of India as an appropriate image for that mystical imageless state for which the Imagination is itself but an image.

---

[219] See chapter 2, p. 62 and n. 98.   [220] *WWJ*, x, 362. In this essay, Jones, considering music and poetry, argues for that identity of passion and sound which he is later to find exists both in Hindu music and in Indian and Persian poetry.

In his preface to the 'Hymn to Narayena' Jones says that the first stanza represents 'the sublimest attributes of the Supreme Being, and the three forms in which they most clearly appear to us, Power, Wisdom, and Goodness, or, in the language of Orpheus and his disciples, Love'.[221] So, too, in *The Missionary*, Luxima tells Hilarion that in India divine Wisdom is personified not as cold, severe and rigid, but as 'the infant twin of Love'.[222] The language in which Orpheus, like Luxima, expressed that love (and in which Jones thought it was most truly expressed) was music and it is a comment on nothing so much as the fourth Act of *Prometheus Unbound* itself to say, as Earth says there:

> Language is a perpetual Orphic song,
> Which rules with Daedal harmony a throng
> Of thoughts and forms, which else senseless and shapeless
> were.[223]

The dramatic form of Act I has become wholly refined into lyric.

Lest it be obscured that Orphic song has its moral implications, Demogorgon, his power acknowledged alike by those above in fortunate abodes 'beyond Heaven's constellated wilderness' and those below, 'the happy dead', rises, like an eclipse gathered up into the pores of sunlight, to close out the poem by addressing all forms of life from the greatest to the least seats of intelligence (from 'man's high mind' to 'the central stone of sullen lead', from 'heaven's star-fretted domes' to 'the dull weed some sea-worm battens on'). The magic he instructs them in is that gentleness, virtue, wisdom and endurance are the divine qualities—more specific than those enumerated by Jones—which enable man to control the serpent-power through which alone he can realize Eternity.[224] It is this final Act of *Prometheus Unbound* which puts in a proper perspective Jones's approach to India even while it illuminates the nature of Shelley's passage. Jones sensed that in Indian antiquity was to be discovered a knowledge of man's origins. The way time and place are eventually superseded as Shelley's poem plumbs greater imaginative depths indicates that Indian antiquity is simply an appropriate image for its own, and Shelley's, most central discovery—that man, irrespective of time or place, may realize in the Self the origin and object of all Being.

[221] Ibid., XIII, 303. [222] *TM*, II, 66–7. [223] *PU*, IV.415–17. [224] Ibid., IV.510–78.

AFTERWORD
Alun Lewis: 'The Earth is a Syllable' and Death in the Green Tree

in which Lewis's short story is read
in terms of the Upanishad from which it
takes its title and his death considered
in the light of both.

      Ah yes, he died in the green
Tree . . .   O had he seen
In a flash, all India laid like Antony's queen,
Or seen the highest, for which alone we are born?

     Vernon Watkins: 'Sonnet on the Death of Alun Lewis'.

And the Celt knew the Indian . . .

        Shelley: *Prometheus Unbound.*

AFTERWORD

Alun Lewis: 'The Earth is a Syllable' and Death in the Green Tree

After E.M. Forster, the only British writer to find the Imagination physically confronted (as well as, like L.H. Myers,[1] metaphysically extended) by India was Alun Lewis, whose early death in the jungle is frequently regarded as a sad loss to literature. One of his last stories, 'The Earth is a Syllable',[2] acknowledges its debt to the Upanishads both by its title and within the story itself. If the most highly acclaimed of Lewis's stories, 'The Orange Grove',[3] might reasonably be read as his passage to India, 'The Earth is a Syllable' deserves to be considered as his passage to more than India.

The story takes its title from a short and important Upanishad, the *Mandukya*, but it also includes a reference to the older *Brihad Aranyaka*, to which the *Mandukya Upanishad* is itself indebted.[4] What the story shares with the two Upanishads (the two which also especially attracted the attention of Yeats)[5] is a concern to discover the stages of enlightenment a man may pass through before his death. Perhaps the closest approach poetry has made to mysticism (if it is not the closest mysticism has come to according recognition to poetry) is to say, as does the first line of the *Mandukya Upanishad*, that the whole Earth is the syllable *Om*, a mystic utterance thought not only to be inclusive of all sound in the mouth and thus all language but to be the *Logos* which is creation. This sacred syllable is said to be too holy to be

[1] *The Root and the Flower* (London, 1935); *The Pool of Vishnu* (London, 1940). [2] *In the Green Tree* (London, 1948), pp. 85–90. [3] Ibid., pp. 111–25. [4] Hume, pp. 391–3. [5] See chapter 4, pp. 128–9 and n. 32; Introduction to Bhagwan Shri Hamsa, *The Holy Mountain*, trans. Purohit Swami (London, 1934), pp. 22–3. Both Upanishads are included in Yeats's translation (with Purohit Swami) of *The Ten Principal Upanishads* (London, 1937).

pronounced in the presence of anyone else and more efficacious if never pronounced at all. It is, in short, an experience of the Absolute. According to the *Rig Veda* the gods found in *Om* the safe refuge which not even poetic metres could provide them.

'The Earth is a Syllable' is the story of a soldier who, as he lies mortally wounded in an unspecified part of the jungle, experiences the various stages of consciousness towards enlightenment. The only other character in the story, a foil for him, is the disgruntled cockney driver of the ambulance. The driver is a man who dislikes quiet and epitomizes what the *Mandukya Upanishad* calls the 'common-to-all-men' state of consciousness, that of ordinary waking reality where men are conscious only of what lies outside themselves. He has emerged unscathed from every theatre where the war has been fought and it is clear he will survive both to get more girls into trouble and to enjoy the material benefits of the Welfare State. In this state of materialism, says Mandukya, a man will obtain whatsoever he desires. But then this insidious idea that it is a man's fate to get, rather than to be denied, what he desires, Yajnavalkya had previously said applied to a man whatever the state of his consciousness—so long as he is still bound by his *karma*. The wounded officer, who in contrast to the driver has been constantly thwarted in his desire to see action, has been preserved because it is his destiny, when he finally does catch up with the war, not to kill but to die. It is his destiny to die not randomly nor because, in any facile sense, he has a death-wish, but because in the hour of his death he is to reach a state of enlightenment where his continued physical existence is no longer important.

The dying man resembles Lewis to a remarkable degree. He is an officer who has been involved in the world more than the driver can guess. A writer, he has known what it is to be without work and in educational talks organized for his men he has done his bit to try and construct a better society for the future. Like Lewis, he has written and theorized about death and, like him, has left behind at home a wife, though, to his relief, no child.[6] Now on his way back to an advanced dressing station, he is aware he is about to die and reflects he had always known he would die if he caught up with the war in Burma. In the jungle he is quite at peace, free of the political ambience of the 'Quit India' movement, which occasions his retort that 'it's the world we can't

[6] Ian Hamilton, Introduction, *Alun Lewis: Selected Poetry and Prose* (London, 1966), pp. 40–1.

quit'. On this evening the wind (according to Yajnavalkya the thread on which the cosmic elements are strung) puffs up 'with a hot dry sigh' creating dust. The dying man begins to shift into the dream-state, what Mandukya refers to as the second stage of consciousness. The social problems he had faced, he realizes, were less important than the moral ones: 'The terrible struggles had been quieter and less obvious than voyages and armoured regiments'. Yet is there not, he asks himself further, an amoral freedom beyond the duality of 'saying Yes or No to Life', a freedom which leads the Upanishad to speak of Earth as a syllable?

The dust storm has been the agent which extinguishes the cooker on which tea was brewing, thereby forcing the driver, with his rhyming cockney slang, into an unconscious parody of Upanishadic non-dualism: 'Well, we'll have to go without a cup of you an' me'. The driver turns in and the officer, already withdrawn, is glad to be left alone with 'whatever he had'. 'His lamp', we are told, 'still burned calmly and it might last an hour yet . . . It was very still except for the pain. There was a translucent golden influence at the core of his being'. The lamp here is obviously that of the Self, referred to by Yajnavalkya in his teaching to Janaka, which remains to light a man when both sun and moon have set, when the fire has gone out and all voices are still. It is the lamp of the soul, spoken of in the *Bhagavad Gita*, 'whose light is steady, for it burns in a place where no winds come', the possession of the *yogi* who 'has found joy and Truth, a vision for him supreme. He is therein steady: the greatest pain moves him not'.[7] It is the lantern whose light, according to Plotinus, remains untroubled when fierce gusts beat about it because it is 'the radiance in the inner soul of the man', experiencing which the wise man asks no pity for all his pain.[8] The darkness about the soldier (and it is a darkness which Yajnavalkya says is greater than that endured by the ignorant) begins, where Plotinus in one place puts it, this side of his own feet.

The opening line of the *Brihad Aranyaka* comes to the soldier's mind close upon that of the *Mandukya Upanishad*: 'The dawn is the head of a horse'.[9] The horse in this context is a sacrificial horse, the cosmic horse which is periodically sacrificed to death so that the universe may be renewed. The man in dying will become the world and, just as he was drawn like a moth to the war, moths now fly over his face like souls wandering in search of the liberation he is about to find. The *Mandukya Upanishad* de-

[7] *BG*, 6, 18–19. [8] *Enn.*, I.iv.8. See chapter 1, p. 30. [9] *BA*, 1.1.1.

scribes the second stage of consciousness as the 'brilliant', that in
which, as in a dream, a man is conscious of what is within and is
exalted beyond contraries. It is the state indicated by Yajnavalkya where the images of waking life—in this story, those of the
moths and the lamp, of the horse's head and the dawn and of the
wife and distant home, shining alike in sun and snow—are open
to be reordered by the Self: 'When one goes to sleep, he takes
along the material of this all-containing world, himself tears it
apart, himself builds it up, and dreams by his own brightness, by
his own light. Then this person becomes self-illuminated'.

The *Mandukya Upanishad* describes the third stage of consciousness as the 'cognitional', a state free of all dreams and all
desires in which a man erects this whole world and is absorbed
into it. This is a direct recapitulation of the teaching of Yajnavalkya who said that at this stage a man, like a god or a king,
apprehends his identity with the universe. Moreover, Yajnavalkya does additionally offer an image for the state itself: it is, he
says, like that of a man who, in the embrace of a loving wife, no
longer knows what is within or without. Yajnavalkya had previously found an image for this state of universal love. When the
Self is ready to be liberated, he had told Janaka, Indra and his
wife Viraj (the First Principle conceived of as separate) leave
their respective abodes within the two eyes, merge within the
heart and reascend through channels which (later tradition will
specify) pass through the skull into *Brahman*. This is an image *for*
the state of enlightenment, not an image seen *in* the state, and its
significance is clarified by the words of Yajnavalkya when, on
leaving his wife who is dear to him for a solitary life in the jungle,
he says: 'Lo, verily, not for love of the wife is a wife dear, but for
love of the Soul [the universal self, or *atman*] a wife is dear'.[10]

It is in this context that the penultimate state of mind of the
man in 'The Earth is a Syllable' may be perceived. He is thinking
of his wife in the village under the hill, but the relationship is no
longer merely personal: it has become unexclusively impersonal.
There has been what Plotinus calls 'a passing of image to archetype', love has become Love and Love is Knowledge. The dying
man is no longer bound by time and space: 'he wasn't in Burma
now, he was in the night, in the common ground of humanity,
and he wasn't alone now'. He knows that he will enter the silent
village with his wife and throw the darkness back over the hill—
just as the heart is lit with a great light when Indra and Viraj re-
enter it and they are no longer bound by mortality, by the body.

[10] The references to Yajnavalkya's teaching may be found in chapter 4, pp.
130–6.

Yajnavalkya says of the ultimate state that as the Self goes free of the constraints of the body, the various physical organs and qualities lose their vitality, their reality. Mandukya says that this state is the origin and the end of all things. Both sages declare that it is wholly beyond duality and description. Superconsciousness is not subject to apprehension within, let alone without. Nothing can be said of it beyond giving a bare description of what has been sloughed. Hence the final line of 'The Earth is a Syllable': 'The driver found him five yards away from the truck'.

When one speaks of the influence of the Upanishads it is important not to be misunderstood. Mandukya and before him Yajnavalkya relate what happens to a man as he becomes progressively enlightened: theirs is a personal record of an impersonal experience. Both offer an interpretation of life, the value of which any individual may test out for himself. Quite possibly Mandukya is indebted to Yajnavalkya (or his tradition) for his terminology: the mystical states of consciousness, we can only assume, he has had to experience for himself—though this similar experience could, possibly, have produced similar terminology. Whatever the origin of the terminology, the experience of mystical states appears to be identical. In 'The Earth is a Syllable' Lewis reveals his familiarity with both the *Brihad Aranyaka* and the *Mandukya Upanishad*. But from all that we know of his integrity as a writer, it is inconceivable he would construct a formula story in which he imagines a dying soldier in terms of the stages of consciousness enumerated in these Upanishads. No-one who has read his letters from India can doubt his fundamental seriousness as a writer and as a human being. We are left with the alternative of reading 'The Earth is a Syllable' as we read the *Mandukya Upanishad*—as universal autobiography, as a record of what happens to the personal self as it is transformed into the impersonal, or universal, self.

In the letters Lewis wrote to his wife after he had left her for India he writes frankly about the death both sense he is leaving her for, urgent as it is for him to explain that he sees it neither as death nor as a leaving of her:

Gweno, death doesn't fascinate me half as powerfully as life. . . Death is the great mystery, who can ignore him? But I don't *seek* him. Oh no— only I would like to 'place' him. I think he is another instance of the contrary twist we always meet sooner or later in our fascinations—like the atrophy that time we walked up the hill in the dark and that you with your Life spirit battled so hugely to dispel, astounding yourself I know, and you were big enough to take me as a stranger and 'make' me again—and isn't Death a stranger that one 'takes'?

Little more than a month before his death he writes:

I know I don't always make my letters cheerful. . . I've put a huge burden on you always, through my poems, which have spoken more openly
of the danger and the jeopardies than either of us could or would with
the living voice. I don't want them to mean foreboding to you or to me.
They're universal statements, if they're anything. They feel the world,
and they mean all that is involved in what is happening. You and I acquired the right to our own destiny when we were together: we made our
peace in the face of the unknown, and it will stand in despite. So deep
down we have no need to worry. I know we do: naturally: like hell: but I
can't tell you the peace you planted in me any more than I can tell you
I'll come back in the end.

The keynote to his Indian experience is sounded in the first
published letter Lewis sends from that country. He passes what
he takes to be a little statue of Buddha (though later apparently
learns that it was, as is more likely, Vishnu)[11] and, following an
experience so similar to that undergone in a Marabar cave he
cannot even be sure he has had one, he complains that he has
'no peace to discover slowly the intricate paths to the universal
tranquillity that gives unbounded freedom'. In the light of this he
sees himself as 'a fussy little officer sahib'—an image of his professional career in the army strong enough to cause him to turn
down promotion and to refer to new postings, in a phrase congenial to Buddhism, as turns within the wheel. His letters constantly testify to what he calls 'the simple restlessness that is a permanent state of mind now'. Writing helps but words are resistant:
once he speaks of being in 'a warm, introspective dream' which is
'the outer circle of a poem, if you like', but in it he makes 'no
real attempt to pierce to the kernel and take up the intolerable
struggle for the honeycomb of words'. He enjoys reading the best
contemporary writers on India—Forster, Thompson, Archer and
Elwin,[12] as well as the Upanishads, but he finds his real peace in
the jungle. In August 1943 he had written to his wife from his
officers' training camp in Karachi: 'All the creature comforts are
here and I loathe them all. I feel now that the only place worth
going to is the jungle'. This might be Yajnavalkya taking leave of
his wife, Maitreyi, to seek enlightenment as a *vanaprastha* in the
jungle, the more so since Lewis is aware that the old life his wife

[11] For the correction of Buddha to Vishnu, see 'To Rilke' and 'Karanje Village',
Selected Poems of Alun Lewis, ed., Jeremy Hooker and Gweno Lewis (London,
1981), pp. 67–70.   [12] Edward Thompson, *Night Falls on Siva's Hill* (London,
1929); *An Indian Day* (London, 1933), *et al.*; W.G. Archer and Verrier Elwin,
eds., *Man in India*.

and he lived belonged to 'the hypercivilized world' (the sort where one considers buying a Toulouse-Lautrec).

So Alun Lewis goes into the jungle. His last letters record two things of material interest: he senses that a phase of his life is ending and he remarks that he is neither writing nor trying to write any more. In a letter of 9 January 1944 he says:

I've got a feeling that another phase of my life is ending now, and the climacteric is near. I'm glad, and I feel something working blindly towards a position from which it can see and plan, and have faith and work. enduringly, not among things that crumble as they are made and [are] meaningless in history and in the heart. Let it come: it's the old cry for the saviour, let it come.

Again, in a letter written a fortnight before his death, Lewis says: 'I want to write you a clear glad message, late in the night, at the end of something and the beginning of something else. I'm writing out of clarity of spirit and letting Life have a chance'. Before going into the jungle, Lewis had hoped that the new phase of his life might include the composition of a novel based on his Indian experience such as Forster had written. But he added that the requirements of such a task were inimical to the passive state of mind in which his writing was done: 'Usually I don't know anything about a poem or story until suddenly I discover that it's written itself . . .'. Furthermore, in the same letter he says that his memory (in the context, surely, the Platonic memory, or Imagination) is taking a new and definite shape to itself: it is discarding all that is ephemeral and unnecessary—'it's going native'.

By January, however, Lewis admits that India is proving resistant to the pen and writes that he will wait for a stronger and more constructive purpose to guide him: 'Oh, if only I had the composure and self-detachment to write of all these things. But everything is fluid in me, an undigested mass of experience, without shape or plot or purpose'. Three weeks later he writes again: 'God knows where happiness or spiritual safety lies: not here, not with me, not now . . . I can't find myself, any more than I can become a poet now, or let myself be'. The next day, in his last letter to his parents—one in which he expresses wonder at being so preoccupied—he refers to his 'present sterility' and adds that he can send nothing to the *Welsh Review* because he has neither written anything nor expects to write anything for several months. Shortly before that, in the letter to his wife where he speaks of the peace which will survive whatever it is that forebodes, he tells her, too, that writing is suspended: 'Tonight a clear voice in me said: "Don't try and write any more" '. Lewis assumes that the cessation of his writing, like the conclusion of a phase in his life, is a temporary phenomenon. With the hindsight we have that what appeared to be temporary was in fact to be permanent, it is hard not to conclude that Lewis was prescient and open to intimations that both his life and writing were at an end.[13]

If the voice Lewis heard was in fact that which tells a man his life and writing are at an end, it would not be surprising were the finality of its tone to be missed by any man still living, especially by one with so great a love of life and literature as Lewis, the more so in a letter home to his wife. Yet it is just possible that in one of those stories he speaks of as having written itself, Lewis has left us an authentic record of the voice: that is, if 'The Earth is a Syllable' is to be considered not as a piece of literary journalism but as autobiography which is potentially universal or archetypal. On 22 December 1943, in one of several letters in which he refers to the peace of the jungle, Lewis says of writing a poem or story: 'If I get too far away from the *thing*, the *thought* becomes flabby and invalid, and it weighs on me with a dead weight and all the creative vitality dies in me . . . I'm more careful about this integrity than about anything else, whether personal danger or advantage suffers'. In 'The Earth is a Syllable', Lewis is on the inside of his story in a way that Kipling, for example, in a comparable story, 'At the End of the Passage',[14] is not. Yet, if Lewis *did* experience the events described in 'The Earth is a Syllable', how could the story be written in the moments before he died?

The *Mandukya Upanishad*, having announced that Earth is the syllable *Om*, says just one thing by way of preamble to its exposition of the stages of consciousness a man must traverse to realize his identity with the universe, and that is that *Om* not only comprehends past, present and future but actually transcends threefold Time itself. Whoever experiences that the Earth is a syllable will, therefore, be wholly free of Time. The dying man in Lewis's story transcends place—Burma and Britain become one—and, given the old Indian conception of a space-time continuum, it is possible to see him providing a correlation so perfect as to be identical with an author who, in creating him, has transcended time. Such a reading assumes that 'The Earth is a Syllable' is quite literally real, that it discovered the near future to Alun

[13] 'India', *In the Green Tree*, pp. 29–63; Hamilton, pp. 46–7; Brenda Chamberlain, ed., *Alun Lewis and the Making of the Caseg Broadsheets* (London, 1970), p. 38.   [14] *Life's Handicap* (London, 1891), pp. 159–84.

Lewis (as Apollonius said it might be discovered to a wise man)[15] and that fragments of this discovery pervade the last letters.

There is another, conceptually more difficult, way of speaking of this prescience, and that is to say that in the last moments of his life Lewis achieved such enlightenment that he was able to go back through time to write his story. Some intimation of this decisive moment might well stand behind the last, urgent words to his wife, inclusive as they are of a final benediction: 'Sorry I have to go. And God be in our heads and in our eyes and in our understanding. Buy me a typewriter when someone has one to sell, and I'll buy you a beautiful emerald or maybe a sapphire or maybe something neither of us knows'.[16] The gift of which both of them were then ignorant was, perhaps, the knowledge (embodied, as it necessarily has to be, in fiction) that in the final moments of his life he had understood where and how was to be reconciled the old dichotomy between the personal love he had for his wife and the strange, unaccountable lure of the war which bore him so irrevocably away from her to his death. Here at last he could do what hitherto had eluded him: namely, 'express at once the passion of Love, the coldness of Death (Death is cold) and the fire that beats against resignation, acceptance'.[17]

The volume of Lewis's last letters and stories from India, published posthumously, was appropriately called *In the Green Tree*. The title is taken from an elegiac sonnet by Vernon Watkins who, as a poet assimilating himself to the experience, apprehends that the death of Alun Lewis 'in the green tree' is related to his 'having seen the highest, for which alone we are born'.[18] We have noticed that both Indian *rishis* and Platonists have spoken of the Tree which has its roots in heaven. Yajnavalkya, in his elaboration of this myth, suggested that man had a divine existence which did not terminate when death hewed him down. In the *Bhagavad Gita*, Krishna returns to the same myth to point up the implication that a wise man will seek actively to cut down the Tree:

There is a tree, the tree of Transmigration, the Asvattha tree everlasting. Its roots are above in the Highest, and its branches are here below. Its leaves are sacred songs, and he who knows them knows the Vedas.

Its branches spread from earth to heaven, and the powers of nature give them life. Its buds are the pleasures of the senses. Far down below, its roots stretch into the world of men, binding a mortal through selfish actions.

[15] Berwick, VIII.vii.449–50.   [16] 'Burma', *In the Green Tree*, p. 66.   [17] 'India', ibid., p. 36.   [18] Epigraph, ibid., n.p.

Men do not see the changing form of that tree, nor its beginning, nor its end, nor where its roots are. But let the wise see, and with the strong sword of dispassion let him cut this strong-rooted tree, and seek that path wherefrom those who go never return. Such a man can say: 'I go for refuge to that Eternal Spirit from whom the stream of creation came at the beginning'.

Because the man of pure vision, without pride or delusion, in liberty from the chains of attachments, with his soul ever in his inner Spirit, all selfish desires gone, and free from the two contraries known as pleasure and pain, goes to the abode of Eternity.

There the sun shines not, nor the moon gives light, nor fire burns, for the Light of my glory is there. Those who reach that abode return no more.[19]

If, in matters pertaining to India, the *Bhagavad Gita* is to be preferred to the Mutiny records as a Bible,[20] it will be seen that the life of Alun Lewis was not cut short in its prime before he had written what he had to nor did he, as he affirms in his own words, seek death. Instead, since he was, surely, a man of pure vision without pride or delusion, it is possible that he was one who with the strong sword of dispassion, cut down the strong-rooted tree while it was still green. If this was so, the culmination of his life might be seen as a return to the pure vision from which it is said all life and writing emanate and into which they are re-absorbed—if that image did not, like the archetypal image of the tree, fail to convey how it becomes clear, at the moment of ultimate self-recognition, that no image was ever outside the Vision, was ever less than the total vision, or the total vision ever other than the Seer.

If that seems a bit too fine-spun, there is, alternatively, the report of a military Court of Inquiry that the death of Alun Lewis—like the falling of the plane tree as reported in 'The Road from Colonus'—was an accident.[21]

---

[19] See introductory chapter, p. 7; chapter 2, p. 53; chapter 4, p. 131 and n. 43.   [20] *PI*, XVIII, 169.   [21] Hamilton, pp. 58–9. See also Alun John, *Alun Lewis* (Cardiff, 1970), p. 78; Gwladys E. Lewis, *Alun Lewis, My Son* (Pengarreg, 1968), pp. 50–1. The day Lewis died is said to have been the day when the tide of war turned in favour of the Allies (Lord Mountbatten, *Report to the Combined Chiefs of Staff*, London, 1961, p. 43, §86).

Index

Abelard, Peter, 151, 162
Abu-l-Fazl, 53, 203, 205n, 237
Ackerley, J. R., 14, 235
Aeschylus, 51, 231, 258n, 259, 279,
    281
aesthetics
  Indian and neo-Platonist, 12n,
    13, 60–2, 63n
  see also Imagination
al-Biruni, 53, 54n, 97, 174n
Alexander the Great
  in India, 83, 87, 88, 143, 145–50,
    231–2, 259
  in Greek and European Ro-
    mances, 150–5, 165–6, 176–7,
    195n
  in Ethiopic Romances, 156–64
  in Persian Romances, 178–82
  in English Romantic literature,
    143, 186, 190, 191n, 241
Alexandria
  meeting place of East and West,
    7, 14, 69, 101–2, 145–6, 182, 265
  see also Forster, E. M.; Clement
    of Alexandria
alphabets, invention of, 196–7, 204
Ammianus Marcellinus, 55, 106, 178
Ammonius Saccas, 101–2
Aphrodite
  identified with Lakshmi, 74, 267,
    272
Apollonius of Tyana
  and Plotinus, 14n, 186n
  and English literature, 50, 80n,
    86–7

in Platonist tradition, 69n, 117,
    118, 124
and Christianity, 85–6
visit of, to India, 87–99, 155
and Ethiopian gymnosophists,
    94–5, 200
and magic, 105–6, 108
story of, further elaborated,
    109–11, 119–20
associated with Alexandria, 145,
    182
associated with Alexander the
    Great, 181–2
Apuleius, 105–6, 117–18, 124, 132,
    136, 201, 222
Arabia
  conduit for Indian culture
    reaching West, 64–5, 91, 156,
    159–60, 174, 248, 280
  other references, 181, 244, 255
Aristotle
  and Pythagorean tradition, 98,
    102, 126
  and Alexander the Great, 158,
    179, 181
Aristoxenus
  tells story of Indians in Athens,
    112–13
asceticism, 134, 154–6, 161–2, 169,
    177
  self-immolation, 109–11, 112
  see also Brahmins; gymnosoph-
    ists; yogis
Ashraf, 179, 181–2
Asia, 195, 273